I-PEEL
THE INTERNATIONAL POLITICAL ECONOMY OF EVERYDAY LIFE

I-PEEL

THE INTERNATIONAL POLITICAL ECONOMY OF EVERYDAY LIFE

JAMES BRASSETT | JUANITA ELIAS
LENA RETHEL | BEN RICHARDSON

Great Clarendon Street, Oxford, OX2 6DP,
United Kingdom

Oxford University Press is a department of the University of Oxford.
It furthers the University's objective of excellence in research, scholarship,
and education by publishing worldwide. Oxford is a registered trade mark of
Oxford University Press in the UK and in certain other countries

© Oxford University Press 2023

The moral rights of the authors have been asserted

First Edition published in 2023

Impression: 1

All rights reserved. No part of this publication may be reproduced, stored in
a retrieval system, or transmitted, in any form or by any means, without the
prior permission in writing of Oxford University Press, or as expressly permitted
by law, by licence or under terms agreed with the appropriate reprographics
rights organization. Enquiries concerning reproduction outside the scope of the
above should be sent to the Rights Department, Oxford University Press, at the
address above

You must not circulate this work in any other form
and you must impose this same condition on any acquirer

Public sector information reproduced under Open Government Licence v3.0
(http://www.nationalarchives.gov.uk/doc/open-government-licence/open-government-licence.htm)

Published in the United States of America by Oxford University Press
198 Madison Avenue, New York, NY 10016, United States of America

British Library Cataloguing in Publication Data

Data available

Library of Congress Control Number: 2022943963

ISBN 978-0-19-885439-5

Printed in the UK by
Bell & Bain Ltd., Glasgow

Links to third party websites are provided by Oxford in good faith and
for information only. Oxford disclaims any responsibility for the materials
contained in any third party website referenced in this work.

PRAISE FOR I-PEEL

Student Endorsements

'I thought it was very exciting to learn about a subject by linking it to contemporary life, it makes us apply theories to what we experience today, which makes it more understandable.'

> Priscilla Alves Tomaz, 2nd-year Politics and International Relations student at Queen Mary University of London, UK.

'A new, interesting examination of the global political economy catered towards a new generation of students.'

> Megan Irvine, 2nd-year International Relations student at University of Surrey, UK.

'I think it's a great approach—I think that taking aspects of everyday life and explaining them through IPE is a good way of bringing IPE to a level that is intuitive and immediately recognizable.'

> Salma Ghandour, 3rd-year Politics and International Relations student at University of Manchester, UK.

Lecturer Endorsements

'This book is an excellent tool to help us connect our students to their own roles as active participants in the political economic world.'

> Dr Francine Rossone de Paula, School of History, Anthropology, Philosophy and Politics (HAPP), Queen's University Belfast, UK.

'I-PEEL provides an accessible and vibrant approach to International Political Economy. Its use of real life examples familiar to students in real life has the potential to revolutionize the teaching of political economy in a positive direction.'

> Dr Derek Wall, Lecturer, Department of Politics and IR, Goldsmiths, University of London, UK.

'This is an excellent resource for teaching IPE to undergraduates. It seamlessly links key topics in IPE to everyday life, using multimedia tools in ways that are engaging for students, while providing a critical entry point into core themes in IPE.'

Konstantin Kilibarda, PhD Candidate and Lecturer,
School of Labour Studies, McMaster University, Canada.

'This is a student-friendly book that explores major issues in global political economy by starting from people's everyday experiences. It is designed to highlight the relevance of IPE to understanding the world as ordinary people experience it in their daily lives and in that sense it is a valuable tool for demonstrating to students that the abstract concepts that scholars use to understand global capitalism can be used to make sense of their daily lives.'

Dr Christakis Georgiou, Research Fellow, Global Studies Institute,
University of Geneva, Switzerland.

'This textbook brilliantly shows that IPE can be learnt by considering mundane acts and objects used in everyday life. Combining lucid conceptual explanations, rich and varied empirical illustrations, and engaging exercises, it opens new ways of teaching and learning.'

Dr Catia Gregoratti, Senior Lecturer, Department of Political Science,
Lund University, Sweden.

'This is a textbook that will transform IPE classrooms. It moves away from the conventional format of IPE textbooks that have developed over the years, to provide an accessible and engaging format that seamlessly blends real-world examples with complex and wide-ranging theoretical debates. Research-led student activities are rich and showcase the cutting edge of IPE pedagogy. They take the textbook way beyond anything currently available on the market by offering truly novel ideas for learning, which academics teaching with this book can be inspired to develop for their own classrooms.'

Dr Adam Fishwick, Research Director, University of Akureyri, Iceland.

ACKNOWLEDGEMENTS

Too often in academia we speak of individuals rather than collectives. The I-PEEL project, of which this book is a part, has affirmed our belief in the value of scholarly community, and of the widespread existence of shared knowledge production and mutual learning. This ethos has long underpinned our teaching practice in IPE and in this regard we have all benefitted from our engagements in the series of Teaching Political Economy events that were initiated in 2011 by Professor Johnna Montgomerie through the International Political Economy Group of the British International Studies Association. More recently, in the context of the pressures facing higher education during the Covid-19 pandemic, we have also benefitted from engagements with colleagues via social media, including on the Facebook group 'online learning mutual aid', and on Twitter, which among other things helped generate ideas for some of the student activities used in the book. We hope to do justice to this collaborative spirit in the pages ahead, in the picture we paint of IPE and its manifold contributors.

The I-PEEL project began in 2015, kick-started by generous funding from the Institute for Advanced Teaching and Learning at the University of Warwick. Our plan was to create an online teaching tool that provided everyday entry points to the study of IPE. The website was created by Phil Tutty, with additional support in setting up and maintaining the site provided by Ben Scarborough, Honey Fafowora, Luke Bantock, and Ruben Kremers. Feedback on the design was provided by a Student Advisory Board comprised of Daniel Craven, Frederic Heine, Julia Wdowin, Marta Musolino, Prathima Ravindra Appaji, Sonali Gidwani, and Yujae Jun, whilst Aine Clarke helped with marketing. Informal feedback was also sought from students at Warwick who have engaged with the I-PEEL site as part of their course and who provided a continual flow of encouragement, as well as from academic colleagues who integrated the site into their modules.

Content for the site came from academics inside and outside Warwick and was provided for free. This is just one indication of the tremendous amount of goodwill that circulates in our profession. There are too many people to name here individually, but they are all recorded in the Contributors section of the I-PEEL website. We are deeply grateful for their contributions and thank them here collectively. Allied to this scholarly support were the endorsements and positive responses about the site that we received from IPE colleagues including Professor Ben Rosamond, Professor Daniel Mertens, Dr Erin Hannah, Professor Jacqueline Best, and Professor Jean-Christophe Graz. To receive their esteem meant a great deal to us and strengthened our conviction in the project.

Acknowledgements

The translation of the I-PEEL site into textbook form began life in 2018. A first step was to take up the generous offer of Dr Amy L. Atchison to write a chapter on IPE for her edited book *Political Science Is for Everybody: An Introduction to Political Science*. This was a kindred project to our own, and the review process overseen by Amy helped us to refine our understanding of the field and how it should be taught. Around the same time, we also began working with Oxford University Press on a book of our own. Here we were guided initially by Sarah Iles and later by Katie Staal. Both have energized the project with ideas, coordinated a huge amount of reviews, and helped us to keep the momentum going during difficult times. We consider ourselves very lucky to have had them as publishing editors.

To the anonymous academic and student reviewers of the book we also extend profound thanks for the generosity they showed, both in giving up their time to provide detailed feedback and in supporting the project ethos. Their comments helped us to align our ambition to write a new generation of textbook with the needs of students based in different courses, institutions, and countries. They provided the best kind of constructive criticism and have enriched the book immensely. As with the website, student contributions from Warwick have also been fundamental to the book. To Anita Goga, Anna Donoghue, Daniel Campanale, Erin Pitcher, Jess Keenan, Juliette Giscard D'Estaing, Mohammad Karim, Sara Tan, Sofia Sanchez-Garay, Susbin Shrestha, Taaiba Khawaja, and Zach Smerin for their work on the learning activities, thank you for your amazing input. Additional thanks to Anita and Anna for their insightful feedback on the chapters, as well as to Dr Leo Steeds, Louis O'Sullivan, and Sara Kende for their careful proofing of the chapters. Their involvement helped always to remind us who and what this book should be for.

Finally, it would be no little understatement to say that writing a textbook during a pandemic was a challenge. Finding the time and inclination to work on the project was hard, and on many occasions the completion of the book seemed to be drifting further out of view. It was only thanks to the help, inspiration, and love of our families that we got this far. So we dedicate this book to you: to Olivia and Isabella from James; to Phil, Reuben, and Iris from Juanita; to Peter and Linus from Lena; and to Katy, Holly, and Thea from Ben. We hope we have made you proud.

BRIEF CONTENTS

1. **INTRODUCTION** 1
2. **CLOTHES** 27
3. **FOOD** 57
4. **DEBT** 92
5. **CARE** 120
6. **CITY** 152
7. **SOCIAL MEDIA** 185
8. **SHARE** 213
9. **HUMOUR** 241
10. **CONCLUSION** 271

GLOSSARY 284
INDEX 293

FULL CONTENTS

ABOUT THE AUTHORS — xv
ABOUT OUR STUDENT PODCASTERS — xvi
ABOUT THIS BOOK — xix
GUIDE TO USING THIS BOOK — xx
RESOURCES FOR LECTURERS — xxii

1. **INTRODUCTION** — 1
   1.1 **International Political Economy of Everyday Life** — 2
      1.1.1 What do you study in everyday IPE? — 4
      1.1.2 Who do you study in everyday IPE? — 5
   1.2 **Lineages of the Everyday in International Political Economy** — 7
      1.2.1 Liberal, Economic Nationalist, and Marxist lineages — 9
      1.2.2 Feminist, Black, and Poststructural lineages — 13
   1.3 **Learning with I-PEEL** — 18
      1.3.1 How do I use this book? — 19
   1.4 **Conclusion** — 22
      Resources — 23
      References — 24

2. **CLOTHES** — 27
   2.1 **Fast Fashion** — 29
      2.1.1 Follow the thing — 32
      2.1.2 Trading T-shirts — 33
      2.1.3 Donating or dumping? — 35
   2.2 **Exploring Clothes** — 37
      2.2.1 How is low-waged labour constructed? — 38
      2.2.2 Where does corporate responsibility lie? — 40
      2.2.3 How is desire manufactured? — 43

Full Contents

	2.3 **Engaging Clothes**	49
	2.3.1 Develop an ethical clothing campaign	49
	2.3.2 Stories of disposal: from classroom quizzes to student podcasts	51
	2.4 **Conclusion**	53
	Resources	54
	References	55
3.	**FOOD**	57
	3.1 **Chocolate**	59
	3.1.1 Chocoholics? Dietary change and public health	60
	3.1.2 The dark side of chocolate: child labour in cocoa	63
	3.1.3 Competition and coordination in the cocoa market	65
	3.2 **Exploring Food**	67
	3.2.1 What is food security?	68
	3.2.2 How are diets governed?	72
	3.2.3 Where is value distributed?	77
	3.3 **Engaging Food**	82
	3.3.1 An autoethnography of the food consumer	82
	3.3.2 The moral economy of a vegan foodscape	84
	3.4 **Conclusion**	86
	Resources	87
	References	88
4.	**DEBT**	92
	4.1 **Student Debt**	94
	4.1.1 Commodification	95
	4.1.2 Assetization	97
	4.1.3 Financialization	99
	4.2 **Exploring Debt**	101
	4.2.1 What are the different kinds of debt?	101
	4.2.2 Why do people indebt themselves?	104
	4.2.3 Do debts always have to be repaid?	107
	4.3 **Engaging Debt**	113
	4.3.1 Thought experiment on usury	113
	4.3.2 Role-playing a debt relief campaign	114
	4.4 **Conclusion**	116
	Resources	117
	References	118

5. **CARE** 120
   - 5.1 Military Spouses 122
     - 5.1.1 Social reproduction 123
     - 5.1.2 Valuing care work 126
     - 5.1.3 Heteronormativity 128
   - 5.2 Exploring Care 131
     - 5.2.1 Are we experiencing a care crisis? 131
     - 5.2.2 Is caring harmful? 134
     - 5.2.3 How is care work organized in the global economy? 138
   - 5.3 Engaging Care 142
     - 5.3.1 Measuring caring labour through time use surveys 142
     - 5.3.2 Uncovering hidden assumptions through social annotation 145
   - 5.4 Conclusion 147
   - Resources 147
   - References 148

6. **CITY** 152
   - 6.1 Mega-Event 154
     - 6.1.1 Place branding 155
     - 6.1.2 Urban transformation 157
     - 6.1.3 Politicizing the event 159
   - 6.2 Exploring the City 161
     - 6.2.1 What are global cities? 161
     - 6.2.2 How does urban development take place? 168
     - 6.2.3 Who needs the right to the city? 171
   - 6.3 Engaging the City 176
     - 6.3.1 An urban development case study 176
     - 6.3.2 A privilege trail 178
   - 6.4 Conclusion 180
   - Resources 181
   - References 182

7. **SOCIAL MEDIA** 185
   - 7.1 Fitness Influencers 187
     - 7.1.1 Self-branding 188
     - 7.1.2 The attention economy 190
     - 7.1.3 The prosumer subject 192

- 7.2 **Exploring Social Media** — 194
  - 7.2.1 How should social media be regulated? — 195
  - 7.2.2 Do we work for social media? — 198
  - 7.2.3 Can the prosumer be transformative? — 201
- 7.3 **Engaging Social Media** — 204
  - 7.3.1 Deliberating resistance on/to social media — 204
  - 7.3.2 Documentary film review poster — 207
- 7.4 **Conclusion** — 209
- **Resources** — 210
- **References** — 210

8. SHARE — 213

- 8.1 **Ride-Share** — 215
  - 8.1.1 Marketization of everyday life — 216
  - 8.1.2 Gig economy — 218
  - 8.1.3 Platform capitalism — 220
- 8.2 **Exploring the Sharing Economy** — 222
  - 8.2.1 Where does the sharing economy come from? — 223
  - 8.2.2 Who owns what in the sharing economy? — 226
  - 8.2.3 Are there alternative economies of sharing? — 228
- 8.3 **Engaging the Sharing Economy** — 232
  - 8.3.1 The diverse economies framework: reimagining the economy — 232
  - 8.3.2 University community mapping — 234
- 8.4 **Conclusion** — 237
- **Resources** — 237
- **References** — 238

9. HUMOUR — 241

- 9.1 **Radical Comedy** — 243
  - 9.1.1 Resistance — 244
  - 9.1.2 Carnival — 249
  - 9.1.3 Subversion — 251
- 9.2 **Exploring Humour** — 253
  - 9.2.1 Can humour promote global justice? — 254
  - 9.2.2 Can the subaltern joke? — 258
  - 9.2.3 Is humour dangerous? — 261

	9.3	**Engaging Humour**	264
		9.3.1 Make a parody collage	264
		9.3.2 Make your own meme	266
	9.4	**Conclusion**	268
		Resources	268
		References	269
10.		**CONCLUSION**	**271**
	10.1	**Exploring the IPE of Everyday Life**	272
		10.1.1 How have I studied everyday IPE?	273
		10.1.2 Who have I studied in everyday IPE?	273
		10.1.3 What have I studied in everyday IPE?	275
	10.2	**Engaging the IPE of Everyday Life**	276
		10.2.1 Reflect, enact, create: three approaches to activating your I-PEEL mindset	276
		10.2.2 Create your own I-PEEL tile	279
	10.3	**The End of Your Journey—At Least With Us**	281
		Resources	282
		References	282
GLOSSARY			**284**
INDEX			**293**

ABOUT THE AUTHORS

Access our **online resources** to watch a video in which James, Lena, Juanita, and Ben introduce themselves and discuss their work on this book: http://www.oup.com/he/i-peel1e

James Brassett is a Reader in International Political Economy in the Department of Politics and International Studies at the University of Warwick. His research looks at popular culture and the everyday in global politics, especially as it relates to 24-hour news, social media, film, and comedy.

Juanita Elias is Professor in International Political Economy in the Department of Politics and International Studies at the University of Warwick. Her research focuses on Feminist IPE and gendered approaches to the politics of globalization.

Lena Rethel is Professor in International Political Economy in the Department of Politics and International Studies at the University of Warwick. Her research interests include the relationship between finance and development with a focus on Southeast Asia and the emergence and governance of Islamic economies.

Ben Richardson is a Reader in International Political Economy in the Department of Politics and International Studies at the University of Warwick. His research looks at international trade and development with a focus on food and agriculture.

ABOUT OUR STUDENT PODCASTERS

As a reader of *I-PEEL: The International Political Economy of Everyday Life* you can benefit from the experience of seven current IPE students. Our panel share their reflections on the learning activities in each chapter, with useful insights and guidance on how to complete these. You can listen to their thoughts in the audio podcasts for each chapter.

 Access the online resources to listen to our student panel reflect on the learning activities: http://www.oup.com/he/i-peel1e.

Daniel Campanale is currently a final-year Economics, Politics and International Studies (EPAIS) student at the University of Warwick. In 2021 he was awarded one of the Oliver Hart Prizes for best-performing students in the first and second years. His main interests are in government and public policy, with particular focus on the UK housing crisis and potential remedies. He intends to travel after finishing his undergraduate degree.

Anna Donoghue studied Politics and International Studies at the University of Warwick, UK, graduating in 2021. In her final year she wrote a dissertation about fashion as a form of protest in the United States, using Condé Nast publications as a primary resource in her research. She was particularly interested in gender, development, and climate change throughout her degree. Anna is now working in the facilities department of an independent school in London, heading their sustainability initiatives in their route towards net zero.

About Our Student Podcasters

Juliette Giscard d'Estaing studies Economics, Politics and International studies at the University of Warwick, and plans on studying an MSc in European and International Public Policy at the London School of Economics. Her dissertation used European Social Survey data to explore the relationship between Euroscepticism and media consumption, and how it was changed by the eurozone crisis. She has interned at think tanks, in the private sector, and within the Financial Conduct Authority's International Division throughout university. At Warwick, she was Academic Officer for the Economics society, Student Leader for the Girls in Charge initiative, Events Officer for Warwick Women in Economics society, and University Manager for High Fliers Research. She is now a Research Assistant for the FRAMENET project led by Warwick's PAIS department.

Anita Goga graduated from Warwick University in 2021 with a bachelor's degree in Politics and International Studies. Her dissertation was entitled 'The state framing of cyber-threats as issues of national security: a policy review of the implications of the 5G debate'. This allowed her to explore research methods and create a methodology drawing on insights from securitization theory while also conducting a policy review. Anita is currently pursuing a master's degree in National Security Studies at King's College London, where she aims to learn more about how new technologies will impact national security.

Mohammad Mahdi Karim completed his undergraduate degree in Philosophy, Politics and Law (PPL) at the University of Warwick, UK, graduating in 2022. During his degree, he found a passion for and subsequently specialized in taking International Political Economy (IPE) related modules. In particular, he enjoyed looking at the Political Economy of Money and the Political Economy of Islam in Southeast Asia. The latter allowed him to academically study Islamic Finance, an area in which he wants to specialize in his future career as a commercial lawyer at the law firm Allen & Overy. Moreover, he also used his IPE knowledge to represent the UK at the G20's Official Youth Conference 2022, which took place in Indonesia.

About Our Student Podcasters

Susbin Shrestha completed his undergraduate degree in Economics and International Relations at the University of Sussex, UK, graduating in 2021. During his degree, he found the discipline of International Political Economy particularly insightful as an approach to understand and interpret the world; analysis remained economically driven but was liberated from the constraints typically associated with the discipline. He is now pursuing an MA in International Political Economy at the University of Warwick, with a dissertation project focusing on just energy transitions from a neo-Gramscian perspective and will graduate in October 2022.

Sara Tan is currently a final-year Politics and International Studies student at the University of Warwick. Upon graduation she will be pursuing an MSc in International Social and Public Policy at the London School of Economics. As an international student from Singapore, Sara is always keen to develop academic experiences in a cross-cultural context.

ABOUT THIS BOOK

The International Political Economy of Everyday Life

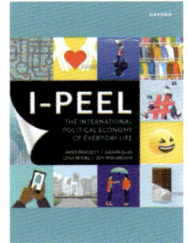

Visual imagery in I-PEEL

I-PEEL: The International Political Economy of Everyday Life is the only textbook to locate the study of IPE in the context of everyday life.

Access the online resources for videos from our authors introducing the I-PEEL approach, discussing the use of visual imagery in the book, and explaining how the book addressess representation, diversity, and inclusion considerations: http://www.oup.com/he/i-peel.com.

A video introducing the I-PEEL website project is also available here: http://i-peel.org/about/.

GUIDE TO USING THIS BOOK

I-PEEL: The International Political Economy of Everyday Life provides a rich learning experience in which issues and concepts are brought to life and set in a real-world context, and in which readers are guided and supported to become active, critical thinkers. Outlined here are the key features and online resources included in the book to ensure that you understand each topic and, importantly, that you can critique this knowledge and form your own views.

 Access the online resources at: http://www.oup.com/he/i-peel1e.

Master the Essentials

Learning Objectives outline what you will learn by the end of reading the chapter. **Reader's Guides** at the start of each chapter ground you in each topic, outlining the issues to be discussed and the knowledge and skills you will gain. They help you to navigate the chapters and highlight the key questions that will be at the forefront of your learning.

Consolidate Your Understanding

Quickfire Quizzes test your knowledge of key IPE facts, and **Reflective Multiple-Choice Questions** allow you to situate your own views and perspectives on IPE issues, both available on the online resources. Each chapter's **Flashcard Glossary**, also available on the online resources, offers further ways to test your knowledge of both the specific and the broader issues associated with the topic.

Put Your Knowledge into Practice

Learning Activities in the 'Engaging' section of each chapter provide you with relevant methodological guidance on how to *do* everyday IPE, such as where to find data, how to apply concepts, and what kind of questions to ask in your enquiry. **Support for Tackling the Learning Activities** can be found on the online resources.

Watch, Listen, and Learn

Author Podcasts allow you to hear directly from the authors as they introduce the key themes and ideas explored in the chapters, and how they relate to the authors' own research and experiences. **Student Reflection Podcasts** provide audio reflections from current IPE students exploring the key themes and ideas put forward in the learning activities for each chapter. Furthermore, **Videos** of news reports, interviews, summaries of key issues, and analysis help you to take your learning further.

Take Your Learning Further

Resources at the end of each chapter provide a useful list of books, journals, articles, and multimedia resources as a jumping-off point for further research.

Access quizzes, support for tackling the learning activities, podcasts, and videos on the online resources: http://www.oup.com/he/i-peel1e.

RESOURCES FOR LECTURERS

The online resources for lecturers are available at: http://www.oup.com/he/i-peel1e.

I-PEEL: The International Political Economy of Everyday Life offers a complete package of information and resources to support your teaching of International Political Economy.

Adopting lecturers can access the following **online resources**:

- A guide to the I-PEEL approach, how it works, and how to incorporate the book into your teaching.
- Customizable PowerPoint® slides, arranged by chapter, for use in lectures or as handouts to support efficient, effective teaching preparation.

1 INTRODUCTION

1.1	International Political Economy of Everyday Life	2
1.2	Lineages of the Everyday in International Political Economy	7
1.3	Learning with I-PEEL	18
1.4	Conclusion	22

Introduction

LEARNING OBJECTIVES

- Discuss the rationale for everyday International Political Economy (IPE)
- Identify the lineages of everyday IPE that draw from different theoretical traditions, including Liberal, Economic Nationalist, Marxist, Feminist, Black, and Poststructural theories
- Describe the I-PEEL approach and its implications for learning about and doing IPE

READER'S GUIDE

This introductory chapter will set the scene for the remainder of the book. It first defines what we mean by an everyday approach to International Political Economy (see Section 1.1) and then outlines some of its historical lineages, showing both its theoretical pluralism and analytical potential (Section 1.2). The chapter ends by setting out how to use the I-PEEL book and showing how it relates to more conventional textbook approaches (Section 1.3). Its aims are to show the connections that exist between the everyday and the international, and to license your own everyday experiences as a basis for learning about and doing IPE.

Access the online resources to watch a video of our authors in conversation, as James discusses what everyday IPE means to him, and how it informs this book: http://www.oup.com/he/i-peel1e.

1.1 International Political Economy of Everyday Life

We are often told that our lives are bound by the fate of the international economy, by movements in world markets, or by the crises of global capitalism. But what does this mean for how we live our life? How did these situations come about? And what are the possibilities for changing them? Insights into these questions can be found across a range of academic fields, one of which is International Political Economy (IPE). A central concern of IPE has been the interrelationship of wealth and power across state borders. In this textbook we want to show how you can use the analytical tools of IPE to interpret and question the world around you. Our approach is to start off with something familiar—the apps on your phone, how you dress, that gourmet cheeseburger you've started ordering—and to 'peel back' the layers of this object, subject, or practice to reveal some of the political and economic processes at work. We call this the I-PEEL approach, and want to invest it with a double meaning. First, as an acronym of the book title: *The International Political Economy of Everyday Life*. Second, as a way of putting the 'I' into the study of IPE, licensing the use of *your* everyday in the study of what might otherwise appear as distant and disconnected topics.

The origin of the I-PEEL textbook lies in the growing attention that scholars in IPE have paid to the everyday from the 2000s onwards (Aitken 2007; Best and Paterson 2010; Davies 2006; Elias and Rethel 2016; Hobson and Seabrooke 2007). A core proposition of this literature is that research in IPE has tended to focus on elite actors like heads of state, abstract structures like global governance, and dramatic moments of high politics like financial crises. As a result, this so-called systemic or regulatory IPE has had less to say about the constitution, legitimation, and contestation of economic activity from below. What 'the everyday' has signalled in this context, then, is a commitment to studying the people, practices, and places normally considered as politically *inconsequential* to the global economy. Be it through the agency of non-elites, the role of popular culture, the sites of routine behaviour, or the stuff of mass consumption, everyday IPE has sought to show that the economy doesn't just exist 'out there' but is continually remade in, and through, our daily lives.

On the one hand, this scholarship has shown how financial institutions and states have encouraged people to take responsibility for their own futures via personal debt, savings, insurance, and investment products—often with highly iniquitous results (Aitken 2013; Harmes 2001; Langley 2008; Montgomerie 2020; Rethel 2010). As these same moral imperatives and calculative technologies seep into other economic areas, this neoliberal form of capitalism can almost seem to be taking over everyday life, extending competitive individualism into every facet of our daily existence (see Chapter 3 for a fuller discussion of neoliberalism). Yet on the other hand, the everyday is also figured as a zone where people adapt and respond to the forces acting upon them, where they show proactive agency alongside passive acceptance. Research in this vein has shown how everyday actions can manifest a struggle to value life differently within the prevailing economic system, and how these and other small-scale actions, intentionally or not, can cohere into powerful undercurrents that transform the global economy (Adebanwi 2017; Hobson and Seabrooke 2007). These two emphases of the everyday—one that points to the routine conformity of daily life and one that reveals acts of contravention and change—can be viewed as a productive tension of this approach, and one which animates the chapters to follow.

1.1.1 What do you study in everyday IPE?

The simple answer to this question is: almost anything! In questioning the excessive focus on elites, everyday IPE has also problematized the necessity of organizing the field around the institutions and issue areas with which those elites were associated. Whilst not denying the importance of the US Secretary of the Treasury and the hegemony of the dollar in international monetary policy, or negotiations at the World Trade Organization to economic protectionism, everyday IPE insists on the merit of embracing ordinary social practices and the unanticipated research questions they throw up. Some examples from the literature include studying financial crisis through home ownership (Seabrooke 2010), global justice via ethical consumption (Watson 2005a), mutual aid via bingo playing (Bedford 2019), climate change via recycling (Acuto 2014), and political resistance via the #MeToo movement (Griffin 2019).

This pluralism also extends to research on popular culture. For instance, some of our own work has looked at Hollywood films about Wall Street and their portrayal of masculinity among the lead characters (who are all men). By exploring what this says to audiences about how men ought to conduct themselves as financial traders and where women belong in this world, this scholarship aims to show how fictional popular culture can still have real-world repercussions (Brassett and Heine 2021; Brassett and Rethel 2015). Other research has stressed how cultural productions and artefacts, from TV soap operas to jewellery, can all be encoded with international political messages about the economy (Brassett 2021; Hamilton 2022; Innes and Topinka 2017).

Take the famous children's books on Paddington Bear, stories about a bear from Peru who is found in Paddington railway station in London by a family. These have been read by Kyle Grayson as a liberal account of why migrants ought to be accepted into English society and what they are expected to do in return. For him, then, they provide an everyday space in which the politics of immigration are raised in common vernacular terms, as well as a subversive image to adorn placards at various protests against the mistreatment of migrants, which, as shown in Photo 1.1, have readily traversed national borders (Grayson 2013). In this way, research on popular culture can also challenge us to think about *where* global politics happens, moving from the 'corridors of power' in government buildings and corporate headquarters to the places where everyday life is inhabited—the home, the classroom, the shop, the street.

Photo 1.1. A protest in 2018 by activists and refugees against the opening of a migrant deportation centre in Darmstadt, Germany.
Source: Pacific Press Media Production Corp./Alamy Stock Photo.

1.1.2 Who do you study in everyday IPE?

A further contribution of the everyday turn in IPE has been to broaden the range of actors considered worthy of study. Actors in this sense refers to participants in a process, and everyday IPE has been particularly keen to recognize the diverse groups of people who (re)produce the global economy. This has often involved interrogating the intellectual boundary separating the economic sphere from the non-economic sphere, which has tended to include certain subjects like 'consumers' and 'financiers' as appropriate for IPE analysis but excluded others such as 'mothers' and 'housewives' on the presumption that these roles are largely irrelevant to the creation and distribution of wealth. This is something that feminist scholarship has challenged, foregrounding structures of **patriarchy** to highlight the often invisible role of women in managing households, raising children, sustaining communities, and more besides (see Elias and Rai 2019; Enloe 1989; Peterson 2003).

One of the rallying calls of feminism has been 'the personal is political'—a slogan used in the second wave of feminism in the late 1970s that was intended to reposition the issues that women faced as societal problems requiring collective political action rather than as individual problems requiring therapeutic intervention or behaviour change (Hanisch 1970). This call has also reverberated through everyday IPE. Issues like street harassment have thus been rendered as both political and economic insofar as they can prevent women from travelling to work and profit companies that trade on the supposed fun to be had from forcing unwanted comments and gestures on strangers (True 2012). Following Cynthia Enloe's pioneering intervention (1989), scholarship in this vein has also made the case that 'the personal is international', again asking us to reconsider where global politics happens. Making the invisible visible in this way carries ethical implications too. If it is only ever the rich and powerful that are studied, there is a risk of naturalizing this hierarchy, and reinforcing the positions and views of those at the top of it. Studying overlooked actors and marginalized groups thus makes an important statement about *whose* lives matter in IPE.

How might this approach play out analytically in political economy studies? Let's consider the response to the Covid-19 pandemic. Of course, there is much to learn from looking at the decisions of state leaders to furlough workers, lend to businesses, and take control of critical economic sectors. But this is far from the whole picture. Providing a different optic, everyday IPE might instead draw our attention to the key workers required to maintain essential services during lockdowns, the daily pressures and risks they faced in doing their jobs, and, in the UK at least, the disproportionate

Photo 1.2. A street mural in Southend, England. During the pandemic the UK government designated certain employees as 'key workers' and expected them to work outside the home throughout lockdowns.
Source: Avpics/Alamy Stock Photo.

number that were working class, women, and ethnic minorities (Francis-Devine 2020). It might also illuminate the uneven impacts of pandemic policy within households as huge amounts of care work were reorganized following the diversion of healthcare services and closure of schools, or the new forms of digital surveillance made possible through the seamless integration of smartphones into people's daily lives (see Campbell-Verduyn 2021; Mezzadri et al. 2021). In short, everyday IPE asks us to think differently about how and *with whom* we address our topics.

1.2 Lineages of the Everyday in International Political Economy

In this section we expand on the disciplinary and theoretical basis of everyday IPE. We begin with two stories that are told about the history of IPE more broadly, which provide the context for understanding how our approach in this textbook relates to the wider field. In the first story, IPE emerged as an offshoot of International Relations in the 1970s as scholars based largely in the discipline of Political Science and located in North America responded to the economic convulsions in the US-centred world order. The explanations they provided were grouped into three theoretical perspectives: **Economic Nationalism**, **Liberalism**, and **Marxism** (Gilpin 1987; Cohen 2007). In brief, approaches based on Economic Nationalism emphasized the role of the state and drew attention to the importance of international rivalries and the constant threat of conflict in shaping interactions. Approaches based on Liberalism emphasized the role of firms and international organizations alongside states, and drew attention to the importance of market exchange and the possibilities for mutual gains between national economies. Finally, approaches based on Marxism, which were firmly at the margins of debate, emphasized the role of classes, drawing attention to the labour exploitation that cut across national borders and how this inequality might be challenged. This tripartite framework still influences how IPE is taught, with many textbooks using it to introduce readers to the field, albeit it with some variations such as referring to Realism instead of Economic Nationalism, or replacing Marxism with critical theories to cover other perspectives from outside the mainstream (see O'Brien and Williams 2020; Oatley 2019).

In the second story of IPE, the field is traced back through the older tradition of Political Economy, typically dated to eighteenth-century Britain and the attempts to comprehend the birth of commercial society or what is now called **capitalism** (Gamble 1995; Watson 2005b). In this longer history, many of the intellectual sources of contemporary IPE come from 'pre-disciplinary' scholarship produced prior to the creation of disciplines in the Social Sciences and Humanities; a categorization which was premised on establishing academic boundaries between the study of Politics, Economics, History, and so on (Jessop and Sum 2001). For those seeking a more fluid or holistic approach to IPE, this reading of the field was thus more accommodating, allowing for the infusion of ideas from areas like Economic Anthropology, Heterodox Economics, and International Political Sociology, to name just a few (see Graz et al. 2019).

Another feature of this reading is that it positions **critical theory** as central rather than residual to IPE. As argued by Robert Cox (1981, 129), one of the protagonists of this second story, critical theory 'stands apart from the prevailing order of the world and asks how that order came about'. He contrasted this to the problem-solving theory of mainstream Liberal and Realist IPE, which instead takes the world as it finds it, attempting to make its prevailing power relationships and institutional arrangements work more smoothly by dealing with particular sources of trouble. For Cox, this theoretical division was also ideological. Whereas critical theory allowed for a normative choice in favour of alternative social and political orders, containing a streak of utopianism to show what this might look like and how to get there, problem-solving theory was ultimately conservative, implicitly aligned with the national, sectional, or class interests comfortable in the current system (Cox 1981). For those wanting an IPE that allowed them to challenge established hierarchies, this history of the field was appealing in that it both foregrounded critical theory and gave it scholarly validity. Indeed, this critical impulse has meant that the second story of IPE has not stood still. Recent historiography has addressed the Eurocentric foundations of Political Economy, calling out its reliance on the world views of white European scholars and calling for greater recognition of non-Western thought (Hobson 2013; Helleiner 2015).

In this textbook we build on this second story to present and promote IPE as a critical interdisciplinary field. We do this for several reasons. First, to encourage you to question the world around you and challenge the unjust hierarchies and inequalities in which you are enmeshed. Second, to highlight the diversity of contemporary scholarship that either describes itself as IPE or could otherwise inform it, a key element of which involves looking beyond both North America and Western Europe to make this a much more global conversation (see Blyth 2009; Tussie and Chagas-Bastos 2022; Vivares 2020). Third, to help ensure that the field of IPE keeps moving forward, renewing itself to offer new insights on urgent issues.

Based on these convictions, we now outline a set of conceptual insights for thinking about everyday IPE in the chapters ahead, drawn from a range of theoretical traditions. These are not the only traditions that could be used but are the ones that we are most familiar with. For this reason, we see this not as a fixed framework for analysis but something more akin to an academic family tree, with lineages that reach back to various people and which evolves with every new generation.

1.2.1 Liberal, Economic Nationalist, and Marxist lineages

We start our conceptual insights with Adam Smith, the best-known scholar of early commercial society, and his notion of the **market**. In many accounts of IPE, Smith is written in as the forefather of the Liberal approach on the basis of his idea that the 'invisible hand' of the market could direct economic tasks to where they could be done most efficiently, both within and between countries, thereby enhancing *The Wealth of Nations* (taken from the title of his 1776 book). As Matthew Watson has argued, this reading of Smith is largely mistaken. Smith did not conceptualize 'the market' as an impersonal system of allocation based on abstract laws of supply and demand but as a real-world space which depended on the willingness of buyers and sellers to exchange in a sympathetic manner, imagining themselves on the other side of transaction so that they could negotiate a morally acceptable market price. In this sense, market relations were not imposed on society from above but had to be enacted by individuals in everyday life (Watson 2005b). Moreover, whilst it is true that Smith recognized the potential for market exchange and the division of labour to increase economic productivity, he also saw the pursuit of increased wealth as a potential source of moral corruption. In warning his readers about the dangers of vanity and profligacy, Smith sought to raise their self-awareness and asked them to 'look inwards to themselves rather than outwards to the state' to bring about societal progress—a political technique which can also be seen in everyday IPE scholarship (Watson 2013, 22; Glaze and Richardson 2017).

As with Liberalism, tracing the lineages of everyday IPE in Economic Nationalist thought involves rethinking what key thinkers stood for. One such thinker in this tradition is Friedrich List, author of the 1844 book *The National System of Political Economy*, which in contrast to the free trade doctrines of Liberalism made the case for more active state intervention in the economy to spur industrialization. It is in revisiting this book that the IPE scholar Eric Helleiner challenges the idea that Economic Nationalism should be understood as state-centric Realist IPE. For him, this missed the distinction that List drew between the state and the nation. Policies like protecting infant industries through trade tariffs or monopolizing the printing of currency in a central bank were advocated not to strengthen the state apparatus but to serve the nation as a community (Helleiner 2002; Helleiner 2021). Viewed in this way, Economic Nationalism revealed itself not just as a governing strategy of elites but also as an everyday practice, witnessed in populist campaigns to buy 'home-made' produce rather than foreign imports or in the use of banknotes to circulate images of heroic figures that symbolize national identity. These daily reminders of nationhood, dubbed '**banal nationalism**' (Billig 1995), are still with us now, explored in contemporary IPE scholarship looking at the reproduction of imagined national spaces in statistics like GDP and in the mobilization of patriotism in corporate marketing strategies that link certain brands to national identity (see Fetzer 2020; and Section 6.1.1 on place branding).

Despite Smith's qualifications and List's nationalist alternative, the nascent field of Political Economy was taken up in such a way as to defend, even naturalize, the very commercial society that it sought to explain. For Karl Marx, founding father of Marxism and another scholar still widely cited in IPE, this naturalization merely served the interests of the bourgeoisie: the capitalist class that owned the means of production and systematically benefitted from the spread of market exchange. This is why his famous 1867 treatise *Capital* had the subtitle *A Critique of Political Economy*. In it Marx argued that one of the most potent elements of capitalism was the way that the proletariat—the class of workers who relied solely on their labour power to make a living—had been distracted from, or even become accepting of, their fundamental exploitation. An important expression of this is what he called **commodity fetishism**. This refers to an understanding of the economy based on market relationships between commodities rather than social relationships between people, which was made possible by the increasing alienation of workers from the product of their work. Because of this fetish it was increasingly difficult to see that proletarians were being impoverished, not because they happened to work in an unprofitable company or lacked the talent to earn a higher wage, but because they occupied a subordinate place in the hierarchy of capitalism. For Marx, then, the everyday experience of life in capitalist society was 'both real and unreal, both actuality and the disguise of actuality' (Highmore 2002, 6). One way this idea has been explored in the contemporary global economy is in relation to Fair Trade products, which are typically priced above the market average so that extra money can be passed on to the farmers and workers at the other end of the supply chain. Scholars have asked whether this *de*-fetishizes commodities by enabling consumers to imagine the social relationships implicated in their purchase, or merely allows the corporations controlling food and drink industries to internalize the feeling of 'doing good' within their business model (Fridell 2007; Lyon 2006; see Section 2.3.2 on the moral economy of food).

Questions about the ideological legitimation of capitalism were taken forward by Antonio Gramsci in the 1930s through his notion of **common sense**. This referred to the everyday reality of popular opinion; a collective, if contradictory, set of ideas which Gramsci thought progressive intellectuals had to engage if they were to give their redistributive political agendas the necessary emotional force. This has since been used as a conceptual device in IPE to show how support for the North American Free Trade Agreement (NAFTA) was built by the business community and its right-wing advocates in the early 1990s. Rather than refer to quantitative economic arguments about jobs growth and so on, NAFTA was depicted in the popular media as a means of unleashing entrepreneurialism and extending economic liberty; values that its

Photo 1.3. Fair Trade certified coffee makes its moral appeal to the shopper, purporting to show them the person behind the product.
Source: René van den Berg/Alamy Stock Photo.

advocates knew would readily appeal to an American public steeped in the **discourse** of liberal capitalism (Rupert 1995). Other scholarship has shown how the American common sense has also been engaged to *challenge* the prevailing class hierarchy. In the Occupy Wall Street movement the rallying cry of 'We are the 99%' put questions of economic inequality front and centre by distilling people's personal experiences of diminishing upward mobility and falling real wages into a pithy soundbite (Crehan 2016). In this lineage, everyday IPE can illuminate the ideological battleground on which class relations are played out, showing how people can be made to conform to but also contest the status quo (see Section 7.2.1 on regulating social media).

The phrase **everyday life** is particularly associated with Henri Lefebvre, who conceptualized the 'everyday' not as what people *do* on a day-to-day basis but *how* activities are subordinated to the imperatives of capitalism and become routine, ordinary, quotidian. Everyday life, then, was not something that had always existed but was a historically produced domain where the dominated sphere of the everyday met the undominated sphere of daily life (Kipfer 2008, 199). Writing in the context of mid-twentieth-century France, he used a study of *Elle* magazine to argue, not without problem, that everyday life was especially pronounced among women. For him, the pages of this lifestyle magazine revealed how women had become subject to the organized passivity brought on by consumer advertising, modern home appliances, and the like (Elden 2004, 117).

Everyday life therefore appeared to Lefebvre as a residue—the life left over once all 'distinct, superior, specialized, structured activities have been singled out' (Lefebvre 1991 [1947], 97). There are clear resonances here with the critical theory of the Frankfurt School scholars, who during the same period were taking aim at the 'culture industry' in Western capitalism for stifling individuality and generating false needs that got people to buy—quite literally—into the political and economic system (see Adorno 1991).

Lefebvre also saw capitalism as an evolving spatial construct, and this led him to consider the production of everyday life as an ongoing process of colonialism, organizing and segregating people into certain ways of living. The location of migrant labour from France's former colonies into 'ethnic enclaves' in its major cities was, for him, a way in which European colonization has evolved an internal dimension (Davies 2016, 34). This argument echoes in contemporary studies on gentrification, which look at how inner-city areas are made into 'respectable' real estate through the creation of pacified consumer spaces that attract higher-paying and often racially privileged residents (Smith 2002). It also indicates one way that an analysis of racialized inequality can be brought into the IPE of everyday life (see Section 6.2.3 on the race-making practices of urban governance).

Photo 1.4. Bo-Kaap in Cape Town, South Africa, was originally known as the Malay Quarter due to the arrival of slaves from Southeast Asia. Now a popular tourist destination, it has become characterized by rising property rates that many long-standing residents can no longer afford.
Source: Ilyas Ayub/Alamy Stock Photo.

1.2.2 Feminist, Black, and Poststructural lineages

We now turn to the lineages of everyday IPE rooted in theoretical approaches located outside the tripartite framework of Liberalism, Economic Nationalism, and Marxism set up in the 1970s. One such approach is Feminism, which took up a different set of questions to those asked by men like Smith, List, Marx, Gramsci, and Lefebvre. As mentioned in Section 1.1.2, a long-standing concern for feminists has been the way that certain tasks get bracketed out from the formal economy and the public sphere of political debate: tasks like cooking and cleaning, which are predominantly carried out by women and girls within the home and without pay in a *gendered* division of labour. **Social reproduction** was the academic term coined in the 1980s to recognize the day-to-day work involved in bearing children, maintaining households, and caring for others *as* work. And not just any work, but work that was vital in ensuring that people and communities could survive, and that capitalism could carry on despite its intrinsic reluctance to internalize costs like nurturing a healthy labour force (Vogel 1983).

For many feminist scholars, then, social reproduction *is* everyday life (Katz, 2001; Elias and Rai 2019; see Section 5.1.1). Intertwining with the Marxist tradition described in Section 1.2.1, they have argued against biological determinism and the supposition that because women give birth they should also take on the burden of raising a family and running a household, and instead sought to denaturalize the gendered division of labour and show how it has been socially constructed. For Silvia Federici (2004) this has involved a continual process of differentiation within society that ordered some groups of people and their labour power as more valuable than others. Not only has this legitimized the exploitation of those at the bottom of the hierarchy; it also incentivized those at the top to align themselves with the structures of patriarchy and heteronormativity that preserved it. Challenging this logic, Federici's 1975 pamphlet *Wages for Housework* was an attempt to transform the subject of the 'housewife' into a revolutionary figure, and the text printed on the book's front cover still reads forcefully today:

> They say it is love. We say it is unwaged work.
> They call it frigidity. We call it absenteeism.
> Every miscarriage is a work accident.
> Homosexuality and heterosexuality are both working conditions …
> but homosexuality is workers' control of production, not the end of work.
> More smiles? More money. Nothing will be so powerful in destroying the healing virtues of a smile.

Introduction

> Neuroses, suicides, desexualization: occupational diseases of the housewife.
> (Federici 1975, 1)

More recent scholarship has made clear that the household is not a static place and that, in fact, waged labour has penetrated the domestic sphere, though not in the way Federici envisioned. Studies of the 'maid trade' have traced the increased commodification and transnationalization of the household through the role of ethnic minority women working as live-in servants or nannies for households in more affluent areas and countries (Ehrenreich and Hochschild 2003; Elias and Gunawardana 2013; LeBaron 2010). Taking particular groups of people like domestic workers as a starting point for analysis resonates with what Cynthia Enloe dubbed **feminist sense**. Different to Gramsci's common sense, this was a methodological call to investigate the international by following diverse women and their 'complex everyday realities' to the places usually dismissed by foreign affairs experts as merely 'private', 'domestic', 'local', or 'trivial' (Enloe 1989, 336).

Echoing Enloe's examples in her book, recent IPE studies have considered the lived realities of Argentine sex workers, Nepalese private security contractors, and Canadian call centre workers, to name just a few (see Elias and Roberts 2018). Such accounts show how macroscopic global dynamics like foreign investment or mass migration are not disembodied abstract processes, but are lived out through gendered social relations. For instance, the growth in international trade in the late twentieth century cannot be understood without appreciating the feminization of the labour force in the major export processing zones—or sweatshops—of Asia and Latin America. This mass mobilization of young rural women into waged work in assembly line production depended both on social renegotiations over where women 'belonged' and a recomposition of patriarchal norms from the family home into the workplace (Elson and Pearson 1981; see Section 2.2.1 on low-wage labour in the clothing industry).

Studies of women's lived experiences of globalization have also shown how much economic activity remains *outside* the capitalist sphere of market transactions, wage labour, and profit-oriented companies. This is an important critical insight. Recognizing the continued existence or even reappearance of practices like barter exchange and self-employment can serve to 'dislocate the naturalized dominance of the capitalist economy and make a space for new economic becomings' (Gibson-Graham 2006, xii). On this view, the varied experiences revealed through a focus on the everyday is not just a litany of overlooked and unjust situations but a place in which to identify alternative (local) forms of economy and take (global) inspiration.

Extending Enloe's notion of feminist sense into considerations of racialized social relations, Patricia Hill Collins has advocated for a theory of knowledge called standpoint epistemology, in which systematically disadvantaged groups are figured with an intimate understanding of the factors producing those conditions. Writing in the tradition of Black Political Economy, her illustrative example of standpoint epistemology was the way that African American women had developed the concept of **intersectionality** to understand how 'gender, sexuality, race, class and nation … mutually construct one another' as systems of oppression experienced in their everyday lives (Collins 2000a, 47; see also Peterson 2003, who similarly writes about the intersection of structural hierarchies).

Drawing on this concept, Collins provides an intersectional analysis of the family to help explain the persistence of racial inequality in the US. This was traced to the perpetuation of 'white families' and 'black families' in society due to the powerful cultural norm of heterosexual intraracial marriage. This in turn enabled the intergenerational transmission of inequality as parents passed on their accumulated wealth to their children in the form of educational fees, property inheritance, and social connections (Collins 2000b, 277–88). In terms of everyday IPE, then, this encourages us to view the interpersonal experiences of daily life as a domain of power relations in which systems of oppression can be recognized and resisted (see Collins 1993). Incidents of racism, sexism, homophobia, and xenophobia that might otherwise be dismissed as trivial are instead cast as critical openings. Take the racial microaggressions disclosed by the students in Photo 1.5. This term refers to the commonplace messages that communicate hostile, derogatory, or negative racial slights and insults toward people of colour (Sue et al. 2007). What might these tell us about the socio-economic advantages of whiteness in schools, universities, and workplaces? And is naming and shaming them as 'microaggressions' an important move towards racial equality?

Finally, from IPE scholarship that has engaged with poststructural theory we get a more diffuse account of power. For Michel Foucault, it was not as simple as saying

Photo 1.5. Portraits from the *Racial Microaggressions* project by Kiyun Kim at Fordham University, New York.
Source: Kiyun Kim.

power is used by this person or that group to dominate and oppress others. Rather, we need to think about how subjects are both produced by and operate within a field of power relations. To illustrate this point, Foucault considered Jeremy Bentham's design for a prison, called the Panopticon.

A central viewing tower would allow a single guard to see all prison cells; however, due to the height and angles of the design, prisoners could not know for sure if they were being watched. The idea was that inmates would behave in accordance with the rules on the assumption that they *could* be under surveillance. As Foucault (1977, 202) put it, 'He who is subjected to a field of visibility, and who knows it, assumes responsibility for the constraints of power; he makes them play spontaneously upon himself; he inscribes in himself the power relation in which he simultaneously plays both roles; he becomes the principle of his own subjection.'

The idea that systems of power rely on **subjectivity** is a useful proposition for thinking about a range of seemingly mundane areas of market life. For example, IPE scholars have associated this kind of power with such technical market devices as credit ratings or normative agendas to educate schoolchildren in 'financial literacy' (Clarke 2015; Gill 1995). In this way they explore how people work on themselves to behave in accordance with market discipline and become a certain kind of person. For example, and drawing directly on the Panopticon analogy, the assumption that credit reference

Photo 1.6. The Model Prison in Cuba was built under the dictatorship of Gerardo Machado in the 1920s and followed the design of Bentham's Panopticon.
Source: Wolfi Poelzer/Alamy Stock Photo.

agencies might be recording information about you encourages adherence to 'good' creditworthy behaviour, lest you be denied a loan later in life. Importantly, though, this is not seen as something imposed from above by the market or the state, but is repeatedly acted out or 'performed' through particular roles. Everyday IPE research on the expansion of home ownership and private pensions in the UK and US, for instance, has argued that these economic developments went together with the evolution of the 'market subject' (Aitken 2007; Langley 2008). As people came to see themselves as mortgagors or investors, they also began to act as individuals with a duty to make informed financial decisions and an entitlement to reap any rewards that flow from these, even if the payoffs owed more to structural factors and sheer good luck than any individual merit. Conceived in this way, market subjectivities not only shape people's way of life but provide the kind of person able *and willing* to engage in the continual reproduction of market exchange (see Section 8.1.1 on the marketization of everyday life).

This idea also complicates binary notions of power and resistance, which position power *against* resistance. For if governance of the global economy happens through the everyday practices of subjects, then aren't those same subjects implicated in its inequalities and injustices? How can they resist what they themselves engender? (Amoore 2006, 261.) This attention to subjectivity and how we act out our selfhood can help us to think

Photo 1.7. Does it matter what it tastes like if it looks good to your followers? Performances of the self on social media can create social expectations for certain lifestyle choices that have far-reaching political and economic effects.
Source: insta_photos/Alamy Stock Photo.

about all manner of issue areas pertinent to IPE: not just as scholars writing about the world, but, more uncomfortably, as complicit subjects existing within it. How do we/you present ourselves as good citizens, and does this also make for bad citizens? What do we/you want our purchases to say about us, and what does this mean for others?

1.3 Learning with I-PEEL

In Section 1.2 we identified several lineages for thinking about everyday IPE. Our intention here was to highlight the diverse conceptual resources on which this approach can draw and thereby encourage a theoretically pluralist **pedagogy** or teaching practice. This is not to say that fundamental differences in how alternative theoretical schools see and study the world can be disregarded, which is one other reason why we did not attempt to synthesize the different lineages of everyday IPE into a single unified framework. What we suggest instead is that productive conversations can be had between theoretical traditions, and that this dialogue may be easier to conduct in the conceptual realm and in regard to familiar real-world phenomena. In this chapter's final section, we outline how we do this in the textbook, through what we are calling the I-PEEL approach.

But first, this is a good moment to level with you about who 'we' are. Embracing an everyday politics requires a certain amount of reflection upon knowledge production itself and the extent to which it can be universalized and applied to all people in all places. To that end, we think it is important to openly acknowledge our own positionality. We all research and teach in relatively secure jobs at a UK university, we were born in the 1970s–1980s, we all identify (and are identified) as white, and we work primarily in English. There's some privilege there, right? By reminding ourselves of this throughout the writing process, we hope to have made the book as inclusive and reflexive as possible. For example, recognizing a persistent male bias in academic citation practices, one thing that we committed to was greater consideration of the gender balance of the authors we cite and engage with. But, of course, we cannot escape our own histories, and nor can we put ourselves outside power relations. So, in the examples we provide and the ideas we prioritize in the book, try to remember that these come from a particular context, and if there are topics or scholars that appear to be excluded, please don't assume it's because they don't belong in IPE. Indeed, they might offer a perspective that the field has been waiting for.

 Access the online resources to watch a video where our authors discuss representation, diversity, and inclusion in this textbook: http://www.oup.com/he/i-peel1e.

To this end, one of the main attractions of everyday IPE for us as teachers is the way it can transform the experiential knowledge that students already possess into academic scholarship. For instance, it is likely that you are well versed in a politics of the everyday through social media usage. Celebrity culture, memes, and Twitter storms now provide a ready flow of critical, reflective, and resistant ideas that constitute a significant part of contemporary political engagement (Dean 2019). This is one reason why we have a chapter on Social Media in the book (see Chapter 7): to demonstrate that seemingly irrelevant actors like 'fitness influencers' can be connected to fundamental questions about wealth and power. In what follows, then, we will try to license your everyday as a basis for learning. We hope this provides an intelligible and meaningful engagement with the IPE literature, whatever your background, and, furthermore, gives you the sense that you are not just a passive recipient of this scholarship but a researcher-in-training, capable of making your own contributions to the field.

1.3.1 How do I use this book?

Access the online resources to watch a video where our authors discuss how the I-PEEL approach was developed: http://www.oup.com/he/i-peel1e.

Before we wrote this textbook, we designed a website. This was our first step in using the lens of 'everyday life' to help students learn about IPE and contains the essence of the approach we adopt here. The website is also called the International Political Economy of Everyday Life and can be accessed at I-PEEL.org. The central pedagogical device of the website was to use everyday objects or practices as a route into the subject matter of IPE. Each entry on the website—what we called a 'tile'—was written by a different scholar in the field and was randomly shuffled on the home page so that each time someone visited the website, they were encouraged to peel back a different tile and embark on another learning journey. In doing this, we wanted to disrupt the sequential ordering of conventional IPE textbooks, which inevitably imply that the topics dealt with first are more important than those dealt with last, or not at all.

In this textbook, then, we want to stress that the objects, subjects, and practices we have chosen as organizing topics for the chapters are meant to be heuristic rather than definitive. We use them to capture your interest and demonstrate the insights (and occasional blind spots) of IPE, not to define what should and should not be studied. We put Clothes (Chapter 2), Food (Chapter 3), and Debt (Chapter 4) first, as these most clearly resonate with IPE's core subject matter of trade, production, and finance, and offer intuitive starting points for an everyday approach. The next two chapters encourage critical engagement with the conventional 'states and markets' approach to IPE. Care (Chapter 5) looks at a form of economic activity that exists largely outside markets, while City (Chapter 6) shows that the nation state is not always the best unit of analysis for understanding changes in state power and capital accumulation. We end with Social Media (Chapter 7),

Table 1.1 Conventional IPE topics and I-PEEL content

Topic	I-PEEL content (and section)
Trade	Clothes trade (2.1), cocoa exports (3.1)
Finance	Student debt (4.1), Islamic finance (4.2.4)
Investment	Place branding (6.1.1), ownership in the sharing economy (8.2.2)
Production	Low-wage manufacturing (2.2.1), prosumers (7.1.3)
Globalization	Global care chains (5.2.2), global cities (6.2.1)
Corporations	Surveillance capitalism (7.2.2), corporate social responsibility (2.2.2)
States	Austerity and the welfare state (5.2.1), state rescaling (6.2.2)
Global governance	Dietary governance (2.2.2), debt cancellation (4.3.2)
Civil society	Alternative economies (8.2.3), satire of Western NGOs (9.2.2)
Gender	Social reproduction (5.1.1), heteronormativity (5.1.3)
Development	'Slum' housing (6.2.3), humour and foreign aid (9.2.1)
Environment	Disposal of clothes waste (2.3.2), unsustainable farming (3.2.3)

Share (Chapter 8), and Humour (Chapter 9) to demonstrate where the I-PEEL approach can take you once you are familiar with it. These are not topics usually covered in IPE but struck us as excellent entry points for discussing the importance of online technologies in reshaping global capitalism and our experiences with(in) it. Despite this loose ordering, the chapters are largely self-contained and can be read out of sequence if needed, allowing them to be consulted alongside other textbooks and key readings that you might be assigned. Table 1.1 indicates some of the connection points between the topics typically covered in IPE courses and the material in the I-PEEL textbook, which if not read in its entirety, could also be used as a starting point or supplement.

Each of the chapters follows the same structure. First is a tile that takes a familiar manifestation of the chapter title to show how it can be understood from an everyday IPE perspective. This section also introduces the chapter's three key concepts. Second is a section that broadens the discussion beyond that specific example and uses the key concepts to analyse a set of IPE questions. We call this section 'Exploring', since we want to convey that these are open-ended investigations: there are other questions to be asked and certainly many different answers that can be given. Third, and finally, are a pair of learning activities. Some of these activities are time-consuming and work best

Table 1.2 What you will learn with I-PEEL

Chapter	Title		Exploring	Engaging
	Object, subject, or practice	Concepts	Analysis	Learning activities
Clothes	Fast fashion	Fast fashion, feminization, corporate social responsibility	How is low-waged labour constructed? Where does corporate social responsibility lie? How is desire manufactured?	Ethical consumption campaign design, presentation or podcast on disposal
Food	Chocolate	Neoliberalism, governmentality, global value chain	What is food security? How are diets governed? Where is value distributed?	Diet autoethnography, foodscape collage
Debt	Student debt	Commodification, assetization, financialization	What are the different kinds of debt? Why do people indebt themselves? Do debts always have to be paid?	Usury thought experiment, sovereign debt role-play
Care	Military wives	Social reproduction, heteronormativity, global care chain	Are we experiencing a care crisis? Is caring harmful? How is care work organized in the global economy?	Time use survey of everyday labour, social annotation of policy document
City	Mega-event	Global city, state rescaling, right to the city	What are global cities? How does urban development take place? Who needs the right to the city?	Urban development case study presentation, privilege trail
Social Media	Fitness influencers	Self-branding, the attention economy, the prosumer	How should social media be regulated? Do we work for social media? Can the social media prosumer be transformative?	Social media resistance group deliberation, documentary film review

(*Continued*)

Table 1.2 Continued

Chapter	Tile		Exploring	Engaging
	Object, subject, or practice	Concepts	Analysis	Learning activities
Share	Ride share	Marketization of everyday life, gig economy, platform capitalism	Where does the sharing economy come from? Who owns what in the sharing economy? Are there alternative economies of sharing?	Iceberg economy exercise, community mapping
Humour	Radical comedy	Resistance, carnival, subversion	Can humour promote global justice? Can the subaltern joke? Is humour dangerous?	Parody collage, make a meme

in groups. For this reason, you may only want to do these if they are assigned as part of a course you are taking. However, we would still encourage you to read about each activity, since they will provide you with relevant methodological guidance on how to do everyday IPE, such as where to find data, how to apply concepts, and what kind of questions to ask in your enquiry. This section is called 'Engaging' as it is designed to translate your experiential knowledge into the language of IPE, and, in the ethos of critical theory, enable you to recognize *yourself* as a political subject (see also Katz-Rosene et al. 2021).

After reading this book, we hope you will be equipped with a conceptual toolkit informed by the lineages of everyday IPE, apprised of ways of applying these ideas, and confident in generating your own research enquiries gleaned from the world around you. We also hope that, while you are able to begin your own studies with the familiar or the intimate, you do not necessarily end there. We are mindful in the chapters to avoid intellectual navel-gazing and instead urge you to consider how economic activity brings you into a relationship with others, the hierarchies of difference on which this depends, and the ethical self-reflection this demands. These are some of the questions we are all left to ponder: Are these relationships 'right' or 'good'? How are they enacted through my everyday practices? And what could I do to live out an alternative?

1.4 Conclusion

International Political Economy can be thought of as the study of power and wealth across countries. Within this academic field, scholars taking an everyday approach have considered the ways that the global economy and global politics are enacted in daily life, inviting analysis of a range of objects and subjects that might otherwise be overlooked. In so doing, they have drawn on various lineages of 'the everyday' in IPE and its cognate fields, using different concepts and theoretical traditions to orient their research. The I-PEEL approach is our attempt to translate this into teaching. It is a pedagogy that starts with the experiences of daily life—including yours—and opens out onto explorations of how social relations of class, gender, race, nationality, and others sustain and subvert global inequalities. It encourages a collective conversation between the different lineages of everyday IPE, unified by a conviction that economic and political outcomes are not natural but socially constructed in, and through, everyday life.

RESOURCES

Adebanwi, Wale (ed.). 2017. *The Political Economy of Everyday Life in Africa: Beyond the Margins*. Woodbridge: James Currey. This book is drawn together around the work of the anthropologist Jane I. Guyer and her attempts to challenge orthodox interpretations of African economies by rereading them through their mundane realities. The introduction is especially useful in setting out how the political economy of everyday life might be understood in an African context.

Best, Jaqueline, and Matthew Paterson (eds.). 2010. *Cultural Political Economy*. Abingdon and New York: Routledge. This book explores the different ways that culture has constituted economic life and shaped the development of capitalism. It features contributions from several authors cited in this chapter (Aitken, Amoore, Davies) and the introduction by Best and Paterson explains how they see 'the everyday' in cultural political economy.

Elias, Juanita. 2010. 'Locating the "Everyday" in International Political Economy: That Roar Which Lies on the Other Side of Silence'. *International Studies Review* 12: 603–9. This article reviews three books that speak to the themes of everyday IPE, one which situates itself in the field of IPE and two which are written from the perspective of Social Anthropology and Labour Sociology. The review outlines some of the ways in which everyday IPE can be done and the different lineages it can draw on.

Elias, Juanita, and Lena Rethel. 2016. *The Everyday Political Economy of Southeast Asia*. Cambridge: Cambridge University Press. This book offers another non-Western application of everyday IPE, exploring the way that economic transformation is sustained and challenged by everyday practices across Southeast Asia.

I-PEEL website (http://www.i-peel.org). This is an open-access resource that presents IPE research through an everyday object, subject, or practice. We contributed tiles on Care (Juanita), Money (Lena), Resistance (James), and Sugar (Ben), and there are many more besides these. In each of the subsequent chapters we recommend two tiles that would make for suitable further reading, but for this chapter we suggest just one, which is Textbook (Matthew Watson).

REFERENCES

Acuto, Michele. 2014. 'Everyday International Relations: Garbage, Grand Designs, and Mundane Matters'. *International Political Sociology* 8(4): 345–62.

Adebanwi, Wale, ed. 2017. *The Political Economy of Everyday Life in Africa: Beyond the Margins*. Woodbridge: James Currey.

Adorno, Theodore W. 1991. *The Culture Industry: Selected Essays on Mass Culture*. Abingdon and New York: Routledge.

Aitken, Rob. 2007. *Performing Capital: Toward a Cultural Economy of Popular and Global Finance*. Basingstoke: Palgrave Macmillan.

Aitken, Rob. 2013. 'The Financialization of Micro-Credit'. *Development and Change* 44(3): 473–99.

Amoore, Louise. 2006. 'There is No Great Refusal: The Ambivalent Politics of Resistance'. In *International Political Economy and Poststructural Politics*, ed. Marieke de Goede, 255–74. Basingstoke: Palgrave Macmillan.

Bedford, Kate. 2019. *Bingo Capitalism: The Law and Political Economy of Everyday Gambling*. Oxford: Oxford University Press.

Best, Jaqueline, and Matthew Paterson, eds. 2010. *Cultural Political Economy*. Abingdon and New York: Routledge.

Billig, Michael. 1995. *Banal Nationalism*. London: Sage.

Blyth, Mark, ed. 2009. *Routledge Handbook of International Political Economy (IPE): IPE as a Global Conversation*. Abingdon and New York: Routledge.

Brassett, James. 2021. *The Ironic State: British Comedy and the Everyday Politics of Globalization*. Bristol: Bristol University Press.

Brassett, James, and Frederic Heine. 2021. '"Men Behaving Badly"? Representations of Masculinity in Post-Global Financial Crisis Cinema'. *International Feminist Journal of Politics* 23(5): 763–84.

Brassett, James, and Lena Rethel. 2015. 'Sexy Money: The Hetero-Normative Politics of Global Finance'. *Review of International Studies* 41(3): 429–49.

Campbell-Verduyn, Malcolm. 2021. 'The Pandemic Techno-Solutionist Dilemma'. *Global Perspectives* 2(1), no pagination.

Clarke, Chris. 2015. 'Learning to Fail: Resilience and the Empty Promise of Financial Literacy Education'. *Consumption, Markets and Culture* 18(3): 257–76.

Cohen, Benjamin J. 2007 'The Transatlantic Divide: Why are American and British IPE so Different?' *New Political Economy* 14(2): 197–219.

Collins, Patricia Hill. 1993. 'Toward a New Vision: Race, Class, and Gender as Categories of Analysis and Connection'. *Race, Sex and Class* 1(1): 25–45.

Collins, Patricia Hill. 2000a. 'Gender, Black Feminism, and Black Political Economy'. *Annals of the American Academy of Political and Social Science* 568(1): 41–53.

Collins, Patricia Hill. 2000b. *Black Feminist Thought: Knowledge, Consciousness, and the Politics of Empowerment*. Abingdon and New York: Routledge.

Cox, Robert. 1981. 'Social Forces, States and World Orders: Beyond International Relations Theory'. *Millennium: Journal of International Studies* 10(2): 126–55.

Crehan, Kate. 2016. *Gramsci's Common Sense: Inequality and Its Narratives*. Durham, NC: Duke University Press.

Davies, Matt. 2006. 'Everyday Life in the Global Political Economy'. In *International Political Economy and Poststructural Politics*, ed. Marieke de Goede, 219–37. Basingstoke: Palgrave Macmillan.

Davies, Matt. 2016. 'Everyday Life as Critique: Revisiting the Everyday in IPE with Henri Lefebvre and Postcolonialism'. *International Political Sociology* 10(1): 22–38.

Dean, Jonathan. 2019. 'Sorted for Memes and Gifs: Visual Media and Everyday Digital Politics'. *Political Studies Review* 17(3): 255–66.

Ehrenreich, Barbara, and Arlie Russell Hochschild, eds. 2003. *Global Woman: Nannies, Maids, and Sex Workers in the New Economy*. London: Granta.

Elden, Stuart. 2004. *Understanding Henri Lefebvre: Theory and the Possible*. London: Continuum.

Elias, Juanita, and Samanthi J. Gunawardana, eds. 2013. *The Global Political Economy of the Household in Asia*. Basingstoke: Palgrave Macmillan.

Elias, Juanita, and Shirin M. Rai. 2019. 'Feminist Everyday Political Economy: Space, Time, and Violence'. *Review of International Studies* 45(2): 201–20.

Elias, Juanita, and Lena Rethel, eds. 2016. *The Everyday Political Economy of Southeast Asia*. Cambridge: Cambridge University Press.

Elias, Juanita, and Adrienne Roberts, eds. 2018. *Feminist Global Political Economies of the Everyday*. Abingdon and New York: Routledge.

Elson, Diane, and Ruth Pearson. 1981. '"Nimble Fingers Make Cheap Workers": An Analysis of Women's Employment in Third World Export Manufacturing'. *Feminist Review* 7(1): 87–107.

Enloe, Cynthia. 1989. *Bananas, Beaches and Bases: Making Feminist Sense of International Politics*. Berkeley: University of California Press.

Federici, Silvia. 1975. *Wages Against Housework*. Bristol: Power of Women Collective and the Falling Wall Press.

Federici, Silvia. 2004. *Caliban and the Witch: Women, the Body and Primitive Accumulation*. New York: Autonomedia.

Fetzer, Thomas. 2020. 'Beyond "Economic Nationalism": Towards a New Research Agenda for the Study of Nationalism in Political Economy'. *Journal of International Relations and Development*. 25: 235–59.

Foucault, Michel. 1977. *Discipline and Punish: The Birth of the Prison*. Trans. Alan Sheridan. New York: Pantheon.

Francis-Devine, Brigid. 2020. 'Coronavirus: Which Key Workers are Most at Risk?', House of Commons Library Insight, UK Parliament, 2 June 2020.

Fridell, Gavin. 2007. 'Fair-Trade Coffee and Commodity Fetishism: The Limits of Market-Driven Social Justice'. *Historical Materialism* 15(4): 79–104.

Gamble, Andrew. 1995. 'The New Political Economy'. *Political Studies* 43(3): 516–30.

Gibson-Graham, J. K. 2006. *The End of Capitalism (As We Knew It): A Feminist Critique of Political Economy*. Minneapolis, MN: University of Minnesota Press.

Gill, Stephen. 1995. 'The Global Panopticon? The Neoliberal State, Economic Life, and Democratic Surveillance'. *Alternatives: Global, Local, Political* 20: 1–49.

Gilpin, Robert. 1987. *The Political Economy of International Relations*. Princeton: Princeton University Press.

Glaze, Simon, and Ben Richardson. 2017. 'Poor Choice? Smith, Hayek and the Moral Economy of Food Consumption'. *Economy and Society* 46(1): 128–51.

Grayson, Kyle. 2013. 'How to Read Paddington Bear: Liberalism and the Foreign Subject in *A Bear Called Paddington*'. *British Journal of Politics and International Relations* 15(3): 378–93.

Graz, Jean-Christophe, Oliver Kessler, and Rahel Kunz. 2019. 'International Political Economy (IPE) meets International Political Sociology (IPS)'. *International Relations* 33(4): 586–619.

Griffin, Penny. 2019. '#MeToo, White Feminism and Taking Everyday Politics Seriously in the Global Political Economy'. *Australian Journal of Political Science* 54(4): 556–72.

Hamilton, Caitlin. 2022. *The Everyday Artefacts of World Politics*. Abingdon: Routledge.

Hanisch, Carol. 1970. 'The Personal is Political'. In *Notes from the Second Year: Women's Liberation*, ed. Shulamith Firestone and Anne Koedt, 76–8. New York: Radical Feminism.

Harmes, Adam. 2001. 'Mass Investment Culture?' *New Left Review* 9 (May/June): 103–24.

Helleiner, Eric. 2002. 'Economic Nationalism as a Challenge to Economic Liberalism? Lessons from the 19th Century'. *International Studies Quarterly* 46: 307–29.

Helleiner, Eric. 2015. 'Globalising the Classical Foundations of IPE Thought'. *Contexto Internacional* 37(3): 975–1010.

Helleiner, Eric. 2021. *The Neomercantilists: A Global Intellectual History*. Ithaca: Cornell University Press.

Highmore, Ben. 2002. 'Introduction: Questioning Everyday Life'. In *The Everyday Life Reader*, ed. Ben Highmore, 1–36. Abingdon and New York: Routledge.

Hobson, John M. 2013. 'Revealing the Eurocentric foundations of IPE: A Critical Historiography of the Discipline from the Classical to the Modern Era'. *Review of International Political Economy* 20(5): 1024–54.

Hobson, John M., and Seabrooke, Leonard, eds. 2007. *Everyday Politics of the World Economy*. Cambridge: Cambridge University Press.

Innes, Alexandria J., and Robert J. Topinka. 2017. 'The Politics of a "Poncy Pillowcase": Migration and Borders in Coronation Street'. *Politics* 37(33): 273–87.

Jessop, Bob, and Ngai-Ling Sum. 2001. 'Pre-disciplinary and Post-disciplinary Perspectives'. *New Political Economy* 6(1): 89–101.

Katz, Cindi. 2001. 'Vagabond Capitalism and the Necessity of Social Reproduction'. *Antipode* 33(4): 709–28.

Katz-Rosene, M. Ryan, Christopher Kelly-Bisson, and Matthew Paterson. 2021. 'Teaching Students to Think Ecologically about the Global Political Economy, and *Vice Versa*'. *Review of International Political Economy* 28(4): 1083–98.

Kipfer, Stefan. 2008. 'How Lefebvre Urbanized Gramsci: Hegemony, Everyday Life and Difference'. In *Space, Difference and Everyday Life: Reading Henri Lefebvre* ed. Kanishka Goonewardena, Stefan Kipfer, Richard Milgrom, and Christian Schmid, 193–211. New York and Abingdon: Routledge.

Langley, Paul. 2008. *The Everyday Life of Global Finance: Saving and Borrowing in Anglo-America*. Oxford: Oxford University Press.

LeBaron, Genevieve. 2010. 'The Political Economy of the Household: Neoliberal Restructuring, Enclosures, and Daily Life'. *Review of International Political Economy* 17(5): 889–912.

Lefebvre, Henri. 1991. *The Critique of Everyday Life: Volume I*. London: Verso.

Lyon, Sarah. 2006. 'Evaluating Fair Trade Consumption: Politics, Defetishization and Producer Participation'. *International Journal of Consumer Studies* 30(5): 452–64.

Mezzadri, Alessandra, Susan Newman, and Sara Stevano. 2021. 'Feminist Global Political Economies of Work and Social Reproduction'. *Review of International Political Economy*. DOI: 10.1080/09692290.2021.1957977.

Montgomerie, Johnna. 2020. 'Indebtedness and Financialization in Everyday Life'. In *The Routledge International Handbook of Financialization*, ed. Philip Mader, Daniel Mertens, and Natascha van der Zwan, 380–9. New York and Abingdon: Routledge.

Oatley, Thomas. 2019. *International Political Economy*, 6th edn. New York and Abingdon: Routledge.

O'Brien, Robert, and Marc Williams. 2020. *Global Political Economy: Evolution and Dynamics*, 6th edn. London: Red Globe Press.

Peterson, V. Spike. 2003. *A Critical Rewriting of Global Political Economy: Integrating Reproductive, Productive and Virtual Economies*. New York and Abingdon: Routledge.

Rethel, Lena. 2010. 'Financialisation and the Malaysian Political Economy'. *Globalizations* 7(4): 489–506.

Rupert, Mark. E. 1995 '(Re)Politicizing the Global Economy: Liberal Common Sense and Ideological Struggle in the US NAFTA Debate'. *Review of International Political Economy* 2(4): 658–92.

Seabrooke, Leonard. 2010. 'What Do I Get? The Everyday Politics of Expectations and the Subprime Crisis'. *New Political Economy* 15(1): 51–70.

Smith, Neil. 2002. 'New Globalism, New Urbanism: Gentrification as Global Urban Strategy'. *Antipode* 34(3): 427–50.

Sue, Derald Wing, Christina M. Capodilupo, Gina C. Torino, Jennifer M. Bucceri, Aisha Holder, Kevin L. Nadal, and Marta Esquilin. 2007. 'Racial Microaggressions in Everyday Life'. *American Psychologist* 62(4): 271–86.

True, Jacqui. 2012. *The Political Economy of Violence Against Women*. Oxford: Oxford University Press.

Tussie, Diane, and Fabricio Chagas-Bastos. 2022. 'Misrecognised, Misfit, and Misperceived: Why Not a Latin American School of IPE?' *Review of International Political Economy*. DOI: 10.1080.09692290.2022.2056902.

Vivares, Ernesto, ed. 2020. *The Routledge Handbook to Global Political Economy: Conversations and Inquiries*. Abingdon and New York: Routledge.

Vogel, Lise. 1983. *Marxism and the Oppression of Women*. New Brunswick, NJ: Rutgers University Press.

Watson, Matthew. 2005a. 'Towards a Polanyian Perspective on Fair Trade: Market-based Relationships and the Act of Ethical Consumption'. *Global Society* 20(4): 435–51.

Watson, Matthew. 2005b. *Foundations of International Political Economy*. Basingstoke: Palgrave Macmillan.

Watson, Matthew. 2013. 'The Eighteenth-Century Historiographic Tradition and Contemporary "Everyday IPE"'. *Review of International Studies* 39(1): 1–23.

2 CLOTHES

2.1	Fast Fashion	29
2.2	Exploring Clothes	37
2.3	Engaging Clothes	49
2.4	Conclusion	53

LEARNING OBJECTIVES

- Understand how the globalization of garment production relates to the feminization of low-wage labour
- Consider the possibilities and limitations of corporate social responsibility initiatives aimed at 'cleaning up' the sector
- Rethink your relationship with fast fashion via an ethical consumption campaign and use storytelling techniques to consider the issue of clothing waste

READER'S GUIDE

Clothing is a topic that is widely discussed in IPE textbooks and academic research in relation to histories of global capitalism, the regulation of international trade, the growth of export-led industrialization as a development strategy, and the exploitation of low-waged workers. In Feminist IPE, the female garment factory worker has also been central to studies examining the reproduction of gender inequalities within global circuits of trade and investment. Picking up these threads, the chapter begins with a discussion of how the garment industry and its workers were impacted by the Covid-19 pandemic, focusing in particular on the vulnerabilities faced by women workers in the UK city of Leicester (Section 2.1). This introduces the concept of fast fashion, situating it within a historical discussion of the globalization of the garment industry during the second half of the twentieth century. Using examples of particular items of clothing—T-shirts and jeans—we delve into the broader politics of international trade that have shaped where in the world the production and disposal of clothing have been located. The next section, 'Exploring Clothes', uses the concept of feminization to look at how and why particular configurations of gendered labour relations dominate the global garment industry (Section 2.2). The discussion then moves to explore whether efforts to 'clean up' the garment sector have been successful, and raises questions about the extent to which we, as consumers, are willing to turn a blind eye to labour and human rights abuses in the garment industry in order to keep up with the latest trends. The final section of the chapter, 'Engaging Clothes', looks at the politics of anti-sweatshop campaigning (Section 2.3). It considers the role that storytelling, using techniques such as podcasting, can play in bringing to life one of the more under-researched aspects of the garment trade: what happens when we dispose of our clothing.

> **KEY CONCEPTS**
>
> Fast fashion; feminization; corporate social responsibility

Access the online resources to listen to a podcast where Juanita introduces and explores the key themes of this chapter: http://www.oup.com/he/i-peel1e.

2.1 Fast Fashion

When the Covid-19 pandemic lockdown forced closures of shops, bars and restaurants, and other workplaces, and large numbers of people were working or being educated from home, many people no longer saw a need to spend as much of their income on clothing. One impact of the pandemic, then, was that declining demand—especially for occasion wear and office wear—saw many major Western retailers simply cancel their contracts with garment suppliers located in poorer parts of the world, such as Bangladesh and Cambodia, often with devastating consequences for workers (Care International 2020). But it also appears that many of us simply changed our consumption habits. We did not stop shopping. We wanted to buy comfortable leisurewear to work or study at home, and although the shops were closed, we were able to purchase this online. In this context and facing disruptions to international transportation and shipping because of the pandemic, major online retailers instead turned to suppliers based closer to home.

During the 2020 lockdown in the UK, the centre of Britain's domestic garment and textile industry in Leicester was thrown into the spotlight when a cluster of cases of the virus were linked to clothing factories in the city. Seeking to fulfil orders placed by one of the UK's major online retailers, Boohoo, shown in Photo 2.1, factories continued to operate as normal despite the restrictions and even carried on as Covid-19 outbreaks occurred among the workforce (Labour Behind the Label 2020). More than £1 billion was wiped off the value of Boohoo when its share price plunged following revelations about working conditions among its suppliers, although this later rebounded when the company reported a 41 per cent increase in revenue thanks to pandemic sales (Hanbury 2021). This example of the Leicester factories reveals some significant

Photo 2.1. Boohoo website offering discounted fast fashion at your fingertips.
Source: Louisa Svensson/Alamy Stock Photo.

issues that will be further investigated in this chapter: the functioning of garment supply chains in an era of 'fast fashion'; the conditions and regimes of work in the sector; and, in particular, the centrality of gender and race to the production of low-waged and exploitative forms of work. At the same time, we also show how everyday practices of fashion consumption not only link us as buyers of clothing to the global political economy but potentially make us complicit in the forms of labour and environmental injustice seemingly endemic to the industry.

The UK garment industry has long been in decline as a major employer. An industry that had employed over 450,000 workers in the 1970s was employing less than 90,000 workers in the early 2000s, as retailers and their UK-based suppliers rapidly shifted production offshore to low-wage manufacturing sites (Elias 2004; Bearne 2018). Nonetheless, in many parts of the Global North, including the UK and the US, low-waged garment manufacturing work has stubbornly remained. Wages are kept low through gendered and racialized workplace regimes whereby women—especially migrant women—are employed at rates that often fall below minimum wage and in poor working conditions. The ability to pay low wages is sustained by recruitment practices whereby firms look to employ workers who would struggle to secure alternative, better-paid employment. Labour Behind the Label, a campaign group that aims to secure better working conditions for garment workers worldwide, reported that over 33.6 per cent of workers in the Leicester garment factories were born outside the UK (from South Asia, Somalia, and

Eastern Europe), and many were especially vulnerable due to their undocumented migration status, lack of English language skills, and inability to access support mechanisms from both the wider community and specific organizations such as trade unions (Labour Behind the Label 2020). In Section 2.2.1 we reflect in more detail on how such intersecting inequalities feed into low-waged, and feminized, labour regimes.

Retailers seeking to keep costs low and ensure a regularly updated supply of the latest trends have come to rely on clothing produced by a disparate network of suppliers based in low-wage locations across both the Global South *and* the Global North. The ability of retailers to set up their supply chains in order to ensure that customers can purchase fashionable garments at low prices is generally described as **fast fashion**. This approach was pioneered in particular by the brand Zara, part of the Inditex group, which brought **just-in-time production** to fashion retailing. It is a business model that is based upon not only the expectation of ever-growing customer demand for cheap clothing but also exceptionally short production runs. For example, Zara went against the convention of having two to four fashion seasons per year in favour of at least twelve (Dicken 2015, 465). The shift to online fashion consumption has increased our appetite for fast fashion, especially as sites selling clothes also link shoppers to quick forms of credit provision like klarna.com, so if you can't afford the latest trends right now, you can always just borrow the money instead (see also Section 4.2.1 on household debt).

Cheap, fast-moving fashions invariably generate waste. In 2016, the magazine *Newsweek* reported that over a twenty-year period the volume of clothing that consumers in the US were throwing away each year had doubled from 7 million to 14 million tons. Some of this waste finds its way to the second-hand clothing market (see Section 2.1.3), but a great deal of it ends up in landfill or as ocean waste (Wicker 2016). Alongside clothing being seen as ever more disposable, we should also consider how the low-waged workers *themselves* are viewed by their employers as disposable (Wright 2006). In Leicester, for example, an extremely vulnerable group of workers—many of whom lacked documented employment status—were rendered disposable—that is, were seen as easily replaceable. This was evidenced in the way in which workers were forced to continue working in the context of a pandemic, exposing them to a deadly virus long before vaccines had been developed.

Questions need to be asked about how and why work in this sector operated through such extreme conditions of worker exploitation. This chapter will reveal that what happened in 2020 in Leicester was not a unique case and cannot be entirely blamed on a handful of 'bad' factory managers and owners. Exploitative and dangerous working conditions and poverty wages underpin our clothing consumption practices, and efforts to 'clean up' garment supply chains have done little to fundamentally change working conditions. The rise of fast fashion certainly plays an important part in the labour and environmental impacts of the industry, but as shown in Photo 2.2, these problems are not new: they are rooted in long-standing histories of exploitation.

Photo 2.2. A nineteenth-century cartoon satirizing the sweatshop conditions in Britain's clothing factories.
Source: Pictorial Press Ltd/Alamy Stock Photo.

The emergence of textiles and clothing production on an industrial and global scale cannot be understood without examining the trade's inhumane practices of labour exploitation, including the brutal legacies of slavery and indentured labour, as well as the long history of 'sweated labour' in the cotton mills and clothing factories of the Industrial Revolution (Riello 2013). Nonetheless, efforts to rethink and challenge consumption practices persist, and there is a genuine desire from certain industry insiders as well as activists and consumers to transform the sector. This chapter asks you to consider your own consumption practices and the extent to which consumers as a group are able to bring about change.

2.1.1 Follow the thing

You are more than likely reading this textbook wearing either a T-shirt or jeans. These classic garments are enduring staples of modern fashion. Take a look at the labels in these items of clothing. Where were they made? Where did you buy them? Were they bought new in a store or online? Or did you look to save money by purchasing your clothing second-hand? How will you dispose of these clothes when they are no longer useful or fashionable? Looking at how a particular commodity or 'thing' like a pair of jeans or a T-shirt is made, traded, consumed, and disposed of is a useful exercise that uncovers much about the dynamics of contemporary capitalism.

On the one hand, it might lead us into a discussion of 'big picture' IPE debates. This could include examining how the expansion of the garment sector was central to the rapid industrialization that has taken place across East and Southeast Asia since the 1970s, and how global trade rules were designed in ways that sought to both limit and accommodate this global shift. On the other hand, 'following the thing' (Cook et al. 2004) can also reveal more intimate human stories, such as the way that the cruelties of international trade are woven into the fabric of our garments through workplace violence, exploitation, and poverty. The Marxist concept of **commodity fetishism** can be useful in terms of understanding how the 'commodity form' (that is, the *thing* that we purchase) exists separately in our imagination from the social relations of production (that is, how and by whom it was produced and the class relations and struggles that governed its production). We purchase commodities like clothing knowing that these items have more than mere use value (keeping us warm and dry); they also have a symbolic value (status, the desire to be seen as fashionable). However, when we consume these items, we think very little about how this commodity's actual value has been derived from labour exploitation or environmental degradation (see also Section 1.2.1 on the commodity fetish as an integral part of the everyday experience of capitalism).

To illustrate the different methodological approaches to following a commodity, consider two books written about T-shirts and jeans. Pietra Rivoli's *The Travels of a T-Shirt in the Global Economy* (2015) argues that by looking at the production and consumption of this everyday object we can learn about 'markets, power and politics of world trade'. Meanwhile Andrew Brooks's *Clothing Poverty: The Hidden World of Fast Fashion and Second-Hand Clothes* (2015), starting with a discussion of second-hand jeans, centres its analysis on what happens to clothing once it is disposed of. Both books provide fascinating, albeit contrasting, perspectives on how the trade in everyday items of clothing provides insights into the wider issues of trade regulation, international development, and labour exploitation.

2.1.2 Trading T-shirts

Rivoli, an economist, writes from a liberal perspective, one that is strongly committed to the benefits of **free trade**. She notes that the trade in clothing and textiles has never been a site of unfettered free trade based on principles of comparative advantage—rather, widespread practices of **Economic Nationalism** have characterized the historical development of production and trade in clothing and textiles. In the seventeenth century, for example, the rapid expansion of French silk production was fostered by state policies that banned imported silks and by strict fashion rules within the royal court of Louis XVI that, in turn, led to a booming luxury clothing market, establishing Paris as Europe's fashion capital (Thanhauser 2022). In the eighteenth and nineteenth centuries, control over cotton production and exports were fundamental to the exercise of British colonialism—for example, in terms of the massive expansion of cotton growing based upon slave labour in Mississippi and Alabama, which supplied the mill towns of northern England with raw material and led to the devastation of India's once thriving global cotton industry as the British flooded the market with cheap textiles (Riello 2013).

In more recent times, global power inequalities have played out within the system for regulating international trade, which up until the late 1990s was subject to significant levels of trade protectionism that counteracted the principle of comparative advantage. In the post-World War II era, states had made ever-widening commitments to free trade under a series of agreements known as the General Agreement on Tariffs and Trade (GATT), the forerunner to the current World Trade Organization (WTO). But while Western leaders frequently extolled the benefits of free trade, at the same time they sought to find new ways to protect domestic industries from the threat of 'cheap foreign imports'. This protectionist impulse within Western states in the post-war period led to a series of trading arrangements designed to protect textile and clothing production that eventually became, in 1974, the Multi-Fibre Arrangement (MFA), a system of 'voluntary' export restraints and quotas designed to place temporary limits on garment and textile exports. The idea was that the MFA would give industrialized countries in the Global North with large garment and textile industries time to adjust to the growth of these industries in newly industrializing parts of the world.

Because garment production is characterized by a low-tech, low-wage, and labour-intensive production model, the industry is generally regarded as a highly mobile, 'footloose' industry. From the 1960s onwards, many states across the Global South sought to expand their industrial base through policies of **export-led industrialization**, and garment manufacturing has often been at the centre of these plans. An unintended consequence of the MFA was that it actually encouraged the rapid globalization of the garment industry. For example, when garment firms based in Hong Kong and Korea saw their growth restricted by quotas, they moved to establish factories in other states that had excess quota and often even lower labour costs (Dicken 2015, 462). As manufacturers and brands located in the Global North sought to increasingly outsource their production to such lower-cost countries, leading to a sharp decline in employment in the sector, the coalition of interests between states, businesses, and workers that had supported the MFA was gradually undermined (Heron 2012). The phasing out or 'unravelling' of the MFA over a ten-year period as part of the agreement reached at the 1994 Uruguay Round of the GATT saw some countries, such as Bangladesh and Turkey, which had developed the industrial capacity to mass-produce garments under the MFA regime, rapidly expand production. As Figure 2.1 shows, countries with low labour costs, many of which are located in East and Southeast Asia, dominate the global export of clothing. However, many parts of Europe are also major clothing exporters. Countries such as Romania, Spain, Bulgaria, Portugal, and the UK have significant garment industries whose competitive advantage is based on both the low wages paid to

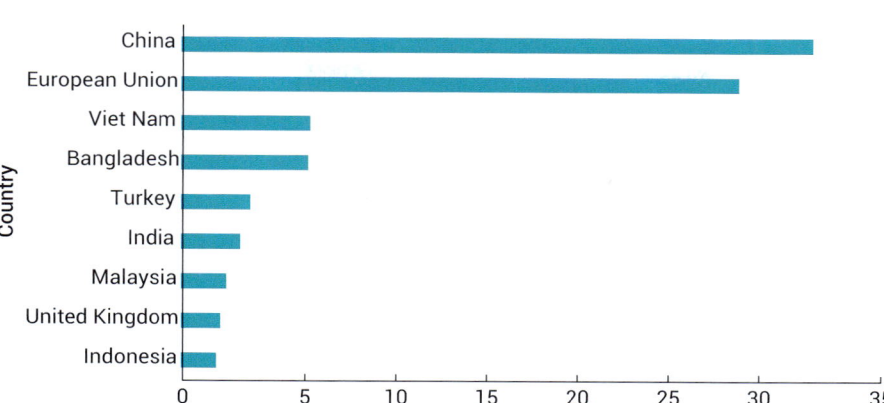

Figure 2.1. Leading countries' share of garment exports.
Source: World Trade Organization (WTO) 2021, 78.

employees and their geographical location within some of the world's most lucrative clothing markets.

Rivoli is especially interested in how political power operates through trade negotiations and the unintended consequences to which these give rise. She notes, for example, how US power was wielded within the framework of the MFA via the allocation of carefully controlled import quotas to politically favoured Cold War allies. At the same time, however, the US's efforts to protect domestic cotton production led to massive investment in the production of artificial fibres in Asia like nylon and polyester, which would ultimately undercut US producers. If we understand free trade, then, as an *absence* of the political interference in markets through state regulation, it is clear that this is not a feature of the historical development of the global garment industry. However, this idea that equates politics with regulation is challenged in Andrew Brooks's *Clothing Poverty: The Hidden World of Fast Fashion and Second-Hand Clothes* (2015). Starting with a discussion of the trade in second-hand jeans, Brooks's book uncovers how the relatively unregulated market for second-hand clothing is nonetheless a site within which structural power dynamics reflective of global development inequalities play out.

2.1.3 Donating or dumping?

For Brooks, the decision *not* to protect local markets and to allow the emergence of a free market in second-hand products is just as political as the decisions that underpinned the MFA. When people in North America or Europe donate used clothing—usually

Photo 2.3. Second-hand football boots on sale at Kantamanto Market in Ghana.
Source: WENN Rights Ltd/Alamy Stock Photo.

to charities or recycling companies—they often have no idea that this clothing is likely to be sold on, and that their donation provides the 'raw material' for a global trade in second-hand garments worth over a billion dollars a year (Brooks 2015, 4). Donated second-hand clothing is compressed into bales and sold on to dealers who import it into poorer countries. On arrival the bales of clothing are 'graded' for quality and sold on to second-hand markets. Some of the world's largest second-hand clothing markets are located in West Africa, including Ghana's Kantamanto Market in Accra (shown in Photo 2.3), with its 5,000 individual shops and a labour force of 30,000 (Ricketts 2020). Whilst this might sound like a positive economic story, Brooks argues that this trade in fact operates as a **dumping** mechanism that has not only decimated local garment production in many parts of the world by undercutting prices but also given rise to its own labour issues insofar as small-time traders and sorters engaged in the industry barely make a living.

In light of such challenges, many states have sought to ban imported second-hand clothing, often with the aim of developing their own clothing industries. This was recently proposed by the East African Community—a regional organization representing Burundi, Kenya, Rwanda, South Sudan, Tanzania, and Uganda—but only Rwanda was successful in implementing such a ban, and has since faced considerable pressure from the US to overturn it. The second-hand clothing markets located across some of the poorest states of the Global South may well provide low-cost clothing for urban

Photo 2.4. Used clothes in a desert landfill in Alto Hospicio, Chile, in 2021. In the nearby free trade zone of Iquique, thousands of tonnes of used clothing arrive for sorting, some of which is resold and some of which is disposed of here.
Source: dpa Picture Alliance/Alamy Stock Photo.

poor populations, but this is hardly a virtuous cycle of waste management. As shown Photo 2.4, so much of the used clothing arriving at second-hand markets is not sold but ends up in municipal landfill sites or is simply illegally dumped, with 'dumping' this time referring to quick and easy disposal. Inevitably, the sheer quantities of waste clothing have increased rapidly with the shift to fast-fashion production.

2.2 Exploring Clothes

Following the journeys of T-shirts and jeans through the global economy has helped us to unpack the fast-fashion industry and provided entry points into broader debates in IPE related to trade regulation, international development, and labour exploitation. In this section we shift perspective and stand back from individual commodity studies to comprehend the everyday IPE in which these production–consumption–disposal circulations are embedded. We begin with the issue of labour exploitation, focusing on the constitutive roles of gender and race in constructing low-waged labour.

2.2.1 How is low-waged labour constructed?

Clothing manufacturing processes have remained largely unchanged for over a century, with garment production long regarded as a site of feminized work. Women dominate the industry, representing more than 80 per cent of the workforce, employed largely as sewing machinists on garment production lines (ILO 2019, 19). The industry is labour-intensive and requires cheap workers to keep costs down, with women often regarded as an easily available pool of cheap labour. But how do we explain these gendered structures of employment and low pay? The answer lies in understanding how the demands of capital for low-paid workers intersect with gendered social norms and practices to produce low-waged feminized work (Elias 2004).

Feminist political economists have developed analyses and concepts that help us to understand how particular ideas, or norms, about the essential nature of women's work sustain systems of low pay. These norms include widely held assumptions about women's 'secondary' labour market status: that is to say, that women are working to merely *supplement* the income of the household provided by the male breadwinner. Women are thus seen as neither deserving higher rates of pay nor requiring job security, being figured instead as part of a 'flexible' workforce that could be easily drawn into the labour market for a short period of time. From the 1970s onwards, an ever-increasing number of countries saw women take up factory employment as states moved to rapidly expand their manufacturing base by developing export-oriented garment industries. In light of this trend, the economist Guy Standing (1999) observed a global **feminization** through flexible labour. This is the idea that the globalization of production was sustaining a quantitative increase in low-waged and irregular forms of work which lacked basic protections and job security. This is characterized as feminization because it is linked not only to rising female labour force participation as a share of overall employment but also to the idea that there are growing numbers of jobs that bear the conventional characteristics of women's work, in the sense that they are irregular, insecure, and low-paid forms of employment.

Alongside these ideas about women's secondary labour market status and flexibility are other sets of gendered assumptions that shape women's experiences of employment in the sector. One of these is that women have 'nimble fingers' and are somehow naturally suited to 'fiddly' work such as sewing (Elias 2004). But it is important to consider how the ability to sew or operate a sewing machine is something that girls and young women often learn to do from an early age. This 'socially invisible' acquisition of skills through domestic labour contributes to the perception that sewing work is unskilled labour (Elson and Pearson 1982, 93–4). The undervaluing of women's contribution as workers is seen more broadly in terms of how women are often confined to lower-paying roles within manufacturing industries. It is worth noting that when economies shift away from industries such as garment manufacture into less labour-intensive and more technologically focused industrial sectors in which pay and working conditions are generally much better, there is a concomitant *de*feminization of the manufacturing workforce in terms of the numbers of women employed (Kucera and Tejani 2014).

In addition, employers in the garment sector often express a preference for female workers because they are perceived as less likely to cause problems on the production line or to go out on strike. Numerous studies have, nonetheless, revealed the *myth* of the docile female factory worker, pointing to long histories of women's involvement in labour activism (Pangsapa 2007; Plankey-Videla 2012). On this view, the supposed docility of female factory workers is less a natural phenomenon than the product of intensive forms of workplace surveillance and disciplining. For example, it has been observed how factory managers often deploy paternalistic management techniques that seek to reproduce ideas of familial loyalty within firms that help to justify demands for long hours (Lynch 2016). In some instances, commitments by firms to 'protect' female workers can lead to *de facto* forms of bonded labour as women are housed in factory-linked hostels or dormitories that serve to control their movement outside factory complexes (Mezzadri and Majumder 2020, 14).

In thinking through the locally specific ways in which feminized low-wage labour is produced, we also need to consider how gender intersects with racial and ethnic inequalities. There is a long tradition of writings that have emphasized how the construction of racial hierarchies 'enshrines the inequalities that capitalism requires' (Melamed 2015, 77).

Photo 2.5. Garment workers in Anhui, China Female factory workers are often depicted as docile employees, devoid of emotions like boredom, anger, or aspiration.
Source: Imaginechina Ltd/Alamy Stock Photo.

The Black Marxist thinker Cedric Robinson (2021 [1983]), for example, used the term **racial capitalism** to describe how capitalism benefits from, and simultaneously reproduces, racial hierarchies that render certain groups less valuable, and thus more disposable, than others. The gender inequalities charted in the preceding discussion need to be understood as operating *within and through* racial capitalism, since both race and gender are central to the construction of garment work as low-paid, disposable labour (Bhattacharyya 2018). Questions need to be raised, therefore, about the extent to which the toleration of poor working conditions in garment production by consumers in the West reflects assumptions and structures rooted in the practices of racial capitalism and colonialism. That is, how my desire to purchase new clothing is seen as more important than the desire of the worker—be they in Leicester or Dhaka—to be paid a living wage and experience safety at work. To return to the phrase used in Section 1.1.2, we ought to ask whose lives matter in the clothing sector and why there is this differential valuation.

2.2.2 Where does corporate responsibility lie?

Discussions of labour abuse and exploitation in the garment sector often highlight the complicity of consumers in sustaining labour abuses. Take as an example the events surrounding the collapse of the eight-storey factory complex in Bangladesh called the Rana Plaza in April 2013, in which over 1,000 people died, the vast majority of whom were women (see Photo 2.6). Seeking to keep production costs as low as possible in order to compete for contracts with major retailers, factory owners had cut corners with health and safety standards, building additional storeys onto a factory building that was not designed to support this extra weight. Major retailers whose clothing was being produced at Rana Plaza sought to distance themselves from the factory collapse: the problem, as they saw it, was caused by unscrupulous factory owners and corrupt local officials who had permitted the building's development.

But such a perspective obscures the role that major retailers play in establishing a diffuse system of production in which it is conveniently unclear where 'corporate responsibility' lies. Major garment retailers own shops and brands: they generally do not own the factories in which garments are made. The actual production of garments tends to be subcontracted down the supply chain. In spite of having stated commitments to **corporate social responsibility** (CSR), major European and North American clothing brands have often engaged in a form of wilful ignorance of the social conditions in which their clothes are made. The ownership structures and geographical distance separating retailers and brands from garment producers can be described as a 'spatial fix' that enables companies to benefit from the low production costs found in low-wage developing countries whilst simultaneously disassociating them from the reputational risks and everyday struggles around wages or working conditions that characterize labour-intensive production (Merk 2011).

Photo 2.6. The 2013 Rana Plaza disaster. The Rana Plaza complex housed five garment factories. It had been designed with six storeys and had been intended only for shops and offices, not factories.
Source: Mamunur Rashid/Alamy Stock Photo.

As the literature on **global value chains** (GVCs) points out, within the 'buyer-driven' supply chains that characterize the clothing industry, those firms at the top of the value chain are able to exert downward pressure on suppliers which are forced to compete on the basis of costs, especially labour costs, to remain competitive (see Section 3.1.2 for an expanded conceptual discussion on GVCs in relation to food). This competition has been described as a 'race to the bottom' which has created downward pressure not only on wages across different countries involved in the clothing trade but also on working conditions and workers' rights (Anner 2020). In addition to the subcontracting of production to networks of suppliers, there is also a subcontracting of labour, whereby intermediaries or brokers source workers, often migrants, for employment in factories (LeBaron 2020, 45–53).

As consumers, we can look at the websites of our favourite brands and see their clear statements on corporate ethics and social responsibility. Voluntary **codes of conduct** in the garment sector have been around since the early 1990s, with major brands such as Nike and Levi's amongst the first to adopt such codes as a response to growing consumer concerns about the prevalence of forced and child labour in their supply chains. But, given the diffuse nature of garment production, to what extent can we be sure that clothing has been produced ethically in firms with commitments to what the International Labour Organization (ILO) calls decent work? That is, that workers have 'quality' jobs in which they earn a fair wage and have job security, basic employment rights, equality of opportunity, and prospects for career development?

One thing to consider is about what is missing from these statements of CSR. For example, a firm might claim to have regular audits to check up on its suppliers' factories, but what do these audits involve? Are they just 'tick box' activities overseen by a third party, or will time be spent talking to workers in factory settings to uncover potential labour abuses? Voluntary codes of conduct are reflective of the emergence of a privatized system of labour governance in many global industries in which much of the day-to-day work of regulating supply chains is undertaken by an ever-growing industry of auditors contracted from the private sector. However, due to the conflict of interest whereby the auditors are paid by the companies whose supply chains they are investigating, the audits can be less than robust. Rana Plaza had seen regular audits and inspections, yet these had failed to report back on poor working conditions, the lack of health and safety standards, and the employment of child labour (LeBaron 2020, 1–3). In the wake of the scandal about the Leicester garment factories mentioned in Section 2.1, Boohoo also admitted that its supplier audit and compliance procedures were not fit for purpose and required 'necessary enhancements' (Boohoo Group PLC 2020, 4).

We might also ask, do corporate codes of conduct include any commitments to improving pay and working conditions for garment workers in their supply chains? It might be hard to find these commitments because, after all, they can potentially increase production costs. But even when commitments are in place to pay living wages to workers, research has suggested that, in practice, genuine commitments to improving working conditions are lacking, and firms may simply signal their involvement in initiatives aimed at improving pay and working conditions to fend off criticism (LeBaron et al. 2021). Given the highly feminized nature of garment sector work, we should also ask whether corporations have established minimum standards when it comes to thinking about issues that specifically impact women—for example, protections for pregnant workers or efforts to combat sexual harassment in the workplace. The fact is that these types of commitments are unlikely because corporate codes of conduct are usually written in a 'gender-blind' manner that fails to recognize the specific problems and grievances faced by women (Pearson 2007).

The significance attached to promoting decent work in global supply chains is underscored in the United Nation's **Sustainable Development Goals** (SDGs), with SDG8 focused on 'decent work and economic growth'. However, as with the ILO's approach to promoting decent work, the SDGs are based upon non-binding targets and commitments. Critics of this approach have therefore suggested we have to move beyond aspirational commitments to improving labour standards in favour of a more comprehensive international labour governance regime backed and enforced by states and international organizations. This might involve embedding commitments to labour standards within bilateral trade agreements or using domestic law to better prosecute firms and brands that are complicit in labour violations (LeBaron 2020). When it comes to voluntary codes of conduct—no matter how well intentioned, and even when they are supported by state actors—deep-seated scepticism remains about whether they can ever serve to clean up the endemic exploitation found in garment supply chains. For example, since the early 2000s many garment firms in Sri Lanka have got on board with government-led initiatives to market the country as a location for ethical garment production or 'Garments Without Guilt'. The sector has sought to embrace higher-end garment manufacturing with guarantees to retailers that sourcing clothing from Sri Lanka is responsible practice. As a consequence, Sri Lankan garment firms are a far cry from stereotypical images of 'Third World sweatshops' (a term that implies that labour and working practices in the Global South are akin to the 'backward' small factory workplaces of the Industrial Revolution in Europe): they are typically well organized and managed, modern, air-conditioned factory spaces. But appearances can be deceiving: low wages are endemic, with unrealistic worker production targets leading to overwork, unpaid overtime, and low or underpaid wages (Gunawardana 2016; Ruwanpura 2022).

Alongside state-led interventions from the top down, we might also consider the important role of bottom-up worker-led initiatives to improve supply chains. Trade unions in particular can transform labour systems by bringing worker voices and concerns into labour governance (Tran et al. 2017). Set up following the Rana Plaza disaster, the Bangladesh Fire and Building Safety Accord seeks to move away from corporate-led voluntarism to a more binding form of labour governance initiated by Bangladeshi and global trade union federations with the support of the ILO and the activist organization Clean Clothes Campaign. The accord has been renewed twice and extended to cover additional countries under its new name the International Accord for Health and Safety in the Textile and Garments Industry. However, many key players in the garment industry, such as the US firms Gap and Walmart, have not signed up to the accord, preferring to pursue non-binding, voluntarist approaches to the governance of their supply chain.

2.2.3 How is desire manufactured?

As discussed in Section 2.2.2, IPE analysis of the clothing sector frequently draws attention to the major retailers and brands that wield huge financial leverage and use this to squeeze profits from their supply chain. However, it is not necessarily the case that workers based at the top of the value chain are working in well-paid and secure forms of employment. For example, the clothing retail sector is yet another highly feminized sector of the economy marked by high levels of job insecurity, low wages, poor working conditions, and ever-increasing forms of workplace surveillance (Van Oort 2018). The kinds of work that people undertake not only in the factories that produce our clothes but also in the places where are clothes are designed, marketed, and sold to us is something that is also worthy of investigation.

Scholars engaged in this area of research have referred to it as the 'production of consumption' (McRobbie 1997; Pettinger 2015). These jobs are often at the forefront of debates around the future of work, especially in Western states in which traditional manufacturing work has been superseded by work in the service sector. Discussions of the future of work have at times tended towards a highly celebratory discourse about the rise of a post-industrial cultural economy in which workers are engaged in creative work. In the garment and fashion industry, this might include people working in the design, advertising, and marketing of clothing, or even as fashion models, make-up artists, and social media influencers (see also discussion of the prosumer in Section 7.1.3). Although it might be celebrated as creative and intrinsically rewarding work, the sector is not immune from practices of labour exploitation. As well as the poor working conditions experienced by retail workers or the drivers on zero hours contracts who deliver your latest online purchases to your door, the fashion industry more widely is marked by highly precarious, and frequently highly feminized, work (see also discussion of the gig economy in Section 8.1.3). Perhaps indicative of the endurance of precarious feminized work in the sector, in the wake of the #MeToo movement, two major fashion retail groups in the UK, Ted Baker and Arcadia Group, were hit with significant allegations of sexual and racial workplace harassment.

The work of enhancing the symbolic value of products by making them desirable is undertaken by designers, marketers, brand managers, salespeople, and retail workers. Focusing on these workers provides insights into not only the capitalist relations of work but also those of consumption. In other words, to understand the clothing industry and fast fashion, we should not only focus on the conditions of work in the sector or its organizational structures; we also need to consider the meaning systems—feelings of pleasure and desire—at work when we purchase and wear new clothing. Take, for example, how we use clothing to 'fashion' and express our identities. Perhaps we are seeking to 'fit in', wearing particular styles of dress to appear professional in the workplace, or perhaps we use clothing to express a unique or even subversive form of identity or expression of creativity. A hallmark of fast fashion is how these desires have been harnessed to accelerate clothing consumption. Zara's constant stock updates, or H&M's collaborations with cutting-edge designers, require consumers to return ever more frequently to its shops and/or websites for fear of missing out on the latest 'must-have' item. As Chua Beng Huat) shows in his ethnography of Singaporean shoppers, this can have profound effects on how we behave and relate to one another:

> Fashion is characterized by constant and rapid change. Its cultural value is perishable and, therefore, requires repetitive consumption. To be 'in fashion', one needs to keep pace with these changes ceaselessly; one must be vigilant, watching the latest trend, make the purchases and wear the clothes before others do. (Huat 2003, 60)

The crafting of class identities in particular is emphasized in work on fashion consumption. The emergence of mass-produced fashion and large-scale fashion retailing

Photo 2.7. Shoppers hit the sales on Singapore's famous Orchard Road shopping district.
Source: Hemis/Alamy Stock Photo.

in the late nineteenth century in part reflected a 'democratization' of fashion, but it also led to the emergence of increasingly sophisticated standards around what constituted appropriate and respectable dress as a growing middle class sought to use the symbolic power of fashion to assert their status (Perrot 1994 [1981], 4). How dress is used as a signifier of class aspiration is a key theme explored by Carla Freeman (2000) in her ethnographic study of Barbadian low-paid female office workers, in which workers signalled their 'professional' status through the purchase of fashionable office wear.

This brings us to another theme in relation to the everyday political economy of clothing: the role that engagement in fashion plays in the production of a neoliberal subjectivity centred on consumption practices and the successful performance of beauty (McCracken 2018: 493). Neoliberal subjectivity can be seen as an idealized notion of individual behaviour and one of the mechanisms through which everyday life under capitalism is governed and disciplined (see Section 1.2.2 on creditworthiness and Section 3.2.2 on healthy bodies). More generally, fashion marketing often mobilizes ideas of the empowered female consumer in which the ability of a woman to purchase clothing *for herself* is viewed as a marker of personal success. Simidele Dosekun's (2019) research amongst upper-class women in Lagos, Nigeria, for example, takes as its subject a group of urban women who fashion themselves in a 'spectacularly feminine style' that asserts a personal brand based around ideas of empowerment and self-management.

The celebratory discourse around women using their own disposable income to purchase stylish clothing does nonetheless tap into important claims about female financial autonomy that challenges dependence on male family members. It also speaks to a concern to cast off tired old stereotypes about what women should or should not be 'allowed' to wear, which involve the policing of female bodies, especially those of young women. But at the same time we need to think carefully and critically about brands that cherry-pick ideas associated with Liberal Feminist thought, making glib assertions about empowerment and choice. In India, for example, one high street fashion brand, Max Fashion, implored its potential customers, '*Behen! Kuch bhi pehen!*' ('Sister! wear whatever you choose!') because 'they may judge you for what you wear. But you can't care. Take charge!' (Max Fashion 2019). Are statements like this best understood as bold assertions of female autonomy and empowerment, or is this more a case of brands simply paying lip service to feminist rhetoric in order to sell more clothes to a growing female middle class (Paul 2019)?

Even with the fun and glamour associated with fashion consumption, shopping for clothing is very much a mundane part of our everyday lives, something that we do without really reflecting about how it connects us to the global political economy. Shopping for clothing is an affective experience central to modern capitalist life; we are constantly aware of the emergence of new trends and are invited to spend money or to take on credit to purchase it. In our everyday environment we see how city centres are sites in which clothing stores proliferate, like the one in Photo 2.8, shaping our experience of the built environment (Crewe 2017).

Photo 2.8. Clothing shops like this Nike store in Shanghai are a key feature of our urban environment.
Source: Lou-Foto/Alamy Stock Photo.

The point that scholars like sociologist Lynne Pettinger try to make is that such consumption practices are *created*, and not by neutral market forces but by workers who are actively engaged in producing consumption. Pettinger (2015, 216) thus observes 'the mismatch between studies of work and studies of consumption' that fail to make this connection. By making visible the work that surrounds consumption we start to think about the everyday practices through which market life, in this case our consumption habits, are produced and sustained. In doing so, we can also see how the work that goes into creating fashionable brands enables a particular affective response, one through which consumers are able to *disassociate* a product from the conditions in which it was produced. In this sense, the spatial fix that enables brands to disassociate themselves from poor labour conditions in their supply chains might be paralleled in the emotional detachment entailed by the fashion drive. As Pettinger writes:

> Nike . . . does not produce the highly engineered trainers, or high-tech running kit that it sells: its designers craft the products and the aesthetics of its own selling spaces; its creatives produce marketing, such as the tagline 'Just do It', to generate feelings in potential consumers. Production is subcontracted, and distant supply chains may generate 'threats' to the Nike brand when the poor working conditions and low pay common to such ways of organizing production are brought to public attention. It is testament to the emotional and aesthetic appeal of the brand that many customers may be aware of the poor working conditions, but find the trainers themselves irresistible. (Pettinger 2015, 216)

This takes us back then to the concept of commodity fetishism introduced at the start of this chapter (Section 2.1.1); perhaps we have a very good idea about the systemic labour exploitation that goes on within the supply chains of garment firms, but we choose not to think about it. The preponderance of child and forced labour in garment supply chains is widely commented on not just in the campaign work of organizations like Clean Clothes Campaign but even in popular culture. In movies that satirize the fashion industry like *Zoolander* (2001) and *Greed* (2019), we see how the wealth of fashion moguls rests upon systematic worker exploitation and unethical labour practices (and, in terms of thinking about the conditions of work for those engaged in the production of consumption, these films also point to endemic sexual harassment within their fashion empires). And yet we continue to buy more and more clothing. Or maybe we *have* read the commitments to CSR that almost all garment retailers and brands have signed up to and we are reassured that it's OK to keep shopping. But to what extent are such initiatives merely an aspect of the production of consumption, a sophisticated form of marketing that enables us as consumers to feel less guilty about our purchases?

We can think about our emotional detachment towards fashion in another way—in terms of how we don't wish to engage with the legacies of colonial power relations at work within clothing trends. Fashion brands have been long criticized for their 'cultural appropriation', a process described by the Black Feminist scholar bell hooks (2015, 380) in her essay 'Eating the Other' as involving 'cultural, ethnic, and racial differences' being 'continually commodified and offered up as new dishes to enhance the white palate'. In the case of fashion this might involve taking ideas and inspiration from non-Western societies without attribution and profiting from this. An example is the use of traditional bright West African Ankara print fabrics in the designer Stella McCartney's spring/summer 2018 collection in Photo 2.9, which attracted a level of criticism. This example is given not to suggest that any non-West African people wearing these prints are wrong to do so but, rather, to draw attention to how big players in the Western fashion industry have extracted value from a cultural product.

Photo 2.9. A model on the catwalk at Paris Fashion Week for Stella McCartney's spring summer 2018 collection.
Source: Sipa US/Alamy Stock Photo.

How we as individuals might seek to challenge the reproduction of gendered and racialized economic practices in both the production and consumption of clothing is a dilemma that we will ask you to reflect upon in more detail in Section 2.3.1 below. When clothing brands state that they are committed to ethical business practices, these commitments usually come about due to concerted consumer pressure on firms to clean up their supply chains. But to what extent does consumer outrage serve to reproduce ideas about the female factory worker as mere voiceless victims of global capitalism? And to what extent does it serve to position those in the Global North campaigning around these issues as 'saviours', a concern that is frequently expressed in relation to various forms of Western humanitarianism? For postcolonial feminist writers such as Chandra Mohanty (2003), building solidarities between female workers in the Global North and the Global South needs to be a key part of global feminist activism against neoliberal globalization. Mohanty's writings push us to think beyond the victim/saviour binary and, rather, to think about building transnational feminist agendas based upon 'political solidarity and common interests' (Mohanty 2003, 144). However, can practical solidarities be built between the producers and the *consumers* of clothing: where might common interests lie, or is there an inherent tension at the heart of practices of 'ethical' consumption?

2.3 Engaging Clothes

2.3.1 Develop an ethical clothing campaign

Garment production and consumption create links between producers and consumers—our purchasing choices impact the lives and livelihoods of workers located near and far. One political question that arises from this is the extent to which consumers can exert pressure to bring about changes to the conditions in which clothing is made. As we saw in Section 2.2.2, leading garment firms have sought to address negative publicity by adopting corporate codes of conduct and producing statements of corporate social responsibility. But what kind of negative publicity cuts through to the boardroom where decisions are made? When do individual consumer choices cohere into collective pressure on companies? And who decides whether 'ethical' consumption is really happening?

Some key actors to consider here would be activist networks like the Dutch-based Clean Clothes Campaign, the UK-based Labour Behind the Label group, and the more social, media-oriented Fashion Revolution, all of which use tactics to push consumers, and brands, to recognize the human stories behind fashion production. We cited the Labour Behind the Label report on Boohoo earlier on, which used testimonials from

Photo 2.10. A 'catwalk' event held in Berlin in April 2018 as part of Fashion Revolution Week, set up to commemorate the Rana Plaza disaster and to push for better working conditions in the garment industry.
Source: dpa Picture Alliance/Alamy Stock Photo.

workers about the illegal opening of factories during lockdown and denial of wages to shame the company in the media. A different form of political mobilization can be seen in the public 'catwalk' event shown in Photo 2.10, which also features the hashtag #WhoMadeMyClothes. This has been used on social media to raise concerns about the working practices in garment supply chains, but also involved images of garment workers holding signs saying 'I Made Your Clothes' in order to encourage more socially conscious fashion consumption practices.

Artistic interventions and performances can also invite consumers to reflect on their purchasing practices by exposing them to the human costs of fast fashion. One such example is Spanish Artist Yolanda Domínguez's art installation 'Fashion Victims' (available at www.yolandadominguez.com/en/portfolio/fashion-victims/), in which shoppers in busy shopping district of Madrid were confronted with well-dressed fashionable women lying face down in the street and covered in rubble. The piece plays on the term 'fashion victim'—one that we associate with consumers of fashion—to expose another group of fashion's victims, namely workers caught up in disasters such as Rana Plaza. It does so by subverting these two notions of victimhood, showing a white Western woman among the debris of a collapsed clothing factory, inviting shoppers to see how consumption and production are connected, and challenging them to see themselves as implicated subjects of labour exploitation (see also Section 9.1.3 on the use of subversion to rework the politics of globalization).

We invite you to explore the issue of ethical garment consumption though a class-based exercise. A starting point for this exercise is to look at your own clothing labels and to think about why your clothing was made in particular parts of the world. Perhaps you could map this out as a class and use this information to inform a wider discussion of clothing production, trade, and gendered divisions of labour, or how best to rethink the choices that you make as a consumer of clothing (see also Ayres 2019, Carlson 2009).

Having reflected on your own consumption practices, the next stage is to develop a campaign to improve working conditions in the sector. In doing so, you will need to consider the form that your campaign will take (a report, petition, artistic intervention, or stunt?) and the target of that campaign (consumers, factories, brands, shareholders, or governments?). As you discuss these campaigning questions, take into account the following questions:

- What are the advantages and disadvantages of hashtag- or meme-based activism such as that pursued by campaigns like Fashion Revolution?
- How do you avoid presenting workers as voiceless victims of global capitalism?
- If you are calling for a boycott of clothing manufactured in a particular country, what might be the downside of this for workers in the sector?
- How could your campaign or intervention be oriented towards asking consumers to rethink their consumption practices—for example, using shock tactics to create feelings of guilt?
- Is it possible to link your campaign to ideas noted in the chapter on Share (Section 8.1.3) concerning alternative capitalism? For example, by encouraging consumers to embrace 'slow' fashion, or to become less invested in practices of consumption and to treasure and preserve what they already have?

2.3.2 Stories of disposal: from classroom quizzes to student podcasts

As discussed in Section 2.1.3, the disposal of clothing via the second-hand clothing market is hugely problematic, leading to never-ending problems of waste management, environmental degradation, and the undermining of local clothing production. Alongside a concern with labour conditions in supply chains, many campaigners like those in Photo 2.11 have thus also raised concerns about the environmental impact of fashion, in part relating to the environmental impact of production itself, but also in

Photo 2.11. Environmental protestors in Cornwall, UK, drawing attention to the environmental cost of fast fashion.
Source: James Pearce/Alamy Stock Photo.

relation to clothing waste. As we mentioned earlier, states like Rwanda have also put in place policies to ban second-hand clothing imports, although pressure on them to remove this raises the question of whether a multilateral approach is needed, such as a binding international treaty to regulate the disposal of donated/discarded clothing.

One simple activity that can be undertaken in or before class is to take a look at the 'Your Plan, Your Planet' quiz on Google, an interactive game that highlights the environmental impacts of waste accumulated in households (see Section 2.5). The short quiz relating to the garment sector provides a stark picture of just how much clothing is being produced and thrown away every year.

Building on this, a more in-depth activity is to pick a topic that can tell a story about the IPE of clothing disposal. Spend some time thinking about the particular issue that you want to focus on in your story—in the spirit of this book, try to conceive of your story as starting from an everyday example or practice in order to develop wider themes and claims. You might focus on regulatory efforts to limit the trade in second-hand clothing in East African countries, local initiatives to distribute second-hand clothing such as the use of school uniform banks, or corporate social responsibility schemes by big retailers to try and cut down clothing waste. You should also think about the form that your story will take. It could take the form of a standard class presentation, or perhaps a blog that your classmates are able to comment on; or, as we set out below, one particularly innovative form of presentation, and even assessment, is to develop a podcast in which you curate your 'story of disposal' using interview material and other sound recordings. Below, we outline some ideas about how to use the podcast format—an activity that, given the work involved, may well work best as a piece of assessed work.

Podcasting is a useful way of presenting interview materials in an innovative and interesting way. An example of how podcasts can be used as a student activity (in this case for assessment) is provided by Ilan rua Wall (2019), who used podcasts to position the student as a producer of their own stories and encourage them to think about how stories are communicated by layering sounds, music, interviews, and voice-overs in ways that creative an immersive experience. Here are a few pointers for how you might approach the task of creating your own podcast:

- Maintain the interest of the listener. Think about the sound recordings that you will use to draw the listener in and maintain their interest—could you use music, sound effects, or even a short dramatization? How will you break up and edit the audio material; could you, for example, use voice-overs to direct the listeners' attention to key themes and issues?

- Technical decisions. You will think about recording and editing software and what recording equipment to use. Is there recording equipment available to borrow from your university, or is the recording function on your mobile phone up to the job? Research what free-to-download editing software might help with the recording and editing of your podcast. There are also certain recording basics that you'll need to get to grips with. This includes making sure that you and your interviewee speak directly into the microphone, not tapping the table or humming in agreement when another person is speaking.

- Ethical issues. If you plan to use interviews as part of your podcast, then you will also need to consider ethical issues—what permissions will you need to get from the interviewee, how will you ensure **informed consent**, and what guarantees do you need to make to them to ensure that they are completely happy with discussing their area of expertise for a recording? This could include conditions of anonymity and approval of the recording. Speak to people that you might know who have produced podcasts or student radio shows in the past and see what advice they can offer you.

2.4 Conclusion

In concluding this chapter, it is useful to provide some reflection on what the study of clothes and fashion brings to the study of everyday political economy. A key thing to note in this regard is that Feminist IPE scholarship has long sought to locate the female factory worker within discussions of the global economy. Indeed, it was women involved in the production of jeans who served as one of the examples in Cynthia Enloe's path-breaking argument that 'the personal is international' (Enloe 2014); an intellectual position which we introduced in Section 1.1.2 as one of the foundation stones of everyday IPE (see also Peterson and Runyan 1993; Pettman 1996). In this chapter we have sought to build on this scholarship, taking a broader perspective that connects together a discussion of the working conditions found in garment manufacturing to consumption practices and the desire for fashion. This was introduced initially via a discussion of commodity fetishism, and later in the chapter we reflected on how the work that goes into producing consumption is a key factor in enabling us as consumers to turn a blind eye to the well-documented abuses and injustices at work within clothing production, as well as to the economic and environmental effects of our practices of clothing disposal. But does this mean that we need to reject fashion? Everyday political economy is one area of the study of IPE in which attention has been paid to 'small pleasures and joyful acts', which may well include the purchase and wearing of clothing (Elias and Roberts 2016, 790). In this chapter, a fundamental question that we want you to reflect on is whether or not you think that we can reimagine our relationship with clothing consumption. Is it possible to have garments without guilt?

 Access the online resources for quizzes, student reflection podcasts, and support for tackling the chapter's learning activities: http://www.oup.com/he/i-peel1e.

RESOURCES

Tile recommendations from the I-PEEL website: 'clothing' (Samanthi J. Gunawardana) http://i-peel.org/homepage/clothing/; 'garbage' (Michele Acuto) http://i-peel.org/homepage/garbage/.

Dead White Man's Clothes https://deadwhitemansclothes.org/intro. A multimedia project exploring what happens to clothing when it is disposed of. Most research is undertaken in Accra, Ghana.

Your Plan, Your Planet https://yourplanyourplanet.sustainability.google/. An interactive website that invites the user to reflect on their clothing consumption.

The True Cost. 2015. 92 minutes. A documentary film directed by Andrew Morgan that exposes the labour and environmental costs of fast fashion.

Greed. 2019. 104 minutes. A satirical film directed by Michael Winterbottom exploring the life of a billionaire fashion mogul. It raises concerns about the ruthless labour exploitation that underpins the industry, tax avoidance, and other forms of unethical corporate conduct.

Dicken, Peter. 2015. '"Fabricating Fashion": The Clothing Industries'. In *Global Shift: Mapping the Changing Contours of the Global Economy*, 7th edn. London: Sage. A comprehensive overview of shifting patterns of garment production and how these relate to changing regulatory contexts.

Ruwanpura, Kanchana. 2021. *Garments Without Guilt? Global Labour Justice and Ethical Codes in Sri Lankan Apparels*. Cambridge: Cambridge University Press. A nuanced exploration of the possibilities and limitations of embedding ethical practices within garment production.

REFERENCES

Anner, Mark. 2020. 'Squeezing Workers' Rights in Global Supply Chains: Purchasing Practices in the Bangladesh Garment Sector in Comparative Perspective'. *Review of International Political Economy* 27(2): 320–47.

Ayres, Jen. 2019. 'Wardrobe Revisioning: How Understanding the Clothes You Have Can Be More Satisfying than Buying More'. *Dismantle*, May.

Bearne, Suzanne. 2018. 'Manufacturing a New UK Clothing Industry', *Drapers Online*. August, https://www.drapersonline.com/insight/analysis/manufacturing-a-new-uk-clothing-industry (last accessed 28 April 2021).

Bhattacharyya, Gargi. 2018. *Rethinking Racial Capitalism: Questions of Reproduction and Survival*. London: Rowman & Littlefield International.

Boohoo Group PLC. 2020. 'An Agenda for Change in UK Garment Manufacturing', Press Release, 25 September 2020. https://www.boohooplc.com/sites/boohoo-corp/files/boohoo-group-publication-of-and-response-to-independent-review.pdf

Brooks, Andrew. 2015. *Clothing Poverty: The Hidden World of Fast Fashion and Second-Hand Clothes*. London: Zed Press.

Care International. 2020. 'What is the Impact of COVID-19 on the Global Garment Industry?' Media Release, 8 April, https://www.careinternational.org.uk/what-impact-covid-19-global-garment-industry (last accessed 5 May 2021).

Carlson, Jon D. 2009. '"What are you Wearing?" Using the Red Carpet Question Pedagogically'. *International Studies Perspectives* 10(2): 198–215.

Chua Beng Huat. 2003. *Life is Not Complete Without Shopping: Consumption Culture in Singapore*. Singapore: Singapore University Press.

Cook, Ian et al. 2004. 'Follow the Thing: Papaya'. *Antipode* 36(4): 557–785.

Crewe, Louise. 2017. *The Geographies of Fashion: Consumption, Space and Value*. London: Bloomsbury Academic Press.

Dicken, Peter (2015) *Global Shift: Mapping the Changing Contours of the Global Economy*, 7th edn. London: Sage.

Dosekun, Simidele. 2019. *Fashioning Postfeminism: Spectacular Feminism and Transnational Culture*. Champagne: University of Illinois Press.

Elias, Juanita. 2004. *Fashioning Inequality: The Multinational Firm and Low Wage Employment in a Globalizing World*. Aldershot: Ashgate.

Elias, Juanita, and Adrienne Roberts. 2016. 'Feminist Global Political Economies of the Everyday: From Bananas to Bingo'. *Globalizations* 13(6): 787–800.

Elson, Diane, and Ruth Pearson. 1982. '"Nimble Fingers Make Cheap Workers": An Analysis of Women's Employment in Third World Export Manufacturing'. *Feminist Review* 7(1): 87–107.

Enloe, Cynthia. 2014. *Beaches Bananas and Bases: Making Feminist Sense of International Relations*, 2nd edn. Berkeley: University of California Press.

Freeman, Carla. 2000. *High Tech and High Heels in the Global Economy: Women, Work, and Pink-Collar Identities in the Caribbean*. Durham: Duke University Press.

Hanbury, Mary. 2021. 'Fast-fashion giant Boohoo unscathed by COVID-19 crisis and modern slavery allegations as sales surge in 2020, analysts say'. *Business Insider*, 5 May.

Heron, Tony. 2012. *The Global Political Economy of Trade Protectionism and Liberalization: Trade Reform and Economic Adjustment in Textiles and Clothing*. London: Routledge.

hooks, bell. 2015. *Black Looks: Race and Representation*, 2nd edn. New York: Routledge.

International Labour Organization (ILO). 2019. 'The Future of Work in Textiles, Clothing. Leather and Footwear'. ILO Working Paper No. 326. Geneva: ILO.

Kucera, David, and Sheba Tejani. 2014. 'Feminization, Defeminization, and Structural Change in Manufacturing'. *World Development* 64 (December): 569–82.

Labour Behind the Label. 2020. *Boohoo and Covid-19: The People Behind the Profits*. Bristol: Label Behind the Label.

LeBaron, Genevieve. 2020. *Combatting Modern Slavery: Why Labour Governance is Failing and What we Can Do About It*. London: Polity.

LeBaron, Genevieve, Remi Edwards, Tom Hunt, Charline Sempéré, and Penelope Kyritsis. 2021. 'The Ineffectiveness of CSR: Understanding Global Garment Company Commitments to Living Wages in Global Supply Chains'. *New Political Economy* 27(1): 99–115.

Lynch, Caitrin. 2016. *Good Girls Juki Girls: Gender and Cultural Politics in Sri Lanka's Garment Industry*. Ithaca: Cornell University Press.

McCracken, Angela B. V. 2018. 'The Global Political Economy of Beauty'. In *Handbook of the International Political Economy of Gender*, ed. Juanita Elias and Adrienne Roberts, 486–502. Cheltenham: Edward Elgar.

McRobbie, Angela. 1997. 'Bridging the Gap: Feminism, Fashion and Consumption'. *Feminist Review* 55(1): 73–89.

Max Fashion. 2019. Ultimate Women's Day Fashion Anthem. Max Kehta hai, 'Behen Kuch Bhi Pehen!' [video] https://www.youtube.com/watch?v=p7Ypffp8LZU.

Melamed, Jodi. 2015. 'Racial Capitalism'. *Critical Ethnic Studies* 1(1): 76–85.

Merk, Jeroen. 2011. 'Production Beyond the Horizon of Consumption: Spatial Fixes and Anti-Sweatshop Struggles in the Global Athletic Footwear Industry'. *Global Society* 25(1): 73–95.

Mezzadri, Alessandra, and Sanjita Majumder. 2020. 'Towards a Feminist Political Economy of Time: Labour Circulation, Social Reproduction and the "Afterlife" of Cheap Labour'. *Review of International Political Economy*. DOI: 10.1080/09692290.2020.1857293.

Mohanty, Chandra. 2003. *Feminism Without Borders: Decolonizing Theory, Practicing Solidarity*. Durham: Duke University Press.

Pangsapa, Piya. 2007. *Textures of Struggle: The Emergence of Resistance Amongst Garment Workers in Thailand*. Ithaca: Cornell University ILR Press.

Paul, Maggie. 2019. 'Brands Must Stop Pushing Consumerism Under the Garb of Women Empowerment'. *The Wire*, March.

Pearson, Ruth. 2007. 'Beyond Women Workers: Gendering CSR'. *Third World Quarterly* 28(4): 731–49.

Perrot, Philippe. 1994. *Fashioning the Bourgeoise: A History of Clothing in the Nineteenth Century*. Trans. Richard Bienvenu. Princeton: Princeton University Press.

Peterson, V. Spike, and Anne Sisson Runyan. 1993. *Global Gender Issues*. Boulder: Westview Press.

Pettinger, Lynne. 2015. *Work, Consumption and Capitalism*. London: Palgrave Macmillan.

Pettman, Jan Jindy. 1996. *Worlding Women: A Feminist International Politics*. London: Routledge.

Plankey-Videla, Nancy. 2012. *We Are in this Dance Together: Gender, Power and Globalization at a Mexican Garment Firm*. New Brunswick: Rutgers University Press.

Ricketts, Liz. 2020. 'Dead White Man's Clothes'. *Fashion Revolution*. https://www.fashionrevolution.org/dead-white-mans-clothes/#:~:text=Liz%20Ricketts%20is%20co%2Dfounder,she's%20been%20observing%20since%202011 (last accessed 5 May 2021).

Riello, Giorgio (2013) *Cotton: The Fabric that made the modern world*. Cambridge: Cambridge University Press.

Rivoli, Peitra. 2015. *The Travels of a T-Shirt in the Global Economy: An Economist Examines the Markets, Power and Politics of World Trade*, 2nd edn. New Jersey: John Wiley.

Robinson, Cedric J. (2021) *Black Marxism: The Making of the Black Radical Tradition*, 3rd edn. Chapel Hill: University of North Carolina Press.

Ruwanpura, Kanchana. 2022. *Garments without Guilt? Global Labour Justice and Ethical Codes in Sri Lankan Apparels*. Cambridge: Cambridge University Press.

Standing, Guy. 1999. 'Global Feminization Through Flexible Labor: A Theme Revisited'. *World Development* 27(3): 583–602.

Thanhauser, Sofi (2022) *Worn: A People's History of Clothing*. London: Allen Lane.

Tran, Angie N., Jennifer Bair, and Marion Werner. 2017. 'Forcing Change from the Outside? The Role of Trade-Labour Linkages in Transforming Vietnam's Labour Regime'. *Competition and Change* 21(5): 397–416.

Van Oort, Madison. 2018. 'The Emotional Labor of Surveillance: Digital Control in Fast Fashion Retail'. *Critical Sociology* 45(7–8):1167–79.

Wall, Ilan rua. 2019. 'Podcasts as Assessment: Entanglements and Affect in the Law School'. *The Law Teacher* 53(3): 309–20.

Wicker, Alden. 2016. 'Fast Fashion is Creating an Environmental Crisis'. *Newsweek*, 1 September.

World Trade Organization (WTO). 2021. *World Trade Statistical Review 2021*. Geneva: WTO.

Wright, Melissa. 2006. *Disposable Women and Other Myths of Global Capitalism*. London: Routledge.

3 FOOD

3.1	Chocolate	59
3.2	Exploring Food	67
3.3	Engaging Food	82
3.4	Conclusion	86

Food

LEARNING OBJECTIVES

- Explain the concepts of neoliberalism, governmentality, and global value chain
- Analyse the meaning of food security, how diets are governed, and where value is distributed in the agri-food sector
- Evaluate your daily diet using autoethnography and create a foodscape of the moral economy of veganism

READER'S GUIDE

Food has featured prominently in IPE scholarship, with a particular focus being the international trade of agricultural commodities and its developmental implications in the Global South. At the everyday level, meanwhile, attention has centred on moral economy questions about how market rationality is acted out and contested through practices of food consumption. To show how these different themes can be linked together, the chapter begins with a case study on chocolate (Section 3.1). This looks at the corporate brands behind the globalization of chocolate, the associated transformation of dietary patterns, and the attempts to ameliorate exploitation in cocoa production through ethical consumption. The next section, 'Exploring Food', shows how these trends can be drawn together conceptually with reference to neoliberalism, a key term in IPE and in Food Studies generally (Section 3.2). It considers the meaning of food security, how diets are governed, and where value is distributed in the agri-food sector. It also builds on the IPE literature by drawing on scholarship in other fields that looks at the relationship between food and the body, emphasizing the unequal embodiment that can result from different structural hierarchies. The final section is 'Engaging Food', which introduces research methodologies used to study the everyday, namely autoethnography and foodscaping, and shows how these can be used to reflect theoretically on your daily diet and the moral economy of veganism (Section 3.3).

KEY CONCEPTS
Neoliberalism; governmentality; global value chain

 Access the online resources to listen to a podcast where Ben introduces and explores the key themes of this chapter: http://www.oup.com/he/i-peel1e.

3.1 Chocolate

M&M's World Shanghai is a superstore dedicated to the chocolate sweets manufactured by Mars, a multinational company based in the US. When it opened in 2014, Mars executives depicted the store as a cross between a theme park and a sales outlet, a place which would offer a 'unique retail experience . . . that engages and excites fans of the M&M's® brand from all over the world' (Mars Retail Group 2014). Visitors could gaze at a Great Wall of Chocolate made up of a million M&M's, have their photo taken with life-size M&M's dressed up as terracotta warriors and pandas, and even scan their face to create their own M&M avatar to use on social media. While international tourists to Shanghai were part of their target audience, the big commercial ambition of Mars was to build brand affiliation among Chinese nationals. That year only 0.2 kg of chocolate per person was sold in China, compared to 2.2 kg per person in the US (Cohen and Patton 2015). Combine that with China's large population and continued economic growth, and we begin to understand why Shanghai was the first place Mars chose for an M&M's World outside the US and UK.

Mars is not the only chocolate manufacturer to have set its sights on China. Following the liberal reforms of Chinese leader Deng Xiaoping in the 1980s that opened the country's economy to foreign firms, the world's big five chocolate manufacturers of Hershey, Mars, Mondelēz, Nestlé, and Ferrero all began to view China as 'the next great frontier, a market of almost limitless potential' (Allen 2010). However, these Western companies faced an immediate cultural challenge. Chocolate was little more than an exotic curiosity in China, so how could they persuade people to embrace this foreign food and consume it in large quantities?

Initial attempts involved grafting chocolate onto the customary practice of gift-giving, marketing it as a luxury present suitable for weddings and celebratory events like Valentine's Day and its Chinese equivalents. For Chinese men, expensive-looking chocolates have now become a socially recognized way of conveying their romantic love, suggesting both the success of this strategy and its gendering effects (see *The Straits Times* 2019).

To really boost sales, though, purchases of chocolate for *personal* consumption were necessary. To this end, young women were targeted directly. The most popular chocolate in China now is the Dove brand owned by Mars. Adverts for Dove have focused very much on the sensual experiences of women, presenting it as a silky-smooth product that would provide chocolate lovers with a moment of indulgence. Mars has also hired female pop stars and models to act as social influencers, and even made a promotional ASMR video where a bar of Dove is slowly unwrapped for the viewer's delight (ASMR stands for autonomous sensory meridian response, the tingling sensation some people get from hearing quiet noises at close proximity and the basis of an entire genre of

Photo 3.1. A customer poses for photos in M&M's World Shanghai, China.
Source: Imaginechina Ltd/Alamy Stock Photo.

YouTube videos). This contrasts with the advertising campaign for M&M's which has been oriented towards frivolity rather than sensuality, appealing more to children as potential eaters and buyers. What links the different campaigns together, though, has been the company's general marketing strategy to 'encourage young people to pursue their own pleasure' (cited in Wang 2018). What we can see here then is how Mars and other foreign firms have made significant investments in constructing different types of 'chocolate consumer' in China, instructing them in what good chocolate tastes like and, most fundamentally, how they could satisfy their desires through the market.

3.1.1 Chocoholics? Dietary change and public health

The marketing push in China seemingly paid off. Between 2000 and 2013 sales of chocolate in the country grew over 400 per cent to US$2.4 billion. And nor was it just in China where this occurred. Encouraged by the big five manufacturers, which by this point produced over half the world's chocolate, similar increases in chocolate sales were recorded in countries including Brazil, India, Russia, and Ukraine. Economists have since described this period as a 'chocolate boom' (Poelmans and Swinnen 2016).

The impacts of this dietary change did not end with the bottom line of company profits. The spread of Western diets has also been linked to the growing waistline of the consuming public. According to the World Health Organization (WHO) since 1975 the number of adults considered to be obese has tripled to more than 650 million (WHO 2020a). Once considered characteristic only of Western countries, levels of obesity have also risen in low-income and middle-income countries. One reason has been the increased consumption of energy-dense foods as more and more people, especially those living in urban areas, have undergone a 'nutrition transition' towards diets based on refined cereals, processed meat, edible oil, and sugar (Popkin et al. 2012). It is easy to see why chocolate has been situated within this historic transformation in the human diet. As well as being an energy-dense combination of cocoa butter and sugar, it is also the type of food that can easily be eaten to excess. The compulsion and craving associated with this product are captured in Figure 3.1, which shows the increased use of the word 'chocoholic' since the 1980s—a portmanteau of 'chocolate' and 'alcoholic' that signals its addictiveness.

The reason why the WHO and other health authorities have taken such an interest in obesity is because a raised body mass index (BMI) is deemed to be a major risk factor for heart attacks, strokes, diabetes, and cancers. These chronic diseases are the biggest killers worldwide, far exceeding deaths attributable to communicable diseases and injury. This is a grim statistic unlikely to change even with the Covid-19 pandemic (WHO 2020b). Consequently, chocolate has been caught up in public health initiatives to reduce the excessive consumption of fats, salt, and sugar. For example, as part of the Healthy China 2030 strategy to reorient the country's healthcare system from disease treatment to disease prevention, national state agencies in China have stated their intention to promote the use of low-calorie sweeteners in place of sugar, and to introduce product labelling on sugar content

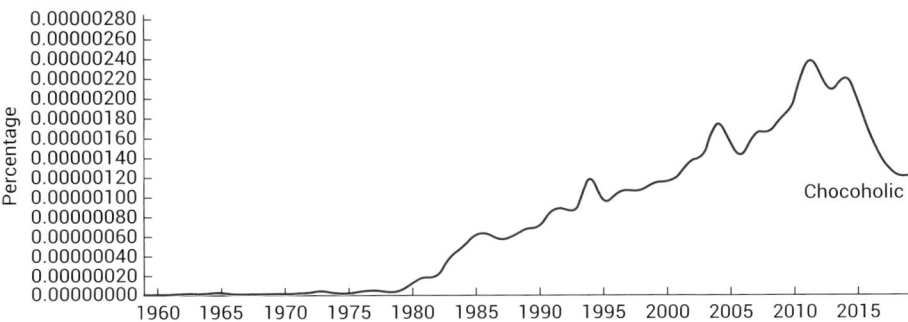

Figure 3.1. Use of 'chocoholic' in English-language books scanned by Google (the authors). These graphs are called Ngrams and are a quick way to chart discursive changes over time. You can generate them for free at: https://books.google.com/ngrams.

to encourage healthier choices (Neo 2019). Demonstrating how such policies have spread internationally, around a third of the world's countries have adopted food reformulation programmes, whilst a quarter require front-of-pack nutritional labelling (WHO 2018). This public policy emphasis on healthy eating and dietary restraint might also be captured in Figure 3.1, albeit this time in the *declining* use of the term 'chocoholic' during the 2010s.

For capital invested in the sale of products deemed to be unhealthy, such policy initiatives are generally considered to be threatening, and in various ways these businesses and their lobby groups have sought to make the case against reform. Taking their cues from the battle over tobacco regulation, strategies to do this have included sponsoring scientific research to present alternative findings on the health impacts of certain diets and proposing the use of voluntary guidelines over mandatory regulation (Nestle 2013). They have been aided in this opposition by the wider ideological and gendered critique of the 'nanny state' from the political right, as shown in Photo 3.2. This has framed public health initiatives as an interference in the rugged individualism of **Economic Man**, a figurative trope defined by the exercise of market choice and **personal responsibility**. These are both key terms in the neoliberal lexicon, to which we return in Section 3.2.2 when we look at how diets are governed, including by ourselves.

Photo 3.2. Two New York newspapers after the law supported by Mayor Bloomberg to limit the size of sugar-sweetened drinks to 16 fluid ounces (just under half a litre) was struck down in the New York Supreme Court.
Source: Richard Levine/Alamy Stock Photo.

3.1.2 The dark side of chocolate: child labour in cocoa

Despite changes in where chocolate is sold, to whom, and in what quantities, the supply of its key ingredient—cocoa—has remained remarkably consistent. For decades it has been concentrated in West Africa, with Côte d'Ivoire and Ghana accounting for over 60 per cent of all cocoa beans produced worldwide (International Cocoa Organization 2020). Unlike other tropical crops that are grown on large plantations by waged labour, cocoa tends to be cultivated by smallholder farmers reliant on family and informal labour. Once harvested and dried, the beans are shipped off to cocoa companies for processing into ingredients and then sold onto chocolate manufacturers and eventually retailers. The fact that most of the processing and manufacturing is undertaken in Europe and the US has thus given chocolate a pronounced development dimension, linking the livelihoods of poor cocoa producers in the Global South to the decisions of wealthy companies in the Global North.

In the early 2000s, this linkage was politicized by media exposés on the prevalence of child slavery on cocoa farms. Though some of the claims were later recognized as sensationalist, confusing legal forms of 'child work' on family farms with illegal forms of 'child labour' in hazardous activities, there was sufficient reason for moral indignation at how the chocolate manufacturers had turned a blind eye to who was growing their cocoa (Berlan 2013). In the US, public pressure built to the point where politicians were planning to introduce mandatory product labelling to designate whether chocolate was free from slavery or not. This stung the chocolate companies into action. To avoid stringent legislation of their sourcing practices, they negotiated the Cocoa Protocol, a voluntary agreement with international organizations, trade unions, and campaign groups to eliminate the worst forms of child labour in the cocoa sector by 2005. However, this **private governance** alternative to a statutory legal framework has been subject to the same criticism made against voluntary approaches to public health, namely, that companies cannot be trusted to self-regulate when this conflicts with their pursuit of profit (see Section 2.2.2 for a broader discussion of corporate social responsibility as a form of private governance in the clothing industry). As evidence, critics point to the continued existence of child labour in the cocoa industry and the continual extension, seemingly without consequence, of the Cocoa Protocol deadline for its eradication (Whoriskey and Siegel 2019).

One way of analysing the persistence of child labour and the limits of private governance has been to study cocoa production using a **global value chain** approach (see Section 2.2.2 for how this has been applied to clothes production too). This involves linking the activities of firms that bring a product from conception to consumption, including things like design and marketing as well as the more obvious processes like manufacturing and logistics that physically transform goods and move them across borders. This is important since, as we saw with chocolate bars in China, intangible assets like brand-name recognition are just as important to generating sales and justifying price premiums as product quality, if not more so. The global value chain approach also politicizes transnational production by highlighting how the activities in the chain are coordinated and where the market value of the final product is distributed, focusing on the use of market barriers by firms to shut out competitors and generate different kinds of economic rent (Gereffi 2018). Studies taking this approach have shown how the 'lead firms' governing the chain and capturing the gains in the chocolate industry have been processors and manufacturers, based on their control of technological rents and brand-name rents. By contrast, following the dismantling of state marketing boards in the 1980s, farmers have been unable to negotiate collectively over cocoa prices and so have been restricted to the role of price-taker (Fold 2002; Barrientos 2016).

The global value chains analysis thus explains *why* certain companies are implicated in the ongoing exploitation of children and suggests different policy responses to address this problem. Take Photo 3.3 by the German-based Make Chocolate Fair campaign. This is one of many that have sought to highlight the small share of the sale

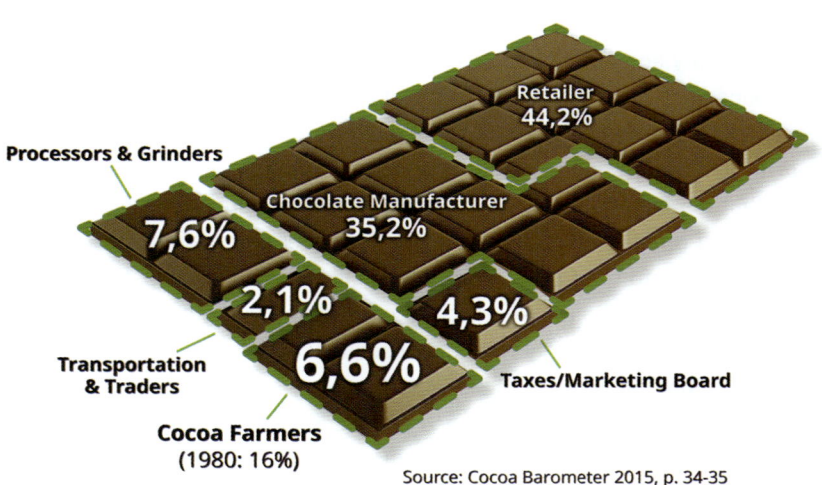

Photo 3.3. Visualization of the global value chain for chocolate.
Source: Make Chocolate Fair.

price of chocolate that goes back to the farmer and how that inequality has widened since the 1980s. From this perspective, the continued use of cheap child labour is seen as a structural necessity caused by the fact that cocoa farmers cannot afford to pay decent wages or make investments in better working conditions. In other words, the higher labour standards that manufacturers and processors demanded from cocoa farmers were made impossible by the low prices they paid them. Consequently, the campaign's demands were directed exclusively at chocolate companies and began with the call for a minimum cocoa bean price to guarantee a living income for small-scale farmers (Make Chocolate Fair 2013).

3.1.3 Competition and coordination in the cocoa market

In the wake of the Cocoa Protocol, chocolate companies have addressed a variety of issues through forms of private governance, including not just child labour but also the endemic poverty of cocoa farmers and the deforestation that has resulted from land being cleared for cocoa tree planting. Indeed, by the end of the 2010s there were over ninety 'sustainable livelihoods' initiatives in Côte d'Ivoire and Ghana alone (Capillo and Somerville-Large 2020). These included third-party labelling schemes like Fairtrade and Rainforest Alliance, which certify production on farms according to certain social and environmental standards, as well as the codes of conduct and sustainability programmes run in-house by the chocolate companies themselves, such as Cocoa Life by Mondelēz, which funds community projects like off-farm entrepreneurial activities.

Taken together, they might be read as indicating a profound shift in the **moral economy** of chocolate, insofar as the industry seems to have accepted at least some responsibility for the social and environmental conditions in which cocoa is produced. We return to the moral economy of food and its appearance in everyday life in Section 3.3.2, but for now consider the reasons why chocolate companies have signed up to so many private governance initiatives. As already discussed, one set of reasons were preventative. Monitoring and regulating conditions among cocoa farmers could help avoid reputational damage caused by media exposés and forestall stringent legislation being imposed by state authorities. Another set of reasons were causal. The future of cocoa was threatened by several factors, including the reluctance of younger generations to impoverish themselves in the sector and the declining yields of old and disease-prone trees. Private governance initiatives were seen by companies as one way to address these problems and secure supply of their key ingredient. Indeed, the Director of the Mondelēz programme later acknowledged that, 'When we set up Cocoa Life it was really a business decision . . . we were not able to grow our business on a weak supply chain' (cited in Nieburg 2020).

This rationale for private governance had been put forward by a number of industry actors concerned that they were jeopardizing their future. One of these was the commodity trader Armajaro, which had warned chocolate companies that if they did not take action to improve the long-term prospects for cocoa production then demand would soon outstrip supply, leading to shortfalls in sales (Barrientos 2016). Armajaro's authority in this world derived from the audacious trades of its CEO, Anthony Ward. In 2010 Ward had bought £658 million worth of cocoa beans and then saw prices rise to their highest level in decades, allowing him to sell at considerable profit and live up to his nickname, 'chocfinger', a reference to the James Bond villain Auric Goldfinger, who speculated on the price of gold (BBC 2010). 'Chocfinger' was unusual both for the size of his trades and the fact that his firm took physical delivery of the cocoa. Most financial traders buy and sell derivative 'cocoa contracts' and have no direct role in the global value chain, distancing them from the site of production. Nevertheless, due to the sheer size of the bets being placed, they have become increasingly influential in determining cocoa prices. Indeed, this **financialization** put paid to Anthony Ward's own cocoa fund, which he closed in 2017 after sustaining losses, laying blame on the 'systems and algorithmic traders' who had no interest in the supply and demand of the physical commodity but nonetheless 'overwhelmed the market' with their trades (White 2017). This financialization of cocoa also filtered back down to the farm gate in the form of price volatility, making it difficult for farmers to forecast prices and forcing them into rushed sales that failed to maximize revenue (Purcell 2018; see Section 3.1.3 on financialization of student debt).

From the West African perspective, enough was enough. After the piecemeal progress seen in private governance initiatives and the repeated protestations by cocoa farmers, one of which is shown in Photo 3.4, in 2019 the governments of Côte d'Ivoire and Ghana sought a more decisive intervention. Returning to the ethos of the state marketing boards that had been used to manage supply prior to the economic liberalization of the 1980s, they announced that they would coordinate sales to drive up prices, withholding entire harvests of cocoa beans from export if necessary. Whether they will be able to honour this pact and take the difficult political action to prevent cocoa farmers and intermediaries from selling at whatever price they can get remains to be seen. The more general point for our purposes, though, is to consider how the dynamics of value distribution in agri-food markets depend as much on coordination as they do on competition. Coordination between companies to stave off the ruinous effects of market competition, and coordination between farmers and workers to improve their lot by negotiating collectively, are arrangements we revisit in Section 3.2.3.

Photo 3.4. In 2006 cocoa producers staged a protest in Abidjan, Côte d'Ivoire, to demand higher prices and more financing for cooperatives. The sign on the right reads, 'Farmers are dying of hunger'.
Source: Reuters/Alamy Stock Photo.

3.2 Exploring Food

In Section 3.1 we touched on the personal responsibility expected of consumers, the transnational power exercised by corporations through advertising and sourcing, and the transformation of commodity markets into sites for financial speculation. Cutting across these different lines of enquiry is the concept of **neoliberalism**. As a salient concept in the field of IPE (we have already mentioned it in Sections 1.1 and 2.2.3) that is also widely applied in studies of food, it is helpful to first explore its different meanings.

One interpretation is that neoliberalism is a utopian project to reorganize the economy based on free markets. Associated with the theoretical work of Austrian economist Friedrich Hayek, its proponents are committed to the traditional liberal idea of individual freedom and believe this is best advanced through the continual extension of market exchange, price competition, and private property. On this view, neoliberalism is seen positively as a way to limit the arbitrary power of the state and establish harmonious international economic relations (Mont Perelin Society 1947).

An alternative and critical interpretation is that neoliberalism is a political project to 're-establish the conditions for capital accumulation and to restore the power of economic elites' (Harvey 2005, 19). Associated with Marxist thinkers, in this reading the emergence of neoliberalism since the 1970s through policies like liberalizing trade and privatizing state-owned organizations has been essentially instrumental. In other words, the roll-back of the state and the roll-out of the market were not pursued for ideological reasons but to allow old or new ruling classes to enhance their wealth. On this view neoliberalism is seen as socially regressive and frequently reliant on police and military force to push through unpopular policy reforms.

A final interpretation is that neoliberalism is a political rationality—a way of governing society by inducing people to act according to economic calculation. Associated with French philosopher Michel Foucault (2008), this approach has traced neoliberalism through the enabling of choice in daily life and its internalization by individuals in pursuit of self-autonomy. Foucault and his followers have sought to interrogate the possibilities of neoliberalism rather than straightforwardly critique it, and thus have tended to have a more ambiguous normative position about whether it should be defended or rejected. In our responses to some of the key questions about the IPE of food in Sections 3.2.1–3.2.3, we return to these different interpretations of neoliberalism and expand on how they operate.

3.2.1 What is food security?

One of the most striking inequalities of the global food economy, embodied by the cocoa farmers in Photo 3.4, is the existence of hunger amidst plenty. Despite huge increases in agricultural productivity over the twentieth century, hundreds of millions of people still lack enough to eat, and in extreme situations starvation from famine remains a grim possibility. Debates on world hunger are often discussed in reference to 'food security'. This term been profoundly political, having been used to both diagnose the causes of hunger and prescribe appropriate policy responses. It is usually traced back to the 1974 United Nations (UN) World Food Conference, which was held in the context of an unfolding famine in Bangladesh and rising prices on commodity markets. At this conference, the problem of 'world food security' was defined as:

> [T]he urgent need to ensure availability at all times of adequate world supplies of basic food-stuffs, particularly so as to avoid acute food shortages in the event of widespread crop failure, natural or other disasters, to sustain a steady expansion food consumption in countries with low levels of per capita intake and to offset fluctuations in production and prices. (UN 1975, 14)

Accordingly, in the Universal Declaration on the Eradication of Hunger and Malnutrition, UN member states agreed to promote national food self-sufficiency through the international coordination of food reserves, development aid, and agricultural policy. What the UN conference thus reinforced was a collective understanding that food security was imperilled by the national shortage of essential commodities, which was best addressed by making more food available through the application of capital-intensive Western farming methods and the acceptance of US grain surpluses as food aid.

Critiquing this account of food security from a liberal position was the economist Amartya Sen. In his pioneering analysis of famines, Sen began by asking an important distributional question: if food shortages affected a whole population, why was it that only some people died of starvation? His answer led him to the notion of entitlement failure. **Entitlements** were defined as the ways in which people legally acquired food. This might be growing it themselves as peasants, working for food as sharecroppers, receiving it as a member of a religious community, or earning money as waged labourers and buying it through the market. Revisiting analyses of the 1974 famine in Bangladesh, which had been widely attributed to flooding, Sen showed that in fact *more* rice had been produced that year than in previous harvests, demonstrating that the availability of food was insufficient as an explanation for famine. He also found that those most susceptible to starvation were in landless households which relied on work as rural labourers or transport service providers to earn income and buy food. The key entitlement failures that Sen picked out were thus reduced employment opportunities and food inflation, which by diminishing wage earnings and making rice relatively more expensive, had combined to price these occupational groups out of the market to devastating effect (Sen 1981).

Translated into policy, the essential response from this perspective was not to make more food available but to identify failing entitlements and rebuild them as quickly as possible. This has involved the distribution of food via non-market mechanisms, such as 'food-for-work' employment schemes for non-disabled people, as well as emergency cash transfers to provide those at risk of starvation with adequate purchasing power. Indeed, over the last decade the UN World Food Programme has moved increasingly in this direction. It now provides over a third of its food assistance as cash, which includes e-cards as illustrated in Photo 3.5, with the remainder distributed in kind as sacks of cereals, pulses, and other essentials (WFP 2020).

Scholarly analysis of the turn to cash transfers has been mixed. Some have seen it as another manifestation of the financialization of food. The World Food Programme's partnership with MasterCard has raised concerns for requiring recipients to use retail outlets that are linked into global financial markets—outlets which typically sell foods grown and manufactured by big businesses in large volumes to the exclusion of local foods from small-scale farmers (Clapp and Isakson 2018). Other critics of cash transfers have argued that they undermine forms of universal public provision, such as free school meals or fuel subsidies for cooking, which might be more effective at reaching

Photo 3.5. An e-card issued to Syrian refugees in Turkey by the World Food Programme.
Source: European Union/ECHO/Caroline Gluck.

those in need and less likely to be treated as a temporary measure prone to sudden budgetary reductions (Lavinas 2013). Following Foucault's definition (as introduced in Section 3.2) and offering a more open-ended interpretation, James Ferguson has suggested that it might be possible to annex neoliberal 'arts of government' to a more redistributive left-wing agenda. This was based on his reading of the Basic Income Grant campaign in South Africa, which had pushed for an unconditional monthly cash transfer to all citizens using the same rhetoric on empowerment through individual choice that characterized debates on food assistance (Ferguson 2010).

Despite Sen's intervention, deep-seated scepticism also exists about the term food security. As we have seen, in its liberal guise it is seen by many—especially those working in the Marxist tradition—as opening the door to anti-hunger policies based on market inclusion via cash transfers, thereby entrenching neoliberalism (Jarosz 2011). It is also seen as effacing the class relations and international relations of global capitalism that put people in positions of structural vulnerability, exposing them to the kind of sudden market disruptions that Sen dissects but does not historically contextualize.

The term food security is considered no less problematic in its nationalist guise, where it is seen as a discursive vehicle for the interests of powerful states (see Section 1.2 for more on Economic Nationalism in IPE). During 2007–8, for example, a global food crisis was declared when the world market price of cereals, dairy, and vegetable oils rocketed to levels not seen since 1974, and food riots broke out in many poor import-dependent countries. World leaders at the G8 Summit were quick to pledge more money for agricultural investment after years of relative neglect. One important difference from 1974, however, was the absence in the accompanying statement of any reference to national self-sufficiency. Instead, state elites committed to 'reduce trade distortions and refrain from raising new barriers to trade and investment' so that food would be available across national borders (L'Aquila Food Security Initiative 2009, 3). This was seen by critics as another way in which food security had been appropriated for neoliberal ends, used in this case to promote an export-led model of industrialized agriculture that served the interests of transnational corporations and affluent consumers in the Global North (Lawrence and McMichael 2012). This was not dissimilar to the security of supply rationale that motivated the chocolate companies and cocoa traders to intervene in the conditions of production in West Africa. Ultimately, then, for these scholars food security is an ideologically compromised concept. For this reason, they have rejected its use in anti-hunger discourse altogether, preferring the term adopted by the international peasant movement of 'food *sovereignty*' (Patel 2009).

Photo 3.6. Convened shortly after the 2009 G8 Summit, the World Summit on Food Security brought together 4,700 delegates at the UN Food and Agricultural Organization headquarters in Rome and reiterated the line on maintaining WTO consistent policies.
Source: Abaca Press/Alamy Stock Photo.

3.2.2 How are diets governed?

Despite their differences, the various interpretations of food security discussed in Section 3.2.1 all tend to equate security with an absence of hunger, understood as not having enough to eat. From a public health perspective this concern has had to be widened to include the nutritional content of *what* people eat. As we saw in Section 3.1 on chocolate, part of this concern has focused on the excessive consumption of energy-dense food leading to unhealthy weight gain. It is important to state at this juncture that both the causes and consequences of obesity are widely contested in the medical literature. Even the very definition of obesity based on a person's body mass index (BMI), calculated as weight divided by height, has been challenged as it neither differentiates between types of body mass—be it fat, muscle, or bone—nor where that fat is located on the body. For this reason, it can lead to systematic misrepresentations of obesity and 'fatness' between different groups, often with racialized consequences in how health is reported. In the US, it is commonplace to read that African Americans have higher levels of obesity than white Americans, with the implication being that they have worse health, and more judgementally, worse lifestyles too. Yet studies have shown that, at the same level of BMI, those in the former group tend to have less body fat overall and less fat surrounding their internal organs than those in the latter group, meaning that the health risks attributed to obesity levels must vary too (Guthman 2014).

Despite such concerns about the universalization of (white) medical norms, influential organizations like the WHO and the United Nations International Children's Emergency Fund (UNICEF) have nonetheless accepted obesity and overweight as a systemic risk to health, adopting terms like the 'triple burden of malnutrition' to stress that getting enough calories is only one part of being properly fed, the other two parts being the right nutrition and the avoidance of excess (UNICEF 2020). As shown in Photo 3.7, this approach produces a global geography of food insecurity, zooming out from the usual focus on impoverished or war-torn states in sub-Saharan Africa, South Asia, and the Middle East as sites of hunger to make the case that 'every country in the world is affected by malnutrition' (Development Initiatives 2018, 14). It also invokes a normative commitment to govern diets, purposefully changing what people eat to reduce the burden of ill health within that population.

Whilst some studies of dietary governance have focused on public policy interventions by state authorities and international organizations to change the regulatory environment in which food is supplied (Haddad 2003; Hawkes et al. 2010), others have given more attention to the role of self-governance by consumers, using the lens of **governmentality** (Cairns and Johnston 2015; Guthman 2008). Coined by Foucault (2008) to refer to the techniques used to govern the conduct of the population, this can be thought of as a fusion of 'government' and 'rationality'. In the context of

Photo 3.7. The annual Global Nutrition Report was designed to track commitments made by the international community to reduce child malnutrition. The scope was widened to include adult malnutrition, using the proxies of overweight and anaemic women.
Source: Development Initiatives.

food, it has involved individualizing responsibility for risks like dietary-related disease and transforming them into problems of self-care and rational choice. In this way, dietary governance is not centrally imposed by the state but instead operates through the diffuse and mundane ways in which people manage themselves in line with state ideals. Think here of your various encounters with fitness classes, step counts, cookery books, and calorie calculators. To the extent that you willingly use these to navigate your food choices, you too might be said to be a subject of neoliberal governmentality.

Accounts of how neoliberal governmentality is acted out through the body have led to the related concept of **embodied neoliberalism** (Guthman and DuPuis 2006). This is a contribution informed by feminist thinking, which emphasizes the lived experience of accepting the logics of self-autonomy and personal responsibility into our emotional and physiological selves. These experiences are not uniformly 'bad'. For example, studies of healthy eating among women found that they described their diets and all the work that went into them—making juices, shopping organic, knowing superfoods—as a positive and empowering act of informed life choice, albeit one that also involved continual surveillance and bodily control (Cairns and Johnston 2015).

However, these positive experiences must be considered alongside those of people unable to embody the neoliberal ideal, often because of a lack of time and money. For many, informal censure is the result. The naming and shaming of people as obese has been particularly potent in this regard. The moral coding of fatness as representing a lack of self-control and the fiscal coding of obesity as a drain on taxpayer-funded health systems has helped to legitimize fat-phobic behaviour and produce disciplinary power across different institutional settings (Glaze and Richardson 2017). In the institutional setting of the workplace, which of course has direct bearing on economic outcomes, studies have discovered the widespread existence of weight discrimination in decisions over hiring, wage setting, promotion, and redundancy. In the US, such discrimination is believed to be comparable to rates of racial discrimination, especially among women engaged in consumer-facing jobs where appearance matters (Puhl and Heuer 2009). Moreover, as a warning of what can happen if one becomes 'fat', weight discrimination can be said to govern *all* bodies, no matter their size (Evans and Colls 2009).

From this perspective, then, one form of resistance to embodied neoliberalism has been to re-evaluate the body and liberate it from societal and patriarchal expectations about how it should look. As shown by the 'I Weigh' social media campaign in Photo 3.8, this discursive re-evaluation remains an ongoing project, and insofar as it involves policing other people's conduct, one with its own political tensions.

Literature in the Marxist tradition offers an alternative interpretation on dietary patterns too, seeing them not so much governed through public policy or individual self-care as structured by the power of agri-food capital (Friedmann 2000; Otero et al. 2018;

Photo 3.8. Instagram post in 2018 from the actor Jameela Jamil, which prompted other women to follow with their own unfiltered pictures and statements of how they weighed/valued things differently.
Source: Jameela Jamil via Tumblr.

Richardson 2015). One example of this structuring would be the way farm lobbies have managed to lock in subsidy regimes that enable the overproduction of agricultural commodities, which in turn provide continual flows of cheap corn, soy, sugar, and milk for use as food ingredients. Another would be the way that multinational corporations like the big five chocolate manufacturers have deployed huge marketing budgets and mass-production techniques to globalize the consumption of **industrial foods**. Despite being based at the different stages in the global value chain, these agricultural and manufacturing fractions of agri-food capital have fitted together in mutually supportive ways. One of the most significant has been the transnational articulation of large-scale plantations producing animal feed with factory farms producing pig and poultry meat. For Tony Weis, this 'industrial grain-oilseed-livestock complex' has been the basis for the unprecedented 'meatification' of the human diet (Weis 2013).

From this perspective, the uprooting of food from its geographical context and its commodification within market relations has also meant that what people eat is determined less by their culture or nationality than by their socio-economic status. In the pithy phrase of Harriet Friedmann (Friedmann et al. 2016), there are now **class diets**: McDonald's chicken nuggets for the poor and organic avocados for the rich, at least in the Global North. This provides a different optic on studies of the nutrition transition. Instead of taking rising income levels and urbanization as its explanatory variables, the class diet lens focuses on the changing social relations of global capitalism. For example, as the primary providers of family meals, the mass entry of women into the waged labour force has encouraged an increased reliance on industrial foods to help meet the double burden of earning income whilst feeding others. The class diet also provides a different optic on the state. Whereas the neoliberal governmentality approach focuses on how the state identifies and manages health risk within the population, the emphasis here is on how the state has enabled new regimes of capital accumulation that have allowed multinational agri-food companies to expand the availability of industrial foods.

Since the 1980s policies to promote agricultural liberalization and protect foreign investors and their intellectual property have provided the legal framework for the globalization of class diets, driven by the core states of the world economy. This has been dubbed a 'corporate food regime', defined by the institutionalization of market relations and private property that privilege agribusiness and undermine peasantries (McMichael 2012, 682). The North American Free Trade Agreement (NAFTA) is often cited as an example of how the corporate food regime functions in practice, whereby a lowering of trade barriers reorientated Mexico's agricultural systems from traditional maize cultivation towards the export of fruits and vegetables for affluent foreigners. The effect on Mexicans, meanwhile, was to encourage consumption of industrial food made using cheap subsidized corn imported from the US, like the corn-syrup drinks shown in Photo 3.9 (Otero et al. 2018). On this view, hopes for more equitable health outcomes

Photo 3.9. A shop vendor in Mexico City, 2015. To address growing health problems, in 2013 the Mexican government levied a tax on sugary drinks of 1 peso per litre. In 2020 the Mexican state of Oaxaca went one further and banned the sale of sugary drinks and high-calorie snack foods to children.
Source: Benedicte Desrus/Alamy Stock Photo.

reside in the material rather than the discursive dimension of diets, led by a class-conscious politics that tackles corporate power by using the state to restrict sales of industrial food and renew the supply of fresh produce from small-scale farmers.

3.2.3 Where is value distributed?

An enduring question in the field of IPE is 'who gets what'? So far in the chapter we have looked at this in relation to the distribution of commodities, namely who gets to eat what food? But another way of posing this question is in relation to the distribution of value, asking who gets to acquire what wealth? As we discussed in relation to chocolate in Section 3.1, one way of answering this is through global value chain analysis. To recap, this approach looks at how the market value of a final product is distributed among the various firms involved in its production. Its method of tracing inter-firm links across national borders has lent itself to the study of how firms located in poorer parts of the world might move into higher value-adding activities, typically measured through increased selling prices. The opportunities and limitations for **upgrading** can thus be taken as defining the prospects for capital and labour in global value chains, and, by extension, whether participation in them will lead to economic development.

Across the primary commodity sector as a whole, it is rare to find cases where wealth is concentrated among producers. One notable exception is in fossil fuels such as oil, due in part to the Organization of the Petroleum Exporting Countries (OPEC), which since the 1970s has coordinated supply to push up prices. Indeed, it was for this reason that the agreement between Côte d'Ivoire and Ghana mentioned in Section 3.1.3 was dubbed 'the OPEC of cocoa'. Certainly, within agriculture most political economy studies conclude that firms further down the chain benefit most (Barrientos 2019). In explaining this phenomenon, the idea of a 'retail revolution' in food has been persuasive (Burch and Lawrence 2005). This points to the way cafés, fast-food restaurants, and supermarkets do much more than just sell food: they influence what people buy and how food is made. Consumption practices have been changed through the relentless promotion of convenience shopping and by marketing tools such as loyalty cards, while production has been governed through private standards on food quality and safety that suppliers must adhere to if they want their products to be stocked on the shelves. The recent entry of big tech firms like Amazon, Alibaba, and Uber into food retail and delivery is seen as further revolutionizing the global food economy through their integration of consumers' online and offline worlds (see also Chapters 7 and 8, Social Media and Share).

In order to examine whether entry into retailer-led global value chains translates into benefits for the workers and farmers involved in them, scholars have drawn a distinction between *economic* upgrading and *social* upgrading. Economic upgrading refers to the process whereby firms move into profitable activities based on value creation or capture, whereas social upgrading refers to the improvement of wages, incomes, and labour standards among the firm's employees and its suppliers. In the case of African agriculture, supermarkets have offered new export markets but on the basis that producers meet exacting standards of cost, quality, safety, and delivery times. For women in the fresh vegetable industry in Kenya, this meant migrating to the peri-urban areas close to airports where greenhouses are located and working under more disciplined labour regimes, albeit at higher wages than they earned previously (Dolan and Humphrey 2000). In the Ghanaian pineapple and South African fruit chains, meanwhile, some waged workers saw important benefits, particularly in the packing and processing stages where women predominated (shown in Photo 3.10), though these were not extended in the same way to the casual workers employed via agencies or the smallholders acting as subcontractors (Barrientos 2019). What these findings demonstrate is that economic upgrading does not automatically lead to social upgrading, and that in some cases like cocoa, economic and social *down*grading can result from the integration into global value chains.

Photo 3.10. Table grapes being packed for export in South Africa.
Source: Eye Ubiquitous/Alamy Stock Photo.

Another distinction drawn by scholars is to differentiate between value-adding activities. In their study on the global value chain for coffee, Benoît Daviron and Stefano Ponte (2005) argued that coffee growers in the Global South have remained relatively poor not only due to the market power of large intermediaries like coffee roasters, which were able to keep prices down by playing suppliers off against one another, but also because the value in a cup of coffee has been increasingly generated through the symbolic and immaterial qualities provided by café culture. In other words, what you are paying for when you buy a cup of coffee is not the coffee itself but the *experience* of drinking the coffee. In this context, attempts by producers to create added value through improving the material quality of coffee beans, such as providing a consistent size or colour, has had limited impact. To the extent that producers might be able to capture some of the value generated further down the chain, Daviron and Ponte concluded that the geographical identity of the beans had to be emphasized and consumers encouraged to become coffee connoisseurs, willing to pay extra for single-origin varieties because it told them a story about a specific place. In effect, producers needed to capture **symbolic value** by imitating the upgrading strategies of vineyards in the value chain for wine.

This general account of the distribution of value in the global food economy has been complicated by a number of alternative perspectives. Methodologically, data on *relative* rates of profit have been used to question the 'supermarket mastery' thesis, showing that in the period 2002–12 the profits of the world's biggest grain traders and agricultural input companies grew much faster than those of retailers and manufacturers. This was attributed to the inflationary dynamics that culminated in the 2007–8 food crisis, caused in part by the diversion of grains and oilseeds into the production of biofuels for sale in energy markets (Baines 2014). For its part, the literature on the financialization of food has shown how questions about value distribution must also consider companies based *outside* the immediate value chain. These include investment funds engaged in agricultural futures markets, as discussed in Section 3.1.3, as well as banks and other lenders financing land purchases and selling services like farm insurance (Clapp and Isakson 2018).

A more frontal attack on the global value chain approach has come from scholarship which treats value not as an expression of social worth registered in a market price but as a reflection of the socially necessary labour time required to produce a given type of commodity (Quentin and Campling 2018). The **law of value** is the term applied to the competitive dynamic in capitalism that compels businesses to produce commodities below the average cost of that socially necessary labour time. Scholars using this Marxist concept are therefore more interested in class relations than inter-firm relations when it comes to questions of whether farmers and workers have improved their standard of living. According to Ben Selwyn (2012), two factors typically overlooked in global value chain studies of social upgrading within Latin American food exporters have been the role of trade unions and egalitarian patterns of land distribution. He argued that where these existed, they have provided workers with a collective bargaining power to negotiate concessions from employers and have enabled farmers to become business owners by forming agricultural cooperatives. Whilst businesses were still subject to the law of value, because of these two factors they had steered away from competitive strategies that forced extra work or lower pay onto those at the bottom of the labour hierarchy.

Supplementing this has been an eco-Marxist critique which asks about the impact of the law of value on the environment (Campling and Havice 2019). This starts from the premise that natural resources like fresh water and fertile soil constitute the **conditions of production** that enable capital accumulation to take place (O'Connor 1988). However, the compulsion to produce commodities below average cost means that firms tend not to renew these conditions but instead take them for granted. For those based in the agri-food sector, this might mean spreading nitrogen fertiliser onto fields and planting them year after year to ensure a continuous high-yielding harvest, only for local rivers to become polluted with agrichemicals and the soil to become exhausted as it is never allowed to lie fallow. Unless the conditions of production can be protected through regulation to control harmful practices or renewed in some other way, such as incorporating newly deforested land into commercial production as discussed in the cocoa industry (see Section 3.3.1), sooner or later an ecological crisis

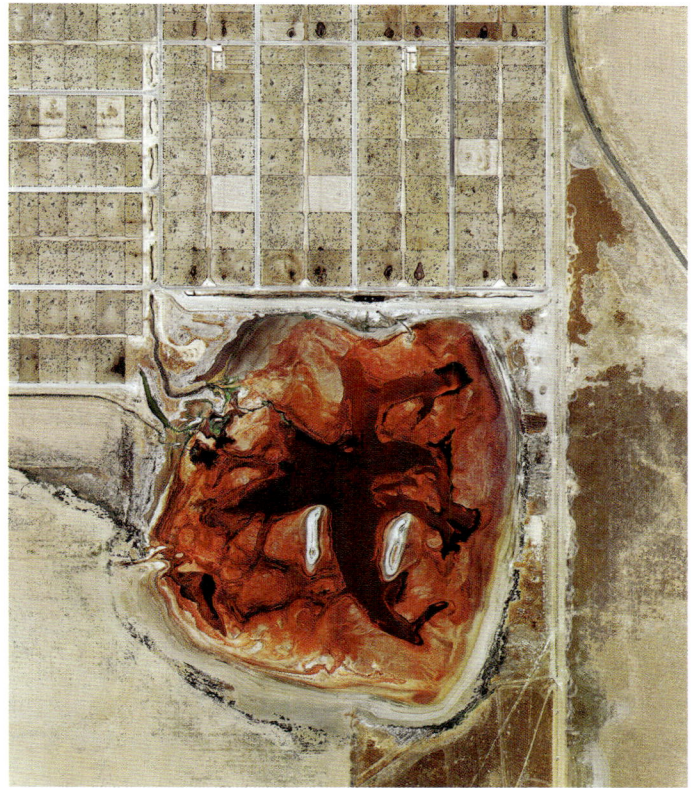

Photo 3.11. 'Coronado Feeders, Dalhart, Texas' by Mishka Henner. This is an artwork made from publicly accessible satellite images, showing cattle pens and an adjacent lagoon turned red by the chemicals used to break down the waste.
Source: Mishka Henner.

erupts affecting both the industry itself and wider society. Photo 3.11 depicts the toxic environment created by intensive cattle farming: the cause of many incidents of water pollution, and one of the sites where this internal contradiction of capitalism appears most acute.

Indeed, some scholars have argued that, with the dawning disaster of climate breakdown, the planetary exploitation of capitalism has gone so far that these contradictions are now beyond resolution. So much damage has already been done and there are so few 'free gifts of nature' left to incorporate into production that commercial losses of one sort or another are unavoidable. The term **negative value** has been used to refer to the build-up of insurmountable barriers to capital accumulation posed by the pollution, depletion, and exhaustion of the environment (Moore 2015). Negative value can thus be thought of as a series of economic sinkholes lying silently in wait in unknown destinations around the world—easily ignored until they suddenly collapse and wipe billions off company balance sheets, rendering established ways of making money completely inviable. In this respect, questions about the distribution of value in food might need to look less at where value is realized and more at where it is imperilled.

3.3 Engaging Food

3.3.1 An autoethnography of the food consumer

In these learning activities we provide some more methods that license your everyday as a basis for studying IPE. We start with Naeem Inayatullah's (2011) promotion of autobiographical writing as a way to acknowledge how personal narratives influence abstract theorization. In his edited book, scholars were invited to use *their* life stories to reflect on why they have come to research the world in a certain way. Interestingly, many of these autobiographies mention food. In her essay, for example, Alina Sajed writes about growing up in communist Romania, where daily experiences of food rationing and an empty fridge were punctuated by occasional encounters with exotic recipes or imports from the West. This translated into a sense that her country was 'backward, uncivilized, and outside of Europe'. Yet, after emigrating to Canada to pursue her career, she found that she still missed many aspects of that old life, including buying 'the freshest fruits and vegetables from peasants' and not being bombarded with 'advertisements, publicity, consumerism, labels, information, pressure, deadlines, offers, sales' (Sajed 2011). Ultimately, Sajed uses this narrative to reflect on how national identity is formed and what it means for a country to be 'developed'.

A similar project of autocritique was undertaken by the geographer Robyn Longhurst, who used feminist readings of Foucault's notion of care of the self to critically examine her experience of dieting. Despite publicly supporting the fat-affirming 'Health At Every Size' movement, Longhurst recognized that she still privately desired to lose weight. Reflecting on this contradiction, she concluded that Foucault's suggestion that we can freely choose an aesthetic to cultivate in our selves does not fully appreciate the power of dominant beauty ideals—in this case, those pertaining to the slim body (Longhurst 2012; see Section 7.1.1 on the way that bodily physiques are cultivated on, and for, social media).

This exercise draws on these self-reflective methods to develop critical insight into 'the food consumer'. The task is to write a reflective essay of 1,000 words on your daily diet. Methodologically, this is more autoethnography than autobiography: you are not writing your life story but offering a discreet 'self-narrative that places the self within a social context' (Reed-Danahay 1997, 9). To get you started, try to recall what you ate yesterday and pick out a certain food, dietary regime, eating pattern, or mode of acquisition like having a meal cooked for you at home or buying it through a food delivery app. Once you have decided on an aspect of your diet to write about, elaborate on how this came to be and why you persist with it. Questions you might consider include:

- How important have economic factors like affordability been in your choices compared to sociocultural ones like honouring tradition or eating the latest superfood?
- Can you detect traces of corporate or state power that might have structured your decisions?
- Did this practice involve elements of globalization, nationalization, or localization at all?
- What *kind* of food consumer are you (impulsive, conscientious, calculative, etc.), and does this subjectivity change when you are in different places with different people?

Once this is complete, read a relevant piece from the references in this chapter, such as those relating to entitlements (Sen 1981), embodied neoliberalism (Guthman and Dupuis 2006), or class diets (Friedmann et al. 2016), and test its analysis against your autoethnography. How neatly does it map onto your account? Are there any aspects

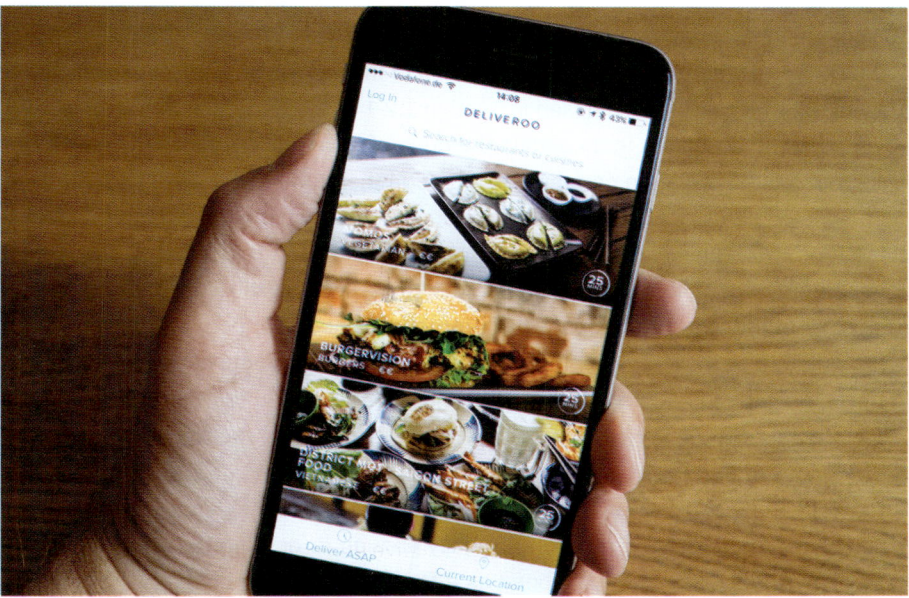

Photo 3.12. Delivery apps are changing when, where, and what we eat—with potentially transformative consequences for the organization of wealth and power in the food economy.
Source: FocusTechnology/Alamy Stock Photo.

of food consumption it has misconstrued or missed altogether? In this way you can use the self as a methodological resource to open up critical perspectives on the way consumer rationality and subjectivity are understood in the existing literature.

3.3.2 The moral economy of a vegan foodscape

Debates on the IPE of food, especially those that invoke the idea of consumer agency, often turn to the question of whether ethically informed decisions can be enacted in capitalist society, or if these will always be trumped by economic considerations like buying at the cheapest price. One way of speaking to this question has been through the prism of **moral economy**. This considers the 'norms and sentiments regarding the responsibilities and rights of individuals and institutions with respect to others' (Sayer 2000). The provision of food has been fertile ground for such enquiries. Drawing on the classic account by historian E. P. Thompson (1971) of the moral economy of food in eighteenth-century England, Naomi Hossain and Devangana Kalita offered an alternative reading of the so-called 'food riots' of 2011 seen in Bangladesh, Indonesia, Kenya, and Zambia. Rather than instances of civil unrest or public disorder, the 'riots' were recast as a justice-based demand for fair prices. Underlying the demand was moral opposition to the perception that food prices were being illegitimately manipulated through hoarding and speculation, with governments seen as duty-bound to intervene and ensure that markets operated fairly (Hossain and Kalita 2014).

The notion of fairness has also been central to the moral economy of the Fair Trade movement, which, as we discussed in Section 1.2.1 of the Introduction, has created a novel trading mechanism that costs in the price of 'doing good', allowing consumers to support distant agrarian communities through their market choices. This has also been enacted semiotically 'through the discursive and visual narratives that saturate these foods with politicized and ethical meanings intended for extensive reading by consumers' (Goodman 2004, 893). In Photo 3.13 we see how the Fairtrade label subtly asks consumers to accept responsibility for the livelihoods of people in poorer countries, conjuring up the image of an empowered 'Third World producer' based in St Lucia to make this other person seem more real and deserving.

The moral economy of food is not always so empathetic, though. In some of our work we looked at the way right-wing politicians and commentators in the UK continually castigated people reliant on charitable food banks or considered to be obese for making poor choices, be it not living frugally enough or gorging themselves on fast food. For us, this discourse functioned as a form of Hayekian neoliberalism. It was a rhetoric and set of accompanying policy reforms designed to instil personal responsibility into society and delegitimize claims for support from the welfare state (Glaze and Richardson 2017).

Photos 3.13 and 3.14. Two sites in the UK where the food economy is moralized: a Fairtrade label for bananas and a volunteer preparing a food bank donation.
Sources: (3.13) Art Directors & TRIP/Alamy Stock Photo and (3.14) Mark Harvey/Alamy Stock Photo.

As Photos 3.13 and 3.14 suggest, we can 'read' the moral economy of food in the world around us. Taken from the field of Geography, the term **foodscape** has been used to refer to the various places where meanings about food are rendered visible: from the supermarket shelf to Instagram posts (Goodman et al. 2010). Such foodscapes help illuminate the cultural specificities of food and explain how consumption practices become embedded in everyday life. For instance, Arve Hansen and Jostein Jakobsen (2020) have used the concept to offer a multiscale account of the 'meatification' dynamic discussed in Section 3.2.2, showing how the supply push of meat through the industrial grain–oilseed–livestock complex has been met by a demand pull in shopping and eating practices. In China and Vietnam, this demand has been generated by supermarkets investing in 'cold chain' logistics so that consumers have not had to rely only on freshly slaughtered meat but can buy it from the chiller or freezer too, and by fast-food chains that have put meat at the centre of the meal rather than as one of several components.

In this activity we want to you look at the flip side of meatification and theoretically reflect on the vegan foodscape. Shifting society towards plant-based diets has been a provocative agenda, raising issues around animal welfare, environmental sustainability, human health, gastronomic taste, cultural preservation, economic affordability, and corporate control, among others. Over the course of a few days try to see how these issues are (re)presented to you in menus, shops, adverts, newspapers, TV programmes, artwork, social media posts, etc. If you have seen things previously about vegan foods or diets that have really stayed with you, then you can include these too. Take pictures or screenshots of these aspects of the foodscape and bring them together in a collage, anonymizing images to protect any personal information and citing sources where appropriate. You should then annotate the collage in terms of what it says about the moral economy, namely 'the responsibilities and rights of individuals and institutions with respect to others'. Questions to consider here might be:

- Are governments or industries called upon to do anything to reduce meat consumption, or are appeals made solely to the 'individual-as-consumer'?
- How are sentiments like guilt, shame, indulgence, and vanity being mobilized?
- What forms of authority are used to validate the appeal or argument being made?
- And who are 'the others' that you are being asked to take responsibility for through your diet?

If you are doing this as part of a class activity, make sure to compare your findings with your peers. This will help you to identify commonalities and differences in how foodscapes are seen and read, which might in turn disclose classed, raced, or gendered patterns. For example, were some people more exposed to this foodscape than others? Did some people see adverts for juicy 'fake meat' burgers while others saw books on raw vegan diets? When two or more people saw the same thing, was it similarly interpreted?

Once you have finished the analysis, use the collage as an evidential basis to address some wider questions about the moral economy of food. Has the promotion of veganism/vegetarianism shown that political change *can* happen through the market? What does this tell us about the effectiveness of different types of moral suasion? And are there particular coalitions that are important to enabling or blocking change? By substantiating the relevance of your findings, maybe via descriptive statistics on consumer trends, and by contextualizing your analysis in the existing literature, this task can also be spun out into a research-based essay.

3.4 Conclusion

Food exists as both a market commodity and a human necessity. It is both profoundly personal and inescapably social. It is both a humdrum daily activity and a historic planetary imprint. An everyday IPE approach helps to unpack these tensions and politicize food in different ways. One such move is to consider the various roles we take on in relation to food, such as being a consumer. In this chapter we discussed how consumer identity might be constructed in the first place, especially by foods sold on the basis of brand identity rather than intrinsic quality, but also how that attachment has been reworked in attempts to bring ethical considerations about a product's origin to bear on shopping purchases. However, we also showed that 'food politics' encompasses more than just consumer power realized by voting with your wallet. The way that we govern ourselves and others in terms of diet revealed important forms of power located in aesthetic ideals, social censure, and moral discourses of personal responsibility. The chapter also sought to use individual encounters with food as a starting point for more systemic analysis, be it the structuring of dietary choices by agri-food capital or the inequalities generated by the global flow of commodities, in which our political analysis gravitated to the role of the state in regulating business and redistributing wealth. And finally, as we showed in the autoethnographic and foodscaping exercises in Section 3.3, research methods utilizing personal experience can help interrogate key figurative constructs like 'the consumer' and better understand how global transformations like dietary (de-)meatification also take place in everyday life.

Access the online resources for quizzes, student reflection podcasts, and support for tackling the chapter's learning activities: http://www.oup.com/he/i-peel1e.

RESOURCES

Tile recommendations from the I-PEEL website: 'coffee' (Zoë Pflaeger Young) http://i-peel.org/homepage/coffee-3/; 'meat' (Ryan Katz-Rosene and Sarah J. Martin) http://i-peel.org/homepage/meat/.

Seaspiracy. 2021. 89 minutes. A documentary film that seeks to expose the fishing industries impact on the world's oceans, rejecting the possibility of sustainable fishing put forward in private governance schemes like the blue MSC label operated by the Marine Stewardship Council.

The Dark Side of Chocolate. 2010. 46 minutes. A documentary film investigating child labour in Côte d'Ivoire and how it sustains the global chocolate industry. It speaks directly to the themes covered in Section 3.1.2 and, like *Seaspiracy*, it also takes aim at private governance schemes.

Clapp, Jennifer. 2020. *Food*. Cambridge: Polity Press, 3rd edn. An excellent introduction to the IPE of food by a key scholar in the field. It covers the rise of industrial agriculture, corporate control, inequitable agricultural trade rules, and the financialization of food, concluding with thoughts on the possibilities for progressive change.

Friedmann, Harriet. 2000. 'What on Earth is the Modern World-System? Foodgetting and Territory in the Modern Era and Beyond', *Journal of World-Systems Research* 6(2): 480–515. Along with Philip McMichael, Harriet Friedmann pioneered the influential 'food regime' concept that situated agri-food production in different eras of the capitalist world system. In this piece she uses the hamburger to explore historical transformations in the human relationship to nature and the ecological contradictions which have resulted.

Guthman, Julie. 2011. *Weighing In: Obesity, Food Justice, and the Limits of Capitalism*. Berkeley: University of California Press. Guthman has helped to bring critical political economy and critical race theory to bear on debates about obesity and in this book foregrounds the paradox of neoliberalism in promoting consumption whilst insisting upon thinness.

Richardson-Ngwenya, Pamela, and Ben Richardson. 2013. 'Documentary Film and Ethical Foodscapes: Three Takes on Caribbean Sugar'. *Cultural Geographies* 20(3): 339–56. Co-authored by the lead author of this chapter, this article uses the foodscape concept to explain how documentaries intervene in the politics of food and why we ought to view them critically by asking whose views are being represented and how they understand power relations.

REFERENCES

Allen, Lawrence L. 2010. 'Chocolate Fortunes: The Battle for the Hearts, Minds, and Wallets of China's Consumers'. *Thunderbird International Business Review* 52(1): 13–20.

Baines, Joseph. 2014. 'Food Price Inflation as Redistribution: Towards a New Analysis of Corporate Power in the World Food System'. *New Political Economy* 19(1): 79–112.

Barrientos, Stephanie. 2016. 'Beyond Fair Trade: Why are Mainstream Chocolate Companies Pursuing Social and Economic Sustainability in Cocoa Sourcing?'. In *The Economics of Chocolate*, ed. Mara P. Squicciarini and Johan Swinnen, 213–27. Oxford: Oxford University Press.

Barrientos, Stephanie. 2019. *Gender and Work in Global Value Chains: Capturing the Gains?* Cambridge: Cambridge University Press.

BBC. 2010. 'Cocoa Investor Buys £650m of Beans'. BBC News, 19 July, https://www.bbc.co.uk/news/business-10682433.

Berlan, Amanda. 2013. 'Social Sustainability in Agriculture: An Anthropological Perspective on Child Labour in Cocoa Production in Ghana'. *Journal of Development Studies* 49(8): 1088–100.

Burch, David, and Lawrence, Geoffrey. 2005. 'Supermarket Own Brands, Supply Chains and the Transformation of the Agri-Food System'. *International Journal of Sociology of Agriculture and Food* 13(1): 1–18.

Cairns, Kate, and Josée Johnston. 2015. 'Choosing Health: Embodied Neoliberalism, Postfeminism, and the "Do-Diet"'. *Theory and Society* 44(2): 153–75.

Campling, Liam, and Elizabeth Havice. 2019. 'Bringing the Environment into GVC Analysis: Antecedents and Analysis'. In *Handbook on Global Value Chains*, ed. Stefano Ponte, Gary Gereffi, and Gale Raj-Reichert, 214–27. Cheltenham: Edward Elgar.

Capillo, Antonio, and Naomi Somerville-Large. 2020. *Cocoa Sustainable Livelihoods Landscape Study: Côte d'Ivoire and Ghana*. London: Fairtrade Foundation.

Clapp, Jennifer, and Ryan Isakson. 2018. 'Risky Returns: The Implications of Financialization in the Food System' *Development and Change* 49(2): 437–60.

Cohen, Luc, and Dominique Patton. 2015. 'Chocolate Demand Melts in China as Stocks and Bribes Decline'. *AG Week*, 20 August, https://www.agweek.com/news/chocolate-demand-melts-in-china-as-stocks-and-bribes-decline.

Daviron, Benoit, and Stefano Ponte. 2005. *The Coffee Paradox: Global Markets, Commodity Trade, and the Elusive Promise of Development*. London and New York: Zed Books.

Development Initiatives. 2018. *2018 Global Nutrition Report: Shining a Light to Spur Action on Nutrition*. Bristol: Development Initiatives.

Dolan, Catherine, and John Humphrey. 2000. 'Governance and Trade in Fresh Vegetables: The Impact of UK Supermarkets on the African Horticulture Industry'. *Journal of Development Studies* 37(2): 147–76.

Evans, Bethan, and Rachel Colls. 2009. 'Measuring Fatness, Governing Bodies: The Spatialities of the Body Mass Index (BMI) in Anti-Obesity Politics'. *Antipode* 41(5): 1051–83.

Ferguson, James. 2010. 'The Uses of Neoliberalism'. *Antipode* 41(1): 166–84.

Fold, Niels. 2002. 'Lead Firms and Competition in "Bi-polar" Commodity Chains: Grinders and Branders in the Global Cocoa–Chocolate Industry'. *Journal of Agrarian Change* 2(2): 228–47.

Foucault, Michel. 2008. *The Birth of Biopolitics: Lectures at the Collège de France, 1978–1979*. Basingstoke: Palgrave Macmillan.

Friedmann, Harriet. 2000. 'What on Earth is the Modern World-System? Foodgetting and Territory in the Modern Era and Beyond'. *Journal of World-Systems Research* 6(2): 480–515.

Friedmann, Harriet, Benoît Daviron, and Gilles Allaire. 2016. 'Political Economists Have Been Blinded by the Apparent Marginalization of Land and Food'. *Revue de la Régulation* 20(2e): no pagination.

Gereffi, Gary. 2018. *Global Value Chains and Development: Redefining the Contours of 21st Century Capitalism*. Cambridge: Cambridge University Press.

Glaze, Simon, and Ben Richardson. 2017. 'Poor Choice? Smith, Hayek and the Moral Economy of Food Consumption'. *Economy and Society* 46(1): 128–51.

Goodman, Michael K. 2004. 'Reading Fair Trade: Political Ecology Imaginary and the Moral Economy of Fair Trade Goods'. *Political Geography* 23(7): 891–915.

Goodman, Michael K., Damian Maye, and Lewis Holloway. 2010. 'Ethical Foodscapes? Premises, Promises, and Possibilities'. *Environment and Planning A* 42(8): 1782–96.

Guthman, Julie. 2008. 'Neoliberalism and the Making of Food Politics in California'. *Geoforum* 39(3): 1171–83.

Guthman, Julie. 2014. 'Doing Justice to Bodies? Reflections on Food Justice, Race, and Biology'. *Antipode* 46(5): 1153–71.

Guthman, Julie, and Melanie DuPuis. 2006. 'Embodying Neoliberalism: Economy, Culture, and the Politics of Fat'. *Environment and Planning D* 24(3): 427–48.

Haddad, Lawrence. 2003. 'Redirecting the Diet Transition: What Can Food Policy Do?' *Development Policy Review* 21(5–6): 599–614.

Hansen, Arve, and Jostein Jakobsen. 2020. 'Meatification and Everyday Geographies of Consumption in Vietnam and China'. *Geografiska Annaler: Series B, Human Geography* 102(1): 21–39.

Harvey, David. 2005. *A Brief History of Neoliberalism*. Oxford: Oxford University Press.

Hawkes, Corinna, Chantal Blouin, Spencer Henson, Nick Drager, and Laurette Dubé (eds.). 2010. *Trade, Food, Diet and Health: Perspectives and Policy Options*. Chichester: Blackwell Publishing.

Hossain, Naomi, and Devangana Kalita. 2014. 'Moral Economy in a Global Era: The Politics of Provisions During Contemporary Food Price Spikes'. *Journal of Peasant Studies* 41(5): 815–31.

Inayatullah, Naeem (ed.). 2011. *Autobiographical International Relations: I, IR*. Abingdon: Routledge.

International Cocoa Organization. 2020. 'Production of Cocoa Beans 2019/20'. *ICCO Quarterly Bulletin of Cocoa Statistics* 46(3): no pagination.

Jarosz, Lucy. 2011. 'Defining World Hunger: Scale and Neoliberal Ideology in International Food Security Policy Discourse'. *Food, Culture and Society* 14(1): 117–39.

L'Aquila Food Security Initiative. 2009. '"L'Aquila" Joint Statement on Global Food Security', L'Aquila, Italy, 10 July, http://www.g8.utoronto.ca/summit/2009laquila/2009-food.pdf.

Lavinas, Lena. 2013. '21st Century Welfare'. *New Left Review* 84(6): 5–40.

Lawrence, Geoffrey, and Philip McMichael. 2012. 'The Question of Food Security'. *International Journal of Sociology of Agriculture and Food* 19(2): 135–42.

Longhurst, Robyn. 2012. 'Becoming Smaller: Autobiographical Spaces of Weight Loss'. *Antipode* 44(3): 871–88.

McMichael, Philip. 2012. 'The Land Grab and Corporate Food Regime Restructuring'. *Journal of Peasant Studies* 39(3–4): 681–701.

Make Chocolate Fair. 2013. *Campaign for Fair Chocolate*, https://makechocolatefair.org/ (last accessed 29 January 2022).

Mars Retail Group. 2014. 'M&M'S World® Celebrates Grand Opening in Shanghai'. Press Release, 11 August, https://www.prnewswire.co.uk/news-releases/mms-world-celebrates-grand-opening-in-shanghai-270785431.html.

Mont Perelin Society. 1947. 'Statement of Aims', https://www.montpelerin.org/statement-of-aims/.

Moore, Jason W. 2015. 'Cheap Food and Bad Climate: From Surplus Value to Negative Value in the Capitalist World-Ecology'. *Critical Historical Studies* 2(1): 1–43.

Neo, Pearly. 2019. 'Healthy China: Ambitious Plans to Cut Dietary Oil, Salt and Sugar Intake Nationwide by 2030'. *Food Navigator Asia*, 5 August, https://www.foodnavigator-asia.com/Article/2019/08/05/Healthy-China-Ambitious-plans-to-cut-dietary-oil-salt-and-sugar-intake-nationwide-by-2030.

Nestle, Marion. 2013. *Food Politics: How the Industry Influences Nutrition and Health*. Berkeley: University of California Press.

Nieburg, Oliver. 2020. '"Cocoa Life Has Not Been Set Up as a Marketing Tool", says Mondelēz International'. *Confectionery News*, 19 August, https://www.confectionerynews.com/Article/2019/10/03/Does-Mondelez-Cocoa-Life-program-up-farmer-income.

O'Connor, James. 1988. 'Capitalism, Nature, Socialism: A Theoretical Introduction'. *Capitalism Nature Socialism* 1(1): 11–38.

Otero, Gerardo, Efe Can Gürcan, Gabriela Pechlaner, and Giselle Liberman. 2018. 'Food Security, Obesity, and Inequality: Measuring the Risk of Exposure to the Neoliberal Diet'. *Journal of Agrarian Change* 18(3): 536–54.

Patel, Raj. 2009. 'What Does Food Sovereignty Look Like?' *Journal of Peasant Studies* 36(3): 663–706.

Poelmans, Eline, and Johan Swinnen. 2016. 'A Brief Economic History of Chocolate'. In *The Economics of Chocolate*, ed. Mara P. Squicciarini and Johan Swinnen, 11–42. Oxford: Oxford University Press.

Popkin, Barry M., Linda S. Adair, and Shu Wen Ng. 2012. 'The Global Nutrition Transition: The Pandemic of Obesity in Developing Countries'. *Nutrition Review* 70(1): 3–21.

Puhl, Rebecca M., and Chelsea A. Heuer. 2009. 'The Stigma of Obesity: A Review and Update'. *Obesity* 17(5): 941–64.

Purcell, Thomas F. 2018. 'Hot Chocolate: Financialized Global Value Chains and Cocoa Production in Ecuador'. *Journal of Peasant Studies* 45(5–6): 904–26.

Quentin, David, and Liam Campling. 2018. 'Global Inequality Chains: Integrating Mechanisms of Value Distribution into Analyses of Global Production'. *Global Networks* 18(1): 33–56.

Reed-Danahay, Deborah. 1997. 'Introduction'. In *Auto/Ethnography: Rewriting the Self and the Social*, ed. Deborah Reed-Danahay, 1–20. Oxford: Berg.

Richardson, Ben. 2015. *Sugar*. Cambridge and Malden: Polity.

Sajed, Alina. 2011. 'Waiting for the Revolution: A Foreigner's Narrative'. In *Autobiographical International Relations: I, IR*, ed. Naeem Inayatullah, 78–92. Abingdon: Routledge.

Sayer, Andrew. 2000. 'Moral Economy and Political Economy'. *Studies in Political Economy* 61(1): 79–103.

Selwyn, Ben. 2012. 'Beyond Firm-Centrism: Re-Integrating Labour and Capitalism into Global Commodity Chain Analysis'. *Journal of Economic Geography* 12(1): 205–26.

Sen, Amartya. 1981. *Poverty and Famines: An Essay on Entitlement and Deprivation*. Oxford: Oxford University Press.

The Straits Times. 2019. 'Chocolate is Big Business in China'. *The Straits Times*, 15 February 2019, https://www.straitstimes.com/lifestyle/food/chocolate-is-big-business-in-china.

Thompson, Edward Palmer. 1971. 'The Moral Economy of the English Crowd in the Eighteenth Century'. *Past and Present* 50: 76–131.

UNICEF. 2020. 'New Insights: 21st Century Malnutrition', https://www.unicef.org/globalinsight/stories/new-insights-21st-century-malnutrition (last accessed 14 July 2022).

United Nations. 1975. 'Report of the World Food Conference', Rome, 5–16 November 1974, https://digitallibrary.un.org/record/701143?ln=en.

Wang, Zhuoqiong. 2018. 'Mars Opens Chocolate-Themed Hotel'. *China Daily*, 26 October. https://www.chinadaily.com.cn/a/201810/26/WS5bd282d2a310eff303284b7f.html.

Weis, Tony. 2013. 'The Meat of the Global Food Crisis'. *Journal of Peasant Studies* 40(1): 65–85.

White, Lucy. 2017. 'Chocfinger Melts; Hedge Fund Famous for Betting on Chocolate Shuts Up Shop', *City A.M.*, 11 December, https://www.cityam.com/chocfinger-melts-hedge-fund-famous-betting-chocolate-shuts/.

Whoriskey, Peter, and Rachel Siegel. 2019. 'Cocoa's Child Labourers'. *The Washington Post*, 5 June.

World Food Programme (WFP). 2020. 'Cash-Based Transfers: Empowering People, Markets and Governments', https://www.wfp.org/publications/2020-cash-transfers-factsheet (last accessed 29 January 2022).

World Health Organization (WHO). 2018. *Global Nutrition Policy Review 2016-2017*. Geneva: WHO.

World Health Organization (WHO). 2020a. 'Obesity and Overweight', 1 April, https://www.who.int/news-room/fact-sheets/detail/obesity-and-overweight.

World Health Organization (WHO). 2020b. 'The Top Ten Causes of Death', WHO Fact Sheet, 9 December, https://www.who.int/news-room/fact-sheets/detail/the-top-10-causes-of-death.

4 DEBT

4.1	Student Debt	94
4.2	Exploring Debt	101
4.3	Engaging Debt	113
4.4	Conclusion	116

LEARNING OBJECTIVES

- Describe the concepts of commodification, assetization, and financialization, and how they apply to the case of student debt
- Explain the power relations of debt at the individual, household, and national level
- Critically analyse debt using thought experiments and role-playing

READER'S GUIDE

Money and finance are key themes in IPE analysis and are included in most IPE textbooks. However, very often analyses focus on so-called 'high finance', namely sovereign debt and international investment flows. By contrast, this chapter begins with a section on 'Student Debt' (Section 4.1). In many countries, borrowing money to pay for tuition fees and living costs is an expected part of going to university. Thinking about the emergence of personal indebtedness in the higher education system—and how this varies across countries and groups—helps to foreground the IPE of debt. The next section is 'Exploring Debt' (Section 4.2). This section widens the scope beyond student debt, first by looking at the different kinds of debt, including sovereign debt and household debt. It then considers the reasons why people go into debt and why debts are repaid (or not). It ends by looking at alternatives to debt, using Islamic finance as a case study. The final section is 'Engaging Debt', which sets out two learning activities (Section 4.3). The first invites you to undertake a thought experiment on borrowing and the moral and power dynamics that underpin interest-bearing loans. The second is a role-playing simulation on sovereign debt, which encourages you to consider demands for debt cancellation from different perspectives.

KEY CONCEPTS

Commodification; assetization; financialization

Access the online resources to listen to a podcast where Lena introduces and explores the key themes of this chapter: http://www.oup.com/he/i-peel1e.

4.1 **Student Debt**

In 2019, the billionaire and philanthropist Robert F. Smith made global news by promising to pay off the student debt of that year's graduating class at Morehouse College, Atlanta, a traditional Black college in the US and the alma mater of Martin Luther King Jr. Smith, a former Goldman Sachs investment banker and founder of Vista Equity Partners, had made his fortune as a tech investor and said that his donation was a way to 'liberate the human spirit' (Hess 2020). Indebted students at that college owed an average of $40,000 each, pricing his act of liberation at an estimated $34 million. Smith followed this gesture by advocating for greater free education in all historically Black colleges, leading the media outlet *Bloomberg Businessweek* to anoint him the 'slayer of student debt' (Kessenidis 2019).

For many students, loans taken out to pay for tuition and maintenance at university are the first major source of personal indebtedness. The definition of this as a *personal* debt is important. Often, the lived experience of being in debt brings with it a sense of burden that can lead in turn to guilt or even shame. Such feelings can be reinforced by the morally charged discourse of debt. For example, when a debt is cancelled, rather than being called an act of 'liberation' as Smith termed it, it is more often described as 'debt forgiveness', as if the person was being pardoned for the sin of not repaying what they owed.

At the same time as magnifying its psychological consequences, the personalization of debt marginalizes its structural dimensions. Smith's donation gained prominence precisely because of the relatively high indebtedness of poor Black students in the US, highlighting the way that debt manifests itself differently along the lines of class, race, nationality, and more (Nova 2019). Moreover, student debt is by no means solely confined to a relationship between lender and borrower. It also links to wider processes of financial innovation and speculation. In this regard, it is notable that just a few months after receiving plaudits for his generous donation, Smith admitted to the US Department of Justice that he had hidden $200 million in offshore accounts to reduce his tax liabilities and had illegally evaded $43 million of taxes owed (Shubber 2020). This is precisely the kind of behaviour that makes it harder for states to fund education through general taxation rather than personal debt.

High levels of student debt are a relatively recent phenomenon, but in the US alone student debt has now surpassed the $1.7 trillion mark, the majority of which is owed to the government's Federal Student Aid organization (Hanson 2022). In the UK, the government's Student Loans Company makes loans every year in excess of £17 billion and to more than 1.3 million students (Bolton 2020). These loans can be subsidized and guaranteed in various ways, making them more or less burdensome on the borrower, but because of the high costs of studying, the amounts owed are still quite large. Student debt is also on the rise in many Asian countries such as Malaysia and

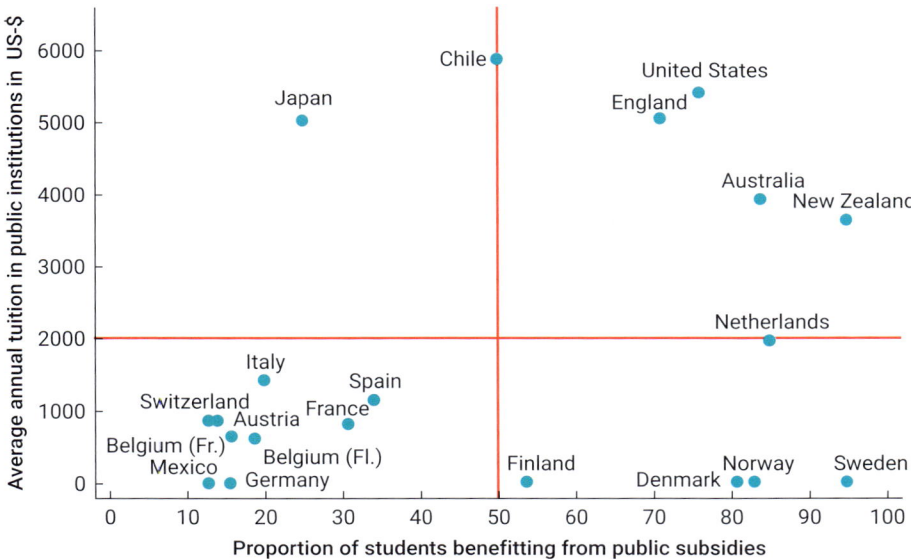

Figure 4.1. The Four Worlds of Student Finance.
Source: Garritzmann 2015, 140.

South Korea, reflecting growth in enrolment numbers—especially in so-called 'emerging markets'—alongside the privatization of higher education provision and rising tuition fees (Asadullah and Chan 2019). In other countries, by contrast, such as Mexico, Germany, and France, tuition fees are relatively low or absent, while in the Netherlands and the Scandinavian countries students may also receive non-repayable grants.

These differences have led Julian Garritzmann (2015) to distinguish between four different types of higher education system, or what he calls 'the four worlds of student finance'. Illustrated in Figure 4.1, this is a typology based on the price of tuition and the proportion of students benefitting from publicly funded financial support, including government-backed loans. To help explain these differences, and in particular the evolution of the Anglo-American economies into 'high-tuition, high-subsidy' systems, as shown in the top-right quadrant, we draw on the concepts of commodification, assetization, and financialization. Let us elaborate these in turn, showing how they shed light on the proliferation of student debt.

4.1.1 Commodification

The first significant move has been to turn education from a public good into a set of discrete degree courses that are sold in a market. IPE scholars refer to this process of turning a good into a commodity that can be exchanged for money in a marketplace as **commodification**. For much of the post-World War II period, free education was initially seen as a contribution to the creation of informed, democratically responsible, citizens—an important issue after the devastating wars of the twentieth century. Similarly, education was viewed as a key means for social mobility and wider socio-economic and national development. Finally, education was also seen as critical in building technological advantage, as witnessed in the 'space race' between the US and USSR to land the first person on the moon during the Cold War period. But changing ideology contributed to a recalibration of the role of the state, in particular in the Anglo-American economies, though some Asian countries such as Japan, Korea, and Malaysia also followed this trend. Governments became increasingly reluctant to subsidize higher education provision through general taxation, especially as more and more students entered university and the costs of supporting them rose accordingly. The view of higher education as a public good faded away, replaced by a belief that getting a degree should be like buying a product. Students should choose the course that suits them, pay for this themselves, and get good value for money.

Such commodification was not a clear-cut question of left or right politics. In the UK, it was the New Labour government under Tony Blair that introduced tuition fees in 1998. Similarly, in Germany it was the Social Democratic government of Gerhard Schröder that pushed for education reform and encouraged subnational states—the German Länder—to introduce fees. These fees were far from inconsequential and tended to increase more rapidly than general prices, giving rise to the new phenomenon of **education inflation**. For example, the upper limit of tuition fees introduced in the UK in 1999 was £1,000, but this soon increased to £3,000 in 2004 and to £9,000 in 2012. Over the last two decades in the US, tuition fees have increased by 2–5 per cent each year *on top* of the general rate of inflation (Ma et al. 2019, 3).

Nevertheless, whilst there was a general trend towards the introduction of tuition fees, the commodification of higher education was not uncontested. In Germany it led to widespread protests, with students occupying university buildings and boycotting lectures, and never gained widespread societal support. Photo 4.1 shows one such student protest: note how the slogans contrast with the consumerist language of choice and value for money adopted by proponents of commodification. Ultimately, decisions to charge for university education were reversed, and one by one state governments abolished fees, with Lower Saxony being the last German state to do so, following a shift to the left in state elections. In the UK, the response to the initial introduction of student fees was more muted, but the tripling of fees by the Conservative–Liberal Democrat coalition government in 2010 led to protests that were violently suppressed when the British police 'kettled' students on the streets of London, trapping them into densely packed spaces. A few months later in Chile, where fees were among the highest in the world, students did the same and had more success than their British counterparts as the Socialist Party government introduced free tuition to the poorest

Photo 4.1. In Ulm, Germany, students made protest crosses to symbolically mark the death of democracy, self-determination, and free education in their university.
Source: blickwinkel/Alamy Stock Photo.

students. However, insufficient state funding for the policy meant that universities did not cover the costs of educating these students and so faced tough choices about how to balance their budgets.

4.1.2 Assetization

A logical development from the transformation of higher education into a commodity was the way that degree qualifications were reconceptualized as an asset that would generate an economic return. According to political economist Paul Langley (2021), **assetization** can be seen as a contingent process that turns all manner of things into assets, namely something that is *investable* because it can generate revenue. Closely linked to this has been the language of **human capital** and imaginaries of corporations and countries being in a 'global war for talent' (see Thrift 2010). In some countries the notion that students should be seen as assets serves as a justification for the government shouldering the burden of paying for their education, whereas in other countries students themselves and their families pitch in to afford a place at university, hopeful that this will pay off in the long run. Think about your own experience: why did you go to university and select your particular degree course? Was it the love of learning alone, or did you also feel pressure to improve your CV? Do you think of education as a good in itself, or as something that must also have market value?

Seeing the possession of a degree qualification principally as an asset, measured according to the financial returns it is likely to generate, is very different from an ethos that sees education primarily as a route to civic participation or national development. Nevertheless, by turning education into an investible asset, borrowing for its purchase can be justified. Consider the advert for the UK's Open University in Photo 4.2. Setting the expectation that a university education will lead to a pay rise helps to persuade potential students that any debts accrued can be paid back out of their future income, encouraging a kind of *self*-assetization in which they themselves become the investment.

Such a process has been identified, for example, in business schools in India, where increased tuition fees and an emphasis on English language teaching have fostered a market subjectivity. This is an understanding of the self that privileges the instrumental pursuit of the maximization of financial returns. What this has meant for students is that they start to gear their studies and extracurricular activities around getting a job with a Western corporation, whilst neglecting social concerns and critical academic perspectives (Varman et al. 2011). Is this something that you can also observe at your university? And how does it impact you and your fellow students? Varman and co-authors also highlight that many students are conflicted by a singular focus on career

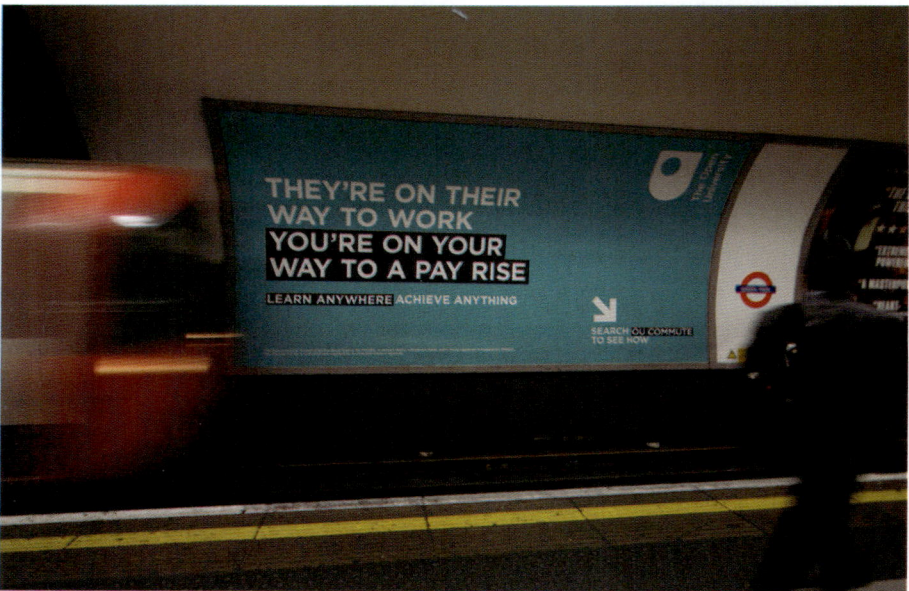

Photo 4.2. An advert for the Open University on a Tube station wall in London.
Source: Chris Batson/Alamy Stock Photo.

goals and draw on alternative discourses of education to resist the advance of market subjectivity (see Section 1.2.2 for more on subjectivity), showing that this is by no means an uncontested process.

4.1.3 Financialization

The final dynamic we consider, and again this is something perhaps most pronounced in the Anglo-American countries, is the way that borrowing has shifted from something frowned upon to a legitimate practice that has allowed students to 'invest' in these sorts of assets. This shift extends beyond student debt to all kinds of borrowing, and has been captured by the notion of **financialization**. The political economist Gerald Epstein defines it in a systemic way, as:

> the increasing importance of financial markets, financial motives, financial institutions, and financial elites in the operations of the economy and its governing institutions, both at the national and international levels.
> (Epstein 2019, 360)

Financialization dynamics are clearly visible in higher education. The UK government has sold on billions of pounds worth of debt owed to the Student Loans Company in a transaction known as **securitization**, meaning that private investors like pension funds and hedge funds will ultimately collect the repayments instead. This was done to improve public finances by cashing in on debt that would take a long time to recover, but was criticized for allowing investors to profit from students, and for instigating a process in which loans would inevitably be designed with financial markets in mind. Indeed, the profit margins are significant. A report by the UK National Audit Office (NAO 2018, 4) discusses student loans sold to financial markets with a face value of £3.5 billion, affecting approximately 411,000 borrowers. The proceeds that went to the UK government from this sale stood at £1.7 billion, less than half of the face value.

Nor is it just student loans that have been securitized and thus become part of financialization dynamics. Universities across the world have borrowed significant sums to pay for a whole range of assets, especially campus facilities like student accommodation, classrooms, and sports centres. Through these debts, universities have become directly connected to global financial markets, pledging their future income from student fees to banks and **bondholders**, that is, the investors who have bought the debt securities—which are basically IOU notes—that they issued. In this context, meeting financial expectations and abiding by loan terms have become a core focus of university operations, affecting decisions like how much they charge for tuition, who they target for recruitment, and what kind of teaching they provide. Increasingly, financial considerations rather than pedagogical (teaching and learning) concerns shape decision-making processes.

Taken together, these three key drivers of commodification, assetization, and financialization have had significant impacts on the terms under which higher education is accessed. As education is turned into a commodity, and students and education-related resources into assets increasingly prone to speculative investment, countries are moving into the top two quadrants of Garritzmann's scheme of high tuition fees (see Figure 4.1). What this suggests is that the growth in university student numbers, which have now passed 200 million worldwide, is increasingly dependent on the ability and willingness of students to indebt themselves—be it to a government-owned company, a privately owned bank, a philanthropic foundation, a family member, or a combination of these. At the same time, the topic of student debt also points to important variations both within and across countries: loans may be an important issue for debate in the UK, the US, and Chile for example, but less so in Scandinavia, where tuition is free, at least for students from EU/EEA countries.

Similarly, and this is something that often gets ignored in discussions of student debt, it has a very uneven gendered and racialized impact. For example, research has

Photo 4.3. Students, graduates, and activists rally in New York City against loans for education. The orange jumpsuit and ball and chains imply that student debt is like a prison sentence. Consider your position on student debt. Do you find it concerning for yourself or for others? What would make you join a protest against it?
Source: David Grossman/Alamy Stock Photo.

estimated that in England—even in well-paying jobs such as the legal professions—it will take female graduates on average ten years longer than men to pay off their student loans, meaning that women ultimately pay significantly more in **interest** (Halterbeck and Conlon 2017). In the US, meanwhile, data from the Center for Responsible Lending shows that 85 per cent of Black students with a bachelor's degree are burdened by student debt, compared to 69 per cent of white students (Nova 2019). This can affect the politics of student debt, making it harder to coalesce around a shared experience and unified set of demands. Photo 4.3 shows a protest against for-profit educational loans in the US. Notice how the signs around the protesters' necks demonstrate a 'unity in diversity', recognizing that while debt is common to all, some are more indebted than others.

4.2 Exploring Debt

Student loans are just one facet of debt and the pathologies associated with it. The patterns of commodification, assetization, and financialization we detailed in the higher education sector are actually emergent and experienced across a diverse range of everyday objects and practices, from farming to home buying, hospitals to airports. Moreover, it is not just students and universities who can take on debt, but a whole array of individuals and organizations. Despite this diversity, debt is always predicated on a set of power relations and, as we will elaborate in the next section, often tends to reinforce inequalities of power rather than subvert them. At the same time, as we discussed in Section 4.1, increasing indebtedness is by no means a foregone conclusion, and we will also look at alternative forms of borrowing, such as Islamic finance (discussed in Section 4.2.3) as an alternative to debt.

4.2.1 What are the different kinds of debt?

Let us begin by looking at the different kinds of debt and debtor. For the emerging academic field of IPE back in the 1970s, it was the **sovereign debt** owed by states that received the most attention, chiefly because of its apparent threat to the stability of the world economy. How did this debt come about? In their search for higher returns on their investments, or what is known as **yield**, banks had begun lending more heavily to countries in the Global South from the 1960s onwards, particularly in the Latin American region. The assumption was that borrowed money could be used to finance industrialization strategies, and could be paid back in the meantime via earnings on traditional exports like agricultural commodities. However, the limited success of industrialization, combined with the oil shocks of the 1970s that forced up the import bill of many countries in the Global South, meant that they struggled to make the repayments on what they owed, and the interest began to pile up. Moreover, loans were typically denominated in US dollars, which made the rate at which local currencies could be exchanged against the US dollar a key feature of **debt sustainability**. When interest rates in the US were hiked up in the early 1980s for domestic economic reasons, it had the knock-on effect of making existing dollar-denominated debt of foreign countries, and any further loans they took, more expensive too.

It was in these circumstances that in 1982 Mexico defaulted on its debt—a public admission that it could no longer meet its repayment obligations. Indeed, so concerned was the US government at Mexico's default that it stepped in to organize a bailout package and continued to play an active role in its debt management through the International Monetary Fund (IMF). One important consideration in this regard was that overconfident American banks had done most of the lending, and writing off the loans as commercial losses would have risked making them insolvent. The bailouts therefore came with conditions designed to ensure that Mexico could resume debt repayments, namely the introduction of free market reforms to encourage foreign investment and reduce government spending. This set the pattern for a number of countries, including Argentina, Brazil, and Chile, that defaulted on and/or renegotiated their sovereign debt in the 1980s—a chain of events known as the 'Latin American debt crisis'. It presaged a 'lost decade of development' when national economic growth all but disappeared in the region. The practice of attaching conditions to implement market-oriented policy reforms in return for crisis loans helped to spread the 'Washington Consensus' throughout the Global South, so called to reflect the key roles played by the IMF, World Bank, and the US Treasury in designing these policies (Babb 2013).

This was but the beginning of a series of recurring debt crises that have shaken the global economy and contributed to significant transformations in the creation of credit and resulting forms of indebtedness (Rethel 2012). This happened against the ideological backdrop of the 'neoliberal revolution' during the 1980s–1990s (see Section 3.2 for more on neoliberalism), which supported a recalibration of the relationship between the state and business in favour of the latter, as well as the rapid expansion of the size and reach of financial markets (Duménil and Lévy 2004). Indeed, many state enterprises came to be privatized and began to raise funds in the capital market. At the same time, changes in financial markets—including the liberalization of bank interest rates, which had previously been set by central banks, and the activities that banks could engage in—spurred a period of intense financial innovation that led to a further expansion of debt markets (Rethel and Sinclair 2012). Public debt owed by states became increasingly replaced by private **corporate debt** owed by companies, although at times of crisis states have tended to step back in and bail out companies, such as big banks Citigroup in the US and Royal Bank of Scotland Group in the UK during the 2008–9 global financial crisis.

However, what we have also seen over the last few decades is the significant growth of **household debt**—house mortgages, car finance, credit cards, personal finance, and, yes, student loans—both supported by, and contributing to, an intensification of financialization (Montgomerie 2009). As the power to borrow has shifted from being a largely sovereign prerogative to being a matter of the everyday, the politics of debt have changed substantially. New kinds of debt instruments have been devised and sold to new kinds of customers, flanked by new laws and policies to regulate this financial activity. The seemingly endless search for new debt markets at the 'fringes of finance' (Aitken 2015) was satirized by artist Darren Cullen in his version of the unsecured payday loans aimed at low-income adults: pocket money loans for children.

By 2021, global debt levels—including all these different sorts of debt—had reached nearly US$300 trillion, about three times global GDP (Ranasinghe 2021). Already high debt levels were quite literally compounded by the coronavirus pandemic that resulted in new heights of government borrowing and, again, new kinds of debtors. For example, the wealthiest members in the EU, Germany and France, agreed to let the European Commission borrow €750 billion for a Coronavirus Recovery Fund. By pledging that around half of this amount would be repaid by the EU *as a collective* and the remainder

Photo 4.4. Leaflets on display in Darren Cullen's pop-up shop Pocket Money Loans in London.
Source: PA Images/Alamy Stock Photo.

by the individual member states, the Commission thus saw its debt status transformed into something more akin to a national government.

Moreover, there have also been significant changes on the lender side, perhaps most importantly a shift from bilateral (i.e. country-to-country) and multilateral (i.e. group of countries) lending to portfolio investment. In the early post-World War II period, governments and international organizations such as the World Bank were core lenders. However, from the 1980s onwards they were increasingly joined by, and soon outpaced by, private lenders and investors such as banks and pension funds (Rethel 2012). This is another way in which our everyday actions, such as saving for old age, connect us increasingly directly to global capital markets, even though we do not have much of a say on how our savings are actually invested by these institutions.

4.2.2 Why do people indebt themselves?

In orthodox Economics, monetary debt can be understood as a form of time management. People borrow to pay for things *now* on the basis that they will be able to pay that money back, with interest, in the *future*. The money may be borrowed for an investment in future earnings, as we saw with the student loan, or to fill a temporary shortfall in income when outgoings still have to be paid, a process known as **consumption smoothing**. One problem with this understanding of debt is that it assumes people are able to calculate the risks of borrowing and will make rational decisions accordingly. It ignores, for example, how loans can be 'pushed' through aggressive selling, distorting the possibility for cost-benefit analysis and leading to excessive indebtedness.

Something of this could be seen in the run-up to the global financial crisis of 2008–9, where in a number of states in the US, such as Florida, loans for home ownership were being sold to borrowers with poor credit histories and/or little income. One reason these **subprime mortgages** were sold so widely was because, despite the risk of borrowers defaulting, banks had found a way to make them look profitable. It involved more complex securitization transactions, whereby the mortgages were bundled together and sliced up into different tranches. By repackaging the mortgages in this way, the banks were able to convince investors that they had sufficiently spread the risk and so found themselves able to continually create and sell on debt, a process known as 'originate and distribute'.

In addition, by moving the default risk off their balance sheets and onto others', the banks appeared as safer bets and could borrow more money to **leverage** their own speculative investments in financial trading. Rules intended to stabilize the financial system by keeping investments in proportion to underlying assets like houses or gold reserves were essentially voided, and debt became bound up with global economic instability like never before. As portrayed in *The Big Short*, the 2015 film about the attempts by renegade investors to bet against or 'short' the securitized mortgages, the lives of ambitious Wall Street traders were thus intimately tied to aspirational real estate owners. What we do not see in the movie, though, is what happens after the renegade investors win their bet: borrowers are faced with mass foreclosure of their homes when the economic fallout of the financial crisis compounded the difficulties they were already facing in servicing their mortgage debt.

Debt and the power to borrow can therefore contribute to increased inequality, not just by making the poor poorer but also by making the rich richer. This relationship does not only hold when comparing different types of borrowers—investment banks compared to low-income homeowners, for example—but also holds when comparing different types of loans. For example, the Malaysian central bank distinguishes between 'loans for wealth accumulation', which include loans to purchase residential and non-residential property and capital market securities, and 'loans for consumption purposes', including loans to purchase motor vehicles, personal financing, and credit cards. Interestingly, in Malaysia the rate of the growth of loans for wealth accumulation exceeds that of the growth of loans for consumption by multiples, with a ratio of 6.9 per cent to 0.6 per cent in 2018 (Bank Negara Malaysia 2020, 13). However, even this more nuanced approach to debt leaves many questions unanswered. For example, how would you classify student debt: is it a loan taken out for wealth accumulation through 'investment' in someone's education or for consumption purposes and the enjoyment of a student lifestyle?

The example of the subprime mortgage market showed how unsustainable debt can be pushed onto people through predatory lending, including where lenders employ deceptive tactics such as offering introductory teaser rates that hide the true costs of a loan. For Silvia Federici (2014) the development of the debt economy and what she refers to as the 'production of mass indebtedness' must also be understood in relation to the more and more precarious nature of work, waning support for the welfare state, and the increasing financialization of social reproduction (see Section 5.1.1 on valuing care work). In this context, debt can be seen as an individualizing practice that both masks and exacerbates hierarchies of difference, as well as rupturing solidarities. As part of a neoliberal discourse people are told that their debts are their own responsibility, whilst structural issues that cause people to take out loans in the first place are ignored. For instance, the Fawcett Society has documented how debt in the UK is a profoundly gendered phenomenon (Westaway and McKay 2007). Is it any surprise that women tend to have more unsustainable debt when they earn less than men over their lifetime, face higher risk of sudden income loss due to unemployment or caring responsibilities, and are much more vulnerable to financial abuse as a form of domestic violence?

Interestingly, in poorer parts of the world microfinance has been hailed by many development organizations as a success story precisely because it targets women.

Microfinance refers to a range of financial instruments designed to be used by people lacking the kind of collateral, credit history, and access to financial infrastructure (such as an ID card and bank account) that commercial banks normally require. The Grameen Bank in Bangladesh became renowned for its alternative approach, which was to lend small sums to people in rural villages hitherto excluded from formal financial markets, organizing the borrowers into small groups to encourage repayments through peer pressure (as depicted in Photo 4.5). The initial borrowers were mainly men, but this switched as they found that women used the money prudently in entrepreneurial activities and were also better at making repayments.

The Grameen model became financially self-sustaining and, helped by the award of the Nobel Peace Prize to its founder, Muhammad Yunus, inspired many other microfinance initiatives. Yet the discovery of viable debt markets among rural women has contributed to an increased financialization of the sector. Commercial banks have partnered with microfinance lenders, while lending and debt recovery practices have intensified in order to boost profitability. Echoing Federici's argument, research on the 2010 debt crisis that unfolded in Andhra Pradesh in India noted how private-sector microfinance loans had grown due to the state withdrawal of public-sector financial services and were used to plug continual shortfalls between earnings and the cost of

Photo 4.5. A woman registering her microfinance loan repayment in Katni District, India.
Source: neeraj chaturvedi/Alamy Stock Photo.

living. This was not consumption smoothing, then, but rather a 'credit-driven survival strategy' that inevitably reached breaking point (Taylor 2012, 607).

Moreover, there are various other forms of debt that are not necessarily recognized or recorded in monetary terms, but that nevertheless reflect uneven global power relations. For example, the environmentalist Andrew Simms has developed the notion of the **ecological debt** of climate change. This is generated by humans 'spending, or rather burning, more of our fossil fuel inheritance than we can afford to in the sense that the atmosphere cannot safely absorb the resulting pollution without being disrupted' (Simms 2009, 7). It is a form of indebtedness driven in particular by countries and individuals in the Global North and one that is being 'repaid' disproportionately by those in the Global South.

4.2.3 Do debts always have to be repaid?

According to the anthropologist David Graeber (2011), debt has been a key feature of social relations throughout the centuries, forming part of the web of mutual obligations that bind humanity together. What Graeber finds rather puzzling is how we came to accept the belief that debts must always be repaid. In his seminal work *Debt: The First 5000 Years*, he traces how, throughout history, periods of greater indebtedness were followed by episodes of **debt relief**, such as the debt jubilees of biblical times that would see foreclosed land returned to its former owners and indentured slaves set free. This can be compared with the urgent need for debt relief in the context of coronavirus-related borrowing, both by poor households and poor countries. Temporary solutions such as mortgage holidays for homeowners and debt service suspension for low-income countries were put in place, both essentially providing a pause in loan repayments. But it was rarely asked why borrowers should bear the brunt of the crisis rather than the lenders, and why loan contracts do not contain clauses that stipulate either debt write-offs or burden sharing in the case of exceptional events like a global pandemic.

Graeber's question prompts us to think about the power relations underpinning debt, and particularly those relations that establish when debts should and should not be honoured. A simple example is the use or threat of physical violence to enforce repayment—a coercive relationship typically associated with illicit forms of lending known as loan sharking, but which might equally apply to the state imprisonment of impoverished people for unpaid debts (see Roberts 2014). But coercive power need not always manifest itself physically. Another criticism made of microfinance is that the use of peer pressure deliberately creates an informal disciplinary mechanism through **joint liability** for the loans. Borrowers unable to repay weekly instalments can thus be faced with 'the scrutiny and shaming practices of the collective in a rural environment in which social dignity is a prerequisite for household wellbeing' (Taylor 2012, 609).

In Graeber's analysis, the notion of debt has historically signified a reciprocal relationship, over time, and as such has been characterized by various sorts of performative functions. This applies to voluntary as well as more coercive creditor–debtor relations. Nearly a century ago the French sociologist and anthropologist Marcel Mauss theorized 'the gift' not as something that is given for free but as a means of renewing social status by putting recipients under obligation to both accept and return the gift in kind. In making this argument, Mauss offered the example of the potlatch, an opulent ceremonial feast practised by indigenous peoples of the north-west American coast in which gifts were given according to social rank:

> The political status of individuals in the brotherhoods and clans, and ranks of all kinds, are gained in a 'war of property', just as they are in real war, or through chance, inheritance, alliance, and marriage. Yet everything is conceived of as if it [the potlatch] were a 'struggle of wealth'. (Mauss 1990, 47)

A more familiar, if somewhat frivolous, example of 'gift debt' can be found in an episode of the US TV series *The Big Bang Theory*. The character Sheldon is dismayed to receive an unexpected Christmas present from Penny, complaining to her that 'I now have to go out and purchase for you a gift of commensurate value and representing the same perceived level of friendship as that represented by the gift you've given me' (IMDb 2008). The comedy is in the fact that Sheldon vocalizes the thoughts on gift-giving that usually get supressed, and in the process exposes the kind of shared social fiction that Mauss also detected in the potlatch.

Building on Mauss's work and drawing on her research in northern Cameroon, another anthropologist, Janet Roitman (2003), shows how the obligations to repay debt, or return gifts, can extend beyond the immediate giver and recipient to regulate society as a whole. She explores the authority figure of the *baaba saare*, translated as 'father of the house'. The *baaba saare* receives credit due to his social position as a married man responsible for an extended family. It comes in the form of lower prices for goods that he buys, and on the expectation that he repays this, not to the shop vendor but to his community, by fulfilling his paternal duties. In contrast to the type of debt which is set out in a legal contract, then, here the rules of conduct for receiving credit can only be understood sociologically.

Putting aside the differences in the way debt is repaid and to whom, there are interesting parallels here with sovereign debt. Consider the way that credit comes from power. Whilst countries in the Global South tend to face the most unsustainable debt, as we will highlight in the learning activity in Section 4.3.2, it is countries in the Global

Photo 4.6. The National Debt Clock in New York was built by the businessman Seymour Durst in 1989 to draw attention to the intergenerational politics of sovereign debt.
Source: Richard Levine/Alamy Stock Photo.

North that are most heavily indebted in absolute, but also often in relative, terms. Just take the example of the US with a total national debt of $27 trillion or nearly 138 per cent of GDP—and, as in Photo 4.6, quite literally ticking up. And this is a figure that does not even include the debt owed by US corporations and households such as student debt. What gives lenders assurance that the American state will honour these debts far into the future, when little can really be known for sure about the strength of its economy and willingness to keep to contract? Perhaps it is not too dissimilar to the notion of *narral*, or confidence in the rules of the market, which underpins exchange in northern Cameroon (Roitman 2003).

Sticking with sovereign debt, we can also see power at play in the way that states politicize debt. After the global financial crisis, the UK government borrowed heavily to bail out banks and stimulate growth as the economy fell into recession. The incoming Conservative–Liberal Democrat coalition government made a commitment in 2010 to eliminate the budget deficit within five years so as to stop incurring additional debt, and did so by prioritizing spending cuts over tax increases. This austerity agenda was strongly contested, not just because of the choices made in how to balance the budget, but in the way that **fiscal consolidation** was justified via the household analogy. This view held that states were like households and had to 'tighten their belts' and show restraint in difficult economic times, as captured in this oft-repeated line by the Chancellor George Osborne: 'We are asking the British people to reduce the record budget deficit and pay off the national credit card' (cited in Stevenson 2011).

This claim was criticized as, unlike a household, governments can—up to a point—create the money they need to spend through their central banks. Moreover, household spending and income are largely independent of one another, but because the government is a much bigger economic actor, when they cut back on spending this can have an economy-wide effect in reducing employment, wages, and ultimately its own tax revenue. In this light, **austerity** was seen less as a necessary economic response to debt and more as an ideologically driven interpretation of it to legitimize the shrinking of the welfare state (Blyth 2013).

In other cases, it has not been the *rate* of repayment that is in question but the very repayment itself. Argentina was one of the countries caught in the debt crisis of the 1980s, and has continued to struggle with debt servicing. In 2001 it defaulted on $93 billion dollars of external debt, in effect saying to its creditors that they had to accept a radical debt restructuring, essentially a vastly reduced repayment, if they ever wanted to get any of their money back. But a minority group of bondholders, including so-called 'vulture funds' that specialize in recovering debt unlikely to be repaid, refused to accept a loss and took Argentina to court in the US, insisting that they should be paid in full. The park sign in Photo 4.7 indicates how this ongoing debt crisis was directly linked in Argentina to the impoverishment of its population, putting the country's government between a rock and a hard place. For behind the courtroom drama was the power of the (America-based) financial markets: the more Argentina challenged the legal verdicts, the less willing investors would be to keep buying government debt. Unlike bankruptcy laws that apply to individuals and firms, there is no established legal and political process for countries to wipe the slate clean and start again.

One approach to finance which helps us to question the permissibility of debt and the often uneven nature of creditor–debtor relations is Islamic finance (Rethel 2011). Islamic finance seeks to create and market products that comply with shariah, a legal system guiding Muslims in their everyday life. One stipulation in this system is the prohibition of *riba*, interpreted as the paying and receiving of interest. Since the payment of interest on debt has been fundamental to all the practices of monetary debt discussed so far, this is potentially a very radical proposition. The underlying thought is that making money from money is unjust, and can lead to exploitation. According to Islamic jurisprudence, on its own money cannot be used to make more money. Only economic activities such as running a business can achieve a return.

When it comes to debt transactions, Islamic finance favours *qard hasan*, literally a benevolent loan. *Qard hasan* is interest-free, typically extended for the social

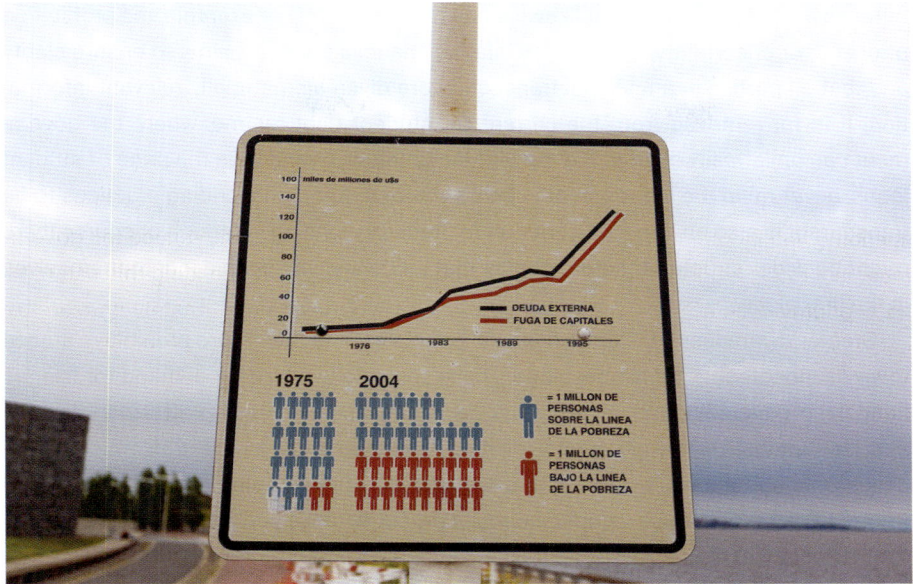

Photo 4.7. A sign in Parque de la Memoria in Buenos Aires, Argentina. It implies that increased external debt and capital flight have led to more people living below the poverty line, and, like the National Debt Clock in the US (see Photo 4.6), it brings the politics of debt to the street level.
Source: Watchtheworld/Alamy Stock Photo.

welfare of the borrower. The borrower is nevertheless obliged to repay the loan as long as circumstances allow it. Indeed, Islam unambiguously stipulates the obligation of lenience towards borrowers who experience duress due to no fault of their own. Thus, in the context of the unprecedented economic hardship caused by the response to the coronavirus pandemic, new guidance had to be provided to Islamic financial institutions so that they could manage their credit–debt relationships in a manner consistent with shariah principles (see Accounting and Auditing Organization for Islamic Financial Institutions 2020). In other transactions, Islamic finance espouses a preference for equity over debt. Along these lines, loans are often structured as sharing agreements where one party provides the capital to another, for example to start a business, and both parties share the profit at a predetermined ratio.

According to its proponents, Islamic finance has the objective of creating a more equitable financial and economic order that at the same time is transaction-friendly. Its advocates see it as a foundation for centring the ethical and moral dimensions of economics and markets. This includes questioning the necessity of debt relations and the proliferation of debt in the global economy. But it also extends to other questions of fairness and social justice that likewise can relate to debt. For example, the prohibition of *gharar*, or uncertainty, another key Islamic financial principle, aims to ensure clarity and that all parties in a financial transaction are given all materially relevant information. It is far removed from the current UK student debt regime, where the government can unilaterally change the repayment conditions—and thus the price of student loans, never mind the interest that is being charged. Requiring lending practices to be transparent is also an important counter to predatory lending, although of course there might be wider structural factors at play that influence why people indebt themselves in the first place.

Greater awareness of Islamic financial principles, and their more prohibitive stance towards indebtedness and speculation, have coincided with rising demand for Islamic financial products. Indeed, recent years have witnessed increasing efforts to develop and institutionalize Islamic capital markets and, above all, to make Islamic finance acceptable and thus investable to the mainstream, an example of which is shown in Photo 4.8. However, many Islamic financial products closely mirror their conventional (i.e. non-Islamic) counterparts, reworking elements that are in violation of shariah principles. For example, an Islamic bank account would not pay interest but might pay savers a profit. Overall then, to date the success of Islamic finance in overcoming the debt economy has been limited.

Photo 4.8. A Muslim trade fair promoting Islamic finance in Le Bourget, France.
Source: Photononstop/Alamy Stock Photo.

4.3 Engaging Debt

4.3.1 Thought experiment on usury

Islamic finance is but one approach that challenges our understanding of debt as an inevitable feature of the global economy. What we think of as debt is in a continual process of social construction, negotiation, and change. Whilst Islamic finance is very specific about the instances in which making a loan or incurring a debt are permissible and how financial transactions can be structured, such as in a way that avoids the paying or receiving of interest, there are a range of other initiatives and strategies that seek to challenge common practices of debt, tackle over-indebtedness, campaign for debt relief, and call out unjust creditor–debtor relations. The exercises in this section are designed to stimulate learning about different forms that debt can take, and how uneven debtor–creditor relationships can be challenged, theoretically and practically, at the individual, household, and national level.

We begin with a thought experiment. This activity can be defined as the mental visualization of a specific scenario for the purpose of answering a more general question about reality (Brownlee and Stemplowska 2017). It is a common philosophical technique, used to expose contradictions in existing arguments or bring forth intuitions not previously considered. For example, Charles W. Mooney (2012) uses it to construct a situation in which the US might seek to default on its sovereign debt so that he can investigate why that decision would be taken and how it could proceed in legal and political terms. His reason for doing this was that no one had explored this question in any depth, partly out of denial that such a scenario could ever arise.

As well as addressing questions normally considered to be out of bounds, thought experiments invite us to draw on our personal experiences to rationalize a suggested response that can be abstracted into more general and impersonal conclusions. This exercise is what we would like you to do in this thought experiment. It concerns **usury**, which is the practice of lending money at an *unreasonable* rate of interest. What is reasonable, of course, is open to debate. On the one hand, interest payments can be viewed as necessary to compensate lenders for foregoing immediate consumption satisfaction and putting aside savings. On the other hand, they can be seen as furthering inequality and creating cycles of indebtedness from which it is difficult to escape.

To explore usury in more detail, read the following scenario and then think through the questions below:

> You make a friend at university who is from a relatively wealthy family. You are in the same sports team and would like to go on the team tour together at the end of the year. Although you cannot

afford it right now, your friend offers to loan you the money and says that you can pay it back later. Offering 'mates' rates', the friend says they will only charge you half the interest that the bank would. 'It's a good deal,' they say.

- Is it acceptable for the friend to charge *any* interest on this loan?
- Next, consider whether this reasoning would hold if you needed the money for 'essentials' like rent rather than 'luxuries' like the team tour. As discussed in the Malaysian example in Section 4.2.2, should the purpose to which the loan will be put make a difference to how much interest is charged?
- Now, can you translate these evaluations into general conditions to determine when loans should be provided with (or without) interest?
- We can also use this scenario to examine the power relations of debt as covered in Section 4.2.3. What means might the friend have to get their money back if you do borrow the money? How might you go about avoiding repayment, should you wish?
- In terms of the performative dimension of debt, how does the request, and potential repayment, of interest change the nature of the friendship?
- And finally, to highlight some of the institutional dynamics as opposed to personal lending relationships, would you use a credit card to pay for this trip? Or take out a payday loan? How would this be different from taking a loan from a friend?

4.3.2 Role-playing a debt relief campaign

Role-playing involves taking on the persona of someone else. It is a common pedagogical technique in the classroom: those of you who have studied Politics or International Relations might already be familiar with simulations of United Nations negotiations where you play a delegate from a particular country and try to reach international consensus on a certain topic. It is also used beyond the classroom for 'real world' actors. Modelled on the clinical simulations used to train medical professionals, Policy Simulation Labs have been run in Bangladesh to provide policymakers with a chance to test out their responses to various political challenges by seeing how different participants would react (see Habib 2020).

The role-playing exercise below is based on a debt relief campaign concerned with assisting highly indebted poor countries that cannot repay their debts. It is a content-based simulation rather than a process-based one, meaning that the focus is on understanding the different interests, arguments, and agency of the representatives involved. Read the following two paragraphs for some context and then choose a role to play.

In 1996 the World Bank, IMF and other creditors established the Heavily Indebted Poor Countries (HIPC) initiative. This was meant to ensure that the poorest countries in the world were not overwhelmed by unsustainable debt burdens, defined as a debt worth less than 150 per cent of the country's annual exports. Previously, calls for debt relief had been deflected with the moral hazard argument. This held that debt cancellation, of either the initial sum borrowed or the interest accrued, would only encourage those same states to become heavily indebted again. In other words, debt relief would create perverse incentives.

However, recurring debt crises and lobbying by NGOs helped create a normative shift, whereby sovereign debt was considered less in terms of economic stability and more in terms of social justice. Adopting the biblical language of a debt jubilee mentioned previously and enrolling religious organizations to support their cause, campaigners recast debt as 'chains' that were shackling impoverished nations and helped to pressurize creditors into cancelling more and more debt through the HIPC initiative (see Photo 4.9; Broome 2009). By 2020, there were thirty-six countries that had $76 billion of debt cancellation approved (IMF 2020). Yet critics have maintained that more must still be done. They have argued that the HIPC initiative does not include enough indebted countries, does not include debt extended by private creditors, does not deliver enough debt relief, and does not deliver it quickly enough.

(a) Jubilee Debt Campaign—a non-governmental organization (NGO) advocating for debt relief.
(b) World Bank—an international organization (IO) with a focus on development; also a major lender to poor countries.
(c) Zambian Ministry of Finance—government authority of a heavily indebted poor country.
(d) Other roles, e.g. journalist, private investor, Zambian NGO.

The task is to come up with a short press statement on the question: what should be done to help highly indebted poor countries that cannot repay their debts? The statement should reflect the role you play, as well as some responses for potential counterarguments put forward by the other representatives, including the media. You can search the internet for examples of press statements from these organizations and consult the sources cited in the student resources. If you are doing this in a group, then get someone to play the role of journalist—ideally the seminar tutor if you are

Photo 4.9. A Jubilee 2000 event at St Paul's Cathedral in London, where 20,000 chain letters were presented calling for the cancellation of Third World debt.
Source: PA Images/Alamy Stock Photo.

doing this in class—as they can pose questions directly and allow you to dismiss any counterarguments verbally. After finishing the role-playing element of this exercise, you may want to come together as a group and reflect on what you learnt in this exercise. Some questions to guide this discussion could be:

- What are the key features of debt that the role-play exposed?
- What are the power dynamics at play?
- Can the international debt regime be changed? If yes, how? If not, why not?
- What do you think the future holds for debt relief in the wake of the Covid-19 pandemic?

4.4 Conclusion

Debt is a core feature of the contemporary global political economy, impacting households, corporations, and governments. It is not an inherently bad thing. Loans and other forms of credit can allow individuals, organizations, and countries to improve their current situation, for example by funding the provision of and access to education and training, without jeopardizing their future. However, this should not distract from the fact that much debt originates from lenders exploiting their privileged position in a hierarchical system.

Poorer borrowers typically pay much higher rates of interest—or, as we have seen in the case of student debt, they have to repay loans and interest over longer periods. They are also significantly more exposed to predatory lending practices. Unequal power relations impact both the levels and affordability of debt, and the conditions under which different economic actors can borrow. As we saw in the discussion of student loans, it is not just the terms of repayment that matter politically but the extent to which university education is predicated on personal indebtedness in the first place. The comparison between the four worlds of student finance, along with the examples of gift exchange and Islamic finance, also pointed to alternatives to debt, such as non-conditional grants and risk-sharing contracts. Whilst none of these are absent power relations or their own pathologies, they show that different ways of organizing economic obligations are possible. They also remind us that debt, in its current form, is neither inevitable nor incontestable.

Access the online resources for quizzes, student reflection podcasts, and support for tackling the chapter's learning activities: http://www.oup.com/he/i-peel1e.

RESOURCES

Tile recommendations from the I-PEEL website: 'borrowing' (Chris Clarke) http://i-peel.org/homepage/borrowing/; 'payday loan' (Rachel Gordon, James Ash, Ben Anderson, and Paul Langley) http://i-peel.org/homepage/payday-loan/.

Inside Job. 2010. 108 minutes. A documentary film directed by Charles Ferguson that provides a sober chronology of the global financial crisis and is especially good at explaining the process of securitization mentioned in Section 4.2.2.

Life and Debt. 2001. 86 minutes. A documentary film directed by Stephanie Black that traces the fallout in Jamaica of the Third World debt crisis mentioned in Section 4.2.1. It helps to provide an appreciation of the socio-economic impact of the loan conditions put in place by the IMF and World Bank.

Graeber, David. 2011. *Debt: The First 5000 Years*. New York: Melville House Publishing. A magisterial discussion of debt and its moral dilemmas by a leading scholar and organizer of the Occupy Wall Street movement; it connects to the discussion of why people indebt themselves in Section 4.2.2.

Montgomerie, Johnna. 2019. *Should We Abolish Household Debts?* Cambridge: Polity Press. Akin to the thought experiments detailed in Section 4.3.1, in this book Montgomerie conceives of her proposals to abolish certain household debts, including student debts, as a way of 'hacking' the global financial system by creatively rewiring it.

Rethel, Lena. 2011. 'Whose Legitimacy? Islamic Finance and the Global Financial Order'. *Review of International Political Economy* 18(1): 75–98. Sets out some of the key principles of Islamic finance and its governance, as discussed in Section 4.2.3, as well as the difficulties associated with positioning Islamic finance as a mainstream-capable alternative.

REFERENCES

Accounting and Auditing Organization for Islamic Financial Institutions. 2020. *Accounting Implications of the COVID-19 Pandemic*. 21 May, http://aaoifi.com/accounting-implications-of-the-impact-of-covid-19-pandemic/?lang=en.

Aitken, Rob. 2015. *Fringe Finance: Crossing and Contesting the Borders of Global Capital*. Abingdon: Routledge.

Asadullah, M. Niaz, and Theresa Chan. 2019. 'Malaysia's Student-Debt Crisis Could Cripple the Economy, Unless the Government Acts'. World Economic Forum blog. 26 June, https://www.weforum.org/agenda/2019/06/asia-s-student-debt-time-bomb/.

Babb, Sarah. 2013. 'The Washington Consensus as Transnational Policy Paradigm: Its Origins, Trajectory and Likely Successor'. *Review of International Political Economy* 20(2): 268–97.

Bank Negara Malaysia. 2020. *Financial Stability Review 2019*. Kuala Lumpur: Bank Negara Malaysia.

Blyth, Mark. 2013. *Austerity: The History of a Dangerous Idea*. Oxford: Oxford University Press.

Bolton, Paul. 2020. 'Student Loan Statistics'. Research Briefing, UK Parliament House of Commons Library, 5 October.

Broome, André. 2009. 'When Do NGOs Matter? Activist Organizations as a Source of Change in the International Debt Regime'. *Global Society* 23(1): 59–78.

Brownlee, Kimberley, and Zofia Stemplowska. 2017. 'Thought Experiments'. In *Methods in Analytical Political Theory*, ed. Adrian Blau, 21–45. Cambridge: Cambridge University Press.

Duménil, Gerard, and Dominique Lévy. 2004. *Capital Resurgent. Roots of the Neoliberal Revolution*, trans. Derek Jeffers. Cambridge, MA, and London: Harvard University Press.

Epstein, Gerald. 2019. *The Political Economy of Central Banking. Contested Control and the Power of Finance*. Cheltenham: Edward Elgar.

Federici, Silvia. 2014. 'From Commoning to Debt: Financialization, Microcredit, and the Changing Architecture of Capital Accumulation'. *South Atlantic Quarterly* 113(2): 231–44.

Garritzmann, Julian. 2015. *The Political Economy of Higher Education Finance. The Politics of Tuition Fees and Subsidies in OECD Countries, 1945–2015*. Basingstoke: Palgrave Macmillan.

Graeber, David. 2011. *Debt: The First 5000 Years*. New York: Melville House Publishing.

Habib, Nazia Mintz. 2020. 'Can Policy Simulations Help Developing Economies Get Back on Track?', *Apolitical: Public Servant*, 1 June, https://apolitical.co/en/solution_article/using-policy-simulations-in-covid-19s-developing-world.

Halterbeck, Maike, and Gavin Conlon. 2017. *The Impact of Student Loan Repayments on Graduate Taxes*. London: London Economics.

Hanson, Melanie. 2022. 'Student Loan Debt Statistics'. *Education Data Initiative*, March 28, https://educationdata.org/student-loan-debt-statistics.

Hess, Abigail Johnson. 2020. 'The Complicated Beauty of Student Debt Forgiveness'. *CNBC Make It*, 24 January, https://www.cnbc.com/2020/01/24/robert-f-smith-talks-debt-at-davos-after-clearing-loans-at-morehouse.html.

IMDb. 2008. 'The Bath Item Gift Hypothesis'. IMDb: *The Big Bang Theory* (TV Series), https://www.imdb.com/title/tt1256021/characters/nm0192505 (last accessed 31 January 2022).

International Monetary Fund (IMF). 2020. 'Debt Relief Under the Heavily Indebted Poor Countries (HIPC) Initiative', IMF factsheet. Updated 25 March 2020, https://www.imf.org/en/About/Factsheets/Sheets/2016/08/01/16/11/Debt-Relief-Under-the-Heavily-Indebted-Poor-Countries-Initiative.

Kessenidis, Dimitra. 2019. 'Robert Smith, Slayer of Student Debt at Morehouse College'. *Bloomberg Businessweek*, 4 December.

Langley, Paul. 2021. 'Assets and Assetization in Financialized Capitalism'. *Review of International Political Economy* 28(2): 382–93.

Ma, Jennifer, Sandy Baum, Matea Pender, and C. J. Libassi. 2019. *Trends in College Pricing 2019*. New York: College Board.

Mauss, Marcel. 1990. *The Gift: The Form and Reason for Exchange in Archaic Societies*. London and New York: Routledge.

Montgomerie, Johnna. 2009. 'The Pursuit of (Past) Happiness? Middle-Class Indebtedness and American Financialization'. *New Political Economy* 14(1): 1–24.

Montgomerie, Johnna. 2019. *Should We Abolish Household Debts?* Cambridge: Polity Press.sss

Mooney, Charles W. 2012. 'United States Sovereign Debt: A Thought Experiment on Default and Restructuring'. *Faculty Scholarship at Penn Law* 1499: 1–67.

National Audit Office. 2018. *The Sale of Student Loans*. London: NAO.

Nova, Annie. 2019. 'The Student Debt Crisis Has Hit Black Students Especially Hard. Here's How'. *CNBC*, 27 July, https://www.cnbc.com/2019/07/27/how-the-student-debt-crisis-has-hit-black-students-especially-hard.html.

Ranasinghe, Dhara. 2021. 'Global Debt is Fast Approaching Record $300 trillion', Reuters, 14 September, https://www.reuters.com/business/global-debt-is-fast-approaching-record-300-trillion-iif-2021-09-14/.

Rethel, Lena. 2011. 'Whose Legitimacy? Islamic Finance and the Global Financial Order'. *Review of International Political Economy* 18(1): 75–98.

Rethel, Lena. 2012. 'Each Time Is Different! The Shifting Boundaries of Emerging Market Debt'. *Global Society* 26(1): 123–43.

Rethel, Lena, and Timothy J. Sinclair. 2012. *The Problem with Banks*. London: Zed.

Roberts, Adrienne. 2014. 'Doing Borrowed Time: The State, the Law and the Coercive Governance of 'Undeserving' Debtors'. *Critical Sociology* 40(5): 669–87.

Roitman, Janet. 2003. 'Unsanctioned Wealth; Or, The Productivity of Debt in Northern Cameroon'. *Public Culture* 15(2): 211–37.

Shubber, Kadhim. 2020. 'How Robert Smith Played Hardball with IRS Over Unpaid Taxes'. *Financial Times*, 17 October.

Simms, Andrew. 2009. *Ecological Debt*. London: Pluto..

Stevenson, Alex. 2011. 'Osborne Digs In Against EU Budget Increase', *Politics.co.uk*, 21 April, https://www.politics.co.uk/news/2011/04/21/osborne-digs-in-against-eu-budget-increase/.

Taylor, Marcus. 2012. 'The Antinomies of 'Financial Inclusion': Debt, Distress and the Workings of Indian Microfinance'. *Journal of Agrarian Change* 12(4): 601–10.

Thrift, Nigel. 2010. 'A Perfect Innovation Engine: The Rise of the Talent World'. In *Cultural Political Economy*, ed. Jacqueline Best and Matthew Paterson, 197–221. Abingdon: Routledge.

Varman, Rohit, Biswatosh Saha, and Per Skålén. 2011. 'Market Subjectivity and Neoliberal Governmentality in Higher Education'. *Journal of Marketing Management* 27(11–12): 1163–85.

Westaway, Jenny, and Stephen McKay. 2007. *Women's Financial Assets and Debts*. London: Fawcett Society.

5 CARE

5.1	**Military Spouses**	122
5.2	**Exploring Care**	131
5.3	**Engaging Care**	142
5.4	**Conclusion**	147

LEARNING OBJECTIVES

- Critically analyse care as a set of relational practices (caring for) and affective experiences (caring about) that can be undertaken inside and outside of households
- Develop an understanding of social reproduction, heteronormativity, and global care chains based on feminist and queer theory
- Apply Feminist IPE insights about care to policy debates by creating a time use survey and undertaking a social annotation task

READER'S GUIDE

This chapter is about care, both caring for and caring about others. The work of caring is often seen as something that is peripheral to the study of IPE. This chapter, by contrast, asserts its centrality. It opens with a discussion of military spouses and the vital everyday role that their care labour plays in sustaining the military as an institution (Section 5.1). This serves as a jumping-off point for looking at three interrelated debates that show why care matters for an everyday approach in IPE: feminist work on social reproduction; the extent to which care can be commodified; and the heteronormative assumptions that underpin understandings of care. In the section 'Exploring Care' (Section 5.2), we examine three crucial areas of feminist work on care that have informed IPE scholarship. These are the 'care crisis', how this crisis is experienced in everyday life as a form of depletion, and the transnationalization of commodified care labour in global care chains. The final section of the chapter is 'Engaging Care' (Section 5.3). This sets out activities that will enable you to reflect on how care can be measured through time use surveys, and, using the technique of social annotation, how policymakers have (and have not) taken up some of the concerns raised by feminists about the significance of unpaid caring labour.

KEY CONCEPTS
Social reproduction; heteronormativity; global care chain

Access the online resources to listen to a podcast where Juanita introduces and explores the key themes of this chapter: http://www.oup.com/he/i-peel1e.

5.1 Military Spouses

Shortly before Mother's Day, the US also celebrates Military Spouse Appreciation Day, with the President making a ceremonial speech and proclamation to mark the event. In 2021, newly elected President Joe Biden used his speech to emphasize the hard work and sacrifice of military spouses, stating:

> Spouses understand that loving a service member means facing the challenges that can accompany their service: from leaving friends behind to changing jobs again; making parenting decisions alone to losing sleep at night; deployments to homecomings to more deployments. Those challenges have been magnified by the COVID-19 pandemic, which has led to lost income, fewer childcare options, and extended deployments. Still, military spouses have done what they do best: adapt, persevere, and keep going.
> (Biden 2021)

The rhetoric around Military Spouse Appreciation Day takes its cue from the same militarized language through which active service personnel and military veterans are understood: making sacrifices for the nation and being thanked for their service. But this similarity masks an important difference. Despite the gender-neutral language of 'spouse', over 90 per cent of the 581,000 civilians married to someone on active duty in the US military were women (Department of Defense 2019, 134). Like other branches of the state, militaries have tended to rely on a **gendered division of labour** in which men enrol in active service while women take care of the domestic duties of the 'home front' (Horn 2010). In celebrating the role of spouses in enabling military institutions to function, Military Spouse Appreciation Day therefore seeks to make women's caring labour count, bringing public recognition to this crucial but often invisible work that goes on in the home. Or does it?

Although military families may receive certain subsidies in the form of housing allocations on military bases, the job of being a military spouse is an unpaid one. On a visit to the Fort Carson military base in Colorado to mark Military Spouse Appreciation Day, Dr Jill Biden, the US First Lady shown in Photo 5.1, declared: 'This community is unlike any other . . . it's bound together by love: love for our country, love for our service members and love for the communities that you all build together' (cited in Castrejon 2021). Critics, however, suggest that we need to look beyond such platitudes and recognize how this veneration of both nationalism and altruism effectively binds large numbers of women to the ever-growing demands of what have been termed the 'greedy institutions' of the patriarchal family and the military (Segal 1986; see also Gray 2022).

Photo 5.1. First Lady Dr Jill Biden greets Erin Nash, a military spouse, as part of Military Spouse Appreciation Day.
Source: Sipa US/Alamy Stock Photo.

Because spouses prop up, through voluntary and unpaid caring labour, a range of key services on military bases, examining their lives throws into sharp relief two themes found in feminist political economy writings on care. First, how care labour is *vital* labour, and second, how the provision of care is organized through a starkly gendered division of labour between paid and unpaid work. Thus, looking at the experiences of military spouses also provides a jumping-off point for examining how the gendered division between unpaid caring labour and paid work outside of the home operates in other areas of the global political economy. As the discussion in this chapter will show, women disproportionately experience vulnerability because of the expectation that they will take responsibility for the invisible household work that enables social institutions—be they the market, the military, or the family itself—to function (Enloe 2010).

5.1.1 Social reproduction

Feminist political economists frequently use the term 'social reproduction' in their writings (Bakker 2007; Luxton 2018). As a concept it captures how there are certain daily activities that are core to the functioning of the economy, but are seen as non-economic or non-productive activities. In other words, we generally conceive *the* economy as encompassing activities that are regarded as 'productive'—they involve things like buying goods, going to work, running a business, and generating wealth. But there are a whole set of other, 'reproductive', activities that, in conventional economic analysis, are placed beyond the production boundary. In essence, then, social reproduction is a way of redrawing that boundary to include 'women's work' *as* work. A useful overview of the kinds of activities that can be understood as falling within the category of social reproduction is as follows:

> Despite some differences of emphasis in feminist analyses, social reproduction can be taken to include the following: biological reproduction; unpaid production in the home (both goods and services); social provisioning (by this we mean voluntary work directed at meeting needs in the community); the reproduction of culture and ideology; and the provision of sexual, emotional and affective services (such as are required to maintain family and intimate relationships). (Hoskyns and Rai 2007, 300)

This definition of social reproduction can be illustrated by referring back to the discussion of military spouses. Here we see that social reproduction consists of more than preparing meals and raising children—the 'goods' and 'services' of unpaid work within the home. It also involves providing emotional support, voluntary labour, and actively performing cultural and ideological norms by participating in activities that reproduce dominant social relations, for example, by being part of a military wives' choir that projects a particular vision of appropriately 'wifely' and patriotic behaviour (Cree 2020).

When Marxist Feminist scholars initially engaged with the concept of social reproduction in the 1970s, they sought to challenge unspoken assumptions that care work was a necessary sacrifice that women made for their loved ones. As we saw in the Introduction to this book (Section 1.2.2), activist scholars such as Silvia Federici were prominent in arguing that housework should be waged, writing:

> Under capitalism every worker is manipulated and exploited and his/her relation to capital is totally mystified. The wage gives the impression of a fair deal: you work and you get paid, hence you and your boss are equal; while in reality the wage, rather than paying for the work you do, hides all the unpaid work that goes into profit. But the wage at least recognizes that you are a worker.... But in the case of housework the situation is qualitatively different. The difference lies in the fact that not only has

Photo 5.2. A representation of how domestic and caring labour in the 'social factory' sustains the waged labour force, created by feminist activists in the UK in the 1970s.
Source: Red Women's Workshop.

> housework been imposed on women, but it has been transformed into a natural attribute of our female physique and personality.
>
> (Federici 1975)

In the twenty-first century, when few women in Western states describe themselves as housewives, many would question the relevance of calls for wages for housework. We can also raise the concern that in some groups of women—especially working-class women and women of colour—the status of housewife was less common in the sense that paid work outside the home had to be taken on out of economic necessity.

Nonetheless, even though Western states witnessed the mass entry of women into the labour force during the second half of the twentieth century, in heterosexual households women continue to perform the greater share of unpaid household labour, and this 'double burden' of combining paid and unpaid work has well-documented knock-on effects for gender equality (Samtleben and Müller 2021; ILO 2018). As the protest in Photo 5.3 attests, many people still find the gendered division of labour in the household to be deeply unfair.

In this vein, social reproduction scholarship provides a theoretical language for thinking about care and locating practices of caring within the study of IPE. It is

Photo 5.3. Participants at an International Women's Day 'Women's Strike' event in Rostock, Germany. The signs read 'refuse to do housework, men clean the toilet! For feminism anyway!' and 'Same work, same wages, all else pure mockery!'
Source: dpa picture alliance/Alamy Stock Photo.

important to recognize, though, that social reproduction and care are not necessarily terms that can be used interchangeably. Care can be understood as a set of activities that we undertake as part of our daily lives that support the physical and emotional well-being of others. But care is also an 'ethical social relationship' (Dowling 2021, 68): we not only care *for* others, we also care *about* them, and in doing so we form attachments—bonds of love and emotion—to those we care for. Care is certainly an aspect of social reproduction, but the thrust of this concept is that we situate the labour of caring for others (or even for ourselves) alongside *all* forms of labour and other everyday activities that are vital to the operation of the capitalist market economy.

5.1.2 Valuing care work

So far in the discussion we have centred an understanding of care as unpaid labour and as an aspect of social reproduction. But the question of how we value care is far more complicated. Much care labour is undertaken by paid workers such as nannies, or home care assistants, and many paid jobs outside the care sector also involve workers exhibiting the demeanour and practices that we associate with caring *about* others. In this section we look at the ways in which care labour has been commodified—made into a marketable service that can be bought and sold—and some of the dilemmas that arise from this.

Returning to the wages for housework discussion in Section 5.1.1, we might look to challenge the idea that labour in the home is something that exclusively involves the unpaid labour of 'housewives'. After all, domestic servants have long been central to the organization of social reproduction within middle- and upper-class households. Black Feminist scholars writing in the context of North America pointed out that even during the so-called 'golden age' of the housewife in the 1950s, African American women were widely employed as domestic workers in the homes of white families. As Angela Davies (2019, 117–18) wrote, 'Cleaning women, domestic workers, maids – these are the women who know better than anyone else what it means to receive wages for housework.' In other words, earning a wage does little to overcome gender, as well as racial, inequality if that work itself is persistently undervalued. As the discussion of global care chains in Section 5.2.3 illustrates, how we value care relates to **intersectional** structures of inequality. Caring is not only gendered work; it is also highly racialized work in which other forms of discrimination based upon nationality, citizenship status, and age all operate.

Whether and how we should value care is a theme explored by feminist economist Susan Himmelweit (1999), who suggests that the very nature of caring makes it impossible to completely commodify this work. There are complex sets of relationships at work in the human interactions that surround caring. We do not simply care *for* others because we expect monetary reward, and we may derive non-monetary rewards, like feelings of pleasure, in the altruistic act of caring *about* others. That said, Himmelweit certainly recognizes the economic value of care labour and, in her more recent work with Jerome De Henau, she makes a convincing case for investment in the infrastructure of the care economy—putting forward a set of policy proposals that would simultaneously address gender inequalities and stimulate the economy. In particular, they emphasize the importance of creating more and better paying jobs with good career prospects for those employed as care workers. Investments in high-quality care are seen as countering the ongoing undervaluing of women's paid and unpaid care labour, which can be witnessed, for example, in the huge numbers of women who dropped out of the formal labour market due to the pressures of caring during the Covid-19 pandemic (De Henau and Himmelweit 2021).

Another issue that might be raised with current understandings of care is the tendency to locate acts of caring within the home or in the social care sector made up of counselling services, nurseries, nursing homes, and so on. In reality, many jobs—whether in the care sector or not—require people to display the emotional conduct of caring. The concept of **affective labour** seeks to capture the work that goes into those everyday human interactions which produce emotional responses in others. Completely new forms of work have emerged within this affective economy, like wedding

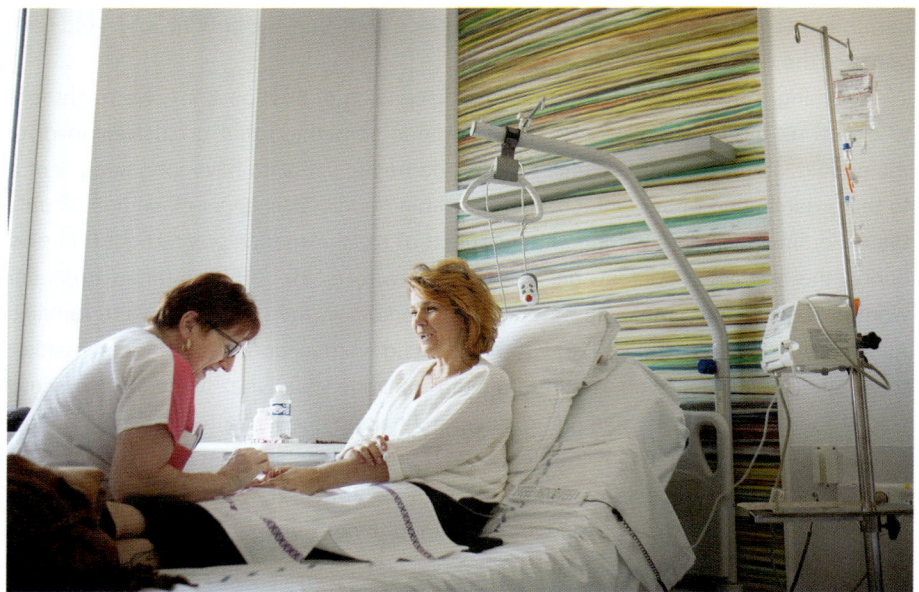

Photo 5.4. A picture taken in the oncology department of a French hospital. It depicts a healthcare assistant who also works in the hospital three days a week as a hospital beautician, providing beauty treatments to patients undergoing chemotherapy.
Source: BSIP SA/Alamy Stock Photo.

planners, breastfeeding consultants, or life coaches. In these professions the primary source of value of this labour lies in how it makes others feel about themselves (see Oksala 2016). The emergence of such professions also reveals how people increasingly buy in affective services for things that would previously have been provided by families and communities, the state, or perhaps not at all (see also Section 9.1.1 on the marketization of everyday life). Take the example presented in Photo 5.4, of a healthcare assistant who works as a hospital beautician on an oncology ward. This indicates how the work of caring for someone is understood as encompassing more than just meeting physical needs—it also builds emotional connection. Work in the affective economy demonstrates how there are always new ways and means of commodifying the experience of being cared for.

5.1.3 Heteronormativity

So far in this chapter we have presented unpaid caring labour within households as something overwhelmingly performed by women. When we think about the households within which this labour takes place, do we make assumptions that these are 'nuclear families', a sociological term referring to heterosexual couples and their biological children? How we conceptualize households and unpaid household labour frequently rests upon an idealized view of what constitutes 'normal' family life. The term **heteronormativity** describes the cultural norms that structure and lend coherence to understandings of love, intimacy, and the family in ways that privilege heterosexuality. Heteronormativity thus also operates as a set of ideas and practices that serve to stabilize the gender division of labour. A **queer theory** lens on political economy asks that we unpack and challenge these assumptions. As V. Spike Peterson argues, by turning our gaze towards sexuality we can also create a space for thinking about how everyday intimacies centred on sexual and familial relations shape, and are shaped by, the global political economy (Peterson 2018, 131).

Going back to the discussion of military spouses in Section 5.1, it is notable that militaries around the world function via the institutionalization of heteronormativity. Given this reliance on the heterosexual household to maintain militaries, alongside the fostering of highly militarized masculinities within the armed forces, it hardly comes as a surprise that militaries have long been exceptionally hostile places for those with non-normative sexual and gender identities. Heteronormativity governs, controls, and disciplines 'unruly' sexual behaviours far beyond the military sphere. As Nicola J. Smith's **queer political economy** writings show, the UK state has long criminalized and penalized groups such as sex workers or single mothers who are viewed as challenging the dominant gender and sexual order (Smith 2016, 2020). And as Gargi Bhattacharyya (2018) reminds us in her work on racial capitalism, these disciplining practices cannot be separated from forms of racialization. For example, ideas of the African American 'Welfare Queen' or of 'backward' and 'dysfunctional' Australian Aboriginal communities reflect dominant ideas that because of a supposed lack of 'family values' such groups have failed to produce the 'right' kind of productive workers, which, in turn, are used to justify draconian cuts to state welfare. (The extensive use of quotation marks is needed because so much of the language in this debate needs to be problematized.)

State welfare regimes have played a more general role through policies which assume that women have the time, inclination, and flexibility to take on ever more caring labour because they are—and should be—in a household supported by a primary income from a (male) breadwinner. Another institution upholding the heteronormative nuclear family as the pre-eminent unit of social organization has been marriage. In many Western states the regulation of sexuality through the institution of marriage has shifted in some important ways—not least through the widening of the legal concept of marriage to include queer couples. This is an interesting development in the sense that it disrupts heteronormativity and some of its related gender practices. For example, studies have shown that same-sex couples are far more likely to have a more equitable division of household labour (Van der Vleuten et al. 2021). But it has also been suggested that gay marriage operates as a form of **homonormativity**, whereby certain groups of gay and lesbian people attain acceptability via their assumption of an identity rooted in values of heteronormative domesticity and capitalist consumption (Duggan 2002).

At the same time, the growing field of queer political economy has challenged the idea that queer identities can be straightforwardly assimilated into an ever more neoliberal, competitive, and consumption-oriented form of capitalism (Nguyen 2021; Raha 2021; Smith 2020). In doing so, this scholarship raises critical concerns about how we can conceptualize care outside of both capitalism and the normative heterosexual family. Histories of queer political struggle present us with different ways of imagining how care is performed, challenging the idea that the heteronormative family unit is always willing and able to provide care. For example, what happens when the nuclear family is a site not of care and love but of violence and repression—something that is often directly experienced by young queer people?

This is explored in the 2021 UK television series *It's a Sin*, which follows a group of gay men living in London during the 1980s HIV/AIDS crisis (see Photo 5.5). A major theme in the show is the rejection that many gay men faced from their biological families, and the rebuilding of kinship and mutual forms of caring for one another in the face of state indifference. *It's a Sin* portrays members of a marginalized community working together to provide care and support to one another, how these new community bonds emerge because of the failure of the state and other institutions like the nuclear family to provide care, and how these bonds foster new forms of political solidarity and activism. As the queer/trans* activist-scholar Nat Raha (2021: 88) argues, the 'caring, domestic and emotional' labour within queer communities needs to be understood as social reproduction

Photo 5.5. Solidarities rooted in mutual aid. Russell T. Davies's 2021 TV mini-series *It's a Sin*, which won plaudits for its empathetic portrayal of a stigmatized community.
Source: Album/Alamy Stock Photo.

because, as she powerfully asserts, it is 'a precondition to our survival'. She illustrates this point using the example from the 1970s of New York's Street Transvestite Action Revolutionaries (STAR), whose work centred on supporting gay, trans, and lesbian young people. Using income earned through sex work, the collective established STAR House, where young homeless queer people could find shelter and support. STAR House can be understood as a reimagining of the household, in which acts of care challenge rather than reproduce gender conformity. More generally, such collective, yet deeply politicized, acts of mutual care are hallmarks of what has been termed **mutual aid**, whereby communities come together to provide collective care and support for one another and, in doing so, reimagine the kind of world they want to live in (Arani 2020).

5.2 Exploring Care

Thus far, we have mapped out various concepts concerning everyday practices of care using military spouses as our initial vantage point. As we turn to explore the theme of care in political economy more broadly, the discussion takes a more disciplinary perspective, connecting the conceptual issues outlined so far in this chapter (social reproduction, commodification of care, and heteronormativity) to key topics in IPE: financial and economic crisis, and labour migration. By looking at financial crises and the ensuing care crises, as well as at global systems of migration for care labour, we gain insights into how the everyday work of maintaining life is increasingly marked by two interlinked processes. First, the withdrawal of the state from public welfare provisioning, which has created ever-growing pressures on economies of care and social reproduction (see also Section 4.1.1 for a parallel discussion of the retreat of the state from public education provision). Second, the ever-intensifying infiltration of capitalist market relations into the realm of social reproduction as households seek to manage risk and find private solutions, such as buying in care labour from an increasingly globalized market for domestic workers (Bakker 2007). These challenges are shown to place particular pressures on women, whose paid and unpaid labour is increasingly relied upon to fill care gaps, resulting in forms of harm to women themselves and to society and communities more broadly.

5.2.1 Are we experiencing a care crisis?

In a lot of IPE scholarship, much significance is placed on the topic of finance, and financial crisis in particular. Some of this literature is overviewed in the chapter on Debt (Section 4.2). You may well be asking yourself, why is it necessary to discuss finance and financial crisis in a chapter on Care? The answer, feminist political economists would point out, is that we cannot divorce the sphere of financial exchange from the underlying relations of production and social reproduction. In other words, we cannot develop our understanding of any area of the economy without also recognizing the processes involved in reproducing people as workers, investors, and consumers of financial products (Roberts 2016). For example, the ability of households to reproduce themselves or 'make ends meet' has become increasingly dependent on the ability to access credit and other kinds of loans. As Chapter 4 on Debt shows, even these small everyday forms of credit-based expenditure link us into the world of global finance.

Moreover, when we start to examine the gendered *impacts* of financial crisis, we gain insights into how macroeconomic shifts are experienced in everyday life—in particular in terms of a crisis of care (Fraser 2017). The impacts of economic and financial crises on women's caring labour have been widely documented. This includes work looking at the gendered impacts of the debt crisis that hit large numbers of developing economies in the 1980s, the Asian Financial Crisis of 1997, financial crises in Argentina and Russia in the early 2000s, and the impact of government austerity programmes in Western states following the 2008 global financial crisis and the 2011 European sovereign debt crisis (Elias and Roberts 2018). During the 1997 Asian crisis, for example, economic downturns led to women having to take on a greater share of paid labour, often in the informal sector, and older girls leaving school to take on care work. Households with lower incomes were less able to afford to access healthcare and struggled to secure an adequate food supply, whilst rising unemployment in cities and declining opportunities for employment in neighbouring states placed pressure on the care labour undertaken in rural households as migrant workers returned home (Elson 2014; Lim 2000).

In Europe, the care crisis is widely understood in terms of the gendered fallout of government austerity programmes that sought to address fiscal deficits via aggressive cuts to public spending. Austerity policies across Europe saw a withdrawal of state-subsidized childcare and older care provision, as well as cuts to maternity pay, with obvious consequences for gender inequality (Rubery 2015). In the UK, cuts to social protections fell disproportionately on lone parents who are overwhelmingly female, while entrenched gendered social norms also meant that women were far more likely to face redundancy in the unemployment that accompanied austerity (Perrons 2021). This is either because they are regarded as a 'flexible' and 'disposable' workforce (see Section 2.1 in the chapter on Clothes for how this has applied to female garment workers), or because the work that they do is viewed as less important, less worthy of protection, than careers in which male employment predominates. This was an assumption tackled head on in the 'rubber glove rebellion' in Greece, shown in Photo 5.6. Interestingly, during the Covid-19 pandemic those working as home and

Photo 5.6. The care economy confronts financial crisis. Cleaners employed by the Greek Ministry of Finance staged ongoing protests from 2014 against government austerity measures in what became known as the 'rubber glove rebellion'.
Source: Nikolas Georgiou/Alamy Stock Photo.

healthcare assistants or cleaners often saw their work reclassified as 'essential', but, in an echo of Military Spouse Appreciation Day, recognition of the vital social and economic contribution of this work generally failed to lead to greater financial rewards or improved working conditions for such groups.

The links between financial crisis and care crisis are at the centre of feminist political economist Emma Dowling's (2021) analysis of the UK's crisis in care provision that has taken hold under austerity. Dowling notes the twofold nature of Britain's care crisis: the withdrawal of the state in terms of funding for care services and social protection; and the progressive undermining of individuals' ability to care for themselves and for others due to welfare benefit cuts, under- and unemployment, and a rapidly ageing population. This results in what she terms a 'care fix', whereby the burden of care work is offloaded onto the family—usually female family members. Dowling's analysis echoes work by the feminist economist Diane Elson on the implicitly gendered assumptions at work within state responses to financial and economic crisis. Specifically, Elson notes how women's labour, unlike men's, is assumed to be 'infinitely elastic', meaning that it is 'able to stretch so as to make up for any shortfall in income and resources required for the production and maintenance of human resources' (Elson 1991, 179). Such assumptions serve to intimately link the world of global finance to the everyday 'life making' struggles of social reproduction. Within this context women's labour in the home acts as a shock absorber. The financial system can remain a realm of risky business decision-making because the risk is passed onto others, 'downloaded to the kitchen' in Elson's pithy phrase (Elson 2002, 3).

In this sense global finance needs to be seen as operating within the context of a gendered political economy that enables risk-taking and acts of extreme financial mismanagement to happen in the first place. As Elson suggests, care work plays this role because it cannot *not* be done. Not to care for a child or an older family member is not an option; someone, usually a female household member, simply has to take on this work. Increased burdens of care labour are therefore tied to the affective dimensions of care. As mentioned earlier, we care *for* because we care *about*. And as Dowling (2021, 16) elaborates, this can be used for political purposes: 'the emotions, feelings and relationships involved, play an important role in enabling the restructuring of care, where people's sense of compassion and responsibility are mobilized in attempts to compensate for or cope with the care crisis'.

In this vein, we can observe how the idea of 'the family' as a social safety net is invoked during times of crisis. The former UK Health Secretary Sajid Javid spoke in 2021 of how health and social care 'begins at home'—that people in need of care should rely on their families in the first instance rather than the state (Javid 2021). Statements like this need to be unpacked. They play upon ideals of family loyalty, care, and compassion, but who is doing the unpaid work of care within households? Are all households able to provide for the care needs of their members? What happens when family units are spaces of violence or oppression? And how does care labour within the household serve to reproduce wider structures of gender inequality? It is well documented, for example, that globally women spend considerably more time that men on unpaid household labour (ILO 2018; Charmes 2019). In reality, then, the care fix is no solution. Increased demands on unpaid labour can lead to physical and mental exhaustion in those who are tasked with undertaking this labour.

5.2.2 Is caring harmful?

A useful concept that enables us to explore how the care crisis is manifested in the everyday lives of those who undertake much social reproductive labour is that of **depletion through social reproduction** (DSR). This seeks to identify the costs and harms that occur when the gap between social reproduction 'inflows' and 'outflows' falls below a sustainable threshold (Rai et al. 2014). When societies fail to adequately value and recognize the importance of social reproduction to the functioning of not just the economy but the reproduction of life itself, there are consequences—consequences that can be understood as harms. Such harms might be experienced by individuals in terms of physical decline or mental health struggles. Depletion might also be observed within households in which members are struggling to combine paid work and unpaid care, resulting in impoverishment through declining household income or in violence through forms of intrahousehold conflict. It is also something that is experienced by communities, like when there are insufficient numbers of people available to run essential community resources and networks. These harms are also gendered harms in that, once again, they disproportionately impact women.

The impact of austerity policies such as those discussed in Section 5.2.1 can also be understood through the lens of DSR. Take, for example, Photo 5.7, taken at a 2011

Photo 5.7. Anti-austerity protestors in London in 2011 highlighting how welfare cuts were impacting women's ability to care for their children.
Source: Janine Wiedel Photolibrary/Alamy Stock Photo.

anti-austerity demonstration in London. Here protestors sought to highlight how welfare benefit changes that targeted single mothers adversely impacted their ability to parent their children, leading to both individual and household-level harms. Gendered harms such as these are, invariably, experienced much more acutely by those living in poverty. Wealthier women are far more likely to be able to mitigate DSR via individualized solutions, buying in services like babysitters and domestic workers (see Section 5.2.3) or buying takeaway food via an app (see Share, Section 8.2.1). These are fixes which can in turn create new forms of inequality, or further accentuate existing ones.

The DSR framework can also shed light on the conditions of work experienced by paid care workers. Returning to a point made in Section 5.1.2 about the commodification of care, even when it is waged care work still tends to be relatively low-paid. And yet many people are attracted to employment in the care sector because of the intrinsic, emotional rewards that caring for others brings. Such a dilemma is exposed in Shereen Hussein's research with long-term care workers in the UK. Workers in her study spoke of how they did not become care workers 'for the money' and expressed overall high levels of job satisfaction. But at the same time, work in the sector was characterized by poverty pay and job insecurity, and was shown to negatively impact the physical and mental health of its workforce (Hussein 2017). This has been described as a 'prisoner of love' problem (England 2005). This proposes that employers are able to get away with underpaying and overworking their care staff because the workers themselves are committed to fulfilling socially important work based on building sustained and rewarding human relationships. It appears, then, that the provision of care through the market may well serve to harm those who do the work of care.

Similar themes emerge when we consider the essential labour of community health workers in the Global South. This is another overwhelmingly feminized group of workers: around 70 per cent of community healthcare workers in sub-Saharan Africa are female (UN Women 2020). Community health workers are mobilized by the state to shore up failing healthcare systems while receiving very little compensation for the work that they do and sometimes even using their own income to support their work (Sekalala 2020). Literature on post-conflict societies in the Global South also points out that the expectation that women's unpaid labour can cushion the effects of humanitarian crisis can itself lead to human costs for those doing the work of caring (Johnson and Lingham 2020; Rai et al. 2019; True 2019).

When women take on more and more social reproductive work in order to meet the needs of their households and communities, there is an accompanying 'ripple effect of harms' (Rai et al. 2019, 564). For example, feminist political economist Maria Tanyag's (2018) research in the Philippines demonstrates how DSR occurs when women are displaced due to violent conflict or environmental disasters. Tanyag notes how DSR is particularly acute in contexts where women are unable to access sexual and reproductive health services and are at risk of sexual violence. Her work emphasizes the physical exhaustion and severe health problems faced by internally displaced women, or the 'bodily costs of crisis' which, in turn, have wider consequences for their communities as the care provisioning so vital to supporting everyday life in locations such as internally displaced person camps, as shown in Photo 5.8, is progressively exhausted (Tanyag 2018, 655). Tackling the perpetuation of such gendered harms lies in recognizing and valuing the everyday gendered work of care in conflict-affected societies, and viewing the regeneration of the care economy as vital to building sustainable and lasting peace (Rai et al. 2019).

DSR as a concept reveals the care crisis as something that is ongoing, an aspect of the violent nature of the everyday political economy under capitalism. Likewise, Katherine Brickell's study of women experiencing eviction and domestic violence in Cambodia engages with the notion of 'crisis ordinary' to capture the conditions within which everyday survival takes place (Brickell 2020). Seeing crisis in this manner—as ordinary, an aspect of everyday life that people are forced to cope with—stands at odds with how we generally think about crises as one-off or extraordinary events. Certainly, this is how financial crises tend to be presented—a view challenged by scholars and activists who have emphasized the ongoing and crisis-prone nature of financialized capitalism (Hozić and True 2016). But whereas politicians show a willingness to stave off financial crises via decisive actions such as banking bailouts, a care crisis can be ignored, or at least seen as a less pressing political issue.

Photo 5.8. A woman displaced by armed conflict cooks at an evacuation centre in Marawi City in the Philippines, 2017.

Source: Reuters/Alamy Stock Photo.

5.2.3 How is care work organized in the global economy?

A key theme already explored in this chapter is the issue of how care labour is not necessarily unpaid labour (Section 5.1.2). Households—especially wealthier middle-class households—will often turn to the market to meet their care needs. It may be difficult to combine work and care responsibilities, or to find high-quality state-run childcare, but these issues can be solved by buying in the services of a domestic worker or a nanny. The provision of household and childcare services by poorer women to richer women is not, of course, in any way a recent development. But what *is* a striking development is the **transnationalization** of domestic worker employment, which is revealed in the movement of large numbers of women across international borders to take up employment as domestic workers, usually on a temporary basis. Data from the International Labour Organization (ILO) indicates that, whilst women represent 44 per cent of all international migrant workers, they account for 73 per cent of migrant *domestic* workers—a much higher proportion (ILO 2015, xiii). Importantly, the transnationalization of domestic worker employment is not simply a matter of the movement of workers from the Global South to the Global North. The ever-growing market for migrant domestic labour has been sustained by the emergence of high- to middle-income economies across Asia and, especially, the Middle East. As we see in Figure 5.1, the biggest destination region for migrant domestic workers is the group of states that the ILO classifies as Arab, followed by those in Southeast Asia and the Pacific.

One way of understanding this transnationalization of domestic worker migration is through the concept of the **global care chain**. In contrast to the global value chain as discussed in Sections 2.2.2 and 3.1.2, this concept centres the creation and distribution of care in its analysis, demonstrating how the migration of largely female workers into caring professions—including domestic workers, nannies, nurses, and home care assistants—has knock-on effects for those household members left behind. One impact of the emotional displacement of care from the homes of poor women in the Global South to upper-middle-class homes in wealthier states, or what Arlie Hochschild (2003, 22) describes as a 'global heart transplant', is the need for migrating care workers to fill the gap left when they are no longer available to provide unpaid care labour in their own homes. This might result in a local woman being recruited to help out with care and domestic labour at home, and she in turn may rely on an older child or mother to fill the gap in her unpaid caring labour, and so the chain continues (see also Parreñas 2001).

Global care chain analysis also highlights the political arrangements that make these linkages possible. Take the example of the Philippines, one of the major senders of care workers overseas and highly dependent on the remittance income that

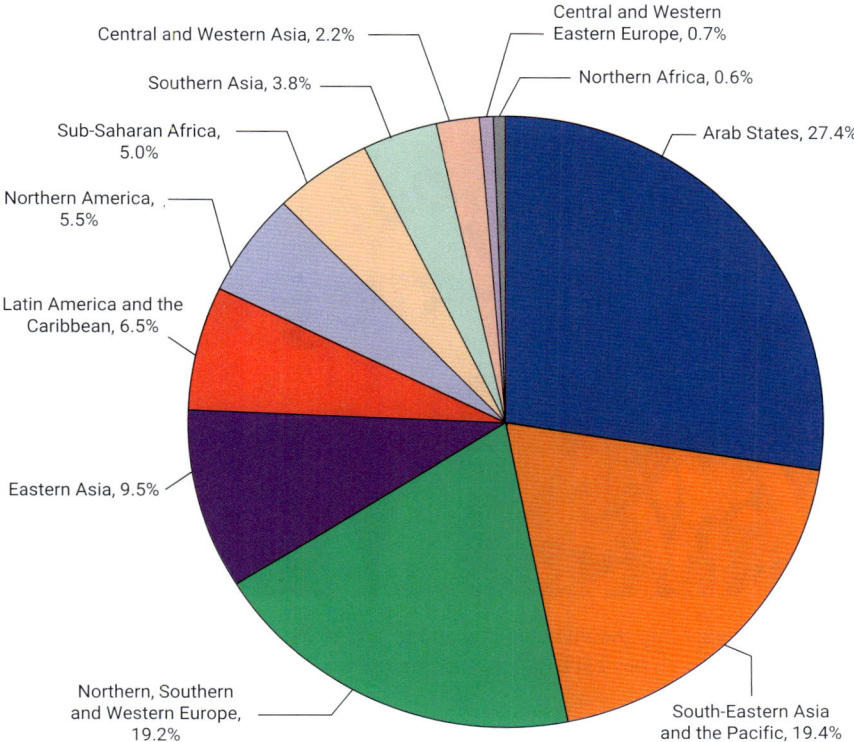

Figure 5.1. How the employment of 11.5 million migrant domestic workers is distributed internationally, based on most recently available data.
Source: International Labour Organization (ILO) 2015.

these and other overseas workers send back home. In 2020 this stood at US$26.3 billion, constituting 9.7 per cent of the country's GDP—and about the same as the entire agriculture, forestry, and fisheries sector (World Bank no date; though see also Section 5.3.1 on how *unpaid* care work is excluded from GDP measurements). Efforts by the Philippine state to encourage its citizens to migrate overseas in order to take up work in the care sector have been highly interventionist. The sociologist Robyn Magalit Rodriguez (2010) thus describes the Philippines as a 'labour brokerage state' in which the state works closely with the private sector on the recruitment, training, and marketing of workers, as well as overseeing bilateral labour agreements with host states to allow domestic workers to enter and work in their countries on a temporary basis. Rodriguez notes that in reality state practices of labour brokerage, ostensibly designed to offer better protection to Philippine migrant workers overseas, are more about protecting remittance flows then substantive commitments to labour and human rights. Domestic work is low-paid labour in which workers have few to no labour protections, with many countries around the world not recognizing domestic

Photo 5.9. Underscoring the vulnerability, abuse, and exploitation of migrant domestic workers, an image from a protest by migrant domestic workers in Beirut, Lebanon.
Source: Reuters/Alamy Stock Photo.

workers in law as 'workers'. As shown in Photo 5.9, this is something that domestic workers themselves have mobilized against.

Other states that dominate the market for migrant domestic workers, such as Indonesia, where personal remittances make up just 0.9 per cent of the country's GDP, are less obviously dependent on this type of income. However, women migrate from Indonesia every year in large numbers to take up employment overseas as domestic workers across Asia and the Middle East. The Indonesian government has implemented very similar labour brokerage practices to the Philippines, which can be taken as a recognition of the significant role that remittance income plays in supporting the livelihoods of poorer households (Elias 2018). Global care chains also have political economic effects on states that are major recipients of migrant care labour. For example, the ability of individual households in richer or middle-income states to access global care chains may play into state decisions not to invest in areas such as childcare provision—a trend noted in some Asian states such as Singapore and Taiwan (Peng 2018).

The global care chain thus presents female care migration as a major political economic flow, of both people and money, and as having significant consequences in terms of the economic development strategies of states. In this sense, the global care chain is just as significant to studies of IPE as the global value chains considered in the chapters of this book on Food (Chapter 3) and Clothes (Chapter 2). In the chapter on Clothes we discussed what it means to take a 'follow the thing' methodology in order to develop a more socially embedded understanding of global value chains, enabling us to trace the complex sets of social relations and hierarchies involved in the production of a particular commodity (Section 2.1.1). But what happens when the commodity that is being produced is a human being?

Olivia Killias attempts this in her 2018 book *Follow the Maid*, which does exactly that: it studies women as they move from the rural villages in Java, Indonesia, to become maids in the wealthy middle-class suburbs of Kuala Lumpur in Malaysia. On this journey, workers experience new sites of exploitation like the recruitment training centre shown in Photo 5.10, where workers are 'housed' ahead of being placed with an overseas household. Once in Malaysia, many face gendered and racialized discrimination within the households that they work in, and often lack the means, legally or financially, to seek redress for employment abuses. Killias also examines how the transnational care chain operates through various intermediary actors such as family members, village heads, state officials, recruitment agencies, employers, and state actors such as Ministries of Labour. These actors do not just enable the movement of workers overseas, but produce the subjectivity of the 'maid' herself. A focus

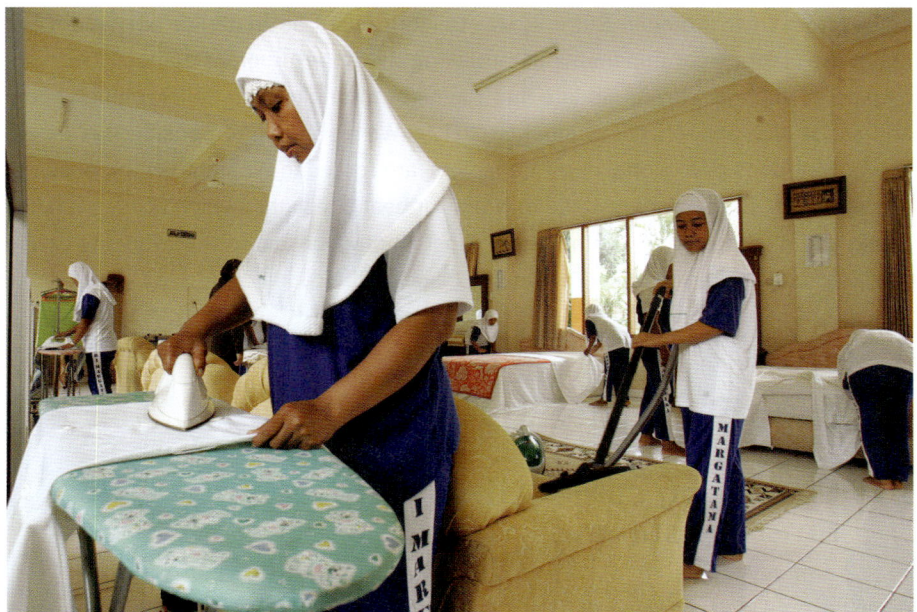

Photo 5.10. Indonesian domestic workers at a training centre in Jakarta ahead of being sent overseas for work.
Source: Reuters/Alamy Stock Photo.

on migrant domestic work thus also reveals how a significant global economic flow rests, fundamentally, on the construction of a precarious and highly feminized workforce (see Section 2.2.1 on how this also underpins the international trade in clothes).

Critics of the care chain approach have raised the concern that it is too neat in how it describes a changing division of domestic labour, whereby the unpaid domestic labour of middle-class women in richer states is substituted by paid domestic labour from poorer countries. Empirically only a relatively small number of households worldwide rely on migrant domestic workers, instead employing local workers often for just a few hours a week. We also need to consider how the global care chain perspective reinforces the idea that care work is something that is only ever performed by women. Certain forms of male-dominated work involve many of the same skills found in domestic and caring professions. For example, drivers or personal-protection security guards need to manage close relationships and social interactions with an employer, often in a domestic setting, and many aspects of their work might be understood as involving caring labour (Chisholm 2017). Moreover, masculinized jobs such as those of handymen or gardeners are frequently overlooked in studies of domestic labour (Kilkey et al. 2013), as are men or those with trans and non-binary gender identities who migrate to take up domestic labour (Brown 2016).

Finally, the global care chain approach often suggests that the transfer of care labour from poorer to richer states results in a care deficit because children are separated from their mothers. But is it as straightforward as that? For example, what about the practices of transnational mothering that many migrant domestic workers engage in, such as staying up late into the night to talk to their children back home and assist with schoolwork (Tungohan 2012)? We also need to consider the extent to which notions of a 'global heart transplant' are rooted in Western-centric assumptions that the nuclear family is the only and/or best site within which childcare takes place, and also consider whether such a perspective obscures the everyday caring practices undertaken by men (Yeates 2012; Locke 2017).

5.3 Engaging Care

5.3.1 Measuring caring labour through time use surveys

Given the growing awareness of the value of unpaid care labour, and the consequences of taking this for granted in terms of gender inequality, it has been argued that unpaid labour needs to be accounted for within official statistical measures such as GDP (Waring 1990). As shown in Photo 5.11, it has long been the case that these have

Photo 5.11. A US satirical cartoon of the 1930 population census highlighting the invisibility of household labour.
Source: Granger Historical Picture Archive/Alamy Stock Photo.

effectively been ignored. Measuring unpaid care might seem to be a tricky thing to do, but advocates of this approach suggest that it has important political advantages. In their view, putting an economic value on care helps to make the case that social policies to support unpaid care work are not simply a matter of addressing gender injustice (which they certainly are) but will also have wider benefits for economic growth, labour productivity, and poverty reduction.

Measuring unpaid care work involves accounting for the *time* spent on particular tasks. A key method for doing this is the time use survey, which asks respondents to report on all activities carried out in a specific time period. In order to engage the theme of care, an exercise that we would like you to undertake is to develop your own time use survey that measures the amount of unpaid labour undertaken in your household (your household being where you currently reside). Time use surveys usually involve asking household members to keep a diary of how they spend their time. Plan how you might design such a diary and think about some of the challenges in gathering this data, such as:

- How to divide the day up into suitable time periods—and, importantly, don't forget to keep in mind the amount of time that it takes to actually complete the survey; participants may not be willing to record how they have spent every minute of the day in great detail.
- How best to capture overlapping activities ('multitasking') and how you might differentiate between various types of daily activities, for example, those that are more active or passive.
- Make sure that you complete the survey yourself so that you too get a sense of how tricky it can be to record your daily activities accurately.

Table 5.1 provides a sample time use diary, in which an attempt is made to capture multitasking by allocating activities as either primary or secondary. Activities that might be understood as forms of social reproduction are italicized. However, you may want to differentiate this category further: for example, tasks that involve caring for others and tasks that are more a form of self-care.

If you are doing this as a class activity, there may be scope to discuss ideas ahead of the task or to reflect on what did and did not work. It may well be the case that the diaries you get back are incomplete, or that certain household members did not wish to take part. This is a normal aspect of survey research. One thing that you could include in your diary is some way of recording how certain tasks make survey respondents feel: did the respondent derive pleasure from helping their younger sibling get ready for school, or was is a stressful experience? Paying attention to our emotional responses to care labour also matters. Taking an elderly parent or grandparent out for

Table 5.1 A sample time use diary

Time	Primary activities	Secondary activities
8 a.m. to 9 a.m.	Get up, *get showered and dressed* (15 mins), *prepare and eat breakfast* (15 mins), *wash dishes* (5 mins), *make lunch for myself and younger sibling* (10 mins), *walk to bus stop* (15 mins).	Listening to the radio, *helping younger sibling get ready for school*, browsing social media.
9 a.m. to 10 a.m.	Take bus and walk the rest of the way to work (15 mins). At work (45 mins).	Chatting to work colleagues, *making tea for myself and work colleague, texting parent to remind them to pick up my prescription from the pharmacy.*

a trip to the park can be a very enjoyable experience, whereas accompanying someone undergoing a medical procedure might be highly stressful. Both tasks may take the same amount of time, but only one is emotionally depleting. Also think about activities that are difficult to classify. An example is that of travelling to and from work: how might we classify an activity such as this? For example, Shirin Rai (n.d.) has suggested that commuting is an activity that connects production to social reproduction, and yet cannot be classified as either. Do you agree?

Once you have your data, what might you do with it? One thing would be to look at the division of time spent on household tasks: who is doing more; why do you think that is? You might look at measuring the value of this labour. One way of doing this is through replacement costs: what would it cost to buy in these services in the private sector? Can you estimate the value of your unpaid labour, or that of other household members? Are there certain things that are impossible to put a price on, and what does that tell us about the intangible nature of care labour, or how care labour is often impossible to commodify? Thinking beyond your immediate household, what do you think the value of this kind of data is, and how do you think having data on time use can inform policy decisions?

5.3.2 Uncovering hidden assumptions through social annotation

A lot of what we have tried to do in this chapter involves unpacking the implicit assumptions about care-related activities that pervade our everyday lives. Care labour has an 'invisible' quality; it is not fully recognized and is not adequately valued. When we reflect upon how care labour has been understood in conventional accounts of the economy, we are often looking to identify the silences on care or the particular, and limited, ways in which care is understood. In this task we will explore how care is and is not discussed in policy settings. For example, economic plans designed to address the fallout of the Covid-19 pandemic frequently failed to address the specific needs and issues faced by women with caring responsibilities. Thus, the impact of many policy responses to the pandemic such as household lockdowns and school closures fell disproportionately on women—because there was an implicit assumption that women had the capacity to take on this extra caring labour (Smith et al. 2021).

This task is a social annotation exercise that asks you to work as a group in order to critically interact with a policy document and to reveal gendered biases and assumptions concerning care labour. Social annotation takes the standard practice of annotating a text (highlighting important passages, commenting on these in the margins, etc.) and turns it into a collaborative endeavour, allowing multiple people to contribute and different readings of the same text to enter into dialogue. Some widely available specialist software makes social annotation very easy to do. The webtool Hypothesis (available at http://web.hypothes.is) often comes highly recommended for this type of exercise, because it allows comments on the text and you can use tags to categorize those comments. But it is just as easy to import a PDF document into a shared space such as Google Drive and add comments on the text. As this is an online activity, you do not need to be physically in the same room but can work together remotely.

One document that might work well for this exercise is the 2020 policy brief produced by UN Women called 'Covid-19 and the Care Economy: Immediate Action and Structural Transformation for a Gender-Responsive Recovery' (Diallo et al. 2020). The brief assesses the impact of Covid-19 on the care economy. When working together to comment on the document, there are a number of questions that you might like to consider (and you could categorize your comments accordingly):

- How do the authors of the policy brief seek to disrupt and challenge dominant framings of how the economic fallout of the Covid-19 pandemic has been understood?
- What are the key pieces of data that underpin the arguments made by the authors, and why might this data have been overlooked by policymakers?
- Who do you think is the intended audience for this policy brief and how have the writers of the brief sought to frame their arguments to speak to this audience (including how the brief has been written to convey the urgency and importance of the issue)?
- How are visual images used in the text and how effective are they in supporting the overarching claims made by the authors?
- How viable do you think the proposals on how to transform care systems are, and what obstacles to implementation might they face?
- What are some of the key themes and concepts from this chapter that come through in this policy brief?

As well as providing you with an opportunity to engage with how care policies are being developed within the context of an international organization, this exercise also encourages you to consider the very notion of policy frames and to consider why it is that UN Women might present the issue of unpaid caring labour in a particular way. We want to encourage you to think about not only how the text itself reveals particular ways of **framing** an issue but also how it is represented visually and how these visual representations of caring labour are intended to impact on particular audiences.

5.4 Conclusion

This chapter began with a discussion of symbolic efforts to better recognize the work of military spouses in the US through Military Spouse Appreciation Day. It was argued that this symbolic gesture serves to normalize a starkly gendered division of labour in which women are expected to perform care labour and are viewed as those best able to do so. The chapter sought to centre its discussion on how care labour is and is not valued, and how this relates to wider gendered, heteronormative, and racialized social relations. In addition, we drew attention to what might be viewed as the 'banal' activities of everyday life (making a sandwich, picking up dirty socks, giving a flatmate a lift to work). These are activities in which we spend a lot of our time, and it is important to consider these activities as work, because doing so pushes us to rethink the boundaries between what we understand as economic and non-economic activities—boundaries which in turn shape valuation processes of recognition and reward. Finally, via a discussion of financial crises and international labour migration, the chapter pushed you to consider how even the most intimate relationships and activities can be tied into global flows and market dynamics. In these ways, then, the discussion of care presented in this chapter sought to press home the radical political potential and analytical perspectives of taking an everyday IPE approach.

Access the online resources for quizzes, student reflection podcasts, and support for tackling the chapter's learning activities: http://www.oup.com/he/i-peel1e.

RESOURCES

Tile recommendations from the I-PEEL website: 'care' (Juanita Elias) http://i-peel.org/homepage/care/; 'housework' (Sedef Arat-Koç) http://i-peel.org/homepage/housework/.

It's a Sin. 2021. Five-part TV series. Directed by Russell T. Davies and discussed in Section 5.1.3, this is a good starting point for thinking about a queer political economy of care.

Nana: The Lives of Live-In Nannies. 2015. 71 minutes. A documentary film directed by Tatiana Fernandes Geara that depicts Dominican nannies working in the US. A powerful illustration of the emotional labour at work within global care chains.

Yaya. 2018. 31 minutes. A short documentary film directed by Hong Kong-based film maker Justin Cheung that explores his relationship with the live-in caregiver from the Philippines who helped to raise him. Available to watch on YouTube at: https://www.youtube.com/watch?v=R8E2fPPs-No.

Dowling, Emma. 2021. *The Care Crisis: What Caused It and How Can We End It?* London: Verso. Using examples from the UK, Dowling looks at the multifaceted nature of the care crisis. The book significantly expands on many of the issues covered in this chapter's discussion of care crisis, including some issues not touched upon in this chapter such as the financialization of care provisioning and the growth of the self-care industry.

Gammage, Sarah. 2021. 'Global Migration and Care Chains'. In *The Routledge Handbook of Feminist Economics*, ed. Günseli Berik and Ebru Kongar, 225–33. Abingdon: Routledge. A short recent overview of the global care chains concept and associated research.

Killias, Olivia. 2018. *Follow the Maid: Domestic Worker Migration In and From Indonesia*. Copenhagen: NIAS Press. An ethnographic study of how migrant domestic workers experience global care chains.

Rai, Shirin M., Catherine Hoskyns, and Dania Thomas. 2014. 'Depletion: The Cost of Social Reproduction'. *International Feminist Journal of Politics* 16(1): 86–105. A useful overview of a key theoretical concept engaged with in our discussion of the care crisis.

REFERENCES

Arani, Alexia. 2020. 'Mutual Aid and Its Ambivalences: Lessons from Sick and Disabled Trans and Queer People of Colour'. *Feminist Studies* 46(3): 653–62.

Bakker, Isabella. 2007. 'Social Reproduction and the Constitution of a Gendered Political Economy'. *New Political Economy* 12(4): 541–56.

Bhattacharyya, Gargi. 2018. *Rethinking Racial Capitalism: Questions of Reproduction and Survival*. London: Rowman & Littlefield International.

Biden, Joseph R. Jr. 2021. 'A Proclamation on Military Spouse Appreciation Day'. Washington DC: The White House, https://www.whitehouse.gov/briefing-room/presidential-actions/2021/05/06/a-proclamation-on-military-spouse-appreciation-day-2021/.

Brickell, Katherine. 2020. *Home SOS: Gender, Violence and Survival in Crisis Ordinary Cambodia*. Oxford: Wiley.

Brown, Rachel H. 2016. 'Re-Examining the Transnational Nanny: Migrant Carework Beyond the Chain'. *International Feminist Journal of Politics* 18(2): 210–29.

Castrejon, Aleah M. 2021. 'Military Spouse Appreciation Day: Dr Jill Biden thanks families for service', https://www.army.mil/article/246452/military_spouse_appreciation_day_dr_jill_biden_thanks_carson_families_for_service.

Charmes, Jacques. 2019. *The Unpaid Care Work and the Labour Market: An Analysis of Time Use Data Based on the Latest World Compilation of Time-Use Surveys*. Geneva: International Labour Organization.

Chisholm, Amanda. 2017. 'Clients, Contractors, and the Everyday Masculinities in Global Private Security'. *Critical Military Studies* 3(2): 120–41.

Cree, Alice. 2020. '"People Want to See Tears": Military Heroes and the "Constant Penelope" of the UK's Military Wives Choir'. *Gender, Place and Culture* 27(2): 218–38.

Davies, Angela. 2019 [1981]. *Women, Race and Class*. London: Penguin Classics.

De Henau, Jerome, and Susan Himmelweit. 2021. 'A Care-Led Recovery from Covid-19: Investing in High-Quality Care to Stimulate and Rebalance the Economy'. *Feminist Economics* 27(1–2): 553–69.

Department of Defense. 2019. *Demographics: Profile of the Military Community*. Washington DC: Department of Defense.

Diallo, Bobo, Seemin Qayum, and Silke Staab. 2020. 'COVID-19 and the Care Economy: Immediate Action and Structural Transformation for a Gender-Responsive Recovery'. *UN Women policy brief series*, https://eca.unwomen.org/en/digital-library/publications/2020/06/policy-brief-covid-19-and-the-care-economy#view.

Dowling, Emma. 2021. *The Care Crisis: What Caused It and How Can We End It?* London: Verso.

Duggan, Lisa. 2002. 'The New Homonormativity: The Sexual Politics of Neoliberalism'. In *Materializing Democracy: Toward a Revitalized Cultural Politics*, ed. Russ Castronovo and Dana D. Nelson, 176–94. Durham: Duke University Press.

Elias, Juanita. 2018. 'Governing Domestic Worker Migration in Southeast Asia: Public–Private Partnerships, Regulatory Grey Zones and the Household'. *Journal of Contemporary Asia* 48(2): 278–300.

Elias, Juanita, and Adrienne Roberts. 2018. 'Financial Crisis in Historical Perspective'. In *Handbook on the International Political Economy of Gender*, ed. Juanita Elias and Adrienne Roberts, 281–97. Cheltenham: Edward Elgar.

Elson, Diane. 1991. 'Male Bias in Macro-Economics: The Case of Structural Adjustment'. In *Male Bias in the Development Process*, ed. Diane Elson, 46–68. Manchester: Manchester University Press.

Elson, Diane. 2002. 'The International Financial Architecture: A View from the Kitchen'. *Femina Politica: Zeitschrift für Feministische Politikwissenschaft* 11: 26–37.

Elson, Diane. 2014. 'Economic Crises from the 1980s to the 2010s: A Gender Analysis'. In *New Frontiers in Feminist Political Economy*, ed. Shirin M. Rai and Georgina Waylen, 189–212. Abingdon: Routledge.

England, Paula. 2005. 'Emerging Theories of Care Work'. *Annual Review of Sociology* 31, 381–99.

Enloe, Cynthia. 2010. *Nimo's War, Emma's War: Making Feminist Sense of the Iraq War*. Berkeley: University of California Press.

Federici, Silvia. 1975. *Wages Against Housework*. Bristol: Power of Women Collective and Falling Wall Press.

Fraser, Nancy. 2017. 'Crisis of Care? On the Social-Reproductive Contradictions of Contemporary Capitalism.' In *Social Reproduction Theory: Remapping Class, Recentering Oppression*, ed. Tithi Bhattacharya, 23–6. London: Pluto Press.

Gray, Hannah. 2022. 'The Power of Love: How Love Obscures Domestic Labour and Shuts Down Space for Critique of Militarism in the Autobiographical Accounts of British Military Wives'. *Critical Military Studies*, doi.org/10.1080/23337486.2022.2033915.

Himmelweit, Susan. 1999. 'Caring Labor'. *The ANNALS of the American Academy of Political and Social Science* 561(1): 27–38.

Hochschild, Arlie. 2003. 'Love and Gold'. In *Global Woman: Nannies, Maids and Sex Workers in the New Economy*, ed. Barbara Ehrenreich and Arlie Hochschild, 15–30. New York: Henry Holt.

Horn, Denise. 2010. 'Boots and Bedsheets: Constructing the Military Support System in a Time of War'. In *Gender, War and Militarism: Feminist Perspectives*, ed. Laura Sjoberg, 57–68. Oxford: Praeger.

Hoskyns, Catherine, and Shirin Rai. 2007. 'Recasting the Global Political Economy: Counting Women's Unpaid Work'. *New Political Economy* 12(3): 297–317.

Hozić, Aida A., and Jacqui True. 2016. 'Making Feminist Sense of the Global Financial Crisis'. In *Scandalous Economics: Gender and the Politics of Financial Crises*, ed. Aida A. Hozić and Jacqui True, 3–20. Oxford: Oxford University Press.

Hussein, Shereen. 2017. '"We Don't Do It For the Money": The Scale and Reasons of Poverty-Pay Among Frontline Long-term Care Workers in England'. *Health and Social Care in the Community* 25(6): 1817–26.

International Labour Organization (ILO). 2015. *ILO Global Estimates on Migrant Workers: Results and Methodology*. Geneva: International Labour Office; https://www.ilo.org/wcmsp5/groups/public/@dgreports/@dcomm/@publ/documents/publication/wcms_808935.pdf.

International Labour Organization (ILO). 2018. *Care Work and Care Jobs for the Future of Decent Work*. Geneva: International Labour Office.

Javid, Sajid. 2021. '2021 Speech to Conservative Party Conference'. 6 October. https://www.ukpol.co.uk/sajid-javid-2021-speech-to-conservative-party-conference/.

Johnson, Melissa, and Jayanthi Lingham. 2020. *Inclusive Economies, Enduring Peace in Myanmar and Sri Lanka: Field Report*. Monash University, https://bridges.monash.edu/articles/report/Inclusive_Economies_Enduring_Peace_in_Myanmar_and_Sri_Lanka_Field_Report/12826130.

Kilkey, Majella, Diane Perrons, Ania Plomien, Pierrette Hondagneu-Sotelo, and Hernan Ramirez. 2013. 'Gender Migration and Domestic Work: An Introduction'. In *Gender, Migration and Domestic Work: Masculinities, Male Labour and Fathering in the UK and USA*, ed. Kilkey Perrons, Plomien, Hondagneu-Sotelo, and Ramirez, 1–19. Basingstoke: Palgrave MacMillan.

Killias, Olivia. 2018. *Follow the Maid: Domestic Worker Migration in and from Indonesia*. Copenhagen: NIAS Press.

Lim, Joseph Y. 2000. 'The Effects of the East Asian Crisis on the Employment of Women and Men: The Philippine Case.' *World Development* 28(7): 1285–306.

Locke, Catherine. 2017. 'Do male migrants care? How migration is reshaping the gender ethics of care'. *Ethics and Social Welfare* 11(3): 277–95.

Luxton, Meg. 2018. 'The Production of Life Itself: Gender, Social Reproduction and IPE'. In *Handbook of the International Political Economy of Gender*, ed. Juanita Elias and Adrienne Roberts, 37–49. Cheltenham: Edward Elgar.

Nguyen, Duc Hien. 2021. 'The Political Economy of Heteronormativity'. *Review of Radical Political Economics*. doi:10.1177/04866134211011269.

Oksala, Johanna. 2016. 'Affective Labour and Feminist Politics'. *Signs* 41(2): 281–303.

Parreñas, Rachel. 2001. *Servants of Globalization: Women, Migration, and Domestic Work*. Stanford, CA: Stanford University Press.

Peng, Ito. 2018. 'Culture, Institution and Diverse Approaches to Care and Care Work in East Asia'. *Current Sociology* 66(4): 643–59.

Perrons, Diane. 2021. *Is Austerity Gendered?* Cambridge: Polity Press.

Peterson, V. Spike. 2018. 'Intimacy, Informalization and Intersecting Inequalities: Tracing the Linkages'. *Labour & Industry* 28(2): 130–45.

Raha, Nat (2021) 'A Queer Marxist Transfeminism: Queer and Trans Social Reproduction'. In *Transgender Marxism*, ed. Jules Joanne Gleeson and Elle O'Rourke, 85–115. London: Pluto Press.

Rai, Shirin M. n.d. 'Commuting'. http://i-peel.org/homepage/commuting/.

Rai, Shirin M., Catherine Hoskyns, and Dania Thomas. 2014. 'Depletion: The Cost of Social Reproduction' *International Feminist Journal of Politics* 16(1): 86–105.

Rai, Shirin M., Jacqui True, and Maria Tanyag. 2019. 'From Depletion to Regeneration: Addressing Structural and Physical Violence in Post-Conflict Contexts'. *Social Politics* 26(4): 561–85.

Roberts, Adrienne. 2016. 'Household Debt and the Financialization of Social Reproduction: Theorizing the UK Housing and Hunger Crises'. *Research in Political Economy* 31: 135–64.

Rodriguez, Robyn M. 2010. *Migrants for Export: How the Philippine State Brokers Labour to the World*. Minneapolis: University of Minnesota Press.

Rubery, Jill. 2015. 'Austerity and the Future for Gender Equality in Europe'. *ILR Review* 68(4): 715–41.

Samtleben, Claire, and Kai-Uwe Müller. 2021. 'Care and Careers: Gender (In)Equality in Unpaid Care, Housework and Employment'. *Research in Social Stratification and Mobility* 77, doi.org/10.1016/j.rssm.2021.100659.

Segal, Mady W. 1986. 'The Military and the Family as Greedy Institutions'. *Armed Forces & Society* 13(1): 9–38.

Sekalala, Sharifah. 2020. 'Categorizing the Gendered Harms to Caregivers During Humanitarian Emergencies: An Analysis of Law and Practice During Ebola Crises'. *Social and Legal Studies* 30(6): 825–47.

Smith, Julia, Sara E. Davies, Huiyun Feng, Connie C.R. Gan, Karen A Grépin, Sophia Harman, Asha Herten-Crabb, Rosemary Morgan, Nimisha Vandan, and Clare Wenham. 2021. 'More than a Public Health Crisis: A Feminist Political Economic Analysis of COVID-19'. *Global Public Health* 16(8–9): 1364–80.

Smith, Nicola J. 2016. Towards a Queer Political Economy of Crisis'. In *Scandalous Economics: Gender and the Politics of Financial Crisis*, ed. Aida A. Hozić and Jacqui True, 231–47. Oxford: Oxford University Press.

Smith, Nicola J. 2020. *Capitalism's Sexual History*. Oxford: Oxford University Press.

Tanyag, Maria. 2018. 'Depleting Fragile Bodies: The Political Economy of Sexual and Reproductive Health in Crisis Situations'. *Review of International Studies* 44(4): 654–71.

True, Jacqui. 2019. 'Introduction: Post Conflict Care Economies'. *Social Politics* 26(4): 535–7.

Tungohan, Ethel. 2012. 'Reconceptualizing Resistance: Migrant Domestic Workers, Transnational Hyper-Maternalism and Activism'. *International Feminist Journal of Politics* 15(1): 39–57.

UN Women. 2020. 'COVID-19 Sends the Care Economy into Deeper Crisis Mode'. 22 April, https://data.unwomen.org/features/covid-19-sends-care-economy-deeper-crisis-mode.

Van der Vleuten, Maaike, Eva Jaspers, and Tanja van der Lippe. 2021. 'Same-Sex Couples: Division of Labor from a Cross-National Perspective'. *Journal of GLBT Family Studies* 17(2): 150–67.

Waring, Marilyn. 1990. *If Women Counted: A New Feminist Economics*. London: HarperCollins.

World Bank. n.d. World Bank Open Data, https://data.worldbank.org/country/philippines (last accessed 1 April 2022).

Yeates, Nicola. 2012. 'Global Care Chains: A State-of-the-Art Review and Future Directions in Care Transnationalization Research'. *Global Networks* 12(2): 135–54.

6
CITY

6.1	Mega-Event	154
6.2	Exploring the City	161
6.3	Engaging the City	176
6.4	Conclusion	180

LEARNING OBJECTIVES

- Relate the concept of the global city to changes in the international financial system
- Explain how state rescaling has enabled urbanization and shaped capital accumulation
- Investigate the role of investors and the state with an urban development case study, and the right to the city by producing a privilege trail of urban space

READER'S GUIDE

City is not a prominent keyword in IPE scholarship. This is because IPE has tended to take the nation state and the global market as its spatial units of analysis. So, whilst lots of IPE research is conducted in cities, looking at the governance of financial institutions in London or the policymaking process in Brussels, for example, there is less about 'the city' itself as a political actor or economic centre. However, as this chapter demonstrates, there are lots of connections to make between IPE and scholarship which has focused on the city, particularly Urban Studies. It begins by looking at mega-events like the Olympic Games (Section 6.1). It shows how these are used in place branding strategies adopted by host cities, how they drive urban transformation through infrastructural investment, and how they have been politicized to challenge social injustice. The next section, 'Exploring the City', zooms out to consider some broader questions raised by our discussion of the mega-event. It looks at the concept of the global city and what that can tell us about the process of globalization; at how urban development takes place, and the role of the state in managing this; and at how the right to the city is being used to articulate and link up struggles against urbanized inequality (Section 6.2). The final section, 'Engaging the City', shows how to put these ideas into practice through a case study of an urban development and a privilege trail highlighting the different exclusions of urban space (Section 6.3).

KEY CONCEPTS

Global city; state rescaling; right to the city

Access the online resources to listen to a podcast in which Ben introduces and explores the key themes of this chapter: http://www.oup.com/he/i-peel1e.

6.1 Mega-Event

Residents of Rio de Janeiro gathered in their thousands to see the result come in. They stood watching a big screen on Copacabana beach, rapt not by a football match or a national election, but a meeting of the International Olympic Committee (IOC). The IOC was deciding which city would host the 2016 Summer Games and, when Rio was declared the winner, the celebrations erupted. The day had already been declared a public holiday, and the party continued long into the night. For the country's President, Luiz Inácio Lula da Silva, the decision affirmed Brazil's new international standing. Amidst tears of joy on hearing the result, he told the assembled journalists: 'We are not a second-rate country anymore, we are a first-rate country, and that is what this victory means' (cited in Gibson 2009).

As well as shifting perceptions of national self-identity, the imminent arrival of the Olympic Games to Rio also initiated a phase of mass urban investment. Not only would sporting venues have to be built, but accommodation and transport links too, all of which would supposedly entail a lasting legacy for the city's residents. As the IOC later recalled, 'foremost in the minds of the candidature team was consideration both of what Rio could bring to the Games, but crucially also, what the Olympic Games could do for the city' (IOC 2017). To this end, alongside the £1.9 billion budget required to run the Games, another £9.9 billion was earmarked for construction and security costs, to be financed from a mix of public sector and private sector sources (BBC 2009).

Yet, even before the Games had begun, questions were being asked about whom this spending was really benefitting. The plan to bring vital infrastructure and public services to the city's informal settlements, known as *favelas*, was soon scaled back, and more money invested in the wealthy suburb of Barra da Tijuca. This was the chosen site for the Athletes' Village, a residential complex that had been earmarked for sale as luxury condominiums after the Games had finished. It also happened to be built on land owned by a billionaire property developer and major campaign donor to Rio's Mayor. By contrast, many *favelas* were slated for demolition, and in cases where residents were reluctant to leave, often because they were offered little in the way of compensation or alternative accommodation, the eviction process hardened. This included the deployment of tear gas and rubber bullets by the police to remove people forcibly from their homes (Caudros 2016).

Doubts over the legacy of the Olympics have only deepened since the Games concluded. The revenue from TV rights and tourism fell short of covering the costs of hosting the event, corruption probes uncovered widespread bribery in building contracts, facilities fell into disrepair as few organizations could afford to take them on, and the fabled new metro and bus lines shown in Photo 6.1 ended up segregating the places they were built through (Yamawaki et al. 2020). Three years after the Olympic

Photo 6.1. Everyday life meets global politics. Residents sit next to a building site of the TransOlímpica, a rapid-transit bus route and toll road connecting the Olympic venues of Deodoro and Barra da Tijuca.
Source: Reuters/Alamy Stock Photo.

flame was extinguished, the city's Organizing Committee still faced hundreds of lawsuits over improper construction and unpaid debts (Morgan 2019).

6.1.1 Place branding

Like World Cup tournaments and World Expo fairs, the Olympic Games can be thought of as a **mega-event**: an organized global spectacle that purposefully transforms the built environment (Müller 2015). As a global spectacle, mega-events seek an international audience and, thanks to the effects of mass media, the size of this can be huge. In the case of the Rio Olympics, it was estimated that coverage of the Games was seen by half the world's population (IOC, n.d.). Such viewing figures are an important part of why mega-events are so commercially lucrative, since they enable brands to reach billions of people through advertisements and sponsorships. And it is not just corporate brands being promoted here, but that of *the city itself*.

A useful concept to unpack this process is **place branding**. This is defined as a set of claims and practices intended to boost the international competitiveness of a certain territory by narrating it as a desirable location for foreign investors, tourists, and other bearers of spending power (Schwak 2018). Place branding has become part and parcel of the organization of the Olympics, communicated in everything from the Games' logo to the public relations messaging. During the Rio Olympics, for instance, the brand was designed to emphasize the city's natural beauty, diverse 'melting pot' culture, and growing safety for international visitors, as against the perceived danger of the *favelas* (Van den Broucke and Gato 2018). As we shall see later in Section 6.2.2, the involvement of state actors in branding campaigns and their depiction of cities through the eyes of the global elite give this process a profoundly political dimension.

The beginning of the mega-event phenomenon can be traced to the International Expositions of the nineteenth century, in which cities including London and Paris showcased in visually striking ways the technologies and triumphs of their respective empires. What is notable about the mega-event nowadays is how many are based outside Western Europe and the US. In 2010, for instance, there was the Shanghai Expo in China, the New Delhi Commonwealth Games in India, and the football World Cup in South Africa. Hosting these events is expensive, and their geographical spread in part reflects the emergence of new poles of capitalist growth outside the West. But as we saw in the quote from President Lula after Rio was awarded the Olympic Games in Section 6.1, it also reflects a desire to communicate this growth to others. Another significant example is the 2008 Beijing Olympics in China. Estimated to cost a staggering $42 billion, its spectacular opening ceremony (shown in Photo 6.2) was

Photo 6.2. Some of the 10,000 performers involved in the 2008 Beijing Olympics opening ceremony—a four-hour show designed to tell a certain story about modern China to the 1 billion people who watched it worldwide.
Source: Science History Images/Alamy Stock Photo.

interpreted as marking China's arrival as a global power: a display of cultural self-confidence and economic strength to the outside world, as well as a reminder to its own citizens of what bound them together as a nation (see Grix and Lee 2013).

At the same time as mega-events are used to brand the host city and its respective country, conflating the two in the minds of the audience, they also work to differentiate them. This paradox occurs because of the additional resources that mega-events confer upon the host city, accentuating its status as a metropole in which wealth and power are concentrated, whilst peripheralizing provincial towns and rural villages, such that their economic fate revolves around the central hub of the city like bicycle spokes in a wheel. This uneven economic growth certainly characterizes the recent history of China. More than 200 million people migrated from rural to urban areas between 1982 and 2010 in search of economic opportunity, with Beijing one of the top destinations—a movement undoubtedly accelerated by the Beijing Olympics (see Garriga et al. 2020). In this sense, the geographical location of mega-events not only helps track *international* economic shifts, such as the growing share of world GDP accounted for by the BRICS (Brazil, Russia, India, China, South Africa) from the late twentieth century, but also identifies some of the major urban hubs through which global economic flows have been channelled and the *intranational* transformations that have resulted. We explore this further in Section 6.2.1 through the literature on the **global city**.

6.1.2 Urban transformation

So large are the costs of hosting a mega-event that the so-called 'legacy effects' have become an increasingly important means by which bids are justified to city residents and state taxpayers alike. Alongside the purported increases in tourism and investment brought by place branding, long-lasting benefits are also sought through transformation of the built environment. An important precedent was the revitalization of Barcelona through the 1992 Olympics. The creation of a sports precinct on Montjuïc Mountain, the restoration of historic buildings in the Gothic Quarter, and the reconnection of the city with its seafront through the Athletes' Village provided an apparent success story that many cities have since tried to emulate (Wood 2019). One aspect of this large-scale urban planning relevant to IPE is its reliance on multilevel political coalitions. Working alongside national governments and state agencies in the planning process are international non-governmental organizations (INGOs) like the IOC or the international football federation FIFA, transnational firms such as consultancy services and investment funds, and subnational actors like city mayors and councils.

The democratic credentials of such coalitions are frequently questioned, not least when they result in harmful or wasteful projects. Take the 2010 FIFA World Cup in South Africa, which hastened the clearance of 'unsightly' informal settlements prior to the tournament and left behind a string of expensive unused stadiums afterwards. It was reported at the time that FIFA had refused the cheaper option of renovating an existing stadium in Cape Town's working-class Black district and insisted that a new one be built on the city's waterfront. Explaining their decision, one FIFA delegate told local officials: 'A billion television viewers don't want to see shacks and poverty on this scale' (Alegi 2007, 320). As with the demolition of *favelas* ahead of Rio 2016, and before that the *hutongs* in Beijing 2008, the redevelopment of Cape Town thus appeared to be premised on the aesthetic desires of the global audience, 'beautifying' the city for views like Photo 6.3, rather than on the day-to-day needs of the people who lived there. Such political decisions are easier to take in the absence of strong democratic mechanisms that could hold mega-event organizers and urban planners to account.

Given these examples, one proposition to consider is whether mega-event planning is implicitly designed around the idea of 'development without the poor'. In this vision of societal progress, there is no attempt to assist the poorest in society on

Photo 6.3. Cape Town stadium, built for the 2010 FIFA World Cup, was located next to the exclusive Victoria & Alfred Waterfront area with the iconic Table Mountain in the background.
Source: Hoberman Publishing/Alamy Stock Photo.

their own terms. Rather, the purpose is to centre the middle class as the 'politically preferred developmental subjectivity' and to reproduce the kind of 'pacified, morally superior, and governable consumer paradises' with which they are associated: gated communities, green spaces, upmarket shopping malls, café culture, private schools, and so on (Ballard 2012, 568). Such transformations in the built environment also bring with them an everyday dimension, encouraging inhabitants into predictable routines, whilst pushing 'undesirable' activities like public gatherings and informal street selling to the margins. This idea provides a useful entry point to explore the dual meaning of **development**, understood here as both a planned intervention of improvement and an unfolding process of progressive social change. While both these meanings *sound* benign, our brief discussion of the mega-event has shown how they often lead to violent evictions and unequal outcomes. We pick this up again in Section 6.2.2, which looks at how **urban development** takes place, focusing in particular on the role of the state in enabling and extending urbanization.

6.1.3 Politicizing the event

In Sections 6.1.1 and 6.1.2 we showed how the global spectacle and urban transformation of the mega-event can be seen through the lens of IPE, revealing some of the politics of the city that might otherwise remain hidden. In this section we look at how the mega-event has been politicized, in the sense that it has deliberately been made the subject of political debate. **Politicization** involves questioning what is 'perceived to be necessary, permanent, invariable, morally or politically obligatory and essential' (Jenkins 2011, 159). By definition it requires encroaching into areas that are considered to be off limits to politics, like sporting events, and for this reason can prove controversial. Indeed, to prevent such political intrusions, mega-event organizers routinely erect barriers to protest, as well as employ media and legal teams to rebuff any criticism.

Nevertheless, because they are so highly mediated and host states are so heavily invested in their success, mega-events continue to be politicized. One example was criticism of the stadium-building process ahead of the 2022 FIFA World Cup in Qatar. Though this process is normally conceived as a technical and apolitical building challenge, human-rights organizations sought to bring global moral pressure to bear on tournament organizers by exposing the abusive conditions of migrant construction workers that lay behind the shiny new venues. Of course, Qatar is not alone in using migrants from poorer parts of the world to host mega-events. In their study of the 2012 London Olympics, Dan Bulley and Debbie Lisle (2012) referred to them as '(g)hosts'. These were the people who did the work of hosting visitors—driving them around, cleaning their hotel rooms, preparing food for them at venues, and collecting up their rubbish afterwards—but whose presence at the mega-event was deliberately kept in the shadows. That said, the Qatari economy, concentrated in its capital city Doha, does have an extremely high proportion of foreign-born workers, as well as long-standing issues concerning the lack of economic rights for workers employed in sectors like construction. The high number of work-related deaths reported among migrants employed in World Cup preparations was especially concerning, adding a second, more chilling meaning to the idea of (g)hosts appearing at mega-events (see Al Thani 2022; Piper 2022).

Another example of politicization can be seen in the protests by disability rights campaigners during the London 2012 Paralympic Games. Previously seen as secondary to the Olympic Games, the Paralympics in London were broadcast extensively, sold more tickets than ever before, and were hailed as a turning point for how disability was perceived in the public imagination. However, this celebration was seen by campaigners as obscuring the role of the host state and Paralympics sponsors—namely the UK government and the French IT company Atos—in making daily life for many disabled people increasingly difficult. For them, the spectacle had obscured the reality. The focus of their protest was the government's strict new disability welfare assessment regime which had been outsourced to Atos to administer. Under this regime many recipients had been deemed 'fit to work', and so had their welfare benefits

Photo 6.4. During the 2012 Paralympic Games campaign groups including Disabled People Against Cuts protested outside the Atos offices in London.
Source: Guy Bell/Alamy Stock Photo.

cut (Wagg 2016). By protesting at strategically chosen sites in London, namely the offices of Atos and the Department for Work and Pensions, campaigners like those in Photo 6.4 sought to subvert the goodwill generated by the Paralympics and use it to bring shame on those in charge of welfare assessment. One reading of this protest, then, is to see it as an attempt to politicize the Paralympic Games, contesting its existence as a morally inviolable, uncriticizable event, and also to politicize the very meaning of disability. What did it mean to be disabled and what statutory rights should flow from that status? We return to these questions later when we ask how a **right to the city** might be realized for disabled people and other disadvantaged groups like migrants (Section 5.2.3).

6.2 Exploring the City

In this section we widen the scope of analysis beyond the mega-event and put the city in an IPE context—as a node of international coordination, a site of economic activity, and an actor with political agency. As with the other chapters in this book, this involves supplementing IPE literature with work in cognate areas. Here we draw on scholarship linked to Geography and Urban Studies, which has been important in providing the intellectual tools to understand spatial processes like **globalization** and urbanization. One important intervention in this regard was work in the 1990s highlighting the dangers of the 'territorial trap', which scholars were said to fall into when they mistakenly treated states as fixed units of sovereign space that acted as natural containers of a 'national' society. Such **methodological nationalism** was considered ill-equipped to deal with the profound changes happening in the world economy that were reconfiguring the nation state in radical ways (Agnew 1994). Attentiveness to the changing spatial forms taken by states—as well as by markets, firms, communities, and households—is a central feature of the work we discuss in Section 6.2.1, all of which connects these changes to cities and our collective experiences within them.

6.2.1 What are global cities?

Writing in the early 1990s, Saskia Sassen addressed these themes through her pioneering concept of 'the global city'. For her this was an entirely new kind of city, very different to the imperial metropoles and ancient trading ports that had existed for centuries, since it was emerging within a historically unprecedented expansion and integration of the world economy. Exemplified by London, New York, and Tokyo, global cities were characterized by their performance of four key functions:

> first, as highly concentrated command points in the organization of the world economy; second, as key locations for finance and for specialized service firms, which have replaced manufacturing as the leading economic sectors; third, as sites of production, including the production of innovations, in these leading industries; and fourth, as markets for the products and innovations produced.
> (Sassen 1991, 3–4)

One thing this concept of the global city did was to challenge accounts of globalization which saw it as a process bringing about the 'end of geography', in which physical distance and national borders no longer seemed to matter—where anything could come from anywhere. Whilst Sassen accepted that the growth of cross-border trade, investment, and financial exchange had weakened the integrity of the national economy, she argued that global economic activity still had to 'take place' in the geographical sense, and that cities were the spatial form through which that was happening. For her it made little sense to talk about the huge amounts of capital moving through the global financial markets without acknowledging how the vast majority of these transactions were executed in, and routed through, a handful of cities in the triad of Western Europe, the US, and Japan.

This boom in financial market activity was in turn related to the relocation of production through global value chains and the reorganization of corporate structures (see Sections 2.2.2 and 3.1.2 for examples related to clothes and food). According to Sassen, as large corporations transnationalized and spread their operations over many countries, they also began to outsource tasks to highly specialized firms to help them manage the complexity. She called this group of firms, based in areas like accountancy, advertising, and law, the 'corporate services complex'. And because these firms sought to provide a global service, they also established *their* own subsidiaries in strategically important cities beyond the triad. In this way, the corporate services complex both enabled and contributed to the concentration of economic activity in global cities, universalizing their business practices throughout the Global South and channelling the profits of this activity back to their headquarters (see also Boussebaa 2015). One of the companies we often see at graduate recruitment fairs on university campus is PwC professional services, and the way it describes itself on its website gives a neat example of what Sassen articulated:

> With offices in 156 countries and more than 295,000 people, we are among the leading professional services networks in the

world. We help organizations and individuals create the value they are looking for, by delivering quality in Assurance, Tax and Advisory services. In FY21 [Financial Year 2021], PwC firms provided services to 84% of the Global Fortune 500 companies.   (PwC n.d.)

In Sassen's view, then, the world economy looked less like a political map of nation states, each competing for its share of export markets and inward investment, and more like a transnational network of cities, linked through the interactions of their respective financial and corporate services firms. Photo 6.5 offers one way of visualizing this alternative ontology of what makes up the global political economy.

From this perspective it also appeared that the urban scale had ascended the national scale as the geographical basis of capital accumulation, with the upshot that the world's major cities would have more in common with each other than with the constituent parts of their respective countries. The shared fate of global cities can be seen in their built environments, which, despite their unique architectural histories and geographical settings, have tended to assume similar features. The underlying dynamic here was the rapid growth in real-estate prices and the associated emergence

Photo 6.5. A map of night-time global aviation, where the dots show airports and the lines show flights.
Source: underdog_cg/Shutterstock.

of skyscraper offices and luxury accommodation. This in turn was intimately linked to their status as global cities. The concentration of profitable firms and high-income jobs in select urban areas was one factor; another was the role played by the corporate services complex in facilitating foreign investment in property, or what Sassen in the quote at the start of this section called 'the production of innovation'.

Take Kensington in west London, an area home to the global super-elite where the average price of even an apartment has now surpassed £1 million. In their detailed analysis of this local property market, Rex McKenzie and Rowland Atkinson (2020) found that around 80 per cent of all property purchased by foreign entities between 1994 and 2014 was registered in tax havens. These investment schemes had been coordinated by firms within the corporate services complex, including PwC, and were used to reduce tax liabilities and channel wealth into secure assets. Moreover, the authors note how, despite the cost of these properties, many were not even used as the investor's primary residence. Over 9,000 residential properties in Kensington, equal to 10 per cent of its housing stock, had 'no usual resident' based in the borough, and many were even unoccupied. In short, these houses were not homes, but assets (McKenzie and Atkinson 2020).

This research demonstrated how the seemingly disembedded world of 'offshore' global finance was in fact anchored in the city, both through the physical presence of the corporate services complex and the property investments they enabled. By doing so, it offered an applied study of the **global wealth chains** concept. Whereas global *value* chains refer to the linked activities of firms involved in bringing a product from conception to consumption, global *wealth* chains refer to the 'linked forms of capital seeking to avoid accountability during processes of pecuniary wealth creation' (Seabrooke and Wigan 2014, 257; see Section 3.2.3 for more on the global value chain approach). Sharing much in common with analysis of the corporate services complex in orchestrating financial flows, the global wealth chains literature has sought to understand the cross-border connections that allow large companies and wealthy individuals to avoid fiscal claims, legal obligations, and regulatory oversight.

It is an approach that has been taken up in more subversive form by campaigners organizing 'kleptocracy tours' through the streets of London, physically taking members of the public to properties that had been paid for with money stolen by corrupt elites (see Minton 2017). Indeed, when Russia invaded Ukraine in 2022 and economic sanctions were applied by the UK government on the assets of wealthy Russian business leaders known as oligarchs, property ownership came under much greater scrutiny. On the eve of war, the campaign group Transparency International (2022) claimed that in the last six years £1.5 billion worth of property had been bought in London by Russians accused of corruption or with links to the Kremlin, with the most popular destinations being the City of Westminster and the borough of Kensington.

Another location where global finance is anchored in the city is the business district. These districts can be discerned across many of the world's aspirant global cities. In Singapore, which like Doha is essentially a city state, one such district can be seen in the Marina Bay Financial Centre. This opened in 2010 as the centrepiece of state efforts to attract a range of multinational financial and advisory firms into leasing offices and setting up business there. Integral to this mission was creating the right financial aesthetic, namely the steel-and-glass towers and manicured waterfront facilities shown in Photo 6.6, to make it look and feel like a rightful home for capital market activity to be conducted. Managers of the business district also acquired the leading 'emerging markets' bank Standard Chartered as a tenant and hosted major industry conferences so that it would become valued as a site of knowledge exchange. What these specific aspects of the Marina Bay Financial Centre reveal is the everyday sociality of global finance, embodied in capital market professionals, which urban planners have recognized and reproduced to help Singapore become a global city (Rethel 2018).

Another similarity that Singapore has with Doha is a large proportion of foreign-born workers. Over a third of the country's labour force is comprised of 'non-residents', the designated status for people without citizenship or the right to remain indefinitely

Photo 6.6. The Marina Bay Financial Centre, comprised of the three skyscrapers on the left, describes itself as 'an integrated development of the future, in Singapore's vibrant downtown core' (MBFC n.d.).
Source: Moonie's World/Alamy Stock Photo.

(SingStat 2021). In cities including Brussels, Dubai, and Miami, non-resident workers even outnumber the local population (UN-Habitat 2020, 3). A high rate of international migration is another characteristic of the global city, bringing with it a social diversity that again differentiates these cities from other parts of the country.

According to Sassen, among high-income earners this migration produces new ideals of everyday life centred on the appreciation of cuisine, art, and designer goods from around the world. Extending this point, we can also see how cosmopolitan social norms come to feature in the place branding strategies of cities as open, tolerant, and vibrant. For example, when the municipal government in Helsinki, Finland, embarked on a mission to brand the city, it asked for something that could be communicated to 'locals, national and international visitors, those looking to make their home in Helsinki or seeking asylum' (Baird 2018). Reflecting on the process, Mayor Vapaavuori provided his take on the cosmopolitan virtues of the city and its embrace of difference:

> Our aim is to be the most attractive place for individuals and companies who want to make the world a better place to live in . . . Helsinki is helpful, Helsinki is nice, Helsinki is kind of weird, but good weird. We are unique and proud of it. (Baird 2018)

Of course, this is just one side of the coin. Most migrants do not earn sizable salaries in the leading economic sectors of the global city, and for many it will not be tolerance but discrimination and suspicion that characterize their daily encounters. This bears out in the extremes of wealth that exist in cities. In the UK, US, and states across Africa, the Caribbean, and Latin America, levels of inequality are higher in cities than they are in the country as a whole (UN-Habitat 2020, 3). These class divides frequently run along racial and ethnic lines, in which historic patterns of immigration have typically played a formative role. This was tragically exposed in Kensington (one of London's richest boroughs, recall), when the block of council flats known as Grenfell Tower fatally burned down in 2017. In the subsequent enquiry, one of the lawyers representing survivors and bereaved families noted that 85 per cent of the residents who died in the fire were people of colour. For him, racial discrimination in housing was 'the elephant in the room': the thing everyone saw but nobody wanted to mention (cited in Apps 2020; see also Shilliam 2018).

These patterns of racialized habitation can be expressed more systematically in maps of residential segregation. Photo 6.7 details the racial profile of neighbourhoods on the Los Angeles coastline. It shows that the affluent beachside areas are comprised of white-majority neighbourhoods, while more impoverished areas like Compton are comprised of Black-majority and Hispanic-majority neighbourhoods. Once again, these spatial inequalities are tied up with immigration. The Hispanic

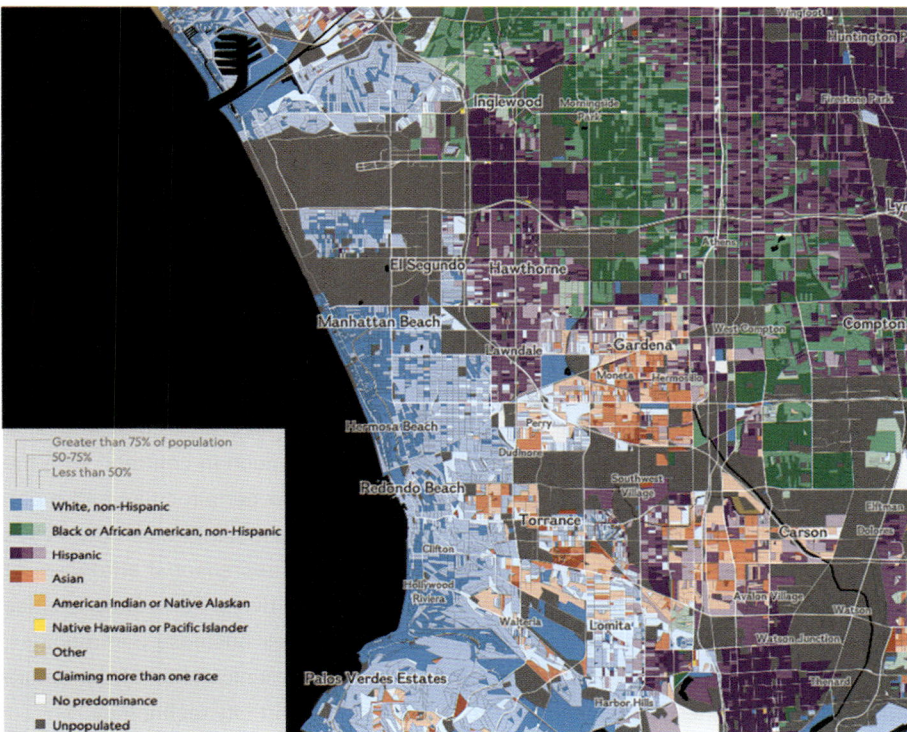

Photo 6.7. A map from the Decolonial Atlas project showing the racial profile of neighbourhoods along the Los Angeles coastline.
Source: Decolonial Atlas.

population in Los Angeles is largely made up of international arrivals from the 1970s onwards, and studies of the wider county have shown that, while the segregation of white and Black populations has slowly decreased since that time, for Hispanic populations it has actually increased (Ong et al. 2016).

But despite their evident marginalization, for Sassen at least, the international migration of racialized 'others' has nonetheless been integral to the emergence of the global city. On the one hand, they have provided much of the hidden labour on which the leading sectors of the economy have depended, like the (g)hosts servicing the mega-events discussed earlier. On the other hand, they have also established diasporic communities of their own: from Salvadoreans in Los Angeles to Indians in Dubai. Through the transnational links established by these diasporas, such as wage remittances sent to family members, Sassen sees them as making their own contribution to the ascendance of the urban scale over the national scale in the world economy (see Section 5.2.3 on remittances in global care chains).

6.2.2 How does urban development take place?

One critique of Sassen's account of the global city from an IPE perspective is that, by focusing on the financial and corporate service industries as the engine of change, it has downplayed the role of the state as a driver of change. This position holds that the state has not only sought to manage some of the contradictions brought about by the global city but deliberately pursued it as an accumulation strategy, promoting select cities within its national borders as 'locational nodes for transnational capital investment' (Brenner 1998, 3). We hinted at this state involvement in our discussion of the mega-event in Section 6.1. There we saw how multilevel coalitions in host cities combined to orchestrate large-scale urban transformations and launch place branding campaigns. Put in conceptual terms, these can be seen as examples of what Bob Jessop called the **entrepreneurial city**. Whilst this shares much in common with the global city concept, what he sought to emphasize was how certain cities had mobilized around the imperative of economic competitiveness, especially since the 1980s (Jessop 2019). This involved the adoption of distinctly *entrepreneurial* strategies of 'creative destruction' intended to keep the city ahead of its rivals. For example, cities have continually increased the pace of connectivity for their business communities, remaking urban space by replacing old transport and communications infrastructure with faster metro lines, high-speed internet access, and smart city technology.

The notion of the entrepreneurial city also stressed the *agency* of the city. Here the city was not just a strategic site where important decisions were made but a political actor in its own right. So, in the same way that we talk of Brazil or South Korea as actors based on their statehood, we might also speak of São Paulo and Seoul as actors based on their cityhood. For Jessop, the city-as-actor was constituted by social forces and organizations joining together around a shared interest in the competitive advantage of that locale, with the resultant entrepreneurial strategies embedded in wider social arrangements such that they took on a collective character. Jessop believed that this 'actorness' was more likely to emerge in cities governed by mayors and councils with greater political autonomy, which could be deliberately created through forms of state decentralization aimed at devolving power away from the core executive. But it did not rely on this process. The city-as-actor could also be comprised of public bodies, political parties, chambers of commerce, citizens' associations, and, perhaps most importantly, branches of the central state that rescaled from a national focus to an urban focus (Jessop 2019).

For Neil Brenner, another political economist interested in the spatial configurations of capitalism, this kind of **state rescaling** was integral to the transformation of the UK economy in the 1980s. In his view, the ambition of the Conservative Party government of Margaret Thatcher to promote London as a global financial centre had led them to abolish the Greater London Council, which at the time was democratically controlled by the opposition Labour Party and steeped in ideas of municipal socialism. This was replaced with an ensemble of unelected parastate agencies and public–private partnerships, administered from the top down to orchestrate a suite of 'mega-projects' in the city including the Isle of Dogs Enterprise Zone, the Thames Gateway project, and the Canary Wharf office development scheme shown in Photos 6.8a and 6.8b. So, despite being stripped of municipal self-government, London was duly elevated in the organizational hierarchy of state territorial power and prioritized as the country's growth pole. In Brenner's analysis, then, the rise of London as a global city resulted from the political victories of financial capital over industrial capital, and of central authority over local authority (Brenner 1998).

The reinvention of Canary Wharf also opens a window onto the historical process of state rescaling, and in particular the role of *colonial* states in shaping cities. Canary Wharf was built on what used to be the West India Docks, a nodal point for trade between the UK and its imperial possessions in the Caribbean. Constructed during the 1800s to receive ships from the British West Indies laden with slave-grown sugar, the docks were at the time the most expensive commercial building project ever undertaken. The transformation of east London into 'the warehouse of the world' was thus intimately tied up with the exploitation at the heart of the transatlantic slave economy (see Museum of London Docklands n.d.).

As well as approving major infrastructural projects like the West India Docks, the British government oversaw a proliferation of urban developments within its colonies. One example is Georgetown, the capital of what was then British Guiana. First

Photo 6.8a. Canary Wharf in East London in 1986.
Source: A.P.S. (UK)/Alamy Stock Photo.

Photo 6.8b. Canary Wharf after the development scheme in 2013, where global financial corporations including HSBC, Citibank, and Credit Suisse can be seen. In 2015 the site was bought for £2.6 billion by Brookfield Property Partners (registered in Bermuda) and the Qatar Investment Authority.
Source: Commission Air/Alamy Stock Photo.

established as a guard post at the mouth of the Demerara River by Dutch colonists, the town (named Stabroek) and its surrounding plantations were taken over in the 1800s by the British, who subsequently intensified both the import of enslaved Africans and the export of sugar. Renamed Georgetown after the British monarch King George III, the city quickly expanded to become the 'hub of British Guiana, its spokes radiating to the rest of the colony' (De Barros 2002, 16). If you look closely at Photo 6.9, alongside the wharves that loaded up sugar and other commodities for export you can see the government buildings and law courts, and behind them the military barracks and parade grounds—all clear materializations of colonial state power. This power was also expressed culturally in the city's cathedrals and cricket grounds, which transplanted religious and sporting institutions into the country. Perhaps the most striking feature of the map though, is the gridiron street plan. This was typical of colonial cities designed by the British, being considered vital to the forms of surveillance and segregation that were intended to keep urban spaces orderly and prevent any anti-colonial resistance (Home 2013, 226).

What the example of Georgetown suggests is how the formation of cities was central to the process of state rescaling that accompanied British colonialism. Consider all

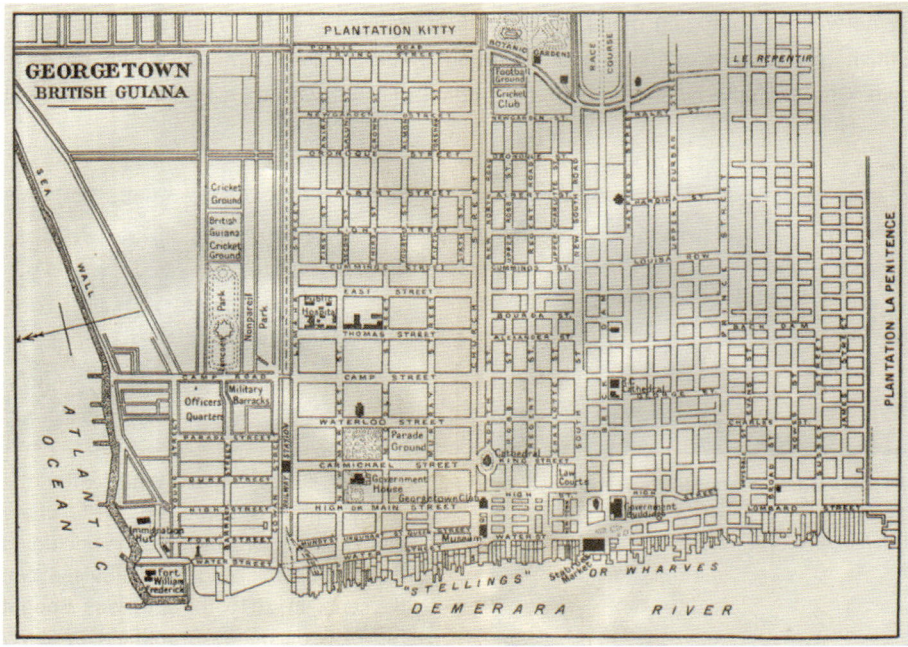

Photo 6.9. A map of Georgetown from *The Pocket Guide to the West Indies* first published in 1910.
Source: Antiqua Print Gallery/Alamy Stock Photo.

the other Georgetowns founded by the British that exist around the world today: from the US in the West to Malaysia in the East. These and other colonial cities formed a global administrative network of urban governance around the needs of the metropole and its extractive economic system of plantation, forestry, and mining enclaves. The legacies of this are evident in postcolonial states today, albeit in romanticized form, where 'colonial districts' in cities are tied to heritage industries and tourism. In Singapore, for example, while modern developments like Marina Bay Financial Centre project a vision for the country's *future*, buildings in its colonial district are used to tell—and sell—a story of its *past*. As detailed on the website of the country's famous Raffles Hotel, named after the colony's founder Stamford Raffles, this past is recalled as a glamourized history of 'regal elegance and Old World appeal' where the hotel functioned as 'as a beacon and haven for world travellers, arriving from all shores to experience its exquisite combination of grandeur and charm' (Raffles Hotel n.d.).

One way of bringing together the varied practices of place branding, the entrepreneurial city, and state rescaling is to consider them as part of the **production of state space**. This refers to the organization of socio-spatial routines into a manageable grid of abstract space, which can be used to govern society and embed capital accumulation (Brenner and Elden 2009). It is a concept drawn from the work of Henri Lefebvre, and it is through Lefebvre that we can get back to the implications of such urban development for everyday life. As we mentioned in the book's Introduction (Section 1.2.1), Lefebvre was interested in how daily activities had become subordinated to the imperatives of capitalism, and for him urbanization was key. In his reading, the modern living designed by urbanists and city planners had separated the rhythms of life from those of nature and fragmented them into separate experiences, each with its designated space (Davies 2006). Work. Shop. Sleep. Repeat. Writing from the vantage point of mid-twentieth-century France, Lefebvre (1984) saw this culminating in a 'bureaucratic society of controlled consumption' in which the state took a central role in 'programming' how people would participate in market life. A technologically updated if somewhat dystopian version of this thesis can be found in the 2008 film *WALL-E*. It is the scene in Photo 6.10 where WALL-E arrives aboard the spaceship designed to save the human race, only to find the species reduced to atomized individuals absorbed their by screens, whizzing around on pre-planned routes to different zones where they endlessly consume commodities delivered by automated service bots. Perhaps not so dystopian after all?

6.2.3 Who needs the right to the city?

So far in this chapter we have emphasized the role of state authorities, city planners, and urban designers in coordinating urban development from the top down. Earlier on

Photo 6.10. A still from *WALL-E*, showing the human inhabitants stuck in their consumer grooves. Notice how the humans are also all depicted as being fat—a comment on capitalist society and its body politics discussed in Section 3.2.2 on food.
Source: Disney's WALL-E (2008). Directed by Andrew Stanton.

we suggested that many such projects have been built on the idea of 'development without the poor', whereby processes of **gentrification** turn urban landscapes into respectable and profitable real estate that caters to the affluent (Smith, 2002). But, of course, the poor do not simply disappear in such scenarios. Many of those priced out or pushed out from these planned developments have been left to find accommodation elsewhere, and in the Global South especially this has given rise to informal housing or encampments. These *unplanned* areas are thought to be home to around a quarter of the world's urban population (UN-Habitat 2018, 3).

Among the biggest is Dharavi in Mumbai, commonly referred to as Asia's largest slum, and the setting of the 2008 British film *Slumdog Millionaire*. As shown in Photo 6.11, Dharavi sits uneasily—unequally—next to the verdant green spaces of the upmarket Bandra Kurla complex, its own topography coloured by the blue tarpaulins used to provide shelter from the monsoon rains. Such informal settlements are typically defined as overcrowded, polluted, unsanitary, and insecure (UN-Habitat 2003). These characterizations need to be handled carefully. As the postcolonial Urban Studies scholar Ananya Roy has pointed out, the pejorative meanings of 'slum' can invite pathological analyses that treat these areas and their residents as if they were a disease on the social body (Roy 2011). If the planned city spaces of the state represent order and integrity, the unplanned spaces of informal settlements can easily be depicted as disordered and disposable.

One danger of this analytically is that it sets the informal settlement apart from the rest of the city, cutting it off from relational processes that envelop both. For example, one cause of insecurity in informal settlements is the fear of eviction, which is linked to both the legal regime underpinning tenure rights *and* the spread of speculative urban

Photo 6.11. Spatial inequality in Mumbai. Dharavi on the right and the Bandra Kurla complex on the left.
Source: Johnny Miller.

development. When occupants in informal settlements are regarded as no more than illegal squatters, they become easy targets for developers wanting to convert the land to prime urban real estate. Dharavi has been no exception to this tendency and has long been slated for a state-approved redevelopment project. Described initially as a way to turn the area into India's Canary Wharf, it has proved to be hugely controversial, not least because of disagreements over how to compensate or relocate the people who own or rent property there (Roy 2011). Offering a general conceptualization of this process, the geographer David Harvey (2008) has described housing evictions as a form of **accumulation by dispossession**, a type of surplus value production that relies on state compulsion and 'legalized theft'. For him it has been at the core of urbanization under capitalism: from the *favelas* of Rio to the *kampungs* of Jakarta (see Photo 6.12).

Whereas Harvey's examples drew attention to the mega-cities of the Global South, the IPE scholar Susanne Soederberg has looked at the rise in evictions across the Global North. One of her studies focused on the borough of Neukölln in Berlin, home to communities of Arabic, Romani, and Turkish immigrants. In the mid-2000s as evictions and homelessness began to increase, she noted how the German Finance Minister publicly referred to parts of the borough as 'slums', joining other politicians in blaming the housing crisis on the failure of immigrants to properly integrate into the

Photo 6.12. Police try to evict residents protesting at the demolition of informal housing in Jakarta in 2016, part of the governor's plan to boost tourism and reduce annual flooding.
Source: Reuters/Alamy Stock Photo.

German job market and national culture. In contrast to this explanation, Soederberg's approach was to consider the **race-making** practices of urban governance and the role of the state in driving spatial inequality.

She pointed in particular to the decisions by the **municipal government** in Berlin to either sell off or raise the rents on their social housing stock, and by the federal government of Germany to reduce welfare and unemployment support. The twin effect of these compelled people to find cheaper, substandard accommodation and take temporary low-wage jobs, thus creating a **surplus population** that was made vulnerable to indebtedness and eviction precisely because of their race, ethnicity, and citizenship status. Echoing the earlier point made by Sassen, for Soederberg the residents of Neukölln *had* been integrated into the city, just on a highly unequal basis. State policies had encouraged them to pay the rents and do the jobs that others would refuse, whilst racial stigmatization presented them as undeserving of welfare. Indeed, this racial 'othering' provided a counterpoint to white German society that could itself be exploited, with pockets of gentrification emerging in Neukölln that seemed 'to derive their desired edginess from the stigmatization of the rest of borough . . . evident in Kreuzkölln's recent naming as a "Hipster Ghetto" complete with its own slum tours' (Soederberg 2017, 480).

The common experiences of eviction and exclusion in cities across the world have led to calls for alternative political ideals that might join these localized struggles together. One of the most prominent has been the **right to the city**. This is another proposition of Henri Lefebvre, and refers to the collective right to make use of urban space and participate in its democratic control. Like the related slogan 'take back the streets', it is not just about accessing those parts of the city presently off limits but allowing people to actively reshape the urbanization process to use space differently. Since the turn of the century, the right to the city has found expression in various legal instruments and policy agendas. It was incorporated into Brazil's 2001 City Statute law and Ecuador's 2008 Constitution, and adopted as a central principle at the UN-Habitat Summit in 2016. It has also influenced the advocacy of Leilani Farha, who, as UN Special Rapporteur on the Right to Adequate Housing, called for an end to urban development 'premised on the idea of eliminating "slums"' and for the introduction of policies that enabled residents of informal settlements 'to become full participants in upgrading' (Farha 2018, 2).

As we saw in the case of the Rio Olympics outlined in Section 6.1, though, even where laws on evictions and popular participation in municipal planning do exist, they are not guaranteed to prevent urban conflict, still less resist the lure of mega-projects in the first place (Rolnik 2013). Lefebvre, too, recognized how easily such laws could be turned into abstract rights that meant little in practice, claiming that only social force could shatter the illusion of legislative reformism. Channelling this force into a militant democracy of ***autogestion*** was, for him, the most productive route to the right to the city (Gray 2018). *Autogestion* referred to a working-class revolt against control from above and for greater self-management (Elden 2004, 229). It embraced a revolutionary socialism which recognized that workers have a life beyond the workplace, encouraging political movements that addressed class inequalities in things like housing, transport, and public space. A contemporary example can be found in what the anthropologist Teresa Caldeira has called 'auto-construction' whereby residents living on the fringes of urban developments in the Global South gradually build not only their own homes but also their own neighbourhoods. In so doing, they have 'engaged in modes of production of space that constitute themselves as simultaneously new kinds of urban residents, consumers, subjects, and citizens' (Caldeira 2017, 9). Or, in Lefebvre's terms, they have begun to author the world around them and, through that, become *dis*-alienated (Charnock 2010).

By changing people's sense of who they are as subjects and citizens, *autogestion* also confronts the state–society relationship. This was evident in the 2013 Gezi Park protest in Istanbul, Turkey, which started as a peaceful sit-in against plans to build over Gezi Park with a shopping mall. Sparked by the heavy-handed response of the police, this dispute over the use of urban space quickly escalated into a city-wide uprising against the national government. Denounced by Prime Minister Recep Tayyip Erdoğan as *çapulcu* or looters, the protestors reappropriated the term and played out this new identity under the movement's adopted slogan, 'Everyday I'm Çapuling'.

Photo 6.13. Reclaiming urban space in the Gezi Park protests of 2013. Six years later, the country's ruling party lost the local election in Istanbul for the first time since Erdoğan came to power, a significant blow to his regime.
Source: Claudia Wiens/Alamy Stock Photo.

Satirical spaces like 'Capulistan' in Photo 6.13 and 'looter classrooms' indicated the emergence of a new political subjectivity, while acts of good housekeeping like litter picking demonstrated their capacity for self-organization. It was in the everyday life of the protest, then, that an alternative vision for Turkish society was forged and found—a collective political experience of empowerment that served as an important counterpoint to the years of state repression that followed (McGarry et al. 2019). Put in general terms, it showed how struggles for the right to the city happen through, and are registered in, a transformation of everyday life (Kipfer et al. 2008). Or, as David Harvey (2008, 23) put it: by remaking our cities we also remake ourselves.

6.3 Engaging the City

6.3.1 An urban development case study

In Section 6.2 we explored how global capital has circulated through the property markets and infrastructural projects of urban areas, enabled and encouraged by state authorities. As a topic that brings together the international, the political, and the economic,

Photo 6.14. New-build suburban real estate in Queensland, Australia. How can we use everyday IPE to explore such developments?
Source: Terra incognita/Alamy Stock Photo.

it is ripe for IPE analysis and has been taken up to good effect in the work of Jason Sharman. Using the global wealth chain concept discussed in Section 6.2.1, Sharman looked at how corrupt politicians and public officials in Papua New Guinea have been able to seize public funds and transfer them into residential property in Australia, its former colonial ruler. Consulting property records in Queensland and cross-referencing these with anti-corruption investigations undertaken by branches of the Papua New Guinea state, he found 203 properties worth AUD86 million that were owned by individuals and companies linked to corruption. Furthermore, sales data revealed that many of these purchases had been arranged through the same few Australian lawyers, real-estate agents, property developers, and banks. By locating the properties via Google Earth, Sharman then found that many were clustered in the same city neighbourhoods. Some corruption-tainted senior officials even lived next door to each other (Sharman 2017).

As you might be thinking, this can be a very difficult area to research in methodological terms, especially when faced with the deliberately opaque and complex legal arrangements of offshore property ownership. In fact, Sharman himself went to the lengths of hiring a private investigator specializing in financial crime to help track down this suspected stolen wealth. What we propose for this research activity is a more modest undertaking: a five-minute video presentation on an urban development case study. To help with data accessibility, we suggest you choose a case that is well documented in the public domain. Examples might include a new building on your university campus, a city-centre housing complex, or a major urban transport system. The idea is to use the case as a way to engage the academic literature on the corporate services complex, global wealth chains, gentrification, and the production of state space covered in the chapter. In particular, we would encourage you to ask:

- Where did the money come from for this development?
- Have local, regional, or national government played an active role in facilitating this?
- What routines of everyday life is it intended to discourage/encourage?
- Does an IPE perspective illuminate anything new about the development that wasn't covered in the project's own public relations material?

In terms of the structure of the video, a suggestion would be to spend one minute introducing the development (its location, purpose, etc.), then one minute on each of the bullet points above. A simple approach to produce a video would be to use PowerPoint slides accompanied by a voice-over, which for five minutes would be around 700 words long. We suggest using the video format for this case study because it allows for the use of images and films to illuminate your analysis. For example, screenshots of media coverage could be used to show how the development has been politicized, while phone videos of site visits might help convey something of its everyday impact.

6.3.2 A privilege trail

One criticism made of Urban Studies in its Marxist guise is that it has prioritized a diagnosis of capitalism over other oppressive social systems such as patriarchy, colonialism, racism, nationalism, heteronormativity, and ableism (Oswin 2016). Each of these systems privilege certain groups in ways that overlap with, but cannot be reduced to, class relations. This intersectionality is important to bear in mind when we are thinking about the right to the city. The exclusions facing residents of informal settlements are not identical to those facing LGBTQ+ communities or religious minorities, and so whilst there might be strategic benefits to political mobilization around a shared ideal, there is also a danger that the resultant policy agendas might speak for some groups but silence others. In short, we need to continually ask ourselves *whose right* to the city is being advanced.

Let us take the example of **ableism**. This can be defined as the beliefs, processes, and practices that produce a particular kind of self and body, which is then projected as the typical or 'normal' human. Consequently, disability is cast as a diminished state of being human (Campbell 2009). Understanding ableism as a norm-setting system challenges the notion of disability as a biomedical fact and encourages us to ask instead how people are actively *dis*abled in society by the collective failure to recognize and accommodate those differences considered atypical or 'abnormal'. Ableism also turns the analytical gaze towards the non-disabled and asks how this category of person is constructed and how they are *en*abled in society by the entitlements this confers. The geographer Vera Chouinard has argued that one way to trace this is in 'the lived environments which incorporate and perpetuate physical and social barriers to the participation of disabled persons in everyday life' (Chouinard 1997, 380). Writing as a disabled woman herself, she highlighted things like the lack of automatic doors and ramps in public buildings, and the reactions to disabled people that effectively question their right to be in certain spaces.

Building on this idea, in this activity we want you to consider how the right to the city is impeded for historically disadvantaged groups by producing a privilege trail. Mimicking the tourist trails set out in travel guides, this should take the reader on a journey through an urban landscape, be it an area of a city, a public building, or a university campus. However, rather than highlighting the 'must-see' destinations, it should instead reveal sites of privilege. These are places that can be used to disclose the everyday yet largely overlooked experiences of dis/advantage that constitute hierarchies of social difference. They could include transport systems designed around non-disabled people, as shown in Photo 6.15, public monuments exclusively of white men, 'hostile architecture' designed to ward off homeless people, spacious parks with clean air that can only be found in affluent areas, streets where women cannot walk at night, or public places where homosexual feelings cannot really be expressed.

One project design question to consider is whether to look at the same kind of privilege across multiple sites, or different kinds of privilege that coexist within the same site. The former would be better if you would prefer to study a particular manifestation of power relations, like ableism or whiteness. The latter would be better if you want to take an intersectional approach and look at, for instance, how metro lines can be experienced as disabling spaces but also as *unsafe* spaces, especially for women (Fenster 2005). The objective of the activity is to think through what the right to the city means in the context of your urban space and how it might be realized. Questions to address include:

- How might your sites of privilege be politicized in the first place?
- Is it the right to make use of existing space or to participate in its democratic control that is needed?

Photo 6.15. A wheelchair user of the Massachusetts Bay subway in the US. Take a look at a metro map and its accessibility for people with different needs. What does it tell you about the right to the city?
Source: Design Pics Inc./Alamy Stock Photo.

- What kind of legislative reform or *autogestion* would bring this about?
- And thinking again of the cross-border dimension that IPE brings, what possibilities exist for international learning or coalition building?

6.4 Conclusion

Thinking about cities is a useful way to avoid falling into the territorial trap of methodological nationalism in IPE. It immediately challenges a view of the world as split into neatly bounded nation states and encourages us to consider alternative kinds of economic space and political authority. Compared to analyses of the global economy which look at US hegemony or the rise of China, this gives a very different picture of where power lies and where wealth is located. Through Saskia Sassen's concept of the global city, we explored the argument that the urban scale has gained ascendance over the national scale as the geographical basis of capital accumulation. One important contribution of scholars coming from an IPE perspective to these debates has been to factor in the state. We referred to this work through the concepts of place branding, the entrepreneurial city, and state rescaling to show how states have enabled, managed, and adapted to the concentration of global economic activity in urban space. The urban development research challenge was designed to help you elicit other such examples by looking at the built environment. Of course, cities are not just nodes in the global economy but places where people live, and it was through the inhabitation of urban space that we discussed Henri Lefebvre's notion of everyday life. This was used to help us comprehend the contradictory forces of urban living, whereby daily routines are programmed from above to fit prevailing regimes of capital accumulation but where new ways of being continually emerge from below as people seek out the right to live differently. The idea of 'development without the poor', as expressed in racialized processes of gentrification and slum clearances, was one way we explored this. Another was to look at ableist environments and their systematic privileging of certain kinds of bodies and minds. Consider this next time you walk around the city. What kinds of inequalities do its buildings, infrastructure, and layout disclose? And how might IPE help to explain them?

Access the online resources for quizzes, student reflection podcasts, and support for tackling the chapter's learning activities: http://www.oup.com/he/i-peel1e.

RESOURCES

Tile recommendations from the I-PEEL website: 'place branding' (Juliette Schwak) http://i-peel.org/homepage/place-branding/; 'evictions' (Oscar Berglund) http://i-peel.org/homepage/evictions/.

Cidade de Deus (*City of God*). 2002. 133 minutes. This film depicts the suffocating growth of organized crime in the *favelas* of Rio de Janeiro. One could argue that its focus on violence, poverty, and hopelessness—broadcast around the world by the film's success—was exactly the kind of narrative that the organizers of the Rio Olympics (discussed in Section 6.1) sought to push against.

Brenner, Neil. 2019. *New Urban Spaces: Urban Theory and the Scale Question*. Oxford: Oxford University Press. This book brings together many of the crossover topics between IPE and Urban Studies, which is a transdisciplinary field that is not so much about profiling individual cities as about understanding urban processes and outcomes in general.

Gleeson, Brendan. 1997. 'Disability Studies: A Historical Materialist View'. *Disability & Society* 12(2): 179–202. Despite having huge ramifications for people's quality of life the world over, disability has been largely neglected in IPE. The scholarship of Disability Studies has not yet enriched IPE to the same extent that Urban Studies has. This article provides one possible bridge between the two literatures and also discusses disablement in the industrial city.

Sassen, Saskia. 2014. 'Interview'. *Globalizations* 11(4): 461–72. An interview with Saskia Sassen that relates her body of work to the genealogy of economic globalization and other key topics in IPE.

Soederberg, Susanne. 2021. *Urban Displacements: Governing Surplus and Survival in Global Capitalism*. London: Routledge. Winner of the 2021 book prize awarded by the IPE group British International Studies Association, this offers a systematic analysis of low-income rental housing and its social dislocations, drawing on the author's work in Berlin discussed in Section 6.2.3.

Van Toorn, Georgia, and Ben Richardson. 2021. 'IPEG Interviews in Embodied Inequality: Disability and Neoliberalism with Dr Georgia van Toorn'. 28 September 2021.https://www.bisa.ac.uk/members/working-groups/ipeg/articles/disability-and-neoliberalism-dr-georgia-van-toorn. An interview with a scholar bringing Disability Studies and Political Economy together in terms of neoliberal disability support, which ends with some suggestions about other links that could be forged too.

REFERENCES

Agnew, John. 1994. 'The Territorial Trap: The Geographical Assumptions of International Relations Theory'. *Review of International Political Economy* 1(1): 53–80.

Alegi, Peter. 2007. 'The Political Economy of Mega-Stadiums and the Underdevelopment of Grassroots Football in South Africa'. *Politikon* 34(3): 315–31.

Al Thani, Mohammed. 2022. 'Channelling Soft Power: The Qatar World Cup, Migrant Workers, and International Image'. *International Journal of the History of Sport* 38(17): 1729–52.

Apps, Peter. 2020. 'Survivors' Lawyer Calls for "Racial Discrimination" to be Considered as Factor in Grenfell Fire'. *Inside Housing*, July.

Baird, Richard. 2018. 'Helsinki by Werklig'. *B&PO Opinion*, https://bpando.org/2018/04/19/branding-helsinki/ (last accessed 19 April 2018).

Ballard, Richard. 2012. 'Geographies of Development: Without the Poor'. *Progress in Human Geography* 35(5): 563–72.

BBC. 2009. 'Rio to Stage 2016 Olympic Games'. BBC Sport, 2 October, http://news.bbc.co.uk/sport1/hi/olympic_games/8282518.stm.

Boussebaa, Mehdi. 2015. 'Professional Service Firms, Globalisation and the New Imperialism'. *Accounting, Auditing and Accountability Journal* 28(8): 1217–33.

Brenner, Neil. 1998. 'Global Cities, Glocal States: Global City Formation and State Territorial Restructuring in Contemporary Europe'. *Review of International Political Economy* 5(1): 1–37.

Brenner, Neil, and Stuart Elden. 2009. 'Henri Lefebvre on State, Space, Territory'. *International Political Sociology* 3(4): 353–77.

Bulley, Dan, and Debbie Lisle. 2012. 'Welcoming the World: Governing Hospitality in London's 2012 Olympic Bid'. *International Political Sociology* 6(2): 186–204.

Caldeira, Teresa P. R. 2017. 'Peripheral Urbanization: Autoconstruction, Transversal Logics, and Politics in Cities of the Global South'. *Environment and Planning D* 35(1): 3–20.

Campbell, Fiona Kumari. 2009. *Contours of Ableism: The Production of Disability and Abledness*. Basingstoke: Palgrave Macmillan.

Caudros, Alex. 2016. 'The Broken Promise of the Rio Olympics'. *The Atlantic*. August.

Charnock, Greig. 2010. 'Challenging New State Spatialities: The Open Marxism of Henri Lefebvre'. *Antipode* 42(5): 1279–303.

Chouinard, Vera. 1997. 'Making Space for Disabling Differences: Challenging Ableist Geographies'. *Environment and Planning D* 15(4): 379–87.

Davies, Matt. 2006. 'Everyday Life in the Global Political Economy'. In *International Political Economy and Poststructural Politics*, ed. Marieke de Goede, 219–37. Basingstoke: Palgrave Macmillan.

De Barros, Juanita. 2002. *Order and Place in a Colonial City: Patterns of Struggle and Resistance in Georgetown, British Guiana, 1889–1924*. Montreal: McGill-Queen's University Press.

Elden, Stuart. 2004. *Understanding Henri Lefebvre: Theory and the Possible*. London: Continuum.

Farha, Leilani. 2018. 'Report of the Special Rapporteur on Adequate Housing'. 73rd Session of the UN General Assembly, A/73/310/Rev.1, 19 September.

Fenster, Tovi. 2005. 'The Right to the Gendered City: Different Formations of Belonging in Everyday Life'. *Journal of Gender Studies* 14(3): 217–31.

Garriga, Carlos, Aaron Hedlund, Yang Tang, and Ping Wang. 2020. 'Rural-Urban Migration and House Prices in China'. *Regional Science and Urban Economics* 91(103613): 1–29.

Gibson, Owen. 2009. 'Olympics 2016: Tearful Pele and Weeping Lula Greet Historic Win'. *The Guardian*, 2 October.

Gray, Neil. 2018. 'Beyond the Right to the City: Territorial Autogestion and the Take over the City Movement in 1970s Italy'. *Antipode* 50(2): 319–39.

Grix, Jonathan, and Donna Lee. 2013. 'Soft Power, Sports Mega-Events and Emerging States: The Lure of the Politics of Attraction'. *Global Society* 27(4): 521–36.

Harvey, David. 2008. 'The Right to the City'. *New Left Review* 53 (September–October): 23–40.

Home, Robert. 2013. *Of Planning and Planting: The Making of British Colonial Cities*, 2nd edn. London: Routledge.

International Olympic Committee (IOC). 2017. 'Olympic Games Rio 2016 – The Legacy'. IOC Press Release, 16 March, https://www.olympic.org/news/olympic-games-rio-2016-the-legacy.

International Olympic Committee (IOC). n.d. 'Global Broadcast and Audience Report: Olympic Games Rio 2016', IOC presentation, https://stillmedab.olympic.org/media/Document%20Library/OlympicOrg/Games/Summer-Games/Games-Rio-2016-Olympic-Games/Media-Guide-for-Rio-2016/Global-Broadcast-and-Audience-Report-Rio-2016.pdf (last accessed 19 January 2022).

Jenkins, Laura. 2011. 'The Difference Genealogy Makes: Strategies for Politicisation or How to Extend Capacities for Autonomy'. *Political Studies* 59(1): 156–74.

Jessop, Bob. 2019. 'Entrepreneurial City'. In *The Wiley Blackwell Encyclopedia of Urban and Regional Studies* ed. Anthony M. Orum, 1–10. Hoboken: Wiley-Blackwell, and online.

Kipfer, Stefan, Kanishka Goonewardena, Richard Milgrom, and Christian Schmid. 2008. 'On the Production of Henri Lefebvre'. In *Space, Difference, Everyday Life: Reading Henri Lefebvre* ed. Goonewardena, Kipfer, Milgrom, and Schmid, 1–25. London: Routledge.

Lefebvre, Henri. 1984. *Everyday Life in the Modern World*. London: Routledge.

McGarry, Aidan, Olu Jenzen, Hande Eslen-Ziya, Itir Erhart, and Umut Korkut. 2019. 'Beyond the Iconic Protest Images: The Performance of "Everyday Life" on Social Media During Gezi Park'. *Social Movement Studies* 18(3): 284–304.

McKenzie, Rex, and Rowland Atkinson. 2020. 'Anchoring Capital in Place: The Grounded Impact of International Wealth Chains on Housing Markets in London'. *Urban Studies* 57(1): 21–38.

Marina Bay Financial Centre (MBFC). n.d. Marina Bay Financial Centre website, https://www.mbfc.com.sg/ (last accessed 19 January 2022).

Minton, Anna. 2017. *Big Capital: Who is London For?* London: Penguin.

Morgan, Liam. 2019. 'Rio 2016 Debts Rise More than Three Times to $113 million'. *Inside the Games*, February.

Müller, Martin. 2015. 'What Makes an Event a Mega-Event? Definitions and Sizes'. *Leisure Studies* 34(6): 627–42.

Museum of London Docklands. n.d. 'Warehouse of the World', https://www.museumoflondon.org.uk/museum-london-docklands/permanent-galleries/warehouse-world (last accessed 19 January 2022).

Ong, Paul, Chhandara Pech, Jenny Chhea, and C. Aujean Lee. 2016. 'Race, Ethnicity and Income Segregation in Los Angeles', UCLA Center for Neighbourhood Knowledge, 24 June.

Oswin, Natalie. 2016. 'Planetary Urbanization: A View from Outside'. *Environment and Planning D* 36(3): 540–6.

Piper, Nicola. 2022. 'The International Labour Organization as Nodal Player on the Pitch of Networked Governance: Shifting the Goalposts for Migrant Workers in Qatar'. *Global Social Policy*, https://doi.org/10.1177/14680181211065240.

PwC. n.d. 'About Us', https://www.pwc.com/gx/en/about.html (last accessed 23 March 2022).

Raffles Hotel. n.d. 'Raffles History', https://www.rafflessingapore.com/raffles-history (last accessed 19 January 2022).

Rethel, Lena. 2018. 'Capital Market Development in Southeast Asia: From Speculative Crisis to Spectacles of Financialization'. *Economic Anthropology* 5(2): 185–97.

Rolnik, Raquel. 2013. 'Ten Years of the City Statute in Brazil: From the Struggle for Urban Reform to the World Cup Cities'. *International Journal of Urban Sustainable Development* 5(1): 54–64.

Roy, Ananya. 2011. 'Slumdog Cities: Rethinking Subaltern Urbanism'. *International Journal of Urban and Regional Research* 35(2): 223–38.

Sassen, Saskia. 1991. *The Global City: New York, London, Tokyo*. Princeton: Princeton University Press.

Schwak, Juliette. 2018. 'All the World's a Stage: Promotional Politics and Branded Identities in Asia'. *Asian Studies Review* 42(4): 648–61.

Seabrooke, Leonard, and Duncan Wigan. 2014. 'Global Wealth Chains in the International Political Economy'. *Review of International Political Economy* 21(1): 257–63.

Sharman, Jason. 2017. 'Illicit Global Wealth Chains after the Financial Crisis: Micro-States and an Unusual Suspect'. *Review of International Political Economy* 24(1): 30–55.

Shilliam, Robbie. 2018. *Race and the Undeserving Poor: From Abolition to Brexit*. Newcastle upon Tyne: Agenda Publishing.

SingStat. 2021. 'Labour, Employment, Wages and Productivity', https://www.singstat.gov.sg/find-data/search-by-theme/economy/labour-employment-wages-and-productivity/latest-data (last accessed 19 January 2022).

Smith, Neil. 2002. 'New Globalism, New Urbanism: Gentrification as Global Urban Strategy'. *Antipode* 34(3): 427–50.

Soederberg, Susanne. 2017. 'Governing Stigmatized Space: The Case of the "Slums" of Berlin-Neukölln'. *New Political Economy* 22(5): 478–95.

Transparency International. 2022. 'Stats Reveal Extent of Suspect Wealth in UK Property and Britain's Role as Global Money Laundering Hub', Press Release, 18 February.

UN-Habitat. 2003. *The Challenge of Slums: Global Report on Human Settlements*. Nairobi: UN-Habitat.

UN-Habitat. 2018. 'Metadata on SDGs Indicator 11.1.1', March, https://unhabitat.org/sites/default/files/2020/06/metadata_on_sdg_indicator_11.1.1.pdf.

UN-Habitat. 2020. *World Cities Report: The Value of Sustainable Urbanization*. Nairobi: UN-Habitat.

Van den Broucke, Sarah, Luana Gama Gato. 2018. 'Contesting the Brand: A Media Analysis of the Image of Rio de Janeiro as Host of the 2016 Summer Olympics in Dutch Language Newspapers'. *European Journal for Sport and Society* 15(3): 268–87.

Wagg, Stephen. 2016. '"The Atos Games": Protest, the Paralympics of 2012 and the New Politics of Disablement'. In *Sport, Protest and Globalization: Stopping Play*, ed. Jon Dart and Stephen Wagg, 257–88. Basingstoke: Palgrave Macmillan.

Wood, Astrid. 2019. 'Advancing Development Projects through Mega-Events: The 2010 Football World Cup and Bus Rapid Transit in South Africa'. *Urban Geography* 40(4): 428–44.

Yamawaki, Yumi, Fabio Marcel de Castro Filho, and Giuliana E. G. D. Costa. 2020. 'Mega-Event Transport Legacy in a Developing Country: The Case of Rio 2016 Olympic Games and its Transolímpica BRT Corridor'. *Journal of Transport Geography* 88: 1–14.

7
SOCIAL MEDIA

7.1	Fitness Influencers	187
7.2	Exploring Social Media	194
7.3	Engaging Social Media	204
7.4	Conclusion	209

LEARNING OBJECTIVES

- Use the concepts of self-branding, the attention economy, and the prosumer to problematize the market life of social media
- Reflect on how social media shapes everyday experiences of work and consumption, asking if it is a free and democratic space or a new infrastructure of surveillance
- Explore your own experiences of resistance on/to social media through group deliberation, and how distinctive moral critiques of social media are performed in documentary films

READER'S GUIDE

Social media is not normally a chapter in an IPE textbook, yet our online experiences are increasingly mediated by big tech multinational corporations that monitor our likes and dislikes as online consumers. How we experience and represent social media has profound implications for the ethical possibilities and limits of global market life. This chapter begins with a short section on 'Fitness Influencers' that problematizes social media via the related concepts of self-branding, the attention economy, and the prosumer. These concepts allow us to ask questions about all the effort and emotion expended on online connections, jokes, and outrage (Section 7.1). The second section explores social media via two popular documentaries on Netflix: *Fyre: The Greatest Party That Never Happened* and *The Social Dilemma* (Section 7.2). These documentaries focus on questions of reform and regulation, identifying how social media data carries immense value for corporate marketing, political strategy, credit rating, and other ways of knowing and governing society. This helps to establish an important dilemma: is social media a free, open, democratic space, or a dystopian infrastructure of surveillance that manipulates ever more docile prosumer subjects according to a logic of accumulation? A final section engages this politics of social media by considering different forms of critical agency (Section 7.3). It draws on theories of everyday resistance to ask how new forms of activism work within *and against* the dominant logics of social media.

KEY CONCEPTS

Self-branding; attention economy; the prosumer

 Access the online resources to listen to a podcast where James introduces and explores the key themes of this chapter: http://www.oup.com/he/i-peel1e.

7.1 Fitness Influencers

When the sports apparel company Gymshark went into partnership with General Atlantic, the deal valued this relatively new athleisure brand at over £1 billion (Thomas 2020). It confirmed the rapid growth of a business founded by 19-year-old Ben Francis (shown in Photo 7.1), which combined transferable skills from his unfinished business degree, sewing techniques learned from his mother, and a garage factory that he funded by working as a pizza delivery driver. The rise of Gymshark owes much to its sophisticated use of fitness influencers to establish a brand that speaks directly to a **Generation Z** demographic of online consumers. Its social media presence spans platforms like Instagram, YouTube, and TikTok, which are filled with regularly updated health and fitness content by influencers who supply their followers with workout tips, discount codes, and carb-free pancake recipes. While Gymshark did not invent this model of business that blends seamlessly with the everyday lives of young consumers, its success indicates some of the very real economic possibilities that social media entrepreneurialism has opened up.

From the outset Gymshark enthusiastically associated with fitness and lifestyle influencers to build a social media 'community' with over 12 million followers (Thornhill 2020). A sponsored 'athlete' can enjoy free clothes, paid endorsements, and lucrative

Photo 7.1. Ben Francis, founder of Gymshark. Staged photos like this have had an important role to play in the branding of Francis and his company.
Source: Andrew Fox/Alamy Stock Photo.

deals of the type normally reserved for elite sports stars. Indeed, the company has even cultivated an aspirational ethos that encourages young people to compete to become a sponsored athlete. This use of influencers in the fitness industry is both interesting and problematic. On the one hand, Gymshark athletes promote a healthy lifestyle, sharing their workout routines, fitness journeys, and nutrition advice. They encourage followers to make positive choices, believe in themselves, enjoy their bodies, and focus on well-being. In this sense, regularly updated content with a normatively appealing message—#liveyourbestlife—is a marketing dream for brands seeking endorsements or product placements. Yet, on the other hand, Gymshark is a registered business, influencers need to earn a living, and the online world has a powerful economic logic: more clicks, more likes, more money. How then should we understand the social media influencer?

7.1.1 Self-branding

Influencers occupy an emerging and hybrid position in popular culture. While they may be famous on Instagram or YouTube, it does not necessarily mean that they are household names. The Media and Technology Studies scholar Alice Marwick (2015, 140) discerns in influencers an everyday practice of micro-celebrity: 'a mind-set and a collection of self-presentation practices endemic in social media, in which users strategically formulate a profile, reach out to followers, and reveal personal information to increase attention and thus improve their online status'. So, while some influencers, such as Kim Kardashian, are celebrities in their own right, others have built up relatively large social media followings without the support of mainstream media. Influencers use a combination of techniques to enhance their brand such as staging selfies, providing regular updates on their lives, and producing emotionally charged content—from personal confessions to professional altercations with other influencers. Take, for example, the 'beef' between YouTubers KSI and Logan Paul, which ultimately led to the pair fighting in a series of amateur boxing matches streamed to millions of viewers worldwide.

 The openness of social media can be both inclusive and exclusive. Social media affords an easy way for people to engage with each other, maybe show off a little, and get some affirmation through comments and likes. Yet the visuality of branding can become instrumental, whereby micro-celebs try to boost online audiences and gain social media power. Rather than overturn the 'traditional hierarchies of fame', Marwick argues, 'the Instafamous can reinforce them by appealing to audiences using the familiar trappings of thin but buxom bodies, sports cars, and designer clothes' (2015, 157). Therefore, although anyone can become #instafamous, the social media environment can also gravitate to themes of consumerism, visual perfectionism, and a relentless self-branding imperative.

A central motif of Gymshark-sponsored athletes is that they are classically attractive and have often worked as fitness models. For example, one of their early athletes, Nikki Blackketter, was already a physique competitor who shared workout routines and eating plans. Gymshark athletes, like Lex Griffin and MattDoesFitness, are young models who either compete in bodybuilding or follow a similar regimen. While they all demonstrate healthy exercise programmes, diet plans, and lifestyles, the aspirational visual hierarchy is a common thread. As the company website states, 'If you have that look (a rippling six pack, glutes of a bikini pro, and cheek bones to die for), you have a good shot of being used as a "model" athlete' (Stafford 2017).

Beyond visuality, Gymshark athletes also seek to cultivate a digital relationship with their followers through subscriptions, likes, and responses to feedback videos. In many ways, this is standard advertising practice. Aspirational images and excitement about the 'new release' are all part of the standard repertoire of marketing. However, what is novel with social media is the centrality and intimacy of the relationship that is imagined between the influencer and their audience. It is this relationship, or 'community', that generates value for brands like Gymshark. As Marwick (2015, 141) again argues, the 'presence of an attentive audience may be the most potent status symbol of all'. Or, as the Gymshark website advises would-be influencers, 'If you focus on being consistent with your posting,

Photo 7.2. To cultivate followers, fitness influencers speak directly to their audience, creating intimacy through techniques like first-person narrative and filming in their home.
Source: samuel wordley/Alamy Stock Photo.

add real value to the people who follow you; offering informative content, and enjoy what you are doing, the value you are providing for your followers will soon come back to you as value seen by big brands that want to work with you!' (Stafford 2017).

This need to gain and retain followers can also generate pressure on individual influencers to create more value than their rivals. In the fitness industry, such competitive dynamics can lead to the promotion of ever more sensationalized clickbait. An example of this logic is the common fitness industry myth that there is 'one simple trick' to get the perfect body. For instance, the rise of fitness influencer Chloe Ting (2019) owed much to the way her 'Get Abs in 2 Weeks' YouTube video went viral and now has over 400 million views in an already crowded genre. Alternatively, MattDoesFitness performs 'eating challenges' where he films himself trying to eat 10,000 calories in a day, sometimes just from McDonald's. The same influencers will also record videos of their 'cuts', which involve reducing the number of calories consumed per day over a certain period to reduce body fat, and therefore enhance the appearance of muscle. While such techniques may work in the context of well-structured diet and exercise programmes, the diverse mix of advice can sometimes blur on social media to produce a confusing message. Indeed, by exercising in attention-grabbing ways, some fitness influencers arguably promote *unsafe* practices, such as weightlifting on a treadmill or deadlifting on a skateboard.

If aspects of the fitness influencer universe seem comical, there are nonetheless more serious questions to pose about the potential mental health effects of this unrelenting focus on visual and physical perfection (Nesi, 2020). At least part of the intimacy and aspirational ethos that influencers cultivate with their followers is built on the idea that 'we all' can achieve our health goals. But what happens when that positive message is confused by the competitive dynamics of social media? A combination of intense workouts, extreme eating, and model physiques can promote feelings of anxiety or shame that have been associated with the rise of body dysmorphia, eating disorders, and exercise addiction (Lothian-McLean 2020; Turner and Lefevre 2017). Concerned about the harmful effect of influencer peer pressure, one Gymshark athlete, Natacha Oceane (2021), gave up her sponsorship deal to focus on her own brand of science-based functional fitness. Despite the competitive dynamics of influencing, then, we should also remain sensitive to how social media can be a space of **critical agency**, where users break with societal norms about how they ought to look and act.

7.1.2 The attention economy

The hours spent looking at pictures, reading tweets, following exercise videos, or just scrolling through infinite timelines are part of an emerging political economy of social media that seeks to access and intensify our attention. Understood in terms of self-branding, it is possible to discern an evolving logic of influencing that occupies a special place in this **attention economy**. As argued by Susie Khamis and her co-authors, the proliferation of social media channels means that 'audiences are saturated with so much to choose from' and so 'the premium on distinctiveness and visibility grows . . . [and] an unprecedented number of communicators compete across more screens for increasingly distracted, dispersed, and privatised audiences' (Khamis et al. 2017, 359). In that sense, the everyday practice of giving attention to influencers is symptomatic of a new set of market practices that seek to cut through the saturation of multiple media channels and sell us something. In other words, influencing can be understood as a form of labour and social media as a space of work.

To think this proposition through the fitness influencer, recall that their key objective is to gain and retain followers, to build a community that can be targeted by advertisers. This requires time and unpaid effort to build a reputation for qualities like strength, health, empathy, and wellness. While this investment of time may be a fair price to pay for the potential reward of sponsorship, it is important to recognize that *influencing is not confined to influencers*. The fact that we spend more and more time online, operating within and subject to the attention economy, is also changing the nature of work in other industries. The IPE scholar Phoebe Moore (2018) argues that workers are increasingly required to build an online reputation in order to maintain status and attract further work, but that such (unpaid) reputation management can also foster pressure on workers to appear productive all the time. Think of delivery drivers who need to clear a specific number of packages per hour, or Uber drivers who try to maintain a customer satisfaction score (see also Section 8.1.2 on reputation management in the gig economy). More problematically, Moore argues, the 'logic of algorithmic reputations acquisition further penalizes non-standard workers and leads to unequal life chances. Irregular career patterns can also result from the time out of work for reproductive domestic labour, maternity leave, physical illness, and mental health issues' (Moore 2018).

The general concern here is that the everyday challenges of work faced by fitness influencers—aesthetic hierarchies, the requirement to provide free labour, the mental health effects of needing to be seen and validated—might be indicative of the growing pressure on workers in general to market themselves and maintain reputations. For example, a profession like journalism has also had to adapt to the demands of the attention economy. Think of how newspapers responded to declining print circulations with a focus on curated websites and a strategy of targeting 'big narratives' like the Donald Trump presidency in the US or the Covid-19 pandemic. In turn, some journalists have moved from investigative reporting to a form of opinionated commentating, often behaving as straight controversialists with a clear personal brand that garners attention, such as Tucker Carlson or Piers Morgan. The attention economy can therefore work to prioritize clicks over the kind of critical journalism that might hold the rich and powerful to account (Carson 2014).

More broadly, we might consider whether 'influencing' itself is becoming generalized as a norm of work in the same way that 'networking' and 'emotional intelligence' have become near essential employment criteria across a range of professions. This in turn raises some regulatory questions: should employees be paid for their social media posts if they benefit the company? Should future employers be able to request access to your online activity to assess your influencing ability? And should influencers, many of whom are under 18 years old, be protected by labour rights and employment law?

7.1.3 The prosumer subject

The argument so far in Sections 7.1.1 and 7.1.2 has been that, while the internet may sometimes seem like an open space of freedom and enjoyment, social media can distort such ideals through reputational imperatives that foster a generalized sense of competition for attention. Basic norms of health are rendered according to an aspirational aesthetic, mixed messages prevail, and we are left wondering about the mental health impacts of this new attention economy. An alternative entry point into this topic is to shift our analytical gaze from the influencer to the influenced, asking questions about the market subject at the heart of the attention economy—including you. What do *you* think about the various ways in which your attention is cultivated through social media? What forms of agency do *you* possess to question, refuse, or redirect the everyday politics of social media?

To help answer these we can draw upon the concept of the **prosumer**, a word derived from 'productive consumer', to further specify the social relations of the attention economy (Ritzer and Jurgenson 2010). One way to understand the prosumer is to consider how fast-food restaurants encourage their customers to both carry meals to the table and then dispose of the rubbish afterwards. Another example is the way IKEA encourages people to assemble their own furniture. In both cases, the consumer does a job that used to be performed by an employee, thus helping to produce the good or service being purchased. Applying this concept to social media gives us important analytical purchase on the community that Gymshark athletes seek to foster. Just as the hit TV programme *Game of Thrones* was sensitive to 'the fandom' and 'fan fiction', so fitness influencers must enter a dialogue with their followers in order to understand the content they may desire in the future. On this view, the prosumer is not only consuming the product but also (enthusiastically) creating it. As Detlev Zwick and his co-authors argue, 'the ideological recruitment of consumers into productive co-creation relationships hinges on accommodating consumers' needs for recognition, freedom, and agency' (Zwick et al. 2008, 185).

In the wider world of big tech, this idea of the prosumer is at the heart of the business model, be it for US-based companies like Facebook, Apple, Amazon, Netflix, and

Google (the FAANGs) or China-based Baidu, Alibaba, and Tencent (the BATs). Enthusiastic customers make branded products a part of their everyday lives by using and relating to them, typically encouraged by the companies themselves. Think of advertising campaigns like 'I'm a Mac', or memes like 'Netflix and chill'. The word Google has even slipped into the vernacular as a verb: *to search.* Prosumers have thus become particularly important to new social media ventures. Both Instagram and TikTok were able to garner extremely large early investments, even though they effectively operated at a loss, due to the expectation of future profitability based on the active attention of their users.

How should we understand the prosumer? On the one hand, a critical view might argue that social media prosumers are simply the unpaid value creators for big tech corporations, pointing to issues of exploitation and alienation (Rey 2012). On the other hand, a more optimistic account might suggest that prosumer needs for recognition, freedom, and agency can translate into alternative visions of online life (Chen 2015; Comor 2010). As an example of the latter position, we might consider how Gymshark has attempted to progressively update its brand image to reflect the racial diversity of society and recognize calls for body positivity, partly in response to online criticism. This at least suggests a capacity for prosumers to demand alternative, perhaps more

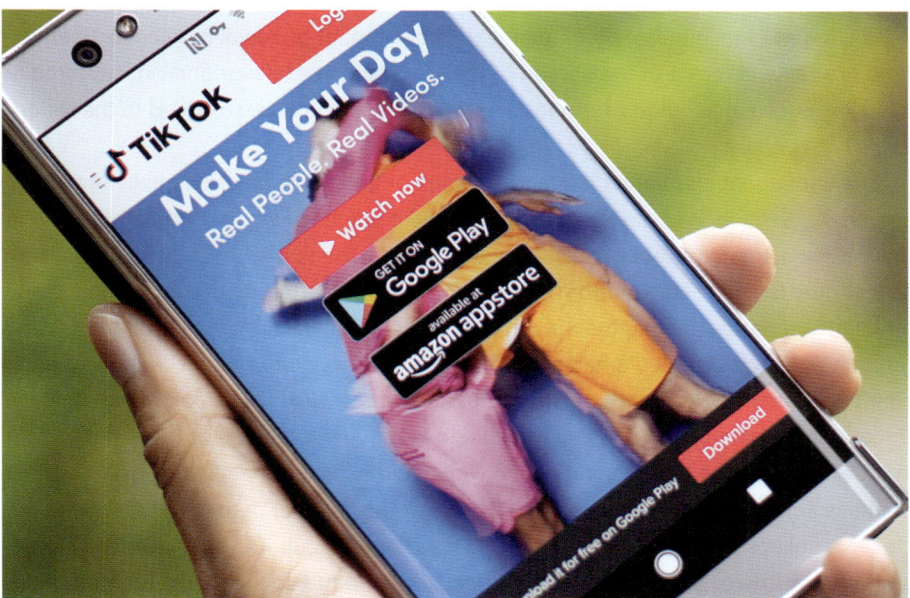

Photo 7.3. The TikTok platform, owned by Chinese company ByteDance, is based entirely on content produced by its users. In 2021 it surpassed Google as the world's most visited website.
Source: Helen Sessions/Alamy Stock Photo.

inclusive, forms of online community that brands can be responsive to. With such possibilities being open questions, Section 7.2 will explore two prevailing images of social media that circulate in popular culture—liberal and dystopian—in order to identify the potential contours of a debate on these more democratic dimensions of the attention economy.

7.2 Exploring Social Media

The rapid growth and interpenetration of different social media platforms, from social networks like Facebook and Instagram to online marketplaces like Amazon and Alibaba, have created a number of challenges for thinking about their impact on global market life. Public debates on social media have tended to focus on the more intense, emotive, and controversial implications of this emerging terrain. Key reference points have been questions of privacy, online harm, organized crime, and the damaging effects of echo chambers on democratic politics. Controversially, social media seems to have a capacity to alter the very terms of politics itself. Think of the rise of hashtag campaigns, the use of Twitter and Instagram by politicians and corporations, or even the generation and popularization of conspiracy theories on forums like Reddit and 4chan. Indeed, in a number of states the political impact of social media has been figured precisely in terms of the spread of disinformation or false reporting, captured in the widely used, if nebulous, term **fake news**, which has now been added to the *Oxford English Dictionary*.

The contingent and unpredictable dynamics of social media are a challenge for research. As Section 7.1.2 suggested, social media practices are evolving rapidly within the attention economy, but precisely because of this the task of political analysis is an urgent one. Social media platforms can seriously impact the reputation of politicians and state leaders, affecting the outcome of democratic elections and referenda. More fundamentally, social media has arguably become a space of politics in its own right, where the nature and form of online interactions foster new forms of political agency. Understanding the politics of social media thus requires a degree of self-examination in order to recognize how we participate within and critically enact its logics. In a study of online activism, Jonathan Dean (2018, 255) argues that 'for many politically engaged citizens, politics is enacted in and through visual media cultures such as gifs, memes and other forms of shareable visual content'. Just as the social media prosumer can co-create value for brands, they can also shape the content of politics by sharing a meme or making a funny video (see Section 9.3.1 on memes in political discourse).

This contingency of social media and politics should also prompt us to reflect on the kinds of methods we employ to understand it. What types of information or empirical data do we use to study social media? Should we collect tweets, or count likes perhaps? Do we also need to consider the meaning of such things? A growing body of work in IPE has sought to answer these types of question by looking to the role of cultural artefacts (Best and Paterson 2010). The nuances of representation, whether in films, advertisements, or even memes, can tell us a great deal about how particular market relations are legitimized and contested (Brassett 2018). To this end, in Sections 7.2.1 and 7.2.2 we will look at two popular documentaries distributed by Netflix: *Fyre: The Greatest Party That Never Happened* (2019) and *The Social Dilemma* (2020). These films are interesting because they each make a claim to know the reality of social media by centring their narratives on a moral critique. While the first promotes the regulation of social media to make it function better, the second is more concerned with the structural effects of social media, questioning how attention is commodified as data about the consumer. Along the way, they also make certain claims about the role of influencers, the desirability of the attention economy, and, most crucially, the political agency of the prosumer subject.

7.2.1 How should social media be regulated?

Fyre is a documentary film that tells the story of how a group of entrepreneurs, app developers, social media marketing companies, and figurehead American rapper Ja Rule combined to build a social media sensation. Led by the charismatic and ambitious entrepreneur Billy McFarland (shown alongside Ja Rule in Photo 7.4), they aimed to host a luxury music festival on a remote island previously owned by notorious Colombian criminal and drug lord Pablo Escobar. Indeed, they frequently use Escobar's name in the marketing of the festival to create intrigue. Their target audience was a new breed of wealthy millennials seeking high-end, Instagrammable 'experiences'. The documentary recounts how they use a sophisticated and expensive strategy of social media influencers to make some 'noise', flying top models like Bella Hadid and Emily Ratajkowski to the Bahamas to record an idyllic promotional film with beach parties, jet skis, and cute pigs that swim in the sea. In coordinated fashion, over 200 influencers then promoted the film on their social media accounts and announced their intention to attend the festival, which would include performances from musicians like Major Lazer and Skepta, and where you could enjoy staying in a luxury yurt, a beach cabin, or even a yacht. In this way, the organizers appear to replicate the standard business models of the attention economy, using famous influencers to entice their community of followers to want to be part of the Fyre Festival.

As an exercise in manipulating the attention economy the promotion scored highly, selling 95 per cent of tickets on the first day. By using so many high-profile influencers, the festival organizers could tap into a pre-existing body of prosumers who resonated

Photo 7.4. Ja Rule (left) and Billy McFarland (right) having fun promoting their festival.
Source: Everett Collection Inc/Alamy Stock Photo.

with the aspirational image of a luxury festival. However, as a practical logistical operation, *Fyre* goes into excruciating detail about how badly organized the resulting project was. Billy McFarland loses the lease on the island because they (illegally) use Escobar's name to promote the festival. Many of the acts are not paid, or even signed up. When the organizers eventually find a replacement island, most of the accommodation is already booked, so they end up using a fleet of hurricane-relief tents. Most problematically, and despite all the difficulties experienced in organizing the festival, they fail to cancel anything and let thousands of ticket holders fly out to what looks more like a disaster zone. The epic failure of Fyre Festival then went viral, receiving more posts, likes, and retweets than the original slick marketing. As shown in Photo 7.5, one attendee exposed this gulf between expectations and reality by contrasting the luxury cuisine he initially paid for with the disappointing cheese sandwich he received on arrival.

The overriding implication of the documentary is that social media is somewhat chaotic and that the immediate political concern is *regulation*. The narrative focuses on the legal aspects of the festival, about whether Billy McFarland was engaged in fraud (which the film argues he was), and about whether influencers should disclose if they are paid to advertise something, as they are now increasingly required to. On this view, any issues identified by *Fyre* are deemed to be correctable or salvageable with appropriate market regulation. In this way, the documentary arguably provides an example of Antonio Gramsci's common sense discussed in Section 1.2 of the Introduction, whereby the apparently critical tone of the documentary gives way to a liberal

Photo 7.5. Promised luxury treatment and unforgettable experiences, festival-goers had to make do with other photos to share on social media.
Source: Everett Collection Inc./Alamy Stock Photo.

belief in the correctability of markets, or what the neo-Gramscian IPE scholar Robert Cox (1993, 5) might describe as 'the common sense of the epoch'. This is the idea that if markets go wrong, it must be due to some issue or defect with the individual agents involved. McFarland is portrayed as problematic, greedy, and arrogant in a manner that echoes the plethora of documentaries about the global financial crisis that blamed the 'hyper-masculine' bankers for taking on excessive risk (Hozic and True, 2016). It is the player not the game that ends up with the blame. The simple answer thus provided is that social media entrepreneurs and their influencers ought to be subject to sober and standardized regulatory frameworks.

Yet *Fyre* also carries a deeper set of reflections on the nature of these new economies of social media. The moral arc of the film is intimately bound up with the lived experiences of the festival attendees—the prosumers. It describes how they buy into the idea of the festival, *actively liking* the idea and the image, following the influencers, and emulating their brands. Obviously, they had to pay for the ticket, but ticket holders were also encouraged to promote the festival on social media, often behaving like influencers themselves. As the festival drew closer, ticket holders were even required to put their money onto the Fyre Festival 'card', so they could enjoy a 'cashless experience' in what turned out to be their disaster-relief tent. Much like the fitness community discussed in Section 7.1, these prosumers were encouraged to co-create the idea of the festival, shaping themselves and their social media lives to embody and promote it.

While the prosumers of Fyre were ultimately duped, the moral lessons of their experiences were subsequently valorized and channelled in the documentary. What initially seems like an entertaining story of the excess of the attention economy—a joke at the expense of naïve ticket purchasers—ultimately becomes, within the film, a critical message about their potential agency. When the festival fell apart, the anger of these disaffected prosumers was turned into social media rage at the organizers that ultimately drew widespread scrutiny and condemnation of this business model. On this view, *Fyre* suggests that prosumers may even restore some of the democratic possibilities of social media by illustrating how online outrage can sometimes redeem these new economies of social media. From the Gramscian perspective, however, we see things differently. Ethical agency in these disaffected prosumers appears less as a source of redemption than one of legitimation, upholding the larger common sense that pervades popular culture: that markets can be made to work if only we protect the consumer from the few bad apples.

7.2.2 Do we work for social media?

An altogether more dystopian account of social media is explored in the Netflix film *The Social Dilemma*, which portrays the relationship between the prosumer and big tech corporations in terms of commodification. Drawing on interviews with former executives and programmers at companies like Google, Facebook, and Twitter, the documentary addresses the implications of allowing social media companies to access and record personal data. Here the attention economy is not presented as a liberal space of self-expression and interaction but as a digital infrastructure for collecting information. Social media prosumers are figured in banal terms as the basic units of data collection and aggregation: Amazon sells cheap stuff in order to find out what other kinds of things we are interested in; Google records search histories so it can sell advertising space on a bespoke basis; and Netflix itself records data about the documentaries you watch, so it can find out what to recommend next. While these functions might seem like part of a strategy to improve the consumer experience, *The Social Dilemma* suggests that there is more to this than meets the eye. Indeed, rather than engaging consumers as producers, as the prosumer concept has it, the real aim might be to turn aspects of consumers into commodities. Or as one of the film's interviewees put it, 'if you are not paying for the product, then you are the product!'

The documentary seeks credibility by drawing on the inside knowledge of people who have worked in the industry. It begins with a former ethical designer at Google who asks a basic question: 'what are the social effects of social media?' He recounts how at one point he did have serious concerns about the problem of

Photo 7.6. In *The Social Dilemma*, a fictional family experiences how echo chambers can lead to isolation and political radicalization, its dystopian aesthetic contrasting with the excesses shown in *Fyre*.
Source: Lifestyle Pictures/Alamy Stock Photo.

addiction to social media but recalls how his actual daily work was more focused on designing email backdrops that had nice colours. A former director of monetization at Facebook recalls how the strategic goal was to emulate Google: to combine a programme that draws millions of people with a system for generating massive profits off the back of it. Indeed, the tone of the film echoes a period of big tech soul-searching that even saw the first President of Facebook, Sean Parker, question the ethics of manipulating attention through social media. In one candid interview he recounted how the technology that runs social media is designed to give users a regular dopamine hit from social validation, inducing a temporary feeling of well-being. In his words, this exploits 'a vulnerability in human psychology' which 'changes your relationship with society, with each other . . . It probably interferes with productivity in weird ways. God only knows what it does to our children's brains' (cited in Solon, 2017). As the computer scientist Jaron Lanier elaborates in the film, it is 'the gradual, slight, imperceptible change in your own behaviour and perception that is the product'.

This narrative thus tells a story of how social media has developed via a series of experiments to see what drives and intensifies user engagement, with insufficient concern for the adverse consequences. For example, the documentary dramatizes how, if you're tagged in a social media photo, you are likely to experience heightened emotions, which may be a good time to show you an advert. Equally, if a social media network alerts you that a friend is online, then you are more likely to engage, and if you comment on their photo or status, then they are also more likely to reply. The subtle trick here—*the imperceptible change in the everyday*—is that messaging technology

Photo 7.7. Think about how you feel when you see the pulsating dots of a chat. Do you not wonder what someone might say and how you might reply?
Source: DCPhoto/Alamy Stock Photo.

now uses a special series of pulsating dots to inform you that the other person is currently typing something. The film describes how social media companies discovered these dots make you more likely to wait in order to see the reply. This is a conditioned response. When applied across the global network, even small changes like using dots to signal someone is typing can increase levels of engagement by orders of magnitude. These and other alerts are now a common technology across messaging apps and social networks, encouraging usage from the moment we wake to the moment we fall asleep.

Drawing these points together, the documentary implies that, far from being engaged in a happy experience of co-creation, the prosumer subject is far more docile. Complex algorithms enable social media companies to use data about what you look at and for how long to garner insights on your past *and future* behaviours. The academic consultant for the documentary, social psychologist Shoshana Zuboff, has argued in her own work that the practices of tech companies have produced a new form of power she calls **surveillance capitalism**. This claims human experience online as free raw material for translation into behavioural data, fabricated into 'prediction products' that anticipate your actions and can be sold not just to advertisers but health insurers, political parties, security services, and more. Enabled by technologies that can both monitor and intensify our engagements, surveillance capitalism presents itself as a structure that exploits the agency of the prosumer as mere engagement (Zuboff 2019).

From the point of view of *The Social Dilemma*, then, the apparent freedoms of social media have come at a massive social cost. Platforms like Facebook and TikTok are free and fun precisely because that maximizes prosumer uptake and attention. Once there, smart algorithms harness behavioural insights to intensify our engagement to yield the most profitable combination of advertising space and personal data about what we are likely to buy, vote, say, and do. Rejecting the redemptive possibilities of social media, the documentary suggests an altogether more critical image of the prosumer as a dupe whose every engagement, active or passive, carries value in the form of 'behavioural surplus' for surveillance capitalism. It is an argument echoed by the artist Laurel Ptak in her project *Wages for Facebook*. Reworking the manifesto statement of Silvia Federici's 1975 pamphlet *Wages for Housework* (see Section 1.2.2), Ptak pointed out the parallel ways in which unpaid labour had been subsumed into capitalism via social media:

> They say it's friendship. We say it's unwaged work.
>
> With every like, chat, tag or poke our subjectivity turns them a profit.
>
> They call it sharing. We call it stealing.
>
> We've been bound by their terms of service far too long – it's time for our terms.
> (Ptak, 2014)

7.2.3 Can the prosumer be transformative?

Cultural narratives of social media relayed by the two Netflix documentaries discussed in Sections 7.2.1 and 7.2.2 centre on new and productive qualities in the prosumer subject. We learn that the normalization of everyday brand engagements through social media can inform the nature and magnitude of economic value, whereby consumer awareness has begun to proxy for the (future) profitability of brands. Yet, more problematically, rapid changes in social media technology have allowed for the generation and sale of vast amounts of personal data, creating new sources of value in the global economy and nurturing new kinds of selfhood dependent on likes and followers.

While *Fyre* tries to unpack the politics of social media through questions of legality and regulation, *The Social Dilemma* highlights the power relations that pervade surveillance capitalism. Both insights lead to important questions about regulating social media through disclosures regarding advertising, or more effective taxation of its revenue and profits. Yet the documentaries also point to other forms of resistance that seek to improve the more problematic logics of social media. For instance, *The Social Dilemma* raises the question of diversity, when a small number of young white men in California design the code for global social media companies that have become the most profitable in history. This could point to the need for more inclusive employment structures within social media, or for interrogation of the kinds of social norms that are presented via the algorithms that structure social media (Noble 2018).

Whilst the two documentaries offer contrasting accounts of, and prescriptions for, the politics of social media, we should remember that there are perspectives beyond the liberal and dystopian dichotomy. One way of engaging these is to reconsider the potential of the prosumer subject. The sociologist Katherine Chen (2015, 451) argues that the prosumer 'also offers transformational potential by enabling meaning-making and agentic action'. She takes the example of 3D printing that has been deployed by prosumers to design and produce new and more personalized products. In the US, children with amputated limbs have been able to design and personalize their own prosthetics, whereas previously they would have had to use basic hooks or claws until they were old enough for more common adult sizes (Chen 2015, 451). For Chen this kind of creative spirit can be adapted and magnified via social media, where blogs and networks are used to spread the word about new initiatives and practices:

> Using Kickstarter, GoFundMe, and other fund-raising venues, they can test interest in their projects and secure advance orders. Prosumers can support projects of their choice by fronting funds through advance orders or underwriting project costs. For example, when artist Nickolay Lamm generated images comparing the proportions of Barbie with a hypothetical doll based on average teen measurements, he received requests to manufacture the doll from doll collectors and parents. After prosumers made more than 13,000 advance orders, he produced the Lammily doll and outfits. In addition, a customization kit allows prosumers to personalize their dolls by affixing glasses, freckles, scars, stretch marks, and even pimples.
> (Chen 2015, 452)

Following Chen's line of thinking, then, the prosumer can be disruptive of established political economy norms and hierarchies, opening the door to new, perhaps more inclusive, social relations. Consequently, social media is understood less as a marketplace in need of regulation, or as a dominant structure that manipulates docile subjects, and more as a productive space of emergence and becoming.

The **prefigurative** quality of prosumers, in which they become an early indication or version of new ways of being, can be seen in the adoption of new technologies in daily life. For example, the increasing availability of **blockchain** technologies make it possible to keep large digital transaction registers anonymous and decentralized. Decentralized networks offer the possibility of full privacy for users, and greater autonomy and choice over how user data is used. Indeed, some companies have reversed the line of surveillance identified by *The Social Dilemma* by using blockchain technology to invite ethical scrutiny of retail products by prosumers. One company that does this is Provenance, which aims to improve the transparency of supply chains by allowing its users to access and verify information with their smartphones, finding out things like where and under what conditions a can of tuna was produced. This plays into the logic of the prosumer by allowing different businesses to showcase the values that make their products unique. While the prosumer is still working, the aim is to use technology to apply user-based ethics to build alternative sources of knowledge about the supply chain that other users can access.

It is an idea that has also inspired Fairphone, an enterprise that aims to build a movement for fairer electronics by presenting every step of the production line on its website, including those normally hidden from view like the mining of minerals, selection of manufacturing partners, and distribution of profits. Apart from promoting a controlled 'ethical' value chain, Fairphone presents smartphones as storytelling devices with the potential to uncover how products are made. Both Provenance and Fairphone advertise their technology as empowering, because it allows prosumers to monitor the enforcement of social standards (Kremers and Brassett 2017; see also Section 2.3.1 on the possibilities of ethical supply chains for clothes).

To return to Chen's position, she concludes that prosumption 'can enhance conceptions of individual and collective agency by challenging the status quo with prefigurative actions' (Chen 2015, 454). While she has in mind the kinds of alternative media and sites of politicization prefigured by movements like Occupy and the artistic and satirical resistances of the Burning Man festival and Billionaires for Bush (see also Section 9.1.1 on humour), such potentialities are also present, and arguably magnified, on social media. Think of the proliferation of critical blogs, collective movements born of hashtags, or the meme-ification of nearly every aspect of modern life. While this chapter began with a discussion of influencers, therefore, the prefigurative possibilities of the prosumer suggest that political agency within social media is in a process of emergence. Is it possible to think about the student as a prosumer? Can you co-create your education or prefigure it through creative actions, as indicated in Photo 7.8?

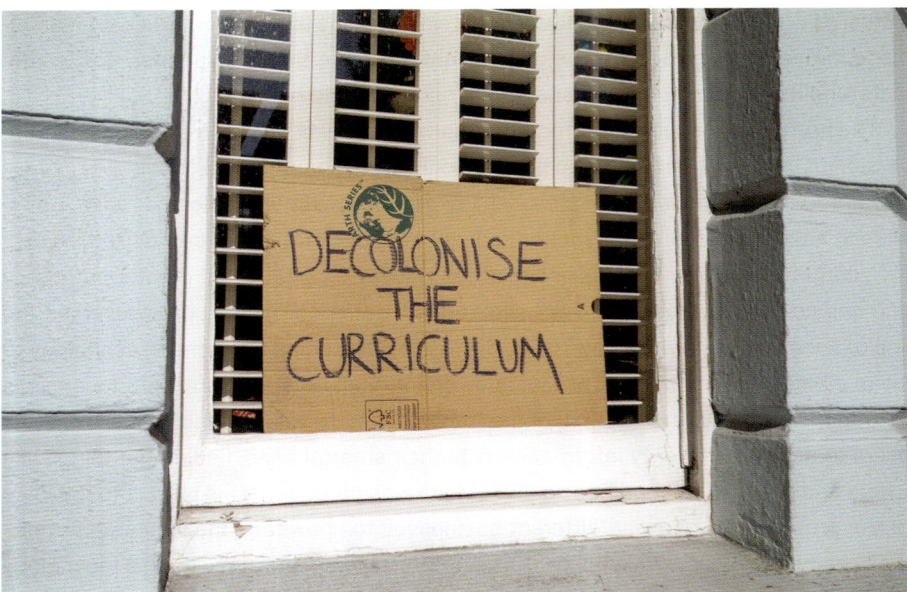

Photo 7.8. Movements led by students of colour like Rhodes Must Fall and Decolonize the Curriculum, each with their corresponding hashtags, have actively contested ideas of established knowledge, or the canon, and how it is produced within universities (see Pimblott 2020).
Source: Moonstone Images.

7.3 Engaging Social Media

7.3.1 Deliberating resistance on/to social media

The activities in this section are designed to stimulate reflection on the different forms that social media can take and the kind of social media subjects—like influencers and prosumers—to which these give rise. Following on from the discussion about the prefigurative possibilities of the prosumer, we begin by looking at the ways in which political resistance is practised on social media, and to some extent toward it. An important dimension of this is how the speed of communication afforded by twenty-four-hour news and social media has meant that critical ideas can 'go viral' within and between publics across the world. The #MeToo movement is a powerful demonstration of how a collective and resistant subjectivity can flourish on social media. By placing the daily violence of sexual harassment in the media and entertainment industries on the news agenda, a credible moment of action was initiated. The hashtag #MeToo gave a platform to people beyond the Hollywood circle to identify abuse in their workplaces and reveal the pervasiveness—or 'everydayness'—of sexism in the economy.

Social media activism can perhaps be understood in line with James C. Scott's (1985) notion of everyday resistance. This holds out the possibility that small everyday forms of dissent or refusal, foot-dragging or sarcasm, or in this case tweets and hashtags, can transform into public campaigns for change. Indeed, Scott argued that we should make such everyday resistances into a habit, one which cultivates an anarchist spirit able to challenge illegitimate authority. Hashtag campaigns can on this basis be understood as both a part of the rhythm and spectacle of the attention economy *and* the potential basis of broad-scale public resistance. For example, although the Black Lives Matter (BLM) movement was founded in 2013, a confluence of social media activism in 2020 meant that the movement rose to global prominence in response to a singular moment of social media outrage at the killing of George Floyd by police. In a rapidly evolving milieu, a number of small everyday resistances came together to inspire a large public movement of global protest. From the posting of a black square by prominent music artists which became #BlackoutTuesday to the circulation of images of American footballer Colin Kaepernick kneeling down during the playing of the US national anthem before games to protest against police violence, the social media form of BLM galvanized public consciousness about everyday racial hierarchies across the globe (see Photo 7.9).

In this way social media resistance was instrumental in fostering a widespread public mood swing to rethink the intersectional politics of everyday life. This also led to

Photo 7.9. A woman holding a placard which means 'Who will be the next? #BLM' during a protest over the death of George Floyd held in Dakar, Senegal, 2020.
Source: Xinhua/Alamy Stock Photo.

changes in how social media itself operated. Companies like Instagram and Facebook moved to change the racial dimensions of their algorithms to try and ensure that Black voices are not suppressed and white voices amplified. There was also widespread endorsement of the importance of the 'Black dollar', whereby platforms actively promoted Black entrepreneurs and creators. Yet whilst it is important that large multinational corporations begin to take intersectional politics seriously, we should not ignore the instrumental dimensions of such rebranding exercises. There is a clear ambiguity in 'corporate activism', which is that it plays upon the common sense of redeemable markets that we contemplated in Section 7.2.1. In the midst of social media outrage, there are heightened levels of prosumer engagement, data is generated, and marketing can be done. For example, companies like Nike invested heavily in associating their brand with the emancipatory politics of 'taking the knee' by featuring Colin Kaepernick in an ad campaign.

A critical IPE perspective that can help to frame these dilemmas is Gramsci's idea of **trasformismo**, which describes how the dominant classes in society try to co-opt forces of resistance. As Robert Cox (1983, 166–7) surmises, '*trasformismo* can serve as a strategy of assimilating and domesticating potentially dangerous ideas by adjusting them to the policies of the dominant coalition'. A good example is the way a previously oppositional and marginal discourse on environmentalism has become a key tenet of mainstream global public policy through ideas like sustainable development. In this vein, several companies that identified with the intersectional politics of BLM were less than proactive in engaging the hierarchies of social difference that pervade their own global supply chains. For example, at the same time as Apple was requiring developers to remove terms such as 'Master/Slave' and 'Blacklist' from its coding platforms, it was reported that the company was also lobbying against a bill that would hold US companies accountable for using Uighur Muslim forced labour in China (Swanson 2020). Does this then play to the logic of surveillance capitalism? Global waves of affective engagement associated with BLM, virtue signalling by corporations keen to gain your attention, or outpourings of anger associated with Donald Trump's presidency ultimately yield more clicks, likes, and retweets. Outrage fosters engagement. The rise of social media resistance may even help to feed the algorithms with fine-grained data about *our dislikes* for future modellers of consumption or voting behaviour.

The purpose of this activity is to **deliberate** whether social media is a useful and viable space for political resistance. Deliberate here has a specific meaning, referring to the need to consider the opinions of others and carefully work through these to reach a reasoned conclusion, which might be different to what you thought at the start. As such, this exercise works best as a group activity, ideally with four–five people to ensure a range of contributions. To help foster deliberation, we outline a series of open-ended discussion points below. You can consider resistance in the specific terms of a particular movement, such as BLM, but should also draw from your own social media engagements, perhaps where you have shared a meme or contributed to a hashtag that showed support for a political movement. In this chapter, we have mainly considered how social media can be a space of everyday resistance, or how imaginative acts of prosumption might prefigure alternative forms of social media that are less dependent on the logics of surveillance capitalism. Perhaps as a final discussion point then, consider whether there is an argument to simply switch off social media.

- Does social media facilitate broadscale and fast-moving resistance by enabling network connections?
- Does the logic of surveillance capitalism mean that such connections are rendered as mere data to be recorded for advertising purposes, stripped of their moral and political force?
- Does it matter if global corporations are using intersectional politics partly as a marketing device: is that a bad thing or something that can be built upon?
- Does resistance always have to build to a large global movement to be considered successful?
- Does refusing social media offer an alternative politics of resistance?

7.3.2 Documentary film review poster

As discussed in Section 1.1.1 in the Introduction, films and TV shows have been part of the popular culture brought into scholarly research on everyday IPE. In this activity we want to build on the exploration of the Netflix documentaries in Sections 7.2.1 and 7.2.2 to show how these can also be used in student learning. As IPE scholar Juliette Schwak (2020) argues, one of the distinct advantages of using films as a basis for teaching is that they highlight questions of structure and agency, portraying individual characters and revealing their ambitions, motives, and scope for action. This resonates with a theme of this chapter, which has been to show how the politics of social media are contingent and emergent, suffused with agential potential.

A number of academics have examined how **documentary films** about globalization can make complex systems of political economy intelligible to wider publics (Brassett and Smith 2010; De Goede 2015; Richardson-Ngwenya and Richardson 2013; Schwak 2020). By making a claim to document the 'reality' of global markets, often critically and with a moral purpose, such films arguably move beyond mere representation to play a role in the social construction of political economy (Clarke and Brassett 2015).

As Rob Aitken (2010, 86) argues, 'economic spaces and practices are not given, nor do they exist in some manner prior to their representations, but are, rather, historically shifting practices brought into being by the representations that are said only to be their effects'. On this view, the way we discuss, represent, or otherwise 'know' emergent political economies like social media can be an important route into understanding their politics and potentialities. For example, as we showed in Section 7.2, the Netflix documentaries still rely on subjective perspectives and narratives to tell a certain story about their subject matter.

Begin this exercise by reading back over the opening of Section 7.2 and reflect on what it means to think about documentary film as a 'claim to the real'. Do such films merely document 'what is there'? Or do documentaries provide an interpretation of reality? What is the nature of that interpretation? Is it moral and ethical, or dystopian and tragic? Other aesthetics might include satire, drama, or romance. Does it point towards or inspire a course of action? Or is it meant to be 'consumed' and forgotten?

Having reflected on these questions, we would ask you to select two or three documentaries on the same subject. You may like to watch the documentaries discussed in this chapter, *Fyre* and *The Social Dilemma*; an interesting third film on social media could be *The Great Hack*. But we would also encourage you to think about this as a method for exploring other areas of IPE, perhaps rerunning this exercise as a primer for reading one of the other chapters in this book. We are living through a period of prolific documentary filming on subjects including finance, trade, food, fashion, and work, to name but a few (see the Resources section at the end of each chapter for further examples).

The task is to present your analysis on a poster, which is better suited to displaying the visual dimension of the material studied, highlighting the key elements of each documentary for comparison. Below are some tips on how to do this:

- Try to reflect on what each film is arguing and what techniques it uses to present the narrative.
- You can use stills from the film to emphasize the fundamental point, such as the images of Billy McFarland having fun at the island beach party.
- You might enlarge the font size of an important quote, such as: 'If you're not paying for the product, you are the product' (*The Social Dilemma*, 2020).
- While aspects of the documentary may rely on sensation or humour, try to work out some basic questions of ontology. What is the nature of the market that is represented? Is it natural and benign, or riven with interests and power? Who are the key market subjects, i.e. consumers, producers, workers? What agency (if any) do they have?

- How does the central narrative understand the nature of politics? Is it about institutions, democracy, and legal process, or do power and accumulation drive things?

- Consider the production and circulation of these films within the very popular cultural circuits they claim to critique. For example, *The Social Dilemma* is a critique of social media that promoted itself via social media. What does it say about the attention economy that it even has a space for critiques of itself? Is the wide availability of documentaries that are critical of globalization on streaming services like Netflix and Amazon a sign that we are in a critical phase of prosumer capitalism? Or is this another manoeuvre within surveillance capitalism that collects data on prosumers, indeed one that this textbook is contingently supporting?

- Finally, would a transformative prosumer stop at this analysis of documentaries, or could you imagine making your own short films to distribute via social media or amongst your class?

7.4 Conclusion

This chapter has explored the everyday political economy of social media via the related concepts of self-branding, the attention economy, and the prosumer. It argued that the way we understand the concept of the prosumer has large implications for whether we conceive of social media and the wider liberal market economy as free and democratic. The politics of social media was then explored via a critical analysis of two popular documentaries distributed by Netflix. While each film portrayed a moral critique of social media and argued for the need for regulation, the chapter questioned whether such critiques relay a particular 'common sense' of liberal capitalism—that markets are ultimately self-correcting and can be redeemed through regulation. More critically, it was suggested that an idea like surveillance capitalism prompts us to think about the changes to prosumer agency that are written into the technological devices that structure social media. Finally, the chapter invited you to engage the politics of social media in terms of your own experiences of social media resistance and by reading documentaries as a method for understanding IPE.

Access the online resources for quizzes, student reflection podcasts, and support for tackling the chapter's learning activities: http://www.oup.com/he/i-peel1e.

RESOURCES

Tile recommendations from the I-PEEL website: 'tracking' (Phoebe Moore) http://i-peel.org/homepage/tracking/; 'web search' (Malcolm Campbell-Verduyn) http://i-peel.org/homepage/web-search/.

Black Mirror. 2011–19. TV series. Created by Charlie Brooker, this series provides a dramatized dystopian commentary on the everyday impact of new technologies on our lives. The 'Black Mirror' in the title of the series refers to the ubiquitous black screens of phones, tablets, televisions, and computer monitors that have permeated our homes. Certain episodes deal directly with the impact of social media. See 'Nosedive' (Season 3, 2016), 'Hated in the Nation' (Season 3, 2016), and 'The Entire History of You' (Season 1, 2011).

Chen, Katherine. 2015. 'Prosumption: From Parasitic to Prefigurative'. *Sociological Quarterly* 56(3): 446–59. This article provides an entertaining and often inspiring analysis that neatly surveys the various debates on the prosumer subject.

Langley, Paul, and Andrew Leyshon. 2017. 'Platform Capitalism: The Intermediation and Capitalization of Digital Economic Circulation'. *Finance and Society* 3(1): 11–31. An influential survey of the emerging debates on the political economy of online platforms, which touches on social media while linking to wider themes explored in Chapters 4 and 8 (Debt and Share).

Lanier, Jaron. 2018. *Ten Arguments for Deleting Your Social Media Accounts Right Now*. London: Vintage. A short and pithy book that provides important insights (and balance) on where and why social media might be failing the users.

Noble, Safia. 2018. *Algorithms of Oppression*. New York: New York University Press. A powerful and insightful piece of research on the legibility of race and gender on Google.

Schwak, Juliette. 2020. 'Film in an IPE Classroom: For a Critical Pedagogy of the Everyday', *Review of International Political Economy* 27(6): 1330–53. Makes the case for using films to reveal the mundane and the unseen of IPE, as well as move beyond Western-centred representations of the economy via films located in other places.

REFERENCES

Aitken, Rob. 2010. '"To the Ends of the Earth": Culture, Visuality, and the Embedded Economy'. In *Cultural Political Economy*, ed. Jacqueline Best and Matthew Paterson, 67–90. New York: Routledge.

Best, Jacqueline, and Matthew Paterson, eds. 2010. *Cultural Political Economy*. Abingdon and New York: Routledge.

Brassett, James. 2018. *Affective Politics of the Global Event: Trauma and the Resilient Market Subject*. Abingdon and New York: Routledge.

Brassett, James, and William Smith. 2010. 'Deliberation and Global Civil Society: Agency, Arena, Affect'. *Review of International Studies* 36(2): 413–30.

Carson, Andrea. 2014. 'The Political Economy of Print Media and the Decline of Corporate Investigative Journalism in Australia'. *Australian Journal of Political Science* 49(4): 726–42.

Chen, Katherine. 2015. 'Prosumption: From Parasitic to Prefigurative'. *Sociological Quarterly* 56(3): 446–59.

Clarke, Chris, and James Brassett. 2015. 'Popular Documentaries About the Global Financial Crisis'. In *Documenting World Politics: A Critical Companion to IR and Non-Fiction Film*, ed. Rens Van Munster and Casper Sylvest. Abingdon and New York: Routledge.

Comor, Edward. 2010. 'Digital Prosumption and Alienation'. *Ephemera: Theory and Politics in Organization* 10(3): 439–54.

Cox, Robert. 1983. 'Gramsci, Hegemony and International Relations: An Essay on Method'. *Millennium: Journal of International Studies* 12(2): 162–75.

Cox, Robert. 1993. 'Critical Political Economy'. Lecture given to the United Nations University conference on Emerging Trends in Political Economy and International Relations Theory, Oslo, Norway.

Dean, Jonathan. 2018. 'Sorted for Memes and Gifs: Visual Media and Everyday Digital Politics'. *Political Studies Review* 17(3): 255–66.

De Goede, Marieke. 2015. 'Documenting Financial Assemblages and the Visualization of Responsibility'. In *Documenting World Politics: A Critical Companion to IR and Non-fiction Film*, ed. Rens Van Munster and Casper Sylvest. Abingdon and New York: Routledge.

Hozić, Aida A., and Jacqui True. 2016. *Scandalous Economics: Gender and the Politics of Financial Crises*. Oxford Studies in Gender and International Relations. New York: Oxford University Press.

Khamis, Susie, Lawrence Ang, and Raymond Welling. 2017. 'Self-Branding, "Micro-Celebrity", and the Rise of Social Media Influencers'. *Celebrity Studies* 8(2): 191–208.

Kremers, Ruben, and James Brassett. 2017. 'Mobile Payments, Social Money: Everyday Politics of the Consumer Subject'. *New Political Economy* 22(6): 645–60.

Lothian-McLean, Moya. 2020. 'The Dangerous Downside of Fitness Addiction'. BBC News, 18 January, https://www.bbc.com/worklife/article/20200117-the-dangerous-downsides-of-a-fitness-addiction.

Marwick, Alice. 2015. '"Instafame": Luxury Selfies in the Attention Economy'. *Public Culture*, 27(1): 137–60.

Moore, Phoebe. 2018. 'Tracking', I-PEEL website, http://i-peel.org/homepage/tracking.

Nesi, Jacqueline. 2020. 'The Impact of Social Media on Youth Mental Health: Challenges and Opportunities'. *North Carolina Medical Journal* 81(2): 116–21.

Noble, Safiya. 2018. *Algorithms of Oppression*. New York: New York University Press.

Oceane, Natacha. 2021. 'Why I left Gymshark, Staying True to Myself + Toxic Coaches'. YouTube video, https://www.youtube.com/watch?v=yYdIif9rs08.

Pimblott, Kerry. 2020. 'Decolonising the University: The Origins and Meaning of a Movement'. *Political Quarterly* 91(1): 210–16.

Ptak, Laurel. 2014. *Wages for Facebook*. Blackwood Gallery, part of the exhibition FALSEWORK, September–December 2014, https://www.blackwoodgallery.ca/program/wages-for-facebook.

Rey, P. J. 2012. 'Alienation, Exploitation, and Social Media'. *American Behavioural Scientist* 56(4): 399–420.

Richardson-Ngwenya, Pamela, and Ben Richardson. 2013. 'Documentary Film and ethical Foodscapes: three takes on Caribbean Sugar'. *Cultural Geographies* 20(3): 339–56.

Ritzer, George, and Nathan Jurgenson. 2010. 'Production, Consumption, Presumption: The Nature of Capitalism in the Age of the Digital "Prosumer"'. *Journal of Consumer Culture* 10(13): 13–36.

Schwak, Juliette. 2020. 'Film in an IPE Classroom: For a Critical Pedagogy of the Everyday'. *Review of International Political Economy* 27(6): 1330–53.

Scott, James C. 1985. *Weapons of the Weak: Everyday Forms of Peasant Resistance*. New Haven: Yale University Press.

Solon, Olivia. 2017. 'Ex-Facebook president Sean Parker: site made to exploit human vulnerability', *The Guardian*, 9 November, https://www.theguardian.com/technology/2017/nov/09/facebook-sean-parker-vulnerability-brain-psychology (last accessed 9 May 2022).

Stafford, Shaun. 2017. 'How Do I Get Sponsored?' Gymshark website, https://central.gymshark.com/article/how-do-i-get-sponsored-shaun-stafford.

Swanson, Ana. 2020. 'Nike and Coca-Cola Lobby Against Xinjiang Forced Labor Bill'. *New York Times*, 29 November.

Thomas, Daniel. 2020. 'Clothing Brand Gymshark becomes UK's Newest £1bn Start-up'. *Financial Times*, 14 August.

Thornhill, John. 2020. 'The Power of Community: How Gymshark is Killing it in the Gym'. *Sifted*, 3 September, https://sifted.eu/articles/gymshark-ben-francis/#:~:text=At%20the%20start%2C%20Gymshark%20did,promote%20their%20own%20personal%20brands.

Ting, Chloe. 2019. 'Get Abs in Two Weeks – Abs Workout Challenge'. YouTube video, https://www.youtube.com/watch?v=2pLT-olgUJs.

Turner, Pixie, and Carmen Lefevre. 2017. 'Instagram Use is Linked to Increased Symptoms of Orthorexia Nervosa'. *Eating and Weight Disorders: Studies on Anorexia, Bulimia and Obesity* 22(2): 277–84.

Zuboff, Shoshana. 2019. *The Age of Surveillance Capitalism: The Fight for a Human Future at the New Frontier of Power*. London: Profile Books.

Zwick, Detlez, Samuel Bonsu, and Aron Darmody. 2008. 'Putting Consumers to Work: Co-creation and New Marketing Govern-mentality'. *Journal of Consumer Culture* 8: 163–96.

8
SHARE

8.1	Ride-Share	215
8.2	Exploring the Sharing Economy	222
8.3	Engaging the Sharing Economy	232
8.4	Conclusion	237

LEARNING OBJECTIVES

- Describe the concepts of marketization of everyday life, gig economy, and platform capitalism
- Explain different principles that can structure economic exchange including householding, reciprocity, redistribution, and the market
- Critically evaluate for-profit and not-for-profit dimensions of the sharing economy using the diverse economies framework and community mapping

READER'S GUIDE

The sharing economy is a relatively new topic of interest in IPE, having come to prominence in the wake of the 2008 global financial crisis as an alternative vision of how economic activity could be organized. However, ideas about the possibilities and pitfalls of economic sharing have long been discussed. Drawing on this tradition, the sharing economy appears less of a utopian project and more like a means to bring everyday life to global capitalism. The chapter starts with a section on 'Ride-Share' (Section 8.1). Ride-sharing is an increasingly popular means of transport that constitutes a significant sector in the for-profit sharing economy. It uses the example of the Indonesian ride-hailing company Gojek to draw out fundamental tensions between solidarity and exploitation that underpin processes of marketization in the sharing economy. The three core concepts it introduces to help make sense of the sharing economy are marketization of everyday life, the gig economy, and platform capitalism. This is followed by the section 'Exploring the Sharing Economy', which examines different forms of economic organization and their historical lineages (Section 8.2). It discusses the rapid growth of a sharing economy organized around the principle of profit maximization in the wake of the global financial crisis and austerity economics. It contrasts this type of sharing economy with more communal forms of economic organization that are oriented around the principles of solidarity and reciprocity of exchange. The final section of this chapter is 'Engaging the Sharing Economy' (Section 8.3). It asks you to identify the many actors and processes that make up your everyday economic life by using the iceberg model from the diverse economies framework. It then sets out an exercise of community mapping to allow you to delve further into identifying what connects your university community with alternative versions of the sharing economy.

KEY CONCEPTS
Marketization of everyday life; gig economy; platform capitalism

Access the online resources to listen to a podcast where Lena introduces and explores the key themes of this chapter: http://www.oup.com/he/i-peel1e.

8.1 Ride-Share

Gojek is Indonesia's first 'unicorn', a start-up company with a private valuation exceeding US$1 billion, so called because of their near-mythical status among investors. This is an extraordinary achievement, but at the same time there is nothing more ordinary, more everyday, than what Gojek does. The company started out in 2009 as a call centre, connecting customers with rides—Indonesia's famous *ojek* (motorcycle taxis)—and mail delivery couriers. In 2015, it launched the Gojek App, extending its bookable services to shopping delivery. Since then, the Gojek App has been downloaded more than 125 million times in Indonesia, leading the company to claim that '1 in 2 Have the Gojek Super App' (Gojek n.d.). Since its launch, Gojek has branched out into many areas. Its **super app** serves as an umbrella for nearly two dozen apps. These include GoMed, which provides medical services such as teleconsultation, pharmacy delivery, and hospital booking; GoPlay, a subscription-based streaming service intended to compete with the likes of Netflix; and GoPay, a cashless payment system that has become one of Indonesia's top five **e-wallet** services (*The Jakarta Post* 2019). Other financial services offered by Gojek to its customers include monthly bill payments, insurance, and even the opportunity to invest in gold.

In just over a decade Gojek has become an indispensable part of everyday life for urbanites across the Indonesian archipelago and its drivers part of the lifeblood of the city. Moreover, in the short time of its existence Gojek has become closely interwoven with the Indonesian national fabric. In 2015, a temporary ban of ride-hailing apps by the Ministry of Transport was revoked the next day following public outcry (*The Jakarta Post* 2015). In 2019, Indonesian President Joko 'Jokowi' Widodo appointed Gojek CEO and founder Nadiem Makarim as Education Minister to help ready the country's 275 million people for the digital age (Istanto 2019). Gojek has also moved into other countries, including Vietnam and Thailand, competing for regional market share with Singapore-based Grab, another Southeast Asian unicorn that grew out of the ride-sharing business. Confirming its expansionary zeal, in 2021 at the height of the Covid-19 pandemic, Gojek announced its merger with Tokopedia, an Indonesian unicorn focused on e-commerce, with plans to list their newly formed company, GoTo, on the stock markets in Indonesia and the US (Ruehl 2021).

Gojek/GoTo and Grab are but two of the many ride-sharing companies that have grown significantly since the 2000s, with US company Uber perhaps being the best known globally. They are part of an emerging economic sector that evokes 'sharing' as a normative ideal, yet is principally motivated by the search for financial profit and

Photo 8.1. Ride-share drivers waiting for customers at a Jakarta train station.
Source: Harismoyo/Alamy Stock Photo.

seeks to realize this through the incorporation of everyday life into its business models. Ultimately, what counts for the ride-share firms is not so much the number of people transported or the mobility achieved but the profitability of its market transactions. In the rest of this section we draw on the concepts of marketization of everyday life, gig economy, and platform capitalism to critically examine the sharing economy from an everyday IPE perspective.

8.1.1 Marketization of everyday life

The sharing economy gets its name because it is premised on the use of peer-to-peer mechanisms to facilitate temporary access to goods and services, matching individuals who agree to provide one another with modes of transport (Gojek, Grab, Uber), homes and garages (Airbnb, Neighbor) or skills (TaskRabbit, Fiverr). The notion of sharing also features extensively in the self-identity and marketing materials of the organizations and platforms doing the matching. But to the extent that the matches are mediated by price and paid for with money, rather than returned in kind with a favour, some see 'sharing' in this context as nothing more than a euphemism for 'selling'. For Anne Jourdain and Sidonie Noulin, the extension of commercial activity through the sharing economy has become an important driver of the 'marketization of everyday life'. They use the phrase to refer to the expansion of the market 'into areas previously not commodified' (Jourdain and Noulin 2020, 2). This is similar to the commodification of education discussed in Section 4.1.1 on student loans, albeit with a greater emphasis on the *mundane* and piecemeal nature of the objects and practices that thus become subject to market exchange.

This dynamic is also reflected in what Arun Sundararajan (2016, 17) identifies as one of the key elements of the sharing economy, namely that it 'creates markets that enable the exchange of goods and the emergence of new services' (see also the commodification of care in Section 5.1.2). Along these lines, one of the most striking things about the sharing economy is how it widens and deepens market relations into every aspect of daily life and how it makes all our lives inherently commodifiable. So, you have a spare room or a car parking space outside your house: lease it to holidaymakers! You have a couple of free hours in the evening and a bike: deliver food! You have

Photo 8.2. The sharing economy and collaborative consumption. Is this marketizing everyday life?
Source: venimo/Alamy Stock Photo.

a car or motorcycle: become a taxi service! Not using your expensive sports equipment: rent it out! In setting out to monetize anything that exhibits excess 'capacity', the sharing economy can on this view quickly blur the lines between the personal and the professional self, and between labour time and leisure time (Sundararajan 2016, 17).

Photo 8.2 illustrates how the sharing economy connects to many aspects of our everyday life, including where we live and sleep, how we get around, and where and how we work. In this respect it is typical of how the sharing economy is represented in the business community as a benign set of opportunities to lease our assets (see PwC 2015). The photo also alludes to how we connect to it through the ownership of property and transfer of use rights as mediated by apps and computers. However, looking more critically, we also see how distinctive social relations are implied: the face of the woman close to the home, versus the face of the man in close proximity to the computer workplace (see Section 5.1.1 on the gendered division of labour). We will return to these social stratifications that underpin and are reinforced by specific arrangements of the sharing economy in Section 8.2.2.

8.1.2 Gig economy

When we examine apps such as Gojek, what we find is quite removed from the presumed reciprocity of sharing a ride with a friend that the term 'ride-share' implies. This is perhaps nowhere as clear as in the precarious nature of work and struggles over labour rights in the sharing economy. The concept of the **gig economy**—according to the *Oxford English Dictionary* 'a labour market characterized by a prevalence of short-term contracts or freelance work'—has been developed to refer to the significant expansion of low-paid and insecure work, especially in the aftermath of the global financial crisis of 2008–9. A former editor of *The New Yorker*, Tina Brown, has been credited with first applying this phrase to workers who were 'transacting in a digital marketplace' (Hasija et al. 2020). The term 'gig' is derived from the name given to the short-term engagements of musicians in one-off paid performances in which they would supply both their artistic service and their instrument. Likewise, underlying ride-sharing apps we see that drivers provide a service for money and often depend on this as their main source of income (White 2018). Moreover, unlike a taxi company which often owns the cars and secures licences for its drivers, ride-hailing apps typically do not own vehicles (although California-based Uber has made significant investments in driverless cars).

Thus, in the case of Gojek the drivers provide their own motorcycle and have to buy the company's famous green helmets—one for themselves and one for their customer—and jacket, typically purchased on credit and paid off in instalments (Ford and Honan 2017). Somewhat ironically, whilst a lot of the marketing of sharing economy products and services emphasizes communal experiences, in practice it relies on a politics of individual responsibilization. Ride-share drivers are made responsible for their own business success, despite this very much depending on the underlying algorithm that matches drivers to riders and prices the journey. Drivers must not only purchase and maintain the required equipment but also carefully manage their online reputation as five-star contractors to ensure repeat custom (see also the online reputation management of social media influencers in Section 7.1.2).

Guy Standing (2014) has figured this trend as part of the fracturing of the working class and the emergence of a new **'precariat'** characterized by precarious employment and income. This is a function not just of low pay but of wider vulnerabilities generated by processes of marketization, including the demise of community benefits in countries experiencing the rapid growth of market society. Much of the sharing economy consists precisely of these forms of labour, which some see as undermining centuries-old struggles for worker rights. In this sense, different manifestations of the sharing economy can also be seen as the outcome of struggles between **libertarian values** that celebrate the free market and communal values that emphasize solidarity. Moreover, the trend towards casualization is not just restricted to so-called 'low-skilled' work. For example, in the UK higher education sector, **casualization** has continued apace, with a growing share of the academic workforce being employed on fixed-term and zero-hours contracts (Megoran and Mason 2020). At the same time, there are also a significant number of students engaging in this sort of work to pay for their studies. For instance, one study conducted in the US suggests that around 7 per cent of Uber drivers are enrolled in college or other higher education programmes (Hall and Krueger 2017, 710).

The development of the gig economy and its associated social class, the precariat, is in turn linked to legal struggles over labour rights. In the case of ride-sharing companies, this has focused on the employment status of drivers and the protections they should be entitled to. In 2016, in a landmark decision, a London employment tribunal ruled that Uber drivers are workers, rather than self-employed, and as such entitled to holiday pay, paid rest breaks, and the national minimum wage (Osborne 2016). In 2021, this ruling was upheld by the UK Supreme Court after Uber appealed. However, despite such basic worker benefits Uber drivers remain at a disadvantage to drivers in the traditional taxi sector, which tends to be more regulated, requiring regular health checks and insurance of drivers, and is bound by tariff agreements that manage driver pay (see Thelen 2018). Echoing this conflict and largely drowned out by the tense vote-counting following the 2020 US presidential election, California voters passed Proposition 22. As employees under labour law, drivers would be entitled to basic protections such as minimum wages, access to healthcare, and the right to organize. However, as a result of much lobbying from the ride-sharing companies, Proposition 22 exempts gig work such as providing Uber rides from the state's labour laws (Mills Rodrigo 2020). In September 2021, Proposition 22 was ruled unconstitutional, a court decision the Californian ride-sharing companies claimed they would appeal.

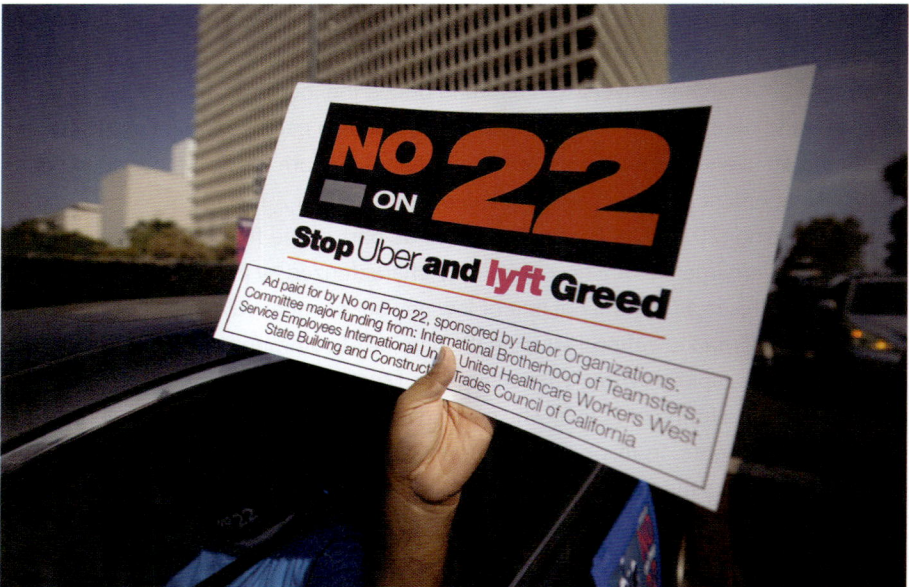

Photo 8.3. App-based gig workers hold a demonstration outside Los Angeles City Hall to urge voters to vote no to Proposition 22, a ballot measure that would classify app-based drivers as independent contractors and not employees or agents.
Source: Reuters/Alamy Stock Photo.

8.1.3 Platform capitalism

The tech giants illustrate how the sharing economy is not just about single-function products and services, such as ride-hailing apps. Instead, these apps and super apps are part of a wider move towards what some IPE scholars have called **platform capitalism**. This term refers to the growing influence—and valuations—of companies whose main business is to intermediate between customers and vendors, or consumers and workers, typically via digital platforms (Srnicek 2016). Most prominent are Amazon, Apple, and Alphabet (Google) in the US, and Baidu, Alibaba, and Tencent in China—though there are numerous smaller companies that often tend to be bought up by one of these. By talking of platform *capitalism* rather than a sharing *economy*, the term also directs our attention to the class inequalities (re)produced through this type of accumulation and the extraction of rents that it supports, as we have seen in the discussion of the gig economy in Section 8.1.2 with regard to the costs and risks put onto drivers.

Paul Langley and Andrew Leyshon (2020) identify three core processes of platform capitalism: reintermediation, consolidation, and capitalization. With the notion of **reintermediation** they seek to capture the fact that the platform, rather than being an atomized market characterized by numerous service providers and their customers, is actually highly stratified, in that all processes are intermediated by the platform. Applied to the Gojek case, we can see this in the way that the company has converted the informal economic practice of *ojek* drivers waiting for their customers close to transportation and shopping hubs into a business model largely steered by algorithms. Meanwhile, Gojek's merger with Tokopedia is perhaps the best illustration of platform capitalism's drive towards **consolidation**. Gojek's leadership have stated several times that ride-hailing in itself need not be a profitable segment of Gojek's business. Indeed, this segment has never turned a profit. Instead, the firm prioritized becoming a platform intermediating as many exchange activities as possible, so that the lack of short-term profit could be allayed by the capture of a rapidly growing number of users. GoTo thus aims to establish a single platform in Indonesia and some neighbouring countries for a plethora of services including banking/payments, shopping, transport, and food delivery.

Consolidation is also a technical feature of platform capitalism. In this regard, a central role is played by the relatively small number of companies that provide the underlying technology. The increased domination of the digital sharing economy by a few companies is also evident in the **capitalization** of digital platforms, in particular the role of private equity investors as well as interlocking investments of the dominant technology and/or sharing economy firms. These features are also evident in the Gojek/GoTo case. Gojek relies on both foreign hardware such as smartphones from brands such as Asus, Samsung, and Xiaomi (Chinese and South Korean companies being the main suppliers of the Indonesian market), and foreign software such as Google Maps. Moreover, despite the important role that Gojek played in Indonesian economic imaginaries and ambitions, many of its investors are based outside Indonesia. They include a range of global financial and technology firms, including Google, Visa, and Tencent—with the newly merged GoTo also counting financial firms such as Softbank and Chinese e-commerce platform Alibaba Group among its largest investors (Cordon 2019; Tani 2021).

Managing investor expectations was clearly an important aspect of Gojek's business model of successive funding rounds. For example, as Gojek was finalizing its June 2020 funding round, in which it obtained investments from the US companies Meta (formerly known as Facebook) and PayPal, among others, it announced that it would cut 9 per cent of its staff—that is, the direct employees who manage the platform, as opposed to the much more numerous 'contractors' who provide the services. At the same time, it was estimated that the closure of its GoLife arm would have knock-on effects on the 60,000 contractors providing services in Gojek's lifestyle division (CNBC 2020). In short, while weak profitability is alleviated for firms by the interest of international equity investors in potential future profits, the incomes and job stability of workers are sacrificed to attract those same investors.

Exacerbating the social divides underpinning the low-regulation gig economy discussed above, the benefits of platform capitalism are highly skewed towards firms and away from workers. This can be seen in their contrasting experiences during the Covid-19 pandemic. Whilst platforms could benefit from reintermediation during the demand shocks of the pandemic, pivoting from ride-hailing to food delivery and online payments, this ability to substitute one source of income for another was not available to workers. Moreover, some workers might face additional challenges. This is exemplified by the plight of female Gojek drivers in urban areas of Indonesia during the pandemic. As schools closed, the caring duties of women increased, reducing their ability to work or adjust to new demand patterns. Male drivers have thus been better placed to weather the changes in demand for Gojek services than women, reinforcing gender inequalities in income (Savirani and Mustika 2020).

As the for-profit sharing economy has grown all over the world, old and new social cleavages have been energized. This includes tensions between the local versus the global, and informality versus algorithmic control, as well as frictions such as workers (drivers) versus consumers. Maha Rafi Atal (2021) has argued that ambiguity—its 'Janus-faced' (contrasting) nature—is a crucial element of the capitalist design of this new sort of economy and explains its ability to slip regulatory controls. The experience of Gojek/GoTo is a case in point: it is at the heart of what its advocates see as a new form of Indonesian capitalism, and at the same time majority-owned by foreign investors and dependent on foreign-owned technologies. However, as we go on to discuss in Section 8.2, not all forms of sharing are driven by profit-oriented motives such as market share and valuation, and there are many examples of alternatives organized around principles of solidarity and reciprocity. Should these expand and become more pervasive, then we might talk about the 'sharing economy' in very different terms.

8.2 Exploring the Sharing Economy

In our everyday life, we experience different forms of cooperation and sharing. For instance, the more commodified forms of the sharing economy have not left student life untouched. Just think of your week: have you booked an Uber ride, had food delivered by Deliveroo, rented a textbook via Chegg, or browsed Airbnb looking for accommodation for your next holiday? Of course, during the same week you might also have got a free lift to campus, borrowed a book from the library, invited your friends over for dinner, and let one of them stay over on your sofa. As these examples illustrate, sharing plays an important role in our economic life, with market and non-market transactions existing alongside one another—or even predicated upon each other.

Indeed, whilst recent economic discourse has popularized the notion of 'sharing', it is neither a new nor an uncontested concept, as we explain in Section 8.2.1. We will refer in particular to the work of Karl Polanyi, an important thinker in IPE, to introduce the concept of sharing at a more theoretical level. Importantly, it is not always clear whether the notion of sharing serves as an alternative to market-based capitalist exchange or as a supplement to market logics. We will explore this question by looking at different forms of economic exchange, before historicizing the contemporary notion of the sharing economy in regard to the fallout from the 2008 global financial crisis and the conjunction of this with new technologies like smartphones. Moreover, as we will elaborate in Section 8.2.2, dynamics of ownership and control in the sharing economy, as elsewhere, are intimately linked to power relations and often tend to reinforce these rather than transcend them, the rhetoric of libertarian values espoused by Silicon Valley entrepreneurs notwithstanding. At the same time, however, this is by no means a foregone conclusion, and in Section 8.2.3 the chapter will also look at alternatives to profit-oriented ideas of the sharing economy, such as cooperatives, as a basis to identify the existing alternatives to market capitalism.

8.2.1 Where does the sharing economy come from?

The terms 'share' and 'sharing' have long been key features of political economy thought and practice and are reflective of different ways in which economic exchange has been socially organized. More recently, they have found renewed resonance in catchphrases such as 'shared prosperity', advocated for example by the World Bank (2017), and, indeed, the 'sharing economy'. As we have seen in Section 8.1, there is not one agreed definition of the sharing economy. Some scholars have understood it in terms of collective endeavours organized through peer-to-peer exchange and decentralized crowd-based networks (Schor et al. 2016; Sundararajan 2016). Other scholars have concentrated on the importance of technology, especially online platforms, in facilitating contemporary realizations of the sharing economy and the increasingly precarious forms of work that underpin it (Langley and Leyshon 2020; Moore and Joyce 2020). In this section, we first draw on the work of Karl Polanyi to provide a more fundamental theorization of sharing, before offering an IPE perspective of the post-2008 rise of the sharing economy that complement the more technology-focused explanations (see Benkler 2004).

Karl Polanyi (1944, chapters 4 and 5) has drawn attention to how different realizations of the economy, and economic exchange, are embedded in distinctive social relations. He identified four major types of economies of exchange: reciprocity, redistribution, householding, and the market. An economy organized around the principle of **reciprocity** is based on a two-sided form of exchange, operating akin to the notion of potlatch, discussed in Section 4.2.2 of the Debt chapter. It relies on personalized relationships and symmetry. By contrast, **redistribution** relies on more centralized forms of authority, for example a village chief or the state requesting tribute or taxes that are then redistributed. **Householding** is premised on the basis of autarchy or self-sufficiency, taking the (extended) household as its basic unit of analysis, which for your purposes could include student flats as well as family homes.

On this reading, the notion of economy has always incorporated a strong element of sharing: of extracting value and redistributing economic surplus, structured by different patterns of communal organization and social institutions. Importantly, all three of these types of economic exchange—reciprocity, redistribution, and householding—embrace elements of sharing, which puts them at one remove from the ideal-typical conceptualization of *homo economicus*, the utility-maximizing individual at the centre of neoclassical economic thought (see Section 3.1.1 on the appearance of Economic Man in debates on food). Nevertheless, they differ along various dimensions, including those of intentionality and coercion. For example, whilst I might be sharing the outputs of my labour in a redistributive system, this is not necessarily my own preference in the first instance but the outcome of submission to a higher authority that asks, and often coerces, me to do so.

In writing about economic exchange in this way, Polanyi thus emphasizes the importance of seeing different practices of exchange as culturally and historically situated. According to Polanyi, it is really only from the eighteenth century onwards that the market paradigm ascended to its dominance. He traces this development back to political and socio-legal changes in Britain, such as the introduction of the Poor Laws (referring to changes in poor relief such as the infamous workhouse system familiar from the novels of Charles Dickens) and the Enclosures Movement (referring to the appropriation of common land by landowners). Of course, the market as a site of exchange also exists in economic systems organized around the principles of reciprocity, redistribution, and householding, and this is indeed one of Polanyi's key points. However, what is new with the rise of market society, according to Polanyi, is the way that the economy becomes detached from social relations, and removed from social and political control. The market thus increasingly becomes a self-regulated abstract, rather than a historically contingent institution reflecting political choices.

Polanyi's view of the market as a form of economic exchange disembedded from its social relations has drawn various critiques, including for discounting how markets have historically always been embedded in highly gendered and racialized relations (Bhambra 2021; Fraser 2016). In this context, notions of sharing and the sharing economy return our gaze to fundamentals of the economy as grounded in social interactions and relations made invisible by the rise of the market paradigm, such as large aspects of the socially reproductive economy (see also Chapter 5 on Care). Furthermore, it is important to note that the sharing economy is very much reflective of the coexistence and, indeed, co-constitution of different forms of economic organization. This includes the marketization of everyday life in the for-profit sharing economy and upwards redistribution of wealth via centralized algorithms, but also reciprocity in the not-for-profit sharing economy, including with regard to social reproduction and shared care. When it comes to sharing, then, rather than focusing on the market alone, we might be better off studying Polanyi's four types of economies of exchange as coexisting and interrelated.

One question this leads to concerns the social bonds that make certain kinds of sharing possible. The reduction of family networks and communal ties that are often assumed to occur in capitalist, urban environments might privilege market exchange and for-profit sharing, though, as discussed, if you look hard enough, forms of mutual aid and not-for-profit sharing can be found (see Section 5.1.3 in relation to care work). Equally, we should be careful not to equate non-market sharing with 'traditional' or 'peasant' economies. For example, a popular, and increasingly populist in terms of its political usage, concept in Indonesia is that of *gotong royong*, which refers to the mutual cooperation of village life, as depicted in Photo 8.4. Yet scholarly work has shown that the idea of *gotong royong* is very much a political construct that romanticizes tradition to mobilize rural labour and incorporate it in development projects (Bowen 1986) rather than the natural solution to the fallout from the pandemic as recently portrayed by politicians in the country (Office of the President, Republic of Indonesia 2021).

Photo 8.4. Community members cleaning their home environment and drawing new road markings.
Source: onyengradar/Shutterstock).

Another question the Polanyian approach invites us to ask is how market exchange is able to expand and gain legitimacy, even as it causes massive social dislocation. Thinking about the for-profit sharing economy, as discussed in Section 8.1, important catalysts here were the global financial crisis of 2008–9 and the subsequent decade of austerity economics, especially but not only in the UK and US (Srnicek 2016). They accelerated the transition to more precarious forms of labour, boosting the workforce of the sharing economy, and expanded its customer base. However, another important driver were advances in mobile phone technologies. Initially the market leader, Apple, launched its first iPhone in June 2007, swiftly followed by the launch of its AppStore in July 2008. The widespread adoption of smartphones within less than a decade offered an important conduit for the seamless integration of the for-profit sharing economy into—and thus increasing marketization of—everyday life, with a growing number of people buying in services through apps.

8.2.2 Who owns what in the sharing economy?

The key players in this industry are massive **conglomerates** such as Alphabet and Meta with market power in different sectors, a fact often masked by the euphemism of the sharing economy (Atal 2021). Their prominence points to the need for a better understanding of the power dynamics that underpin and are reproduced through the sharing economy. Nevertheless, as we will illustrate, there is also scope for solidarity and resistance. Thus, current manifestations of the sharing economy both further accentuate inequalities and offer resources to contest them.

Widening inequalities are a crucial factor with regard to the question of who owns the sharing economy, in terms of ownership of the platforms organizing the sharing and the firms behind them, as well as the broader patterns of ownership of the assets/content being shared that it propagates. As we have seen in the case of Gojek, much of the funding is derived from private equity investors as well as interlocking investments of technology firms. Both groups of investors have an interest in rapidly capturing market share, sacrificing short-term profits for fast-pace growth. This is tolerated, if not encouraged, by investors because of the expectation of future market dominance and monopoly profit. As the journalist Eric Levitz argues:

> The route to 1,000 percent returns tends to run through a cornered market. Sometimes, the pursuit of market dominance is abetted by network effects inherent in the product. Often, it is aided by capital-rich VCs [venture capitalists] rallying behind a prospective titan, and enabling it to ruin its rivals by offering products and/or services at below break-even prices. (Levitz, 2020)

This is facilitated further by concerted lobbying efforts targeted at undermining regulations directed at the protection of workers and consumers (Moore and Joyce 2020) and fair competition (Atal 2021), and favouring tax cuts for technology firms and private equity/venture capital (Rothstein 2021). If we return to the case of ride-sharing in our opening section, the valuation of Gojek and Grab, as well as the global market leader Uber, exceeds by multiples their assets; they own neither transport devices nor even maps. And they often make losses rather than profits. As of 2021, after launching more than a decade ago, Uber had still not become profitable on a net basis (Bellon and Balu 2021). Indeed, the lack of profitability is perhaps one of the most paradoxical traits of the for-profit sharing economy.

It is important to address ownership in the sharing economy in terms of both the platforms and the goods and services that are being shared. A major benefit of the sharing economy, as put forward by its proponents, is that it leads to the more efficient use of resources—be they cars, flats, computer memory, and so on. These 'idle' resources are put to use through the business models of the sharing economy, leading to everyone's gain (Sundararajan 2016, 8). Nevertheless, it is important to subject this claim to scrutiny and investigate further what resources the for-profit sharing economy commodifies, who owns them, and, in so doing, what it is that is being displaced. The impact of accommodation rental platforms such as Airbnb and of ride-sharing platforms such as Uber is a case in point. They highlight some of the distorting economic and social effects of the growth of the sharing economy.

For example, research has shown that, in cities from Barcelona to Lisbon to New York, the growth of Airbnb and similar short-term rentals has contributed to gentrification and displacement (Cocola-Gant and Gago 2019; Ferreri and Sanyal 2018; see also Section 6.2.3 in City). Rather than leading to the more efficient use of housing space, as in the example of renting out your spare bedroom, the rise of the sharing economy has actually led to the wholesale conversion of residential accommodation into tourist accommodation in often already densely populated conurbations. The rise of companies such as Airbnb has further contributed towards a shift to buy-to-let property investment, with the added benefit for investors that vacated holiday lets can easily be sold on (Cocola-Gant and Gago 2019). This in turn has led to increases in rent and house prices, such that the sharing economy has become both cause and consequence of the uneven distribution of asset ownership, skewed towards the wealthiest strata of global society.

Research on ride-sharing similarly points to the importance of paying closer attention to what it replaces; be it the use of private cars or of public transport, or walking (Leard and Xing 2020). Rather than leading to the more efficient use of existing vehicles, the expansion of ride-sharing has coincided with record car sales in the US. It is likely that the growing demand from ride-share drivers, fuelled by companies such as Uber moving into the business of providing car financing, has been a force in this development (Dubal 2019). Even with regard to seemingly straightforward environmentally

Photo 8.5. A Chinese bike-share graveyard.
Source: frederic REGLAIN/Alamy Stock Photo.

friendly schemes such as bike-shares, questions of benefit and harm are not always clear-cut, as Photo 8.5 illustrates. It portrays hundreds of disposed bikes from failed Chinese bike-share schemes, a phenomenon that Huang (2018) traces back to oversaturation of the market and lack of profitability.

8.2.3 Are there alternative economies of sharing?

As we have seen so far in this chapter, much of the growth of the sharing economy since the global financial crisis has been underpinned by the expectation of future monopoly profits. Yet at the same time there have been renewed attempts to foreground economic practice in cooperative values like community and reciprocity. Which of the two provides the benchmarks for change and why? Cooperation might seem to offer a way to humanize the economy, reduce inequities, and provide an altogether different logic of organizing production, consumption, and distribution. But there have also been numerous attempts to commoditize such values, to use them to legitimize current economic practice, and, if at all, only marginally modify it. How then can we think about alternative approaches to market life?

This and similar debates form a point of departure for discussions of various forms of cooperation and solidarity, but also subversion and resistance, that have emerged in the global economy. They range from acts of individual and collective opposition to the sharing economy, communal activities such as cooperatives, and alternative philosophies that embrace principles of economic organization different from the market. We will discuss examples of each in this section. Together, they create a vibrant tapestry of lived economic agency and diverse political action. Whilst this should not distract from the structural constraints within which they operate, an analytical focus on the everyday allows us both to celebrate and critically interrogate them.

First, acts of resistance do not always—or even in the majority of cases—take the form of organized action. In his book *Weapons of the Weak*, political scientist James C. Scott (1985) analyses how subtle acts of resistance—foot-dragging, evasion, rumours—were used by peasants in a Malaysian village in the late 1970s to resist grand plans of national economic modernization that had little connection to their people's everyday realities (see Section 7.3.1 for a related discussion of Scott). And indeed, we do see these forms of resistance emerge aplenty once more in the sharing economy. Thus, if we go back to the case of Gojek from the opening section, for instance, one example is that of Gojek drivers ordering rides through a second phone, which they then accept through their Gojek accounts, boosting bonus points. According to Ford and Honan (2017), such actions happened on a mass scale after Gojek changed its reward scheme, increasing the number of bonus points required to qualify drivers for an extra IDR50,000 (less than US$4). However, these everyday deceptions were also accompanied by large-scale protests by Gojek drivers, as Photo 8.6 illustrates, reminding us that individual acts of resistance can feed into collective struggles..

Collective struggles against precarious labour can also become institutionalized. One such example is the Self-Employed Women's Association, a trade union for poor, self-employed women workers in India. Established in 1972, it represents the interests of women working in the informal sector, many of them in their own homes. It is the first of many homeworkers' associations that have been set up globally and are loosely connected via HomeNet, an umbrella organization. Similar evolutions can also be seen in the trade union movement in high-income countries. For instance, the Independent Workers' Union of Great Britain has been at the forefront of disputes over gig economy workers. Phoebe Moore and Simon Joyce (2020, 937–40) also point to the important role that trade unions play in resisting and modifying the impact of the gig economy, for example by ensuring that workers are designated as such (and therefore entitled to protections) rather than as contractors.

Second, the local scale is often seen as an important antidote, or counterpoint, to uneven processes of globalization and capitalist extraction. Feminist economic geographers and activists Julie Graham and Katherine Gibson, writing under the pen name J. K. Gibson-Graham (2006), argue in favour of community economies, organized at a local scale around principles of solidarity and care. According to Gibson-Graham, we tend to base our understanding of the economy on the visible part which is

Photo 8.6. In 2016 Gojek drivers protested in front of the company's headquarters in Jakarta. One demand was for Gojek to change the performance assessment algorithm that determined whether or not they received their IDR140,000 (£7) daily bonus.
Source: ZUMA Press, Inc./Alamy Stock Photo.

'capital-centric' and ignore a mass of economic activity that takes place beneath the surface, such as domestic work, informal sharing, volunteering, and cooperative initiatives like swap shops, **local exchange trading schemes (LETs)**, and community gardens. We return to the transformative possibilities of this approach in Section 8.3.1. Nevertheless, it is important to caution against an overly romanticized view of not-for-profit forms of sharing and community, including idealized visions of collective agency enabled by digital technology (Mansell 2016). Drawing on their research on sharing economy schemes based in the north-eastern US, Schor and co-authors (2016) demonstrate that even communally embedded forms of the sharing economy can give rise to significant dynamics of social stratification along the dimensions of class, race, and gender. Their findings thus echo the critiques of Polanyi raised in Section 8.2.1: despite a commitment to 'break[ing] down traditional relationships of power' that many such schemes explicitly espouse, they nevertheless tend to reproduce existing forms of inequality (Schor et al. 2016, 67).

In regard to the digital economy, one such example of not-for-profit collaboration that many are familiar with is that of Wikipedia, a crowd-sourced online encyclopaedia hosted by the Wikimedia Foundation. Figure 8.1 provides a breakdown of the geographical origins of its contributors in 2018, showing that more than half of the editors writing and revising Wikipedia entries are based in Western Europe. Stark gendered differences were also apparent. That same year, 90 per cent of contributors were male (EGalvez 2018). We see similar dynamics in academic publishing too, including in key IPE journals, where women authors and reviewers remain in the minority and scholars from the Global South are hardly represented at all (Bair et al. 2021). Relevant here is the fact that academic journals in the Social Sciences typically do not pay their contributors or editors or reviewers, which makes academic publishing a sort of collaborative endeavour that nonetheless produces a highly profitable capitalistic publishing model. These rather distinctive patterns reiterate the point that even not-for-profit collaboration is marked by social differentiation, and pose important questions about the representativeness of communities engaged in alternative economies of sharing and their relationship to the for-profit sector.

Third, in considering alternative ideas around which alternative economies of sharing could be organized, non-Western philosophies of cooperation and solidarity offer important insights. For example, the notion of *ubuntu* has been highlighted by people such as the South African archbishop, anti-apartheid fighter, and human rights activist Desmond Tutu (1931–2021), as a cultural concept that embraces our shared humanity. However, as in so many of the other examples discussed in this chapter, there have been attempts to commodify *ubuntu* into a market-friendly version of 'Afri-capitalism', which have in turn led to new resistances (McDonald 2010). Silicon Valley has also sought to make this term its

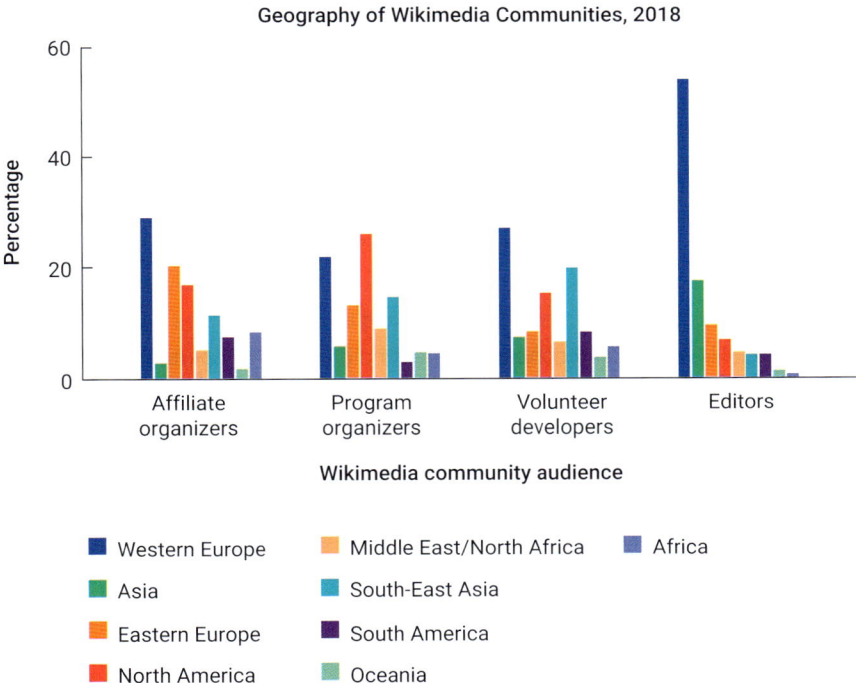

Figure 8.1. Geography of the Wikimedia Communities, 2018.
Source: EGalvez (WMF). 2018. CC BY-SA 4.0.

own—nowadays many people tend to be more familiar with Ubuntu, the Linux operating system, than *ubuntu* as a commitment to a shared humanity. More generally, it is important to note that alternate philosophies can manifest in multiple ways and are not inherently politically progressive, however that might be defined. Nonetheless, we do not say that we should discount them—and indeed there is much that IPE can learn from how people think about—and enact—economies around the world (see also Blaney and Trownsell 2021).

In sum, whilst the development of the sharing economy in the aftermath of the global financial crisis has mainly evolved around the principle of profit maximization, there has also been a proliferation of alternative market forms or, indeed, alternatives to the market. In Section 8.3 we will ask you to reimagine economic life around a range of alternative foundational principles, such as solidarity and cooperation. Once more, this development is reflective of a range of intersecting dynamics, including the rise of inequality and the growing precarity of labour in the gig economy, but also a resurgence of cooperative movements and new tactics of change.

8.3 Engaging the Sharing Economy

8.3.1 The diverse economies framework: reimagining the economy

This chapter has drawn attention to both libertarian ideas that idealize the free market and communal ideas that emphasize solidarity as underpinning different aspects of the sharing economy. The learning activities in this section are designed in a way that encourages you to tease out further the similarities, differences, and interdependencies between these two ideas. Thus, they will allow you, individually and in groups, to explore different economic systems/communities and the principles around which they are organized. How does an economic system built around cooperation and solidarity differ from one that emphasizes scarcity and self-interest? What do these differences mean for everyday life? What scales do they operate at? What role can you play in bringing about change? What are the most promising strategies for and tactics of change, and what are the forms of agency that they foreground?

As a first step towards recognizing the rich diversity of our economic lives, making alternative economies (more) visible is important work. In their book *Take Back the Economy*, Gibson-Graham et al. (2013) set out an agenda for changing how we think about and engage with the economy in order to take economic matters into our own hands. They suggest that an important reason why people do not connect their own agency—our decisions and actions—with how the economy works is that they often dismiss the impact of their own everyday lives as insignificant. In making this point, the authors draw attention to the diverse lived realities and attending power relations that are constitutive of economic life in practice.

Gibson-Graham and co-authors encourage us to 'reframe' ourselves, to think small about the big things like work, business, the market, property, and finance. This makes us recognize, they suggest, that collectively we can harness our everyday agency not just as a consumer but also as a worker, a carer, a producer of food, and so on for the greater good. As they succinctly summarize:

> When we see ourselves as economic actors with multiple roles, we can start to envision an exciting array of economic actions. When we take responsibility for our economic lives and for interconnected others, we can begin to shape the economies in which we live.
> (Gibson-Graham et al. 2013, xix)

They go on to argue that what we assume the economy is in reality is very much just the tip of the iceberg. We might be overly focused on just a few things—profit, competitiveness, and so on—but the larger part of what constitutes the economy, and what makes it so rich and enriching of our everyday lives, falls below the visibility line of the iceberg. The Community Economies Collective initiated by J. K. Graham-Gibson and colleagues is a treasure trove of resources for thinking otherwise about the economy, including examples of the iceberg: https://www.communityeconomies.org.

In Photo 8.7 we have applied this approach to higher education. Higher education includes important markers that are highly visible, ranging from the degree certificate that you will obtain at the end of your course to workers such as us authors employed in the higher education sector, to student finances, and to learning resources such as books and laptops. Hidden below these visible and increasingly commodified elements of higher education (see also Section 4.1.1 on student debt), however, there are a vast range of other issues and resources. This becomes clearer when we ask ourselves questions such as:

- How important is (the lack of) tutelage from friends, family, and mentors for explaining success at university?
- Do you benefit from this sort of help, or are you a first-generation student struggling to navigate the university social milieu, whilst trying to explain to your family what it is that you are actually doing—a sort of reverse burden?
- How are resources and support structures distributed?
- What is it that you actually have to do to be at university that is not necessarily visible to everyone?

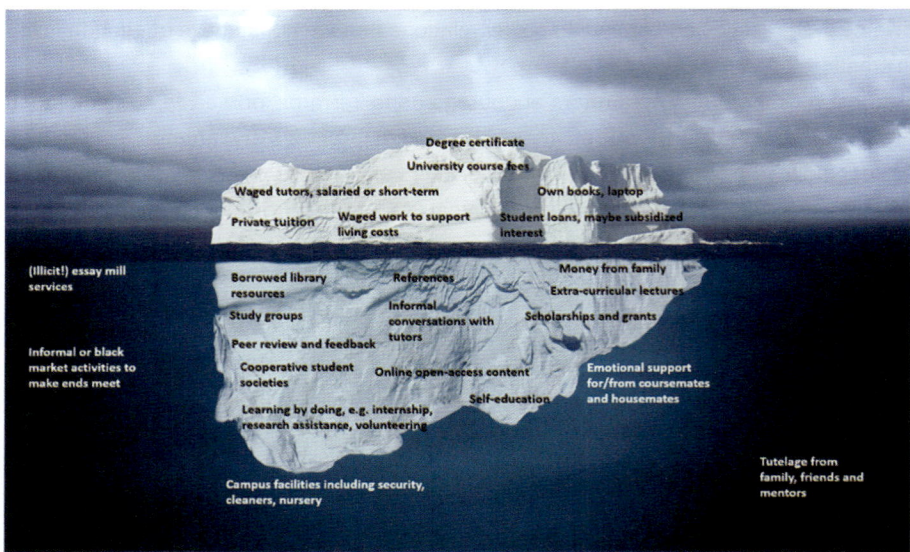

Photo 8.7. A Diverse Economies Iceberg for (UK) Higher Education.
Source: the authors.

Answers to some of these questions might be very personal and you do not have to share them with others, but the fact that these things *do* matter and are kept private is important to reflect on. Think closely about your own experiences and the ways in which you engage with the sharing economy as part of your student life. Now draw your own iceberg: what is visible, and what falls below the visibility line?

As you can tell, there are significant IPE dynamics at play, shaping how you and your everyday actions connect to global capitalism. But this exercise also demonstrates a number of problems and challenges that require further reflection. These relate to some of the shortcomings of dominant representations of the sharing economy, a number of which we have discussed in this chapter, such as its gendered stratification (Section 8.2.1). Moreover, it makes more glaring the absences of many aspects that are crucial facilitators of the sharing economy but tend to be (made) invisible. Of course, although this exercise has been framed as an individual challenge, you do not have to work this through on your own, but can also do so as a group, as part of a community exchanging ideas and coming up with joint solutions.

8.3.2 University community mapping

One way to learn more about your local sharing economy is **community mapping**. This refers to 'the process and product of a community getting together to map its own assets, values, beliefs or any other self-selected variable' (Coghlan and Brydon-Miller

2014, 147). It is a type of action research that is intended to empower researchers and lead to change, using relatively informal processes so that there are few barriers to entry. Action research is a relatively new concept in IPE and is an approach to learning that cuts across disciplinary boundaries (Brydon-Miller et al. 2003). One example of a successful campus community mapping exercise is the University of California-Berkeley Foodscape Mapping Project (see Figure 8.2; Fanshel and Iles 2020; see also Section 3.3.2 on the concept of a foodscape). The project was initiated in 2015 with the aim of 'building equitable and inclusive food systems' against the background of significant levels of food insecurity among the US student population. Indeed, according to a survey of nearly 167,000 US university and college students conducted in 2019, more than a third of participants reported having experienced food insecurity (Baker-Smith et al. 2020, 7).

The Berkeley Project, then, brought together a diverse array of actors, including students and academics as well as staff involved in food production and catering, and university management. One of the outputs it produced was a 'geographic asset map' providing the location of a range of food-related 'resources' ranging from basic-need services to lactation rooms to water refill stations (Fanshel and Iles 2020, 5–7). Have a look at the website, https://food.berkeley.edu/foodscape/geographic-map/ and click on the map icons for further information. Can you tell from the descriptors which of these icons form part of the sharing economy? What is the relative importance of profit/not-for-profit among these outlets? And how do they connect Berkeley students to the global economy?

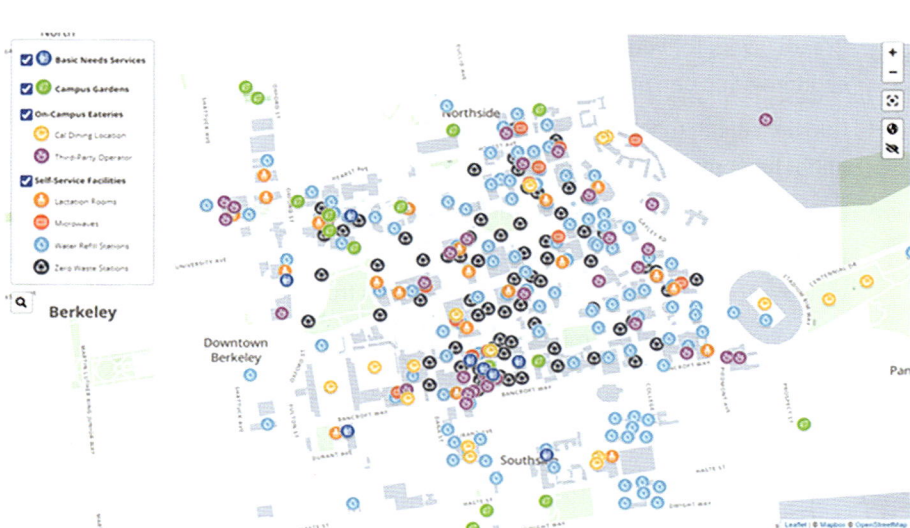

Figure 8.2. University of California-Berkeley foodscape map.

The University of California-Berkeley Foodscape Mapping Project is one example of the use of community mapping in highlighting structural inequalities faced by campus communities. In the following learning activity, we are setting out an easy-to-use guide for developing your own mapping project. This need not be focused on food provisioning. Other maps produced in the Berkeley project focused on campus influencers and decision-making structures (see Fanshel et al. 2018). But whatever aspect you focus on, try to think of this map as a local representation of what connects you—and your university community—to the global economy. In this exercise, we invite you to map your local university sharing economy.

Step 1: Choose your mapping purpose—decide what aspect of the sharing economy you want to focus on.

Step 2: Choose your mapping system—decide the scope of your project and which mapping system is most suitable for it. This could be a map app such as Google Maps, a downloadable map in portable data format (PDF) from your university website, or a hard-copy map (printout).

Step 3: Choose the information you want to collect—and decide how you want to go about it. This could be information such as exact location, descriptors, and visual data such as photos etc. that can be collected either in person or via an online search.

Step 4: Create your own map—analyse, visualize, and communicate the information.

If you use Google Maps as a platform, Green Map (n.d.) sets out the following work processes—but they can also easily be applied to a physical map:

- Give your map a title.
- Create layers for your map, for example to distinguish different types of sharing economy; you can also add descriptors and labels.
- Use the search function to add a place to your map (if you 'walk' your map, there might be some unsuspected surprises).
- Use markers ('placemarks') to add a place to your map and add custom icons.
- If you do this exercise as a larger assessed project, add images—these can be your own photographs or images downloaded from the internet.
- Share your map—but be mindful of whom you want to give access to it.

Following this exercise, in class you might want to consider the following questions:

- How has community mapping sharpened and deepened your understanding of your university community?

- What are the main issues that this challenge has highlighted for you?
- How does your own engagement with the sharing economy reproduce some of the empowering and/or disempowering dynamics discussed in this chapter?

8.4 Conclusion

The sharing economy gained popularity in the aftermath of the 2008–9 financial crisis—but it is also an excellent illustration of the insights that can be gained from an everyday IPE approach. The concept of marketization of everyday life (Section 8.1.1) offers a lens for understanding how the for-profit sharing economy incorporates a growing number of everyday practices and objects—from giving someone a lift to renting bedrooms. Different accounts of the sharing economy emphasize the importance of shared resources, the often precarious forms of labour it produces (the gig economy; Section 8.1.2) or the role and ownership of the technology that underpins it (platform capitalism; Section 8.1.3). As we discuss in this chapter (in Section 8.2.1), economic exchange can be organized according to different principles, such as reciprocity, redistribution, householding, or the market. These reflect different ways in which the economy is embedded in social relations. Moreover, as we highlighted in Sections 8.2.2 and 8.2.3, different types of economic organization give rise to variegated forms of social stratification and resistance. The learning activities sought to bring to the fore interdependencies between the for-profit and not-for-profit sharing economies, inviting you to reflect using the iceberg visibilization technique of the diverse economies framework (Section 8.3.1) and community mapping (Section 8.3.2).

Access the online resources for quizzes, student reflection podcasts, and support for tackling the chapter's learning activities: http://www.oup.com/he/i-peel1e.

RESOURCES

Tile recommendations from the I-PEEL website: 'scarcity' (Sahil Jai Dutta and Richard Lane) http://i-peel.org/homepage/scarcity/; 'sisterhood' (Sara Salem) http://i-peel.org/homepage/sisterhood/.

Nowtopia (2019), directed by Tom Smith: https://www.filmsforaction.org/watch/nowtopia-a-documentary-about-economic-alternatives-2020/. A film on creating alternative economies, as discussed in Section 8.2.3.

Sorry We Missed You (2019), directed by Ken Loach. Demonstrates the precarious—and indeed lethal—nature of the gig economy discussed in Section 8.1.2.

Green Maps provides examples of, and tools for, community mapping see: https://www.greenmap.org/.

For a great thread of (free) reading suggestions on the gig economy, see: https://twitter.com/bigblackjacobin/status/1344406158916923392 (h/t Edward Ongweso Jr).

Gibson-Graham, J. K., Jenny Cameron, and Stephen Healy. 2013. *Take Back the Economy. An Ethical Guide for Transforming our Communities*, Minneapolis and London: University of Minnesota Press. Offers important suggestions for rethinking—and redoing—the economy, and our everyday role in it, as discussed in Section 8.3.1.

Langley, Paul, and Andrew Leyshon. 2020. 'The Platform Political Economy of FinTech: Reintermediation, Consolidation and Capitalisation'. *New Political Economy* 26(3): 376–88. Introduces key concepts for understanding the sharing economy discussed in Section 8.1.

REFERENCES

Atal, Maha Rafi. 2021. 'The Janus Faces of Silicon Valley'. *Review of International Political Economy* 28(2): 336–50.

Bair, Jennifer, Daniela Gabor, Randall Germain, Alison Johnston, Saori N. Katada, Genevieve LeBaron, and Lena Rethel. 2021. 'Editorial: RIPE Diversity Statement 2020'. *Review of International Political Economy* 28(1).

Baker-Smith, Christine Vanessa Coca, Sara Goldrick-Rab, Elizabeth Looker, Brianna Richardson, and Tiffani Williams. 2020. *#RealCollege 2020: Five Years of Evidence on Campus Basic Needs Insecurity*, rev., The Hope Centre for College, Community and Justice, Temple University, February, https://hope4college.com/wp-content/uploads/2020/02/2019_RealCollege_Survey_Report.pdf.

Bellon, Tina. and Nivedita Balu. 2021. 'Uber makes first operating profit as driver shortage eases', 4 November, https://www.reuters.com/technology/uber-posts-first-small-adjusted-profit-ridership-rises-delivery-gets-more-2021-11-04/.

Benkler, Yochai. 2004. 'Sharing Nicely: On Shareable Goods and the Emergence of Sharing as a Modality of Economic Production'. *Yale Law Journal* 114(2): 273–358.

Bhambra, Gurminder K. 2021. 'Colonial global economy: towards a theoretical reorientation of political economy'. *Review of International Political Economy* 28(2): 307–22.

Blaney, David L., and Tamara A. Trownsell. 2021. 'Recrafting International Relations by Worlding Multiply'. *Uluslararası İlişkiler/International Relations* 18(70): 45–62.

Bowen John R. 1986. 'On the Political Construction of Tradition: Gotong Royong in Indonesia'. *Journal of Asian Studies* 45(3): 545–61.

Brydon-Miller, Mary, Davydd Greenwood, and Patricia Maguire. 2003. 'Why Action Research?' *Action Research* 1(1): 9–27.

CNBC. 2020. 'Indonesian ride-hailing firm Gojek cuts 9% of staff', 23 June , https://www.cnbc.com/2020/06/24/indonesian-ride-hailing-firm-gojek-cuts-9percent-of-staff.html.

Cocola-Gant, Agustin, and Ana Gago. 2019. 'Airbnb, buy-to-let investment and tourism-driven displacement: A case study in Lisbon'. *Environment and Planning A: Economy and Space* 0(0): 1–18.

Coghlan, David, and Mary Brydon-Miller. 2014. 'Community Mapping'. *The SAGE Encyclopedia of Action Research*, London: SAGE Publications, DOI: 10.4135/9781446294406.

Community Economies. n.d. 'Diverse Economies Iceberg', http://communityeconomies.org/resources/diverse-economies-iceberg.

Cordon, Miguel. 2019. 'Payments giant Visa joins Gojek's ongoing series F funding round'. TECHINASIA, 17 July, https://www.techinasia.com/payments-giant-visa-joins-gojeks-ongoing-series-funding.

Dubal, Veena. 2019. 'Uber's new loan program could trap drivers in cycles of crushing debt'. *The Guardian*, 5 December, https://www.theguardian.com/commentisfree/2019/dec/05/uber-loan-program-debt.

EGalvez. 2018. 'Gender Across Wikipedia Project Contributors in 2018, Weighted'. Wikipedia, 31 August, https://commons.wikimedia.org/w/index.php?curid=72199511.

Fanshel, Rosalie Z., and Alastair Iles. 2020. 'Transforming the Campus Foodscape Through Participatory Mapping'. *Case Studies in the Environment* 4: 1–16.

Fanshel, Rosalie Z., Alastair T. Iles, and Meg Prier. 2018. *Building Equitable and Inclusive Food Systems at UC Berkeley: Foodscape Mapping Project Report*. White Paper. Berkeley Food Institute

Ferreri, Mara, and Sanyal, Romola. 2018. 'Platform economies and urban planning: Airbnb and regulated deregulation in London'. *Urban Studies* 55(15): 3353–68.

Ford, Michele, and Vivian Honan. 2017. 'The Gojek Effect'. In *Digital Indonesia. Connectivity and Divergence*, ed. Edwin Jurriens and Ross Tapsell. Singapore: ISEAS–Yusof Ishak Institute.

Fraser, Nancy. 2016. 'Contradictions of Capital and Care'. *New Left Review* 100, https://newleftreview.org/issues/ii100/articles/nancy-fraser-contradictions-of-capital-and-care.

Gibson-Graham, J. K. 2006. *The End of Capitalism (As We Knew It). A Feminist Critique of Political Economy*, Minneapolis: University of Minnesota Press.

Gibson-Graham, J. K., Jenny Cameron, and Stephen Healy. 2013. *Take Back the Economy. An Ethical Guide for Transforming our Communities*, Minneapolis and London: University of Minnesota Press.

Gojek. n.d. '1 in 2 Have The Gojek Super App', https://www.gojek.io/superapp/#:~:text=Gojek%20Super%20App.,125%20million%20times%20in%20Indonesia.

Green Map n.d. 'Green Map System Tutorial: How to Make a Green Map on Google My Maps', https://www.greenmap.org/sites/default/files/tutorials/how_to_make_a_green_map_on_google_mymap.pdf.

Hall, Jonathan V., and Alan B. Krueger. 2017. 'An Analysis of the Labor Market for Uber's Driver-Partners in the United States'. *ILR Review* 71(3): 705–32.

Hasija, Sameer, V. Padmanabhan, and Prashant Rampal. 2020. 'Will the Pandemic Push Knowledge Work into the Gig Economy?', *Harvard Business Review*, 1 June, https://hbr.org/2020/06/will-the-pandemic-push-knowledge-work-into-the-gig-economy.

Huang, Freddy. 2018. 'The Rise and Fall of China's Cycling Empires', *Foreign Policy*, 31 December, https://foreignpolicy.com/2018/12/31/a-billion-bicyclists-can-be-wrong-china-business-bikeshare/.

Istanto, Freddy H. 2019. 'Jokowi appoints Nadiem Makarim as education minister. Can the Gojek co-founder streamline bureaucracy in education?', 24 October, https://www.thejakartapost.com/academia/2019/10/24/jokowi-appoints-nadiem-makarim-as-education-minister-can-the-gojek-co-founder-streamline-bureaucracy-in-education.html.

Jourdain, Anne, and Sidonie Noulin. 2020. 'Introduction: The Marketization of Everyday Life'. In *The Social Meaning of Extra Money. Capitalism and the Commodification of Domestic and Leisure Activities*, ed. Naulin and Jourdain. Basingstoke: Palgrave Macmillan, 1–29.

Langley, Paul, and Andrew Leyshon. 2020. 'The Platform Political Economy of FinTech: Reintermediation, Consolidation and Capitalisation'. *New Political Economy* 26(3): 376–88.

Leard, Benjamin, and Jianwei Xing. 2020. 'What Does Ridesharing Replace?', Working Paper 20–03, February. Washington DC: Resources for the Future, https://www.rff.org/documents/2341/WP_20-03_Leard_Xing_Ridesharing.pdf.

Levitz, Eric. 2020. 'America Has Central Planners. We Just Call Them "Venture Capitalists"', *New Yorker* magazine, 3 December, .https://nymag.com/intelligencer/2020/12/wework-venture-capital-central-planning.html.

McDonald, David A. 2010. 'Ubuntu bashing: the marketisation of "African values" in South Africa', *Review of African Political Economy* 37(124): 139–52.

Mansell, Robin. 2016. 'Power, hierarchy and the internet: why the internet empowers and disempowers'. *Global Studies Journal* 9(2): 19–25.

Megoran, Nick, and Olivia Mason. 2020. *Second class academic citizens: The dehumanising effects of casualisation in higher education*, https://www.ucu.org.uk/media/10681/second_class_academic_citizens/pdf/secondclassacademiccitizens.

Mills Rodrigo, Chris. 2020. 'California voters approve measure exempting Lyft, Uber from labor law'. *The Hill*, 4 November, https://thehill.com/policy/technology/524403-california-voters-approve-measure-exempting-lyft-uber-from-labor-law.

Moore, Phoebe M., and Simon Joyce. 2020. 'Black box or hidden abode? The expansion and exposure of platform work managerialism', *Review of International Political Economy* 27(4): 926–48.

Office of the President—Republic of Indonesia. 2021. 'President Jokowi: Gotong Royong Kunci Penanganan Pandemi di Tanah Air', 22 December, https://www.presidenri.go.id/siaran-pers/presiden-jokowi-gotong-royong-kunci-penanganan-pandemi-di-tanah-air/.

Osborne, Hillary. 2016. 'Uber loses right to classify UK drivers as self-employed'. *The Guardian*, 28 October, https://www.theguardian.com/technology/2016/oct/28/uber-uk-tribunal-self-employed-status.

Polanyi, Karl. 1944. *The Great Transformation*, New York: Farrar & Rinehart.

PriceWaterhouse Coopers [PwC]. 2015.' Sharing or paring? Growth of the sharing economy', https://www.pwc.com/hu/en/kiadvanyok/assets/pdf/sharing-economy-en.pdf.

Rothstein, Sidney. 2021. 'Toward a discursive approach to growth models: Social blocs in the politics of digital transformation'. *Review of International Political Economy*, DOI: 10.1080/09692290.2021.1895278.

Ruehl, Mercedes. 2021. 'Indonesia's Gojek and Tokopedia agree $18bn merger'. *Financial Times*, 17 May, https://www.ft.com/content/ce944c28-a6d1-42b9-9da2-12e90cb2ae19.

Savirani, A., and W. Mustika. 2020. '"My kids need me, but we need money too": Female GOJEK drivers in Indonesia'. *Melbourne Asia Review*, 22 October.

Schor, Juliet B., Connor Fitzmaurice, Lindsey B.Carfagna, WillAttwood-Charles, and Emilie Dubois Poteat. 2016. 'Paradoxes of openness and distinction in the sharing economy', *Poetics* 54: 66–81.

Scott, James C. 1985. *Weapons of the Weak. Everyday Forms of Peasant Resistance*. New Haven: Yale University Press.

Srnicek, Nick. 2016. *Platform Capitalism*, Cambridge: Polity.

Standing, Guy. 2014. *The Precariat. The New Dangerous Class*, London: Bloomsbury Academic.

Sundararajan, Arun. 2016. *The Sharing Economy: The End of Employment and the Rise of Crowd-Based Capitalism*, Cambridge, MA: MIT Press.

Tani, Shotaro. 2021. 'SoftBank and Alibaba take top stakes in Indonesia's GoTo'. *Nikkei Asia*, 20 May, https://asia.nikkei.com/Business/Technology/SoftBank-and-Alibaba-take-top-stakes-in-Indonesia-s-GoTo.

The Jakarta Post. 2015. 'Jokowi Defends Ride-Hailing Apps as Transportation Ministry Withdraws Ban'. *The Jakarta Post*, 18 December, https://www.thejakartapost.com/news/2015/12/18/jokowi-defends-ride-hailing-apps-transportation-ministry-withdraws-ban.html.

The Jakarta Post. 2019. 'The Top Five E-Wallets in Indonesia', *The Jakarta Post*, 14 August, https://www.thejakartapost.com/life/2019/08/14/the-top-five-e-wallet-apps-in-indonesia.html.

Thelen, Kathleen. 2018. 'Regulating Uber: The Politics of the Platform Economy in Europe and the United States'. *Perspectives on Politics* 16(4): 938–53.

White, Jeremy B. 2018. 'Many Uber and Lyft drivers now rely on the work as their primary income source, report finds', *The Independent*, 30 May, https://www.independent.co.uk/news/business/news/uber-lyft-jobs-drivers-income-employees-independent-contractors-gig-economy-a8376271.html.

World Bank. 2017. *Growth for the Bottom 40 Percent: The World Bank Group's Support for Shared Prosperity*. Independent Evaluation Group. Washington DC: World Bank.

9 HUMOUR

9.1	Radical Comedy	243
9.2	Exploring Humour	253
9.3	Engaging Humour	264
9.4	Conclusion	268

LEARNING OBJECTIVES

- Reflect on how humour affects our everyday experiences of market life as both a form of entertainment and a critical space of dissent
- Develop concepts of resistance, carnival, and subversion to explore the potential for humour and comedy to contemplate critical alternatives to/within globalization
- Apply your own knowledge of social media memes to subvert hierarchies of social difference

READER'S GUIDE

Humour is an ambiguous topic in the everyday politics of globalization. On the one hand, market life appears to be saturated with jokes, irony, and memes. Comedy is big business with satirical news shows and stand-up comedy specials providing regular popular content for global media giants like HBO and Netflix. On the other hand, the radical substance and often critical or anti-capitalist nature of the comedy can seem to contrast with the high status and salaries of the performers. Humour's commercial popularity is very often—and somewhat paradoxically—related to its resistant and rebellious nature. This chapter takes up this theme with a first section on 'Radical Comedy' (Section 9.1). It draws out three related concepts of resistance, carnival, and subversion to reflect on how joking and pranks can critique, but also reproduce, the inequalities and exclusions of market life. The second section, 'Exploring Humour', analyses the global politics of humour by foregrounding the ethical, social, and political functions of comedy (Section 9.2). Satirical resistance has contributed to seemingly laudable interventions in the sphere of international development, like the Comic Relief fundraiser and the Make Poverty History campaign. Humour therefore seems to carry a productive association with issues of global justice and responsibility. Yet postcolonial scholars, and comedians themselves, have questioned the privileged agency of the white, male, Western comedian typically at the centre of such interventions. More problematically still, the widespread circulation of humour and irreverence within the public sphere might even create an opportunity for the 'weaponization' of irony by populists and authoritarian states. A third section, 'Engaging Humour', asks you to navigate these debates by collaging the use of parody in political communication and coming up with your own subversive meme (Section 9.3).

KEY CONCEPTS

Resistance; carnival; subversion

Access the online resources to listen to a podcast where James introduces and explores the key themes of this chapter: http://www.oup.com/he/i-peel1e.

9.1 Radical Comedy

Recent decades have seen a rise of humour and comedy to occupy an interesting, and somewhat contradictory, space within everyday market life. In the fallout from the global financial crisis after 2008, satirical news shows like *The Daily Show* in the US and Charlie Brooker's *Newswipe* in the UK became important vehicles for channelling public incredulity at the scale and apparent injustice of events (Brassett 2016). More latterly, John Oliver's *Last Week Tonight* has gone on to provide a regular series of tightly scripted comedy case studies of the excesses and inequities of American capitalism, with other countries having their own equivalents, such as Egyptian comedian Bassem Youssef. However, while there might be grounds for optimism in this ability of comedy to make critical and radical ideas a subject of popular entertainment, the commodification of humour and '**commedification**' of public discourse also point to some profound ambiguities (Berlant and Ngai 2017). Is making us laugh contingent on making us pay? Is being funny reducing politics to farce? The spread of humour through key circuits of globalization, including the syndication and global distribution of TV shows via digital streaming services, the use of **irony** in advertising, and the proliferation of memes in political communication all suggest that these are increasingly important and *international* questions to address.

While it may be tempting to dismiss the critical significance of famous and rich comedians, even if they do have some good anti-capitalist one liners, this chapter will foreground the importance of understanding the ambiguities and limits entailed in satirizing markets. On the one hand, the everyday qualities of humour mean that jokes and irony can spread quickly, serving to undermine established or mainstream discourses with a wider public. This can help to challenge the idea that the site of meaningful politics must always be with established actors like the state or international organizations, and can in turn provoke a more creative attitude to thinking about the spaces and nature of political agency. On the other hand, building awareness of the market demand for radical comedy can help to illustrate the kinds of dilemmas entailed in thinking about resistance more broadly. Simply put, what happens when one or other form of resistance becomes popular: is that the goal, or is it merely selling out? This section will explore the way radical comedy uses jokes about debt, inequality, and the power of global corporations to promote an everyday cultural discourse that appears to resist different facets of globalization. While it begins with mainstream satirical news shows, it draws on a longer tradition of **prankster** resistance on the part of protestors, clowns, and artists mobilizing humour for political ends.

9.1.1 Resistance

The famous English novelist and social critic George Orwell (1945) argued that humour can be seen as a form of resistance against unfair or unequal power relations: 'A thing is funny when it upsets the established order. Every joke is a tiny revolution.' The more elevated the target, the more revolutionary the joke; hence good **satire** is often described as that which 'punches up' at the powerful and privileged. However, it is important to recognize that Orwell also prized a second quality in humour: *vulgarity*. The more vulgar a joke, the better—especially when lampooning those people, like politicians or the clergy, who might expect their position of power to afford them reverential treatment. Think of the slapstick caricatures of political leaders in newspaper cartoons. Humour thus works in the context of social understandings of historical and political context, or what the anthropologist Mary Douglas (1968) refers to as the 'joke in the social structure'. Put differently, a good joke can be deeply serious by teasing at the everyday boundaries of what we know and accept (Brassett 2021).

The current explosion of interest in satirical news shows, radical stand-up, and even the online circulation of memes can be instructive for reflecting on the boundaries of what we know and accept within global market life. The British comedian John Oliver shot to fame when he stood in for *Daily Show* anchor Jon Stewart and then became host of his own HBO vehicle, *Last Week Tonight with John Oliver*. The format is by now well established with a mix of serious, news-like monologues delivered straight to camera, interspersed with exaggerated comparisons and pop cultural references by Oliver. What is most interesting for students of IPE, however, is the way discussion so often strays into concerns of power and injustice within markets, such as the problematic role of private enterprise in the prison system or healthcare.

Oliver regularly returns to the subject of private debt and its harmful effect on individuals and society. In one episode, he considers the practice whereby banks sell overdue or 'delinquent' private debt contracts on the open market (Oliver 2016). The debt-collecting industry is described as poorly regulated, with rogue collectors intimidating individuals, and there appears to be a persistent problem with expired or paid debts being reactivated. Popular news coverage of this so-called 'zombie debt', where buried old debt is brought back to life, playfully compares it to *The Walking Dead* about the zombie apocalypse. John Oliver responds: 'Yeh, Zombies are fun. But the comparison is actually quite apt because just like on the *Walking Dead*, zombie debt comes back from the grave, is incredibly hard to deal with, and seems to disproportionately

Photo 9.1. Part of the humour in *Last Week Tonight* is about form. Oliver dresses smartly and talks about serious investigative news topics, but is often driven to hyperanimated swearing, ridiculous gestures, and facial expressions to express his incredulity at the subject material.

Source: Album/Alamy Stock Photo.

impact minorities.' In this way, a reflexive irony is brought to the playful tone of the show, and the ground is cleared for a more critical engagement with the hierarchies of social difference that structure the delinquent debt industry. Speaking to the question of how to respond to being trapped by personal or household debt (as discussed in Section 4.2.3 of the Debt chapter), John Oliver even goes on to set up his own debt-buying company in order to purchase 16 million dollars of medical debt at knock-down prices, which he then forgives live on the show.

While Oliver has done much to bring genuine investigative critiques to a mainstream audience, in this case performing an inspiring stunt about the assumed normality and necessity of paying debt, we might wonder about the instabilities and contradictions of doing this for entertainment purposes. There is clearly an important educative function to *Last Week Tonight with John Oliver,* yet the laughter and applause can seem out of place with the topic sometimes. Does laughing at such difficult subjects make it easier for us to go on with our daily lives? As Slavoj Zizek (2008, 24) argues, 'in contemporary societies . . . cynical distance, laughter, irony, are, so to speak, part of the game. The ruling ideology is not meant to be taken seriously or literally.' In other words, by making debt funny Oliver might have unwittingly given viewers an emotional release, defusing any feelings of anxiety and anger about indebtedness and foreclosing more antagonistic political responses.

A more critical vision of comic resistance considers the potential of such stunts and pranks to contribute to wider political objectives, asking how it might foster processes of agitation and dissent that seek to change things. Contemplating the **direct action** potential of humour, the activist–researcher L. M. Bogad (2016, 32) describes how social movements need to confront the very systems of media relay that satirists partake in:

> Social movements often face a formidable cultural phenomenon in the form of what I call the 'hegemonologue' – the hegemonic monologue of common neoliberal ideology that drones on from big and little screens, with favourite themes being the criminalization or pathologization of dissent, and the inevitability of predatory and unrestricted global capitalism. However, sometimes through luck, pluck and skill, artist activists can create an irresistible image that interrupts this hegemonologue, even if only temporarily. An irresistible image is so compelling or beautifully troubling that even one's ideological opponents must reproduce it, even when it interrupts their narrative in the battle of the story. A clown kisses a riot shield – and tabloids that have been criminalizing the global justice movement for years print the photo. These images on their own may not have tangible results but they do help movements to gain momentum or to weaken the determination of their opponents.

There are numerous examples of how basic comic techniques can create resistant images that circulate through the media. The 'book bloc' was a decentralized movement that came to prominence during student fees protests in Europe. Protesters dressed themselves up as large mock-up versions of critical theory books like Theodor Adorno's *Negative Dialectics* and Herbert Marcuse's *One-Dimensional Man* (see also the Frankfurt School in Section 1.2.1). Not only did their costumes serve as good body armour if the police hit them, but such moments of violence also served as a visual embodiment of the injustice they were protesting about. Similarly, Bogad himself was a member of a group called the Clandestine Insurgent Rebel Clown Army that used comedy to bring a sense of play to protest. In one operation, a crack team of highly trained clowns descended on the Glasgow G8 summit to Make Poverty History. Armed with tickle sticks and baggy trousers, their **'tactical frivolity'** was designed to anticipate and respond to the inevitable pushback from the riot police (Bogad 2016).

Photo 9.2. Lipstick traces on the riot shield of a police officer at the G8 Summit in Edinburgh, 2005.

Source: Bart Pro/Alamy Stock Photo.

When stopped and searched, their deep clown pockets were filled with a vast array of items for the police to itemize and seize: sausages, handkerchiefs, sex toys, etc. At one stand-off, a clown called Trixie approached the armed police and kissed their transparent riot shields. The thick red lipstick left a visible mark on the shield, and the image was captured and circulated through global media for two days.

What is interesting about these techniques of resistance is that they all work by mobilizing the standard images of the media relay: everyday signs and symbols that crystallize a narrative point. Like Orwell's vision of humour, the hierarchy of police power is made to look excessive, anti-intellectual, or—when the police are itemizing the contents of clowns' pockets—just plain ridiculous. In a manner reminiscent of the prosumer subject considered in the chapter on Social Media (Section 7.2.3), there is a suggestion that resistant agency can be creative and productive of new modes of engagement. In this vein, we might consider the example of the Yes Men. These were a group of anti-corporate pranksters that set about finding innovative ways to resist by means of what they called 'identity correction': an approach spawned by a summer they spent working in a toy store rewiring Barbie dolls to speak like G.I. Joes and vice versa (The Yes Men 2004).

In one project, the Yes Men set out to correct the identity of the World Trade Organization (WTO), establishing a website domain name GATT.org and responding to invitations to speak as (apparent) representatives of the WTO (see Section 2.1.2 on the evolution of the GATT into the WTO). They travelled across the world giving speeches to unwitting audiences about the need to press on with trade liberalization. They railed against inconvenient and irritating barriers like 'banning the import of tuna caught in nets that kill dolphins', or 'prohibiting the import of food with carcinogenic pesticide residues', or banning clothes made with 'slave labour' which 'impose arbitrary limits to the functioning of the economy' (The Yes Men 2004, 32). These jokes not only tease at the human rights implications of global value chains but also satirize the form of modern policy discussion: the authoritative (male) speaker in a policy meeting. While such pranks got attention, being described by the WTO as 'deplorable', their final stunt was to call a press conference in Sydney and announce the closure of the WTO itself. Regretfully, they informed a shocked audience that the WTO had failed in its mission to end poverty and create prosperity because theories of free trade contained 'fundamental mistakes', and that they would now try to reinvent it as part of the UN system of human rights (The Yes Men 2004, 160–1). The subsequent media storm saw journalists vigorously worrying about whether the WTO was really finished, whether globalization is a failure, and whether trade should actually promote human rights.

Photo 9.3. Rather than dress as typical protestors with placards, the Yes Men put on suits and carried briefcases, adopting the language of corporate globalization.
Source: Album/Alamy Stock Photo.

9.1.2 Carnival

While pranksters can create innovative techniques of resistance, their actions can sometimes run the risk of preaching to the converted. What if we don't like or agree with the premise of the prank? Is this just joking 'for our side'? Read through to contemporary practices of online 'dunking' and 'pile-ons' in which controversial social media posts trigger a landslide of derision and ridicule, we might wonder about the ethics of mocking those we don't agree with. The poststructural IPE scholar Marieke de Goede (2005) observes that activists are too often expected to form a coherent programme of opposition that can unite against 'global capitalism'. Indeed, she argues that 'reducing the multiplicity of possible refusals and resistances to a single force or movement can be seen as an exclusionary political project in itself' (2005, 380). Sides are taken, jokes become instrumentalized, and pranks are judged on their ability to go viral. Rather than proceed with a vision of resistance that places 'critique first, and the development of effective political programmes second', de Goede instead celebrates the way humour can 'make strange' (2005, 381). What would it mean to make the economy strange?

A key thinker to consider here is the Russian philosopher Mikhail Bakhtin. He looked at the role of the medieval **carnival**, celebrating the way mass movements of people within towns and marketplaces could rupture the normal social order. In line with Orwell's regard for vulgarity (see Section 9.1.1), he praised the way that during carnival time the people could oppose the austerity of the Church and drink, dance, and even defecate in the street. He particularly valued an everyday focus on the 'lower bodily strata' (genitalia, excrement, etc.) for its capacity to challenge the severe self-discipline of a Church which praised modesty and restraint (Bakhtin 1984). We can see similar themes in the way that carnival cultures of the Caribbean have been theorized. Emerging from the tradition of masquerades on slave plantations, in which enslaved people seized the opportunity to lampoon the powerful elites who literally controlled their lives, carnival gave rise to practices of 'resistance to officialdom, linguistic innovation and the disruptive nature of play, parody and humour' such that it now exists as 'a site for everyday conviviality, pleasure, social cohesion and resistance to heteronormativity' (Marshall 2019, 486–7).

Aligned with such readings, de Goede points to the carnivalesque as a 'reversal of the normal social order and an atmosphere of licentiousness during which prohibitions are challenged' to suggest that comic resistance is about far more than an instrumental win:

> In carnivalesque politics, the figure of Capital itself – and the divisions it gives rise to – appears much less stable and

secure: its rationality is laughed at, its power is disturbed and the contradictions within global political economy become apparent.

(de Goede 2005, 382)

A carnivalesque notion of pranking therefore embraces the instability and raucousness of humour *as an end in itself*. At one level, this can foreground the affective presence of clowns and jokers on the streets, how they interact with other protestors or the police to challenge the traditional oppositions of power and resistance. At another level, the carnivalesque licenses a more extensive concept of humour that is open-ended and uncertain. Thus, any discomfort we may feel at certain pranks is precisely the point—to interrupt the settled categories and parameters of normal politics, forcing us to reflect on the genuinely difficult dilemmas and violence of how we come together within global markets.

An interesting example of this kind of carnival atmosphere can be found in the work of the Billionaires, a network of performers who role-played as representatives of the wealthiest 1 per cent. Initially incarnated as the Billionaires for Forbes in a reference to the Forbes 'rich list', they were able to adapt to new issues and events with different titles, such as the Billionaires for Bush (or Gore), the Billionaires for Bailouts, and the Billionaires for Plutocracy. Often dressed in glamorous clothing and with character

Photo 9.4. The Billionaires presented themselves as a caricature of corporate interests, staying in character to get their message across to often confused journalists.

Source: Cavan Images/Alamy Stock Photo.

names like Ivan Aston Martin, Ionna Bigga Yacht, or Meg A. Bucks, their prankster humour was one of overidentification with the thing they opposed (Haugerud 2013). In carnivalesque terms, they used their status as the ruling class to gently mock other campaigners, for example carrying the placard 'This is what Plutocracy looks like', a play on the popular protest slogan, 'This is what Democracy looks like'.

These and other slogans like 'Corporations are people too!' and 'It is a class war and we are winning!' puncture the assumed normalcy of state-level politics by laughing at its imbrications with globalization. However, there is an important uncertainty for Billionaire humour in that, unlike a TV show or comedy gig, the audience is neither self-selecting nor prepared for the joke. As Bogad (2016, 93) elaborates, 'There is no way to control the creative consumption of irony by all individuals, but performers may nevertheless play with audiences' sensibilities, trying to anticipate possible misfires.' Some jokes will fall flat or send mixed messages, but that doesn't necessarily matter. A carnivalesque understanding of pranking is concerned less with impact or coherence and more with the disruption of established knowledge frames.

9.1.3 Subversion

While carnival and play can be important techniques for changing the space and substance of political action, some humour can become subversive in a manner that challenges the accepted reality of capitalist society. In de Goede's terms this can lead to a *making strange* of apparently fundamental components of global market life such as capital, debt, and expertise. In bringing such arguments into IPE, many scholars have drawn on the work of the influential feminist and queer theorist Judith Butler. One example of **subversion** provided by Butler is the use of drag to perform and potentially resignify gender. While the drag artist might exaggerate stereotypical aspects of male and female identity, ridicule sexualities, or push audience interaction in uncomfortable ways, she argues that in 'imitating gender, drag implicitly reveals the imitative structure of gender itself – as well as its contingency' (Butler 1990, 187). Although subversion is momentary and fleeting—indeed, subject to recuperation within capitalist culture as mere entertainment—it introduces an important way of thinking about comic resistance: 'In place of the law of heterosexual coherence, we see sex and gender denaturalized by means of a performance which avows their distinctness and dramatizes the cultural mechanism of their fabricated unity' (Butler 1990, 187–8; see heteronormativity in Section 5.1.3). Rather than seek to judge whether a joke is 'correctly resistant', or even adequately 'funny', we might instead ask about what the joke 'does': how it circulates, what it disrupts, how it is recuperated.

On this view, the anonymous graffiti artist Banksy has made the market value of irony a direct subject of his work. Sometimes he poses as a street trader to sell what appear to be cheap reprints of his work for 5 dollars each, which are later revealed to be original works. On another occasion, he auctioned *Girl with Balloon*, a picture that partially shredded itself at the very moment the sale was agreed. Both actions subvert market value, disturbing established norms around the provenance of artworks and their durability. At the same time, however, all the Banksy pieces went up in price once the joke was revealed, indicating the possibility for market recuperation of such ironic interventions. In more carnivalesque fashion, Banksy has also provided inspiration and support to artists involved in practices of commodity subversion. For example, the **'subvertising'** collective Brandalism installs original artworks in bus stop advertising spaces (which, it turns out, are actually quite easy to gain access to). Some are small additions to existing adverts like 'Warning: Advertising Shits in Your Head', while many are directly critical of brands. One campaign on the use of body image in the beauty industry produced a succinct billboard slogan: 'If your product was any good you wouldn't need sexism to sell it'. As shown in Photo 9.5, more recent actions took on the triumphant memorialization of the British Empire in the UK and its legacies in school curricula.

Photo 9.5. #SubvertTheCity was a coordinated international campaign involving Brandalism to challenge corporate advertising in public space and collectively reimagine what a post-consumerist city might look like (see also Section 6.2.3 on the right to the city).
Source: Mark Kerrison/Alamy Stock Photo.

Part of the politics of resistance is to reflect on what is being resisted. While each of the jokes and satirical plays in this section have focused on small situations, sometimes emerging in spontaneous moments of improvisation, there is also a sense in which they connect up. Indeed, activists like Bogad directly conceive of diverse actions in a manner that can contest something singular like the hegemonologue. On this view, finding the 'joke in the social structure' of neoliberal globalization (see Section 3.2 for a discussion on neoliberalism in the context of food) can contribute to changes in the wider discourse—in the process, reimagining the site of political resistance itself by circulating through performances in the street, on social media, and even in the classroom. However, the ambiguity of this approach must reckon with the contingency of power and the capacity of humour to circulate in different, perhaps unintended, ways. A well-meaning joke might offend or be taken as a smug expression of the privileged position of the one who is able to joke. Comic resistance can thus both critique and affirm power relations. Does this imply that we should stop joking? For Michel Foucault, the idea of resistance was never about an escape from power. Instead, resistance was a question of refashioning the subject *within* power, so that 'the will not to be governed is always the will not to be governed *thusly*, like that, by these people, at this price' (Foucault 1997, 73). From this perspective, prankster resistance is less about 'opposing' or 'overcoming' globalization and more about understanding our intimate entwinement with(in) its pluralities.

9.2 Exploring Humour

In the discussion of radical comedy (in Section 9.1), we showed how humour can challenge boundaries, question hierarchies, and make serious things like the police and the WTO look silly. In productive terms, pranksters have played with the politics of the media relay, how it supports the common sense of markets, and how it can be short-circuited. But the effects of this are by no means certain. As Anton Zijderveld (1983, 58) writes:

> Humour carries an enigmatic quality: it is itself unrealistic and thereby able to demonstrate that reality as we know and live it could be otherwise; that alternatives, as unreal and absurd as they as they may seem to be, are not unthinkable. Humour shares this with utopias, and it is up to the audience to decide, by a laughing response, whether a utopia is nothing but a joke.

This line of argument shifts our gaze from the comedian to the audience, and from the prankster to the public. What difference does it make to them if the joke succeeds? And just as important, what happens if it fails?

In one prank, the Yes Men successfully posed as a spokesman for the Dow Chemical Company (formerly Union Carbide) and appeared in a live BBC News interview on the twentieth anniversary of the Bhopal chemical disaster which killed around 8,000 people and left many tens of thousands with life-changing conditions. Neither Union Carbide nor Dow has ever accepted responsibility for the factory disaster despite a long campaign from survivors. In the interview, the apparent spokesman, Jude Finisterra, takes the opportunity to apologize for everything the company has done and accepts full responsibility for the disaster, going on to promise full compensation to the families. Of course, the bitter irony is that this world of corporate responsibility *does not* actually exist, and Dow has not taken responsibility (see also Section 2.2.2 on corporate responsibility in the clothing industry). There is thus a genuine question as to whether to laugh at this joke. The prank places Dow in the acutely uncomfortable position of wondering whether it should publicly deny that they have apologized. Even those who may be sympathetic to the cause may balk at the tensions revealed: who is the joke for? Should the survivors feel good about this joke 'on their behalf'?

For all that the subversive potential of comic resistance can be productive of new modes of political engagement—in the street, through the media, even at the bus stop—it should be underlined that humour carries a number of ambiguities. Indeed, one prominent theory of humour equates laughter with power and *superiority*: that joking is often at someone else's expense (see Kuipers 2012). While comic resistances may be well intentioned, the question recurs: who gets to joke? The next section (9.2.1) will delve a little deeper into the possibilities and limits of humour by exploring how the market form of comedy has been adapted for different ethical and political causes. One set of campaigns 'use' humour as a way of raising awareness of global inequalities through development campaigns by NGOs. Humour is here regarded as a disarming genre that can resonate with a wider public to promote a sense of global responsibility. The positionality of Western celebrities within such campaigns has been a touchstone for critique and the production of new, potentially more radical, satires.

9.2.1 Can humour promote global justice?

The long-running charity campaign *Comic Relief* has seen comedians like Lenny Henry and comic producers like Richard Curtis organize a regular TV appeal to raise money for people living in poverty around the world, espousing a form of **global justice**. In basic humanitarian terms, it seems unambiguously positive that money is being raised to help fund a set of ongoing engagements with development projects.

However, John Cameron (2015, 277) argues that an overemphasis on 'techniques that aim primarily to attract donations or bolster support for development assistance without questioning the ways in which aid is used' can reinforce paternalist understandings of development. In this understanding, where parentlike donors benevolently assist childlike recipients, charity campaigns may thus come to function as a moralizing distraction from the more exploitative economic relations that exist between the Global North and Global South (see, for example, Section 3.2.1 on sovereign debt). We might well wonder, then, if campaigns like Comic Relief have proven so popular precisely because they cheer domestic audiences with a rosy post-imperial image of a well-meaning Britain.

While there are genuine tensions in Comic Relief, there are also instabilities and carnivalesque moments of *making strange* (Brassett 2009). In one short campaign sketch, for example, Ricky Gervais (2020) is filmed walking through a Kenyan village recounting how 'harrowing' it is that 'half the country live in abject poverty'. But he is now inspired by the fact that 'they don't just roll over and sit around waiting for handouts. They do whatever they can to help themselves. They fight back.' He meets Daniel Eboua, who 'like most Kenyans' lives in poverty. They enter his house and Ricky points to all his worldly possessions, which amount to a few bags and old pots and pans, a fact which he says, 'makes you feel spoilt, doesn't it? When we whinge about the things we whinge about.' And then:

> Gervais: [*Narrated*] Even though Daniel has nothing, he wanted me to have one of his most prized possessions. [*Spoken*] He's just given me a cassette tape of U2. [*Narrated*] And then came the sucker punch.
>
> Daniel: [*Spoken*] When my brother was in the hospital the doctor played him this cassette. The doctor was from England and he played this. I keep it because it reminds me of my brother. My brother died.

Ricky is visibly touched by this gesture and starts to cry. Some light music plays in the background, guitar chords from U2's 'One Love'. And Ricky assures him 'it's not your fault'. At this point his writing partner and co-star Stephen Merchant walks in and the camera pans to reveal that *everything* has taken place in a film studio.

> Merchant: Alright Ricky what are you up to mate, what are you doing?
>
> Gervais: Just doing one of those comic relief appeals from Africa.

Merchant: You're not in Africa though are you, this is BBC Television Centre.

Gervais: Yeh, I don't actually have to go there do I?

Merchant: You can't fake being in Africa.

Gervais: Yeh, I can yeh. Get a blue screen, pop the hut up, Bob's your uncle.

Merchant: No obviously technically you can fake it. You can't fake it morally.

Gervais: Right, I'm not gonna go to a country where you need injections to get into it. That's a good holiday. Also, you get just as good publicity faking it as actually going there yourself. Everyone's a winner.

To anyone familiar with Gervais's comedy, what follows is standard stuff. He mock-humbly suggests that he is one of the world's greatest living comedians and claims that his TV programme *The Office* 'changed the genre'. He finishes with the suggestion of what people at home will think of him: 'hold on though, we love everything he's done, but has he got a heart of gold? He's in Africa, the answer is yes! . . . If he's doing that then we'll continue to buy his DVDs.' Convinced of the argument, Stephen Merchant decides to take part in the video. Then comes celebrity chef Jamie Oliver, who explains that he 'hasn't been seen on TV caring about anything for at least three days'. The progress is completed when Ricky sees a 'homeless' person that turns out to be Sir Bob Geldof, the organizer of Live Aid. While Geldof initially describes the fake video shoot as a 'disgrace', he is eventually persuaded to take part because he has a single coming out. When filming is finished, Daniel takes off his mask to reveal that he is in fact Bono, the lead singer of U2, dressed up as an African in an attempt to surreptitiously promote his band's singles album.

Echoing the discomfort of the Yes Men Bhopal prank, the ironic critique works to question the positionalities of global humanitarianism, both in the sense of a 'they'—the helpless recipients of cash—but, more specifically, the idea of a 'we', including the viewer who donates to Comic Relief. The irony requires interpretive work. Why do so many celebrities want to be associated with charity campaigns? What is the effect of portraying the people they campaign for as 'helpless' but 'proud'? In similar fashion, a spoof campaign called Radi-Aid saw a group of 'cool musicians' from 'Africa' collect used radiators to send to Norway 'to save freezing Norwegians from frostbite' (Cameron, 2015). The musicians then record a charity single to encourage other Africans to share their heat with freezing Norwegians.

Photo 9.6. An official Comic Relief photo showing, from left to right, Jamie Oliver, Andi Peters (who played a Kenyan in the video), Ricky Gervais, Bono, Sir Bob Geldof, and Stephen Merchant.
Source: Comic Relief/Getty Images.

John Cameron (2015, 283) argues that 'what makes this video funny is its incongruity – citizens of a supposedly "Third World" country trying to "save" the residents of a "First World" country through the traditional mechanisms of charity'. While the terms First and Third World are no longer accepted, the hierarchy they implied is often implicit in charity campaigns and is thus explicitly parodied in these satires. Like Gervais's video, Radi-Aid plays on well-established forms of fundraising, reversing the North-to-South transfer of material goods, and thereby the saviour/victim dynamic. In so doing, it reveals both 'the absurdity of the idea that global poverty can be eliminated through charity and the one-dimensional framing in many fundraising campaigns of Africa as a poverty-stricken humanitarian disaster zone' (Cameron 2015). Indeed, the website for the video poses the question clearly:

> Imagine if every person in Africa saw the 'Africa for Norway' video and this was the only information they ever got about Norway. What would they think about Norway? If we say Africa, what do you think about? Hunger, poverty, crime or AIDS? No wonder, because in fundraising campaigns and media that's mainly what you hear about.
> (SAIH Norway 2015)

While the two sketches tease at similar hierarchies in the everyday moralization of development, their humour points in fundamentally different directions. Gervais is content to point to the moral ambiguity of global charity campaigns, especially the role of celebrities in nurturing and benefitting from the spectacle. Although the resistance is edifying, perhaps forcing a critical reflection within the viewer subject, or else contributing to a longer-term revision of Comic Relief aesthetics like avoiding 'white saviour' tropes in their fundraising videos, it is up to us to interpret the political point. In contrast, the Radi-Aid sketch is driven by a clear objective: to change the way NGOs and development actors think about their portrayal of the developing world. The aim is to recover the agency of developing countries and their citizens in the discussion of global justice.

9.2.2 Can the subaltern joke?

While humour can be a space for critical reflection on the positional hierarchies of global justice campaigns, we might still question the Western-centrism of comedy production. Who gets to joke? Very often white men from the Global North. This is a dilemma that runs through nearly all the comedy considered in this chapter, and speaks to a fundamental question in the politics of comic resistance: is satirical agency an expression of power? Bakhtin's celebration of the medieval carnivalesque was contrasted with the decline and neutering of European carnivals over time. He also contrasted the 'joyful, open, festive laugh' of the carnival with the 'closed, purely negative, satirical laugh' of modern comedy, which he argued was 'not a laughing laugh' (Bakhtin 1984, 134–5). On this view, he wondered if modern comedy can ever be 'truly resistant'. Does the clever irony of Western comedians act as a comfort blanket, a 'conscience easer' for the iniquities of globalization?

At least one aspect of the struggle over the terms of comic resistance concerns the recognition of the capacity of non-Western subjects to joke. This might be in terms of the inclusion of non-Western subjects in the very campaigns that speak 'for' them—for example, by providing a forum for African comedians in campaigns like Comic Relief. Or else, we could foreground the important contribution of non-Western comedians to global justice campaigns, for example, through the work of Superbarrio, a Mexican wrestler/working-class hero who attended Occupy demonstrations to fight *lucha libre* matches against landlords, billionaires, and one character called 'Nike Man'. In such spectacles, Bogad (2016, 147) recounts how Superbarrio worked with groups like Reclaim the Streets to 'perform solidarity across tensive borders of identity with immigrant workers'.

Saadia Gardezi (2021) looks to the potential for a critique of coloniality in political cartoons about the West. Taking insight from Gayatri Chakravorty Spivak's (1988)

Photo 9.7. Superbarrio Gómez, a 'real-life superhero' who first appeared in 1987 in support of the campaign for affordable housing by the Assembly of Neighbourhoods in Mexico City.
Source: Sergio Dorantes/Getty Images.

question of whether the **subaltern** can speak, Gardezi delineates a genealogy of Pakistani humour that was initially influenced by the racialized satires of *Punch* magazine imported by the British during its imperial rule of the wider Indian subcontinent. While *Punch* would seem to define the very capacity of Pakistanis to 'speak' humour as the subaltern subject of British imagination, Gardezi draws out how the concept of *Punch* was taken up by local groups and cartoonists in Pakistan to rework the established and racialized terms of cartooning, sometimes 'against' the imperial edifice. Instead of a 'self-consolidating Other of the West', then, Gardezi argues that political cartoons can provide a 'counter discourse', playfully inverting the image of Western power as ethical to satirize its parochial self-regard.

A recent example of postcolonial subversion can be found in *The Samaritans*, a Kenyan satire of Western Non-Governmental Organizations (NGOs). The mockumentary follows 'Aid for Aid', a fictional NGO that specializes in doing lots of nothing. Its staff have to deal with the odd demands and decisions of the UK head office and the hopelessly inept local bureaucrats, while trying to write as many useless reports as possible—all under the guise of 'saving Africa'. While this kind of joke may play on similar themes of positionality explored by Western comedians, the humour is more 'in-between' or 'hybrid'. This is something that Amanda Källstig and Carl Death develop in relation to the South African comedian Trevor Noah, who now hosts the US talk show *The Daily Show*. They place Noah's humour in terms of mimicry—a practice that they argue highlights 'the ambivalence at the heart of colonialism' (Källstig and Death 2020, 7). Essential to this process is that the mimic imitates the colonizer without becoming them, reproducing colonial culture and conduct but with a trace of mockery and menace that preserves the difference of the colonized (see also Bhabha 1984). Or, more directly, Källstig and Death note the Ethiopian proverb, 'When the great lord passes, the wise peasant bows deeply and silently farts'.

In one stand-up sketch, Noah (2019) gently chides his US audience that 'Americans don't seem to know much about South Africa . . . you don't know much about Africa as a whole . . . well you guys don't know much about anything, but that's not your fault cos you're so big and America-centric'. As a South African living in America, he recounts how the only time he's seen anything about Africa is in 'those commercials, those UNICEF ads', which ask you for money: 'I hate those ads, they don't even warn you those things are coming on the TV!' Noah complains they interrupt him enjoying comedy shows with 'this horrible village, it's dirty and old rusting buildings and these sad black people and I'm looking and I'm like "ooooo, where's that? Cleveland?!"' He laments the caricature of a poor Africa with starving children as they always have that same look on their face—'the why haven't you called look?'—and they always have a fly on their eye: 'how does a fly sit on your eye?!'. And Noah satirizes the use of

Photo 9.8. As a South African comedian hosting a US satirical news show, Noah's positionality and humour might be said to disrupt established hierarchies of difference.
Source: Rockstar Photography/Alamy Stock Photo.

celebrities, in Africa via blue screen, who explain the situation to us, because that way 'we'll understand'. While aspects of the joke may seem familiar, Noah takes it further by inserting his own history into the story:

> I hate those ads, I hate the people who make those ads, there's people starving all over the world but you can give them a bit of dignity, and you know what, I hate the people in those ads as well, they make Africans looks bad. And I can say that . . . I don't care, I grew up in a black family in Africa and no matter how poor or hungry we were, we could still do this [he motions to swat a fly away from his eye].

The difficulty of humour can be a way of inhabiting and subverting the wider power structures and postcolonial imaginaries. As Källstig and Death argue, mimicry returned as mockery 'captures something essential and crucially important about the resistive, disruptive potential of some forms of stand-up comedy. In the meeting between a joke, and the people hearing it, a range of possible new interpretations are available' (Källstig and Death 2020, 8). Different audience members will hear jokes differently. Who gets to interpret the joke? We all do. The discomfort of comedy can be the beginning of a conversation.

In similar ways to Noah, the popular Malaysian comic Harith Iskander (2016) uses the potential discomfort of comedy to subvert the racial categories integral to the development of colonial rule in British Malaya, and which are now part of everyday bureaucratic governance in post-independence Malaysia. He recounts a memory from school when he was asked to tick his race as Malay, Chinese, Indian, or Other, and realized that he didn't know what race (he) was. Placing his lived experience at the heart of the postcolonial state, he finds no way to record the combination of his Malay father and English mother, who the teacher tells him is 'not important' for this exercise. In response, Iskander puts an 'M' next to 'Other' on the form to spell 'Mother', but the teacher tells him he cannot have two, he is 'confused'. He goes on to recall that when he left school he travelled around Malaysia and realized that 'a lot of Malaysians are confused'. While Noah leaves his audience to do interpretive work, Iskander takes the same disruption of postcolonial narratives to propose a future resolution, arguing to his audience that if we can 'laugh together' then maybe one day we will only have to tick one box marked Malaysian.

9.2.3 Is humour dangerous?

In ideal form, then, humorous resistance can promote ways of thinking and acting that might change the world by making us reflect on our relations within it. As Simon

Critchley argues, there is something about humour, especially when embodied as laughter, that brings people together:

> Laughter is a convulsive movement, it is like sobbing or like an orgasm, it is involuntary, it sometimes even hurts. It is contagious and solidaristic – think of the intersubjective dimensions of giggling, particularly when it concerns something obscene. In this way, perhaps, we might say that laughter in its solidaristic dimension has an ethical function insofar as the simple sharing of a joke recalls what is shared in our lifeworld practices. (Critchley 1999, 120)

On this view the solidarity of laughter might then be the basis for new publics to be imagined: a site of shared resistance to experiences of poverty or state oppression. Yet, as this chapter has discussed, all these possibilities seem to come with important caveats like who gets to joke and about what. The caveat we consider now instead concerns the capacity of humour to offend and exclude. Is not the solidarity of laughter precisely the solidarity of those who share the joke?

One influential line of academic thinking has focused on the exclusionary politics of humour. There is always a butt of the joke, and therefore humour can also be about social discipline, encouraging conformity with certain behaviours and 'othering' those who appear to deviate from them. Evidence for this can be found in the long histories of racist and sexist comedy, or in the widespread use of stereotypes in advertising and sitcoms (Billig 2005). For all that comic resistances can problematize hierarchies of social difference in certain circumstances, there also seems to be a conservative function whereby humour might shore up and reproduce existing power relations. This problematic is especially acute when we consider the widespread circulation and legitimacy of subversive humour in contemporary market life. Think of widely used jokes about 'Karens', which ostensibly seek to problematize the haughty attitudes of self-entitled middle-class women, yet all too easily collapse into the social policing of women in the public sphere. This echoes a previous period of humour about 'chavs' in the UK, which was essentially a form of humour that stereotyped working-class people as brash, loutish, and crude. Similar dynamics might be discerned in contemporary usage of 'boomers', 'millennials', 'Chads', and 'soy boys'.

Indeed, the everyday legitimacy of irony and memes as a mode of communication has been actively engaged for populist, exclusionary, and authoritarian political purposes. On these terms, humour is recognized as an important way of engaging in public discourse where the *lack of seriousness* is precisely the point. With the subversive play of humour, otherwise problematic or difficult topics can be broached with the ready-made denial of 'it was just a joke' or 'don't you understand irony?' Think of the way populists like former US President Donald Trump used this as a defensive shield

Photo 9.9. The instability of humour was deployed as a tactic in Donald Trump's international diplomacy, announcing economic sanctions on Iran using a *Game of Thrones* meme: 'sanctions are coming'.
Source: Sipa US/Alamy Stock Photo.

to mock political opponents or stereotype people from different ethnic groups, often using the outrage that he provoked as an example for his base that the other side were overly moralizing and angry.

What might be called the 'alt-right' of white nationalism in the US has developed its own genre of memes like Pepe the Frog, innovative techniques of 'shitposting' (deliberately posting provocative or off-topic comments to upset others on social media), and a number of increasingly influential parodies of left-wing 'woke' politics such as 'the left can't meme'. Although the activities of alt-right satirists and 'irony bros' could be framed as part of the normal, albeit innovative, process of campaigning for conservative political agendas, the very uncertainty in irony explored in this chapter can also make it hard to find where the line of acceptability really is. For some critics, the use of memes like 'Let's Go Brandon' (an anti-Joe Biden slogan) can serve as a 'dog whistle' for more extreme constituencies, sending them messages that they can hear but no one else picks up on—a heightened concern in the wake of the 2021 mob attack on the US Capitol.

Finally, the rise of **post-truth politics** and widespread concerns about misinformation have become an important context in the circulation of humour. During the Covid-19 pandemic, light-hearted jokes and silly memes about the unavailability of toilet roll were seen as an important form of relief from the difficult experience of fear and isolation during lockdown. Yet critics of lockdown and vaccine sceptics also played on this use of irony with a host of puns and memes like the 'plandemic' and 'Covid-1984', referencing George Orwell's dystopian book *Nineteen Eighty-Four* about the totalitarian state. Such jokes can arguably work to affirm divides within society, provoking more fear and uncertainty. In wider terms, these kinds of post-truth instabilities have also been described as a strategic weakness in the West which is being actively targeted by authoritarian states that increasingly use memes and pranks in their programmes of disinformation or 'hybrid warfare'. Indeed, the use of humour, irony, and pranks by authoritarian states like Russia has even been framed as a key component of its strategy by NATO, which it uses to destabilize Western societies (Chernobrov 2022).

9.3 Engaging Humour

9.3.1 Make a parody collage

While Sections 9.1 and 9.2 have explored the different ways in which humour can play a role in global market life, this section will turn to engage the creative and proliferative dimension of humour by asking you to collect and design your own memes. In this sense, we will explore the 'commedification' of the global public sphere as an everyday mode of experiential learning. The feminist scholar Saara Särmä (2015) has argued that humour provides an easy and increasingly common way of coming to know global events and political controversies. There are multiple and diverse ways in which jokes and humour can impinge on events, whether through representation or critique or just plain silliness. This can sometimes mean that humour is the primary way in which we come to know the world around us:

> What we know about world politics on the everyday level in the internet age is increasingly anecdotal and accidental. The internet is a specific modality of knowledge; it is random and highly fragmented. Hence, our knowledge of many things remains fragmented if we do not actively search for more information. Because humour and laughter play a role in the circulation process (what is shared, how much, how fast), parodies can sometimes remain our sole connection to an event or issue. (Särmä 2015, 113)

The question then becomes what to do with this mass of ideas, jokes, parodies, and so forth? Särmä draws on **queer theory** and art methodologies to suggest a creative practice of collage, whereby we try to understand something about global politics through the jokes we come by—perhaps randomly, perhaps by design—assembling images and words about a subject in a collage fashion. This takes place in a fast-moving area, bringing critical politics into close contact with popular culture. As Särmä goes on to describe,

> My collages are playful and they respond to questions of knowledge production in the internet era by bringing forth memes and other internet parody images, which anyone can produce and circulate. The notions of what the international is are no longer only mediated to us by mass media, scholarly works, and academic experts. On the contrary, all and any one of us can participate.
> (Särmä 2015, 112)

In this activity we ask you to follow Särmä's lead and collect memes or other forms of internet **parody** and put them into a collage. You are encouraged to be as open as you like in terms of the content and nature of what you collect, whether images are prepared and professionally formatted, or if they involve moments when people have creatively used or deployed the meme or an aspect of its form. The only parameter we would suggest is that you pick a particular IPE theme, event, or issue to provide some focus. So, for instance, following the examples earlier you might look at memes about Donald Trump to think about Economic Nationalism or use Covid-related memes about panic buying to explore economic crisis. But equally, Särmä's method can work from the meme backwards, so if there is a popular meme or internet parody that is circulating, such as the various versions of the 'mind explosion' meme, then this could also serve as the basis for some pop critique. The point is to bring the images together and collage them in a way that is fun and creative.

In a seminar or tutorial, get into groups and present your collages to each other. Discuss what you learned from the memes you found; see whether and how the images tell a story about global market life. Again, impressions could be based on individual memes or/and the effect of random juxtapositions between images that arise in your collage. You might reflect on the following questions:

- What political point(s) do the memes highlight?
- How do they represent the market, the market subject, ethics, and/or politics of their target?
- What impact, perceived or otherwise, did the meme have?
- Would you suggest that the images are resistant, benign, conservative, or reactionary?
- Do they aim to shame or ridicule, and is this is warranted?

- Does the process lead to any kind of change?
- Does the juxtaposition of images and jokes suggest anything unexpected about the subject?

9.3.2 Make your own meme

In a second, related activity we invite you to develop and design your own meme. The subject could be an issue of direct personal concern to you or could relate to some of the topics covered in this book like student debt, dietary pressures, or unethical clothing, as shown in Photo 9.10. Try to find out if there are any examples of memes or parodies of the subject you have chosen to help give you ideas. Feel free to explore different media, whether you want to download a free meme generator that provides a set of formats to play with, or if you are already comfortable with a format like TikTok or mainly text-based sites like Twitter or Facebook. In line with Särmä's work, you might take inspiration from the feminist satires that exist on social media, from her own 'Congrats, you have an all-male panel!', which uses an ironic image of David Hasselhoff to call out public events that feature a panel of speakers without any women (see https://allmalepanels.tumblr.com), to dedicated satire accounts like @manwhohasitall ('Man Who Has It All').

Online satire is bound up with a productive conception of the audience that actively relies upon user engagement, retweets, likes, controversy, and newspaper articles (see also influencers in Section 2.1.1). For instance, @manwhohasitall is structured around a basic but effective subversion: what if you take all the cultural anxieties imputed onto modern women and cast them through a man? The result is an immediate and easily adapted perspective on the instability and ridiculousness of liberal gender norms. To take at random some tweets from this account:

- My friend is a history teacher. She's compiling a list of great historical figures and she needs to add a male to the list. Suggestions?
- Today's Debate: Why can't we believe unmarried childless men are happy?
- Today's Question: What do boys look for in a cycle helmet?
- 'Reading a wonderful little collection of men's poetry taught me how to respect men.' Claire, CEO. Thanks for being such a wonderful ally, Claire, we need more good women like you.
- I'm pitching an article to the men's section of a tabloid about the problem with men's voices and what they can do about it. Suggestions?

Indeed, this last tweet had a funny reply from another user: 'Why are men talking? If it's in the workplace they should do the following: 1) Don't talk unless asked a direct question. 2) Speak in a low pleasant modulated tone. 3) Smile, as he has been acknowledged, and thank the person asking the question.' This capacity for different forms of engagement in and through feminist satire is perhaps a more challenging question for thinking about comic resistance. Increasingly the audience is a productive element in humour: feminist satire as a space of conversation and engagement, where the joke is essentially uncontrollable and subject to circulation, adaptation, and new iterations. There is a pronounced ethos of reciprocity, whereby comedians can both build their respective fan bases and foster new talent in a supportive environment. Bringing this ethos into the learning activity, once you have produced your memes, discuss them in class in relation to themes and issues in IPE, but also try and build on them together and see where the jokes take you.

Photo 9.10. This meme was created by one of the student panel members, Susbin Shrestha, using the meme generator imgflip.com.

9.4 Conclusion

The chapter has explored the everyday political economy of humour via three related concepts of resistance, carnival, and subversion. Humour, irony, and sometimes just playful improvisations can disrupt the established terms of discourse on market relations as serious material and governed by immutable laws. By overidentifying with the core logics of trade and capitalism—suits, masculinity, and media-friendly images—prankster groups explored creative techniques of resistance and subversion. Acknowledging certain ambiguities in comic resistance—not least that it embodies many of the intersections of power that it seeks to challenge—the chapter questioned how humour can contribute to the imagination of global justice. While the reflexive conversation over global justice that irony can promote is of critical value, Section 9.2 argued that we should go beyond the Western, masculine, and 'humanitarian' concerns of existing humour. This licensed a move to think through certain postcolonial forms of comic agency, and a further engagement with feminist satire was developed through the activities of the final section, which asked you to reflect on the affective and pedagogical scope of memes.

 Access the online resources for quizzes, student reflection podcasts, and support for tackling the chapter's learning activities: http://www.oup.com/he/i-peel1e.

RESOURCES

Tile recommendations from the I-PEEL website: 'laughter' (Amanda Källstig) http://i-peel.org/homepage/laughter/; 'humanitarianism' (Lisa Ann Richey) http://i-peel.org/homepage/humanitarianism/.

Brandalism. An international collective of artists that challenge corporate power, greed, and corruption around the world. Available at http://www.Brandalism.ch.

Larry Charles' Dangerous World of Comedy. 2019. Netflix. Four-part documentary series on humour in difficult contexts exploring issues including war, Ebola, racism, misogyny, and homophobia.

The Samaritans. 2014. Kenyan mockumentary TV series based around a fictional NGO 'Aid for Aid' that satirizes the international development industry. Can be viewed at http://www.aidforaid.org.

The Yes Men. 2003. 83 minutes. Directed by Dan Ollman, Sarah Price, and Chris Smith, this documentary is about how anti-globalization activists use culture-jamming techniques to politicize and resist global trade.

Bogad, Lawrence M. 2016. *Tactical Performance: The Theory and Practice of Serious Play*. Oxford and New York: Routledge. Draws upon the author's first-hand involvement in humorous political activism including the 'clownfrontations' of the Clandestine Insurgent Rebel Clown Army (CIRCA) at the 2005 G8 summit.

Brassett, James. 2021. *The Ironic State: British Comedy and the Everyday Politics of Globalization*. Bristol: Bristol University Press. Written by the lead author of this chapter, this book explores how comedy can provide a window into the everyday politics of globalization in the context of the UK.

de Goede, Marieke. 2005. 'Carnival of Money: Politics of Dissent in an Era of Globalizing Finance'. In *The Global Resistance Reader*, ed. Louise Amoore, 379–91. Oxford and New York: Routledge. Explores the special role of laughter and irony in political resistance to the power of global finance and in imagining financial alternatives.

REFERENCES

Bakhtin, Mikhail. 1984. *Rabelais and His World*. Bloomington: Indiana University Press.

Berlant, Laurent, and Sianne Ngai. 2017. 'Comedy Has Issues'. *Critical Inquiry* 43(2): 233–49.

Bhabha, Homi. 1984. 'Of Mimicry and Man: The Ambivalence of Colonial Discourse'. *October* 28: 125–33.

Billig, Michael. 2005. *Laughter and Ridicule: Towards a Social Critique of Humour*. London: Sage.

Bogad, Lawrence M. 2016. *Tactical Performance: The Theory and Practice of Serious Play*. Abingdon and New York: Routledge.

Brassett, James. 2009. 'British Irony, Global Justice: A Pragmatic Reading of Chris Brown, Banksy, and Ricky Gervais'. *Review of International Studies* 35(1): 219–45.

Brassett, James. 2016. 'British Comedy, Global Resistance: Russell Brand, Charlie Brooker and Stewart Lee'. *European Journal of International Relations* 22(1): 168–91.

Brassett, James. 2021. *The Ironic State: British Comedy and the Everyday Politics of Globalization*. Bristol: Bristol University Press.

Butler, Judith. 1990. *Gender Trouble: Feminism and the Subversion of Identity*. London: Routledge.

Cameron, John. 2015. 'Can Poverty Be Funny? The Serious Use of Humour as a Strategy of Public Engagement for Global Justice'. *Third World Quarterly* 36(2): 274–90.

Chernobrov, Dmitry. 2022. 'Strategic Humour: Public Diplomacy and Comic Framing of Foreign Policy Issue'. *British Journal of Politics and International Relations* 24(2): 277–96.

Critchley, Simon. 1999. 'Comedy and Finitude: Displacing the Tragic-Heroic Paradigm in Philosophy and Psychoanalysis'. *Constellations* 6(1): 108–22.

de Goede, Marieke. 2005. 'Carnival of Money: Politics of Dissent in an Era of Globalizing Finance'. In *The Global Resistance* Reader, ed. Louise Amoore, 379–91. Abingdon and New York: Routledge.

Douglas, Mary. 1968. 'The Social Control of Cognition: Some Factors in Joke Perception'. *Man* 3(3): 361–76.

Foucault, Michel. 1997. *The Politics of Truth*. New York: Semiotext(e).

Gardezi, Saadia. 2021. 'Imagining Security in Pakistan'. Paper resented at the British Academy Workshop 'Laugh or Cry? Anxiety, Humour and Global Politics', held at the University of Warwick, 23 September.

Gervais, Ricky. 2020. 'Ricky Gervais' African Appeal, Comic Relief'. YouTube video, https://www.youtube.com/watch?v=KK819106cfc.

Haugerud, Angelique. 2013. *No Billionaire Left Behind: Satirical Activism in America*. Stanford: Stanford University Press.

Iskander, Harith. 2016. 'The Question of Race and Ethnicity'. YouTube video, www.youtube.com/watch?v=1a4ryGy5HzQ.

Källstig, Amanda, and Carl Death. 2020. 'Laughter, Resistance and Ambivalence in Trevor Noah's Stand-up Comedy: Returning Mimicry as Mockery'. *Critical African Studies* 13(3): 338–55.

Kuipers, Giselinde. 2012. 'Schadenfreude and Social Life: A Comparative Perspective on the Expression and Regulation of Mirth at the Expense of Others'. In *Schadenfreude: Understanding Pleasure at the Misfortune of Others*, ed. Wilco W. van Dijk and Jaap W. Ouwerkerk, 259–74. Cambridge: Cambridge University Press.

Marshall, Emily Zobel. 2019. 'Power, Performance and Play: Caribbean Carnival and the Cultural Politics of Emancipation'. *Caribbean Quarterly*, 65(4): 483–90.

Noah, Trevor. 2019. 'Starving Africans and Oprah's School'. YouTube video, https://www.youtube.com/watch?v=l4Q6kYZx1Ck.

Oliver, John. 2016. 'Debt Buyers'. YouTube video, https://www.youtube.com/watch?v=hxUAntt1z2c.

Orwell, George. 1945. 'Funny, But Not Vulgar'. *Leader Magazine*, 28 July.

SAIH Norway. 2015. 'Africa for Norway – New Charity Single Out Now!'. YouTube video, https://www.youtube.com/watch?v=oJLqyuxm96k.

Särmä, Saara. 2015. 'Collage: An Art Inspired Methodology For Studying World Politics'. In *Popular Culture and World Politics: Theories, Methods, Pedagogies*, ed. Federica Caso and Caitlin Hamilton, 110–119. Bristol: E-International Relations.

Spivak, Gayatri Chakravorty. 1988. 'Can the subaltern speak?' In *Marxism and the Interpretation of Culture*, ed. C. Nelson, and L. Grossberg. Basingstoke: Macmillan Press.

Yes Men, The. 2004. *The Yes Men: The True Story of the End of the World Trade Organization*. New York: Disinformation Co. Ltd.

Zijderveld, Anton. 1983. 'Trend Report: The Sociology of Humour and Laughter'. *Current Sociology* 31(3): 1–100.

Žižek, Slavoj. 2008. *The Sublime Object of Ideology*. London: Verso.

10 CONCLUSION

10.1	Exploring the IPE of Everyday Life	272
10.2	Engaging the IPE of Everyday Life	276
10.3	The End of Your Journey—At Least With Us	281

Conclusion

LEARNING OBJECTIVES

- Identify ways in which a focus on the 'the everyday' enriches IPE analysis
- Describe how your own experiences can be brought to bear on the field of IPE empirically and methodologically, and what this means in terms of its diversity
- Create your own I-PEEL tile using the insights gained from the book

READER'S GUIDE

In this short Conclusion we summarize key aspects of your learning journey through this book. In the first section, 'Exploring the IPE of Everyday Life', we remind ourselves what it means to take an everyday approach to the study of International Political Economy, and review the core concepts introduced and operationalized in the eight thematic chapters (Section 10.1). In the second section, 'Engaging the IPE of Everyday Life', we summarize the learning activities you were set and the analytical and practical skills they equipped you with, before outlining the book's final activity: creating your own I-PEEL tile (Section 10.2.2).

10.1 Exploring the IPE of Everyday Life

In her field-defining book *States and Markets*, Susan Strange described International Political Economy as the study of global systems of production, exchange, and distribution, with a view to understanding what those mean for the basic values of wealth, security, freedom, and justice. For Strange, as for many other IPE scholars of her time including Robert Gilpin and Robert Cox (discussed in Section 1.2), the mix of values that people experienced were fundamentally about power (Strange 1988). What we have sought to do in our book is to connect this academic field and its animating questions to everyday life. For example, alongside states and markets we have also looked at households as important sites of power. Alongside production, exchange, and distribution, we have also considered the contested economic sphere of consumption. And instead of beginning with distant institutions or abstract issues, we have started with the familiar, taking everyday objects, subjects, and practices as both entry points into IPE and things to be studied in themselves. This, in essence, has been the I-PEEL approach.

10.1.1 How have I studied everyday IPE?

The book began by outlining some of the intellectual lineages of everyday IPE, which established the grounds for its theoretical diversity and openness to different ways of seeing the world (see Section 1.2). As a result, we deployed a number of usages of 'the everyday' across the chapters, often as an adjective to terms such as approach, actors, life, practice, and so on. However, writing a textbook is an unavoidable exercise in what Ben Clift and co-authors identify as 'boundary work' in that it has to intervene in 'how the contemporary field of IPE gets understood, discussed, and legitimized' (Clift et al. 2020, 1). In this light it is important to emphasize that, whilst the everyday presents a distinct entry point to the study of IPE, taking such an approach by no means rejects the idea that there are other such entry points or levels of analysis. Indeed, we hoped to have shown in the 'Exploring' sections of the chapters how these can sometimes be complementary, with analyses crossing from the everyday to the systemic and back again. What we think everyday IPE can do, then, is help open up the field of IPE to new sets of questions and pathways of enquiry, as well as offer tools for analysing and understanding the changing nature of the international, the political, and the economic.

A simple way of visualizing this is to use word clouds, which are derived from the most frequently used terms within a given text. Figure 10.1a is based on the Introduction of this book, while Figure 10.1b is based on a corpus of 645 English-language articles from key IPE journals. While some terms are common to both—global, power, market—there are also clear differences of emphasis, with this book foregrounding terms including women, work, and capitalism. Have a look at the word cloud generator in the Resources section and try running your own essays through it. What does it reveal about the focus of your analysis?

10.1.2 Who have I studied in everyday IPE?

As mentioned in Section 10.1.1, the chapters in this textbook are not organized around theoretical approaches or 'big' IPE issues. Rather, each one starts with an everyday object, subject, or practice. We presented these in the form of what we termed opening 'tile' sections: short engagements combining analysis and commentary with visual sources. These sections were designed to take you on a journey, so that through your

Conclusion

Figure 10.1a. Word cloud of the Introduction to I-PEEL.
Source: Image produced by the authors.

Figure 10.1b. Word cloud of the IPE literature (Seabrooke and Young 2017, 301).

initial engagement with something commonplace you were provided with a concrete entry point to understanding the content and relevance of IPE scholarship. In so doing, rather than focusing just on political and economic elites, we sought to foreground the experiences of everyday actors, often overlooked but far from irrelevant: Gojek drivers in Jakarta who simultaneously enact and oppose platform capitalism, US military spouses who through their caring labour make possible violent military intervention, comedy activists who mock capitalism through its memes, or fitness influencers who promote healthy lifestyles whilst selling themselves as a brand. Neither 'hero' nor 'villain', these figures each embody that tension in the everyday that we mentioned in the book's Introduction (see Section 1.1). This is a tension between conformity and contravention, between reproducing and resisting those broader political economy processes in which we all find ourselves enmeshed.

At the time of writing, all four of us were based at the University of Warwick in England. Nevertheless, our intention was to speak to a global community of IPE scholar-students and reflect some of the diversity of IPE thought and practice. To this end, and often guided by our own research work, we have sought to incorporate examples from different regions and communities. And yet there is no way around the fact that we have unavoidably brought our own biases and privileges to the writing of this book. One of the most deep-seated of these is the centrality of English language to our engagement with IPE, with three of us also being native English speakers. In this respect we are encouraged that the I-PEEL website (Section 1.3.1) has been taken up as a pedagogical resource in countries where English is not spoken as a first language, suggesting that the approach does have something of a global appeal. At the same time, we would like to point to the crucial importance of translation work in bringing scholarship, and scholars, across linguistic barriers, especially those that exist around anglophone academia (see Section Resources).

10.1.3 What have I studied in everyday IPE?

In advancing a mode of analysis grounded in everyday objects, subjects, and practices, much of the empirical subject matter is driven by the case selection. Choose chocolate, student debt, or any of the other tile topics at the start of each chapter, and that is what you will find out more about. While these are interesting and important in their own right, what is likely to be of more *general* use in your studies are the twenty-four core concepts that we introduce in this book. This is because these concepts are relevant not just to the substantive focus of their respective chapters but also to wider debates in IPE and cognate fields.

A first group of concepts sought to characterize key features of contemporary global capitalism such as neoliberalism (Section 3.2), commodification (Section 4.1.1), financialization (Section 4.1.3), and the emergence of the attention economy and gig economy (Sections 7.1.2 and 8.1.2). A second group brought to the fore the processes, networks, and webs of social relations that make these features possible, including feminization (Section 2.2.1), global value chains, and global care chains (Sections 3.1.2 and 5.2.3), social reproduction (Section 5.1.1), the global city (Section 6.2.1), and platform capitalism (Section 8.1.3). A third group of concepts focused on the rules, norms, and techniques of governance, ranging from corporate social responsibility (Section 2.2.2) and state rescaling (Section 6.2.2) to governmentality (Section 3.2.2) and heteronormativity (Section 5.1.3). A fourth group of concepts considered the ways in which we as individuals are enrolled in global capitalism through practices of fast fashion (Section 2.1), assetization including of oneself (Section 4.1.2), self-branding (Section 7.1.1), and the marketization of everyday life (Section 8.1.1). Finally, a fifth group of concepts helped to think through challenges to these transformations, be it via the right to the city (Section 6.2.3), the prosumer (Section 7.1.3), resistance (Section 9.1.1), carnival (Section 9.1.2), or subversion (Section 9.1.3).

In offering these case studies and concepts, we hope to have demonstrated the merits of the I-PEEL approach to studying global capitalism. Following on from this, throughout the book, and particularly in the activities in the 'Engaging' section of each chapter, we also sought to show how *your* experiences can be used to develop existing scholarship, bringing new questions or perspectives to bear on the field of IPE. The next section recaps these exercises and sets one final challenge, designed to help you make that scholarly contribution.

10.2 Engaging the IPE of Everyday Life

The I-PEEL approach was developed as a response to our experiences of teaching face-to-face, small-group, discussion-based seminars. In our teaching, we asked our students to reflect on their own everyday practices, consumption habits, responses to particular images, and so on, and found that this made for fruitful class discussions that complemented and enhanced the required readings. Yet the world of learning does not stay still, in particular given the impact of the Covid-19 pandemic on teaching delivery and the rise of the virtual classroom. Students and teachers had to adapt, often rapidly so, to ever-shifting learning conditions. Given this, we have formulated the activities in this book in a way that allows for a certain flexibility in how they are undertaken, whether online or offline, individually or collectively. Nevertheless, their aim remains the same: to allow engaged reflection, to think and do IPE differently, and to translate academic interest into practical action. In the remainder of this section we briefly summarize the key learning activities and methods introduced in this book, before setting out some guidance as to how you can create your own tile to finish off your I-PEEL learning journey.

10.2.1 Reflect, enact, create: three approaches to activating your I-PEEL mindset

I-PEEL encourages an active and activist learning approach, and we have included a number of exercises and learning activities to this end. These activities served to develop your ability to think critically and independently, ultimately with a view to becoming a 'knowledge producer' yourself. We suggest that these activities can be loosely grouped into three categories—reflect, enact, create—each with its own emphasis in developing and testing different skill sets.

Throughout the book we have encouraged you to use class discussion to prepare for these activities, and for sharing and reflecting on their outcomes. But it is important to note that many of these activities could also be done independently. Even if there is no module credit attached to them, we encourage you to do them for their own sake. The activities we included in this book are not the usual essay questions intended to prompt subject-specific writing, but a deliberately varied set of tasks to help you apply the ideas and techniques discussed in fun and engaging ways.

A first group of activities in the 'Engaging' section of the chapters invited you to *reflect* on your own daily economic practices and how they connected you to global capitalism. With this group of activities, we hoped to give you the self-confidence to draw on your own experiences as a valid source of data.

Table 10.1 Reflective activities in I-PEEL

Activity	Objective	Type of Exercise
Food autoethnography (**Section 3.3.1**)	Write an informal essay on your motivations and capabilities to develop critical insight into yourself as a consumer	Independent study exercise (~1 hour)
Usury thought experiment (**Section 4.3.1**)	Draw on our personal experiences to rationalize a suggested response that can be abstracted into more general and impersonal conclusions	Independent study or classroom exercise (~30 minutes)
Time use survey (**Section 5.3.1**)	Capture time spend by you and other members of your household on caring along with other activities	Independent study exercise (several days, depending on design of time diary)
Social media resistance deliberation (**Section 7.3.1**)	Think through the question of your online presence and how this relates to practices of resistance on/to social media	Independent study or classroom exercise (~1 hour)
Diverse economies iceberg (**Section 8.3.1**)	Visualize the diverse range of economic activities that underpin and make possible your own economic actions	Classroom exercise (~30 minutes)

A second group of 'Engaging' activities asked you to *enact* various economic scenarios, often putting yourself in the position of others, to learn about how we do and think IPE, and how this can be done differently. Through these exercises, which connect to our understanding of students as researchers-in-training, we sought to encourage empathetic interaction and imagination.

Table 10.2 Enacting activities in I-PEEL

Activity	Objective	Type of Exercise
Develop an ethical clothing campaign (**Section 2.3.1**)	Inspect the labels of your clothing to learn where they come from and consider what form and targets an ethical clothing campaign might take	Independent or group study exercise (~1 hour)
Vegan foodscape (**Section 3.3.2**)	Render visible one aspect of the moral economy of food as depicted in the world around you	Independent or group study exercise (~half day)
Debt relief role-play (**Section 4.3.2**)	Take the persona of someone else to develop an understanding of their interests, arguments, and agency	Classroom exercise (~1 hour, can be played in iterations)
Social annotation of a policy document (**Section 5.3.2**)	Work collaboratively to comment on the assumptions and biases of a policy document in respect to care work	Group study exercise (~half day)
Privilege trail (**Section 6.3.1**)	(Virtually) Walk an urban landscape and identify how it privileges some and excludes others	Independent or group study exercise (~half day)
Parody collage (Section 9.3.1)	Collate images/text of jokes, memes, and other parodies on an IPE theme to generate ideas on how we encounter global politics through humour	Independent or group study exercise (~half day)

A third group of 'Engaging' activities required a lot more action, inviting you not just to reflect and to enact but also to *create*. With these exercises, we wanted to show in particular how non-textual work like visual displays or verbal presentations can be academic, and moreover serve as powerful resources for activism. Many of these exercises may best have been conducted as group-based term projects, although our student research assistants also tackled them on their own. Perhaps as a final note, it is important to see these activities and the way we have grouped them together as a

Table 10.3 Creative activities in I-PEEL

Activity	Objective	Type of Exercise
Stories of clothing disposal (Section 2.3.2)	Curate a story of disposal to communicate with a wider audience	Term project (~2 weeks)
Urban development video presentation (Section 6.3.2)	Produce a study on an urban development project, tracing the international flows of moneys involved	Term project (~1 week)
Documentary film review poster (Section 7.3.2)	Design a poster to convey the political position policy prescriptions of a documentary film about social media	Independent or group study exercise (~1 day)
Community mapping (Section 8.3.2)	Identify and develop obstacles to and resources for community-based action, for example with regard to food justice	Term project (~1 week)
Meme-making (Section 9.3.2)	Design your own memes that subvert existing hierarchies and ways of knowing	Classroom exercise (~2 hours) or longer if played as a campaign

heuristic or rule of thumb. So, for example, the privilege trail invited you to reflect and engage your own privilege, but of course this exercise may also be extended and serve as a resource for community action.

10.2.2 Create your own I-PEEL tile

As a final research activity and to put into action everything you have learnt on this journey, we invite you to create your own tile. To recall, a tile is the name we gave to the entries on the I-PEEL website (http://i-peel.org/) which use an everyday object, subject, or practice as an entry point to IPE analysis. Creating your own tile will help you to develop several skills, including articulating multimedia sources and conveying complex topics through concise writing.

Let us first set out a basic format to help structure your tile. Based on the model we adopted for the website, we suggest you write 1,500 words, split into four thematic sections:

- Start with the object/subject/practice and set up the central question you will address
- Introduce a relevant concept to help do this

- Speak to the question about the object/subject/practice through the concept
- Outline some academic implications of your analysis.

In regard to the central question, the I-PEEL website features these on the home page, visible when you hover over the tile. For example, the question for Dieting is 'Why is weight loss seen as an individual responsibility?' and for Knotweed it is 'How can nature gain economic value?' The website tiles are also saturated with images, which we encourage you to use too. In particular, we suggest finding images that enhance your analysis: these might be graphs that convey complex data, photos that capture power relations at work, or memes that demonstrate the popular cultural reach of a topic. It is good practice to treat images in the same way as text: make sure you are using publicly available sources and cite where they came from.

The first option of what to write about is 'mobile money'. We suggest this as a set topic, given its likely familiarity to you and also because of its connections with many of the key concepts adopted in this book. Mobile money refers to financial transactions conducted using a mobile phone and has become ubiquitous as an everyday practice the world over. There is a sizeable literature on the Kenyan money transfer service M-Pesa, for instance, with advocates and critics debating its effects on poverty reduction and gender equality (for IPE analyses see Bateman et al. 2019; Natile 2020). This in turn relates to broader themes such as the politics of financial inclusion, the reproduction of the heteronormative family through transnational remittances, and the power of financial technology or 'fintech' in international development (see Bernards and Campbell-Verduyn 2019; Gabor and Brooks 2017; Kunz 2018). Of course, these lines of enquiry are not confined to the Global South or to questions of development. In our research we have considered how mobile payments have been used in the Global North to craft 'user experiences' so as to produce an intimate connection between online brands and consumers' everyday life, but which at the same time open up possibilities for new forms of impersonal solidarity within the digital economy (Kremers and Brassett 2017; see also Maurer 2015). In short, mobile money offers a number of starting points for exploring the (everyday) IPE literature.

The second option, which we would very much encourage you to try, is to pick your own topic. There are two ways to go about this. One is to work backwards from an argument you want to make or concept you want to apply towards something that lends itself to this as an illustrative example. For instance, a discussion of international inequalities arising from unequal exchange could begin with consumer products dependent on imports from the Global South, such as a cup of coffee or an electronic toy. The other way is to choose something that is of intrinsic interest that you want to study for its own sake. If these are also objects/subjects/practices involving relatively new technologies such as robotic housekeepers, undergoing rapid

Photo 10.1. Mobile, card, cash, or credit . . . does the mode of payment make a difference?
Source: EyeEm/Alamy Stock Photo.

transformations as in post-pandemic homeworking, or largely unexplored topics like the trade in human hair, then there is also a good chance that you can begin to push at the boundaries of IPE, finding gaps in the existing literature. If it feels like this when you are writing the tile, why not see if you can take it up as an extended essay or dissertation project? Many PhD theses are born of such assessments, and many research agendas of PhD theses.

10.3 The End of Your Journey—At Least With Us

This book invited you on a journey to study IPE using everyday objects, subjects, and practices as entry points. Thanks for staying the course—we hope you enjoyed learning more about what connects you to global capitalism, and how we can change it. In our pedagogic approach, we sought to break down barriers between 'scholar' and 'student' and inspire you to think and reflect about how global market life is political, and to engage it through a number of practical exercises and research challenges. In our work we were very much guided by our experience over the years of working through these topics with our own students, from whom we have learnt so much.

Whilst our journey with you is coming to an end, we are confident that it has equipped you with the conceptual and methodological tools to embark on your own exploration of the International Political Economy of Everyday Life.

 Access the online support for tackling the chapter's learning activity: http://www.oup.com/he/i-peel1e.

RESOURCES

Alternautus. '(Re)Searching Development: The Abya Yala Chapter'. A blog and online journal that brings Latin-American intellectual reflections on development to larger English-speaking audiences. http://www.alternautas.net/

Diagonales Atlantiques/Diagonales Atlánticas This is a glossary of key IPE terms, in both French and Spanish (and available for translation into English). It makes us question how our language mediates how we approach and understand the global economy. https://sepia2.unil.ch/wp/diagonal/

Follow the Things. This website invites you to ask the question, 'Who makes the things that we buy?' You can use it to trace various objects, including UK banknotes and coins, electrical goods, and health and beauty products, among others. http://followthethings.com/

Free Word Cloud Generator. MonkeyLearn. This online tool allows you to generate your own word clouds. https://monkeylearn.com/word-cloud/

Padlet. This provides a real-time collaborative web platform in which users can upload, organize, and share content to virtual bulletin boards and could be used in the development of a tile.

Tumblr.com. This is a straightforward blog-style website that can be used to upload and host your own tiles.

REFERENCES

Bateman, Milford, Maren Duvendack, and Nicholas Loubere. 2019. 'Is Fin-Tech the New Panacea for Poverty Alleviation and Local Development? Contesting Suri and Jack's M-Pesa Findings Published in *Science*'. *Review of African Political Economy* 46(161): 480–95.

Bernards, Nick, and Malcolm Campbell-Verduyn. 2019. 'Understanding Technological Change in Global Finance through Infrastructures'. *Review of International Political Economy* 26(5): 773–89.

Clift, Ben, Peter Marcus Kristensen, and Ben Rosamond. 2020. 'Remembering and Forgetting IPE: Disciplinary History as Boundary Work'. *Review of International Political Economy*, DOI:10.1080/09692290.2020.1826341.

Gabor, Daniela, and Sally Brooks. 2017. 'The Digital Revolution in Financial Inclusion: International Development in the Fintech Era'. *New Political Economy* 22(4): 423–36.

Kremers, Ruben, and James Brassett. 2017. 'Mobile Payments, Social Money: Everyday Politics of the Consumer Subject'. *New Political Economy* 22(6): 645–60.

Kunz, Rahel. 2018. 'Remittances in the Global Political Economy'. In *Handbook on the International Political Economy of Gender* ed. Juanita Elias and Adrienne Roberts, 265–80. Cheltenham: Edward Elgar Publishing.

Maurer, Bill. 2015. *How Would You Like to Pay?* Durham, NC: Duke University Press.

Natile, Serena. 2020. *The Exclusionary Politics of Digital Financial Inclusion: Mobile Money, Gendered Walls*. Abingdon and New York: Routledge.

Seabrooke, Len, and Kevin. L. Young. 2017. 'The Networks and Niches of International Political Economy'. *Review of International Political Economy* 24(2): 288–331.

Strange, Susan. 1988. *States and Markets: An Introduction to International Political Economy*. London: Pinter.

GLOSSARY

1. INTRODUCTION

banal nationalism the ideological habits which indicate the nation on a daily basis in the lives of its citizenry, thereby enabling established nations to be reproduced

capitalism an economic and political system organized around the continual expansion of capital accumulation via generalized commodity production and private ownership of the means of production

commodity fetishism a concept developed in the writings of Karl Marx that refers to an understanding of the economy as based on market relationships between commodities rather than social relationships between people

common sense for Antonio Gramsci this refers to the collective, albeit contradictory, set of ideas that exists in popular opinion

critical theory a perspective which seeks to stand apart from the prevailing order of the world, asking how that order came about, whose interests it serves, and how it should change

discourse the web of meanings which define the limits, variations, and effects of what can be said or written in a given context

Economic Nationalism an approach to IPE that has emphasized the role of the state, drawing attention to the importance of international rivalries and the constant threat of conflict in shaping interactions

everyday life for Henri Lefebvre this is a historically produced domain where the dominated sphere of the everyday meets the undominated sphere of daily life

feminist sense for Cynthia Enloe this refers to the methodological impulse to study global politics through the everyday realities of diverse, non-elite groups

intersectionality the effects that ensue when multiple axes of differentiation intersect in historically specific ways

liberalism an approach to IPE that has emphasized the role of firms and international organizations alongside states, drawing attention to the importance of market exchange and the possibilities for mutual gains between national economies

market the physical or virtual site where goods and services are exchanged, but also a way of organizing economic relations

Marxism an approach to IPE that has emphasized the role of classes, drawing attention to the labour exploitation that cuts across national borders and how this inequality might be challenged

patriarchy rule by the father, a social system organized around the dominance of men and their preferences

pedagogy the methods and practices used to teach an academic field

subjectivity a socially constructed selfhood in which an individual's identity is both historically contingent and politically consequential

2. CLOTHES

codes of conduct statements of minimum standards with regard to labour and environmental issues that firms assert they will voluntarily adhere to

corporate social responsibility (CSR) a voluntary and non-binding approach to business practice whereby certain minimum ethical commitments are adopted, usually relating to labour, environmental, and human-rights standards

dumping when products are exported to another country and sold below the usual price, undermining the competitiveness of domestic producers

export-led industrialization a development strategy that has typically involved the rapid expansion of low-wage manufacturing such as garment and consumer electronics production and the use of specific state incentives such as tax breaks and the establishment of export-processing zones

fast fashion the continual updating of fashion trends, usually associated with the availability of cheap clothing produced in relatively small production runs based on the application of just-in-time production principles

feminization how certain types of work come to be dominated by female workers, usually jobs associated with declining rates of pay, poor conditions of work, and the assumption that workers are 'flexible'

free trade the absence of barriers such as tariffs or export controls to trade

just-in-time production a model of manufacturing that leverages developments in logistics and distribution technologies in order to minimize wait times in the production process

Sustainable Development Goals (SDGs) a set of seventeen development goals to be achieved by the member states of the United Nations by 2030

3. FOOD

class diets modes of food consumption that are organized on the basis of people's position in the capitalist hierarchy rather than by their nationality, religion, gender, age, etc.

conditions of production the fundamental things needed in order for production to take place, including stable ecologies, healthy workers, and functioning infrastructure

Economic Man a portrayal of humans as utility-maximizing and narrowly self-interested individuals, sometimes referred to in Latin as *homo economicus*

embodied neoliberalism the effects on the body of internalizing the governing logics of self-autonomy and personal responsibility

entitlement in relation to food security, a dependable means by which a person legally acquires food

foodscape the places where meanings about food are rendered visible

global value chain the linked activities of firms involved in bringing a product from conception to consumption across national borders

governmentality the techniques used to govern the conduct of a population through positive means rather than coercive ones

industrial foods factory-made food and drink which are standardized, durable, highly processed, and of limited nutritional value

law of value the competitive dynamic in capitalism that compels businesses to produce commodities below the average cost of the socially necessary labour time taken to make them

moral economy the norms and sentiments regarding the responsibilities and rights of individuals and institutions with respect to others

negative value the combination of rising costs of production and the planetary instability of climate change that constitutes biophysical limits to capital accumulation which cannot be externalized

neoliberalism variously a utopian market order, a political project to restore class power, or a way of governing society by inducing people to act according to economic calculation

personal responsibility a moral injunction to take control of your life and accept that outcomes are down to individual decisions

private governance rules and standards agreed, monitored, and enforced by non-state actors, which act as an alternative or complement to public regulation established by states

symbolic value the price premium derived from intangible quality attributes in a commodity communicating social meaning or status

upgrading moving into higher value-adding activities to increase the economic benefits of participation in a global value chain

4. DEBT

assetization a contingent process that turns a thing (or quality) into an asset in which investors can invest

austerity a moral and economic agenda to live more frugally, which as government policy often involves fiscal consolidation

bondholders the investors and owners of debt securities

collateral an asset that can serve as a security for a loan

commodification the process of turning a thing into a commodity that can be bought and sold in the market

consumption smoothing the idea that consumption patterns are stable over a person's life course, with indebtedness offset by the expectation of future earnings, and the expectation of lower earnings in the future offset by saving for old age

corporate debt debt owed by companies

debt relief the partial or total forgiveness of debt, which can include extending the repayment schedule for a loan

debt sustainability the ability of debt being repaid without recourse to new borrowing

ecological debt the consumption of nature/natural resources beyond nature's ability to regenerate these resources and absorb the waste that is created in the consumption process

education inflation the rapid increase in the price of education, including, for example, university tuition fees

financialization a process whereby financial markets, financial actors, and financial motives increase their relative influence in the economy

fiscal consolidation a policy aimed at reducing budget deficits and government spending

household debt the debt owed by individuals and households

human capital the idea that we can apply a value to human knowledge and skills—and that they can generate a return

interest the rate of money that you pay/ receive for taking/making a loan

joint liability a mechanism where two or more people are liable for an obligation such as a loan repayment

leverage using borrowed money for an investment

microfinance relatively small sums of financing provided to people who lack formal sources of income or a credit history

moral hazard the idea that a party in a transaction might alter its behaviour to the detriment of the other party once a contract has been agreed

securitization a process in which loans are bundled and sold on to investors

sovereign debt the debt owed by a government

subprime mortgages a mortgage loan to a person with a poor credit score

usury the practice of lending at an interest rate that is deemed excessive

yield the return on an investment

5. CARE

affective labour the labour involved in generating affective responses in others, often classified as a form of immaterial labour that produces non-material goods such as services

Black Feminism a stream of feminist work associated with the writings of mainly African American scholars which draw attention to the centrality of race in understanding the dynamics of gender inequality

depletion through social reproduction (DSR) a concept that seeks to identify the costs and harms that stem from the lack of recognition for social reproduction which occur when the gap between social reproduction 'inflows' and 'outflows' falls below a sustainable threshold

framing something that political actors do in order to influence how issues are perceived by those that they are intended to influence

gendered division of labour can relate to women taking responsibility for domestic labour, with men more likely to work in paid employment, as well as forms of occupational segregation whereby men and women are confined to different job roles within specific workplaces

global care chain the transfer of care labour from poor(er) to rich(er) nations and the knock-on material and emotional effects of the 'care deficits' that are left behind in households dependent on migrant remittances

heteronormativity the cultural norms that structure and lend coherence to understandings of love, intimacy, and the family in ways that privilege heterosexuality

homonormativity how heteronormative ideals, values, and practices come to be privileged and performed by homosexual people

informed consent a key principle of ethical research conduct which insists that research subjects know how and why the researcher is collecting this data and agree that it can be used for specific purposes

intersectional relating to intersectionality, namely the effects that ensue when multiple axes of differentiation intersect in historically specific ways

Marxist Feminism a body of feminist work that draws upon Marxist ideas and identifies the centrality of women's unwaged labour to the functioning of capitalism and how gender subordination serves as a form of exploitation

mutual aid a form of organizing based on reciprocal exchange of voluntary labour that is also viewed as an act of solidarity whereby communities unite against a common struggle

queer political economy situates queer theory within studies of the economy and market life, identifying how the regulation of sexuality is embedded within wider economic systems and exploring how non-normative sexual identities challenge and provide the basis for thinking alternatively about economic systems

queer theory an approach to knowledge that asks that we unpick commonly held assumptions about how sex, gender identity, and sexuality neatly map onto one another, and how such assumptions shape the way in which we understand the social world

social reproduction refers within feminist political economy to the often unpaid and undervalued work involved in bearing children, maintaining households, and caring for others, which reproduces the labour power and social cohesion on which capitalism depends

time use survey a tool for social research which asks participants to record their daily activities, usually in diary form, which have been used to account for unpaid labour in the home

transnationalization an extension of political, economic, and social processes across national borders, often without the direct involvement or oversight of the state

6. CITY

ableism the beliefs, processes, and practices that produce a particular kind of self and body, which is then projected as the typical or 'normal' human

accumulation by dispossession a type of surplus value production in the Marxist sense that relies on state compulsion and legalized theft, including through evictions

autogestion a revolt against control from above and a movement for greater self-management

development a widely used term that can refer either to a planned intervention of improvement or to an unfolding process of progressive social change

entrepreneurial city a city that pursues entrepreneurial strategies to enhance its competitiveness vis-à-vis other cities and economic spaces in the global economy

gentrification the transformation of disreputable urban spaces into respectable and profitable real estate, named after the old class of 'well-bred' people in Europe known as the gentry

global city a city that functions as a command point in the organization of the global economy

globalization a process of increased interconnectedness across national borders and at global scale

global wealth chains linked forms of capital seeking to avoid accountability during processes of pecuniary wealth creation

mega-event an organized global spectacle that purposefully transforms the built environment

methodological nationalism a perspective that takes the nation state as the unit of analysis, often assuming that this is the natural form of social and political organization

municipal government the institutions created by states to govern incorporated localities, including town councils and city mayors

place branding a set of claims and practices intended to boost the international competitiveness of a certain territory by narrating it as a desirable location for capital

politicization exposing and questioning what is taken for granted, or perceived to be necessary, permanent, invariable, morally or politically obligatory and essential

production of (state) space the organization of socio-spatial routines into a manageable grid of abstract space that can be used to govern society and embed capital accumulation

race-making the processes through which race and racial categories are reproduced and contested

right to the city the collective right to make use of urban space and participate in its democratic control

state rescaling a reshuffling of the geographic scales at which different state institutions and policies seek to govern, typically incorporating the local, regional, national, and global scales

surplus population for Karl Marx a population bigger than required for capitalism to reproduce itself, but tolerated since it provides an industrial reserve army to be exploited when needed

urban development investment into the fixed capital of urban space like buildings, land, and infrastructure, usually in accordance with the designs and rules of city planners

7. SOCIAL MEDIA

attention economy a concept that focuses on how advertising must adapt to an increasingly dispersed media landscape by finding new ways to gain the attention of consumers

blockchain a decentralized ledger of transactions stored across a peer-to-peer network, used to provide the accounting infrastructure for cryptocurrency and other kinds of digital exchange

critical agency the capacity of individuals or groups to reflect upon and shape the conditions of possibility for action in society

deliberate in political theory, a practice of reasoned democratic debate which involves considering the opinions of others

documentary films non-fiction motion pictures that shape and interpret factual material for purposes of education or entertainment

fake news false or fabricated information that is broadcast or published as news for fraudulent or politically motivated purposes

Generation Z the demographic cohort after millennials, born around 1995–2010

prefigurative the idea that certain actions can be an imaginative instantiation of something new to come; instead of planning what to do, what you are doing can become the plan

prosumer derived from productive consumer

self-branding marketing oneself to create a uniform public image that conveys your value(s)

surveillance capitalism a critical theory of digital technologies that focuses on the extraction of surplus value from social media users who provide free information or data to big tech companies which can be refined and sold to advertisers

trasformismo a critical IPE concept drawn from Antonio Gramsci that highlights the way authorities accommodate critical or resistant ideas within their ruling ideology in order to reduce the appeal of actors who espouse them

8. SHARE

capitalization (of platforms) high levels of investment, especially from technology companies and financial firms such as venture capital

casualization the shift from long-term employment contracts to short-term contracts and casual forms of employment

community mapping a participatory action research approach that brings together a group of people creating a map

conglomerates firms with business operations in different sectors of the economy

consolidation combining assets, liabilities, and other financial items of two or more entities, often with a view to increasing market share and reducing market competition

diverse economies a framework for understanding the multiplicity of economic action

e-wallet a vehicle of electronic payments, typically linked to a bank account

gig economy a labour market characterized by the prevalence of short-term contracts or freelance work

householding a form of economic exchange centred around both production and consumption occurring within the remit of the (extended) household

libertarian values a social preference for individual freedoms and political autonomy (often in opposition to the state)

local exchange trading schemes (LETs) community groups through which people exchange goods and services

marketization of everyday life the process of creating marketable products and services from previously non-monetized daily practices such as giving someone a lift

platform capitalism the growing influence and valuations of companies whose main business it is to intermediate between customers and vendors, or consumers and workers, typically via digital platforms

precariat a reworking of proletariat that refers to a social class characterized by precarious employment and income

reciprocity a form of economic organization that relies on reciprocal exchanges among members of a community and between communities

redistribution a form of economic exchange where resources are centrally pooled, often via coercive authority, and then distributed to members of the community

reintermediation in the context of platform capitalism, this form of economic organization is highly stratified, as the platform makes itself a central coordinator of transactions

super app an app that serves as an umbrella for multiple apps (as opposed to single-purpose apps)

9. HUMOUR

carnival a popular mode of celebration where social norms are suspended or actively inverted; the concept of carnival is associated with a set of everyday resistances to hierarchy and discipline

'commedification' a transformation of the public sphere in which politicians and other political actors are increasingly expected to adopt humorous modes of communication

direct action where political activists seek immediate remedy to perceived injustice, as opposed to indirect action, which appeals to governing authorities through established channels

global justice a concern with justice, or who deserves what, between individuals on a global scale rather between nations or states as in international justice

hegemonologue coined by L. M. Bogad from 'hegemony' and 'monologue' to refer to the prevailing consensus on the inevitability of globalization and the retrograde nature of resistance to it

irony the expression of meaning by using language or tone to imply the opposite; while similar to sarcasm, ironic techniques require work by the audience to find their own meaning in the joke

mimicry the action or skill of imitating someone or something, especially in order to entertain or ridicule

parody an imitation of the style of another composition with deliberate exaggeration or inappropriate application for comic effect

post-truth politics a political culture of public anxiety about the disregard for truthfulness and honesty

prankster a person who plays practical jokes or does mischievous acts

satire the use of humour, irony, or exaggeration to expose or critique some stupidity or venality in the target of the satirical piece

subaltern in postcolonial studies, refers to colonial subjects that are economically, socially, politically, or otherwise marginalized within hierarchies of power and so not heard even as oppositional voices in political debate

subversion a moment where essential elements of a system are brought into performative contradiction; used especially in this chapter to refer to comic techniques that caricature systemic logics to both acknowledge their constructed nature and anticipate potential alternatives

subvertising the practice of making spoofs or parodies of corporate and political advertisements

tactical frivolity the strategic use of jokes, humour and 'silliness' to draw out or diffuse underlying tensions in resistance; used especially in this chapter to refer to campaigns that seek to avoid or defend against police violence in non-violent ways

INDEX

Note: Tables and figures are indicated by an italic t and f following the page number.

3D printing 202
4chan 194

A

ableism 179, 181
accumulation by dispossession 173
action research 234
activism *see* protests and activism
Adorno, Theodor 246
advertising *see* marketing
affective labour 127–8
Airbnb 222, 227, 229
Aitken, Rob 208
Alibaba 78, 193–4, 220–1
Alphabet 220, 226
  see also Google
Amazon
  food sector 78
  globalization documentaries 209
  impact 194
  platform capitalism 220
  prosumers 192
  The Social Dilemma 198
Apple 192, 206, 220, 226
apps
  food delivery 83
  sharing economy 215, 217–18, 220, 226
  super 215, 220
Arcadia Group 44
Argentina 102, 110, 111, 132
Armajaro 66
Asian Financial Crisis (1997) 132
assetization 97–101
Asus 221
Atal, Maha Rafi 222
Atkinson, Rowland 164
Atos 160–1
attention economy 190–2, 194–5, 198, 205, 209
austerity 109–10, 132–6, 226
Australia 177
auto-construction 175
autoethnography, food 82–4, 277t
autogestion 175–6

B

Baidu 193, 220
Bakhtin, Mikhail 249, 258

banal nationalism 9–10
Bangladesh
  clothes sector 29, 34, 35f, 40–3, 50
  famine 68, 69
  Fire and Building Safety Accord 43
  food riots 84
  microfinance 106
  Policy Simulation Labs 114
Banksy 251–2
  Girl with Balloon 252
Barbados 45
Belgium 166
Bentham, Jeremy 16
Bhattacharyya, Gargi 129
Biden, Jill 122–3
Biden, Joe 122, 263
Big Bang Theory, The (TV series) 108
Big Short, The (film, 2015) 104–5
bike-share 228
Billionaires 250–1
Black Feminism 127
Black Lives Matter (BLM) 205–7
Black Political Economy 14–15
Blackketter, Nikki 189
Blair, Tony 96
blockchain 203
Bogad, L. M. 246, 251, 253, 258
bonded labour 39
bondholders 99, 110
Bono 256–7
Boohoo 29–30, 42, 50
book bloc 246
Brandalism 252
Brazil
  chocolate consumption 60
  right to the city 175
  Rio Olympics 154–6, 158, 175
  Rio's development 173
  sovereign debt 102
Brenner, Neil 168–9
Brickell, Katherine 137
British Guiana 169–70
Brooker, Charlie 243
Brooks, Andrew 33, 35–6
Brown, Tina 217
Bulgaria 34
Bulley, Dan 159
Butler, Judith 251

Index

C

Caldeira, Teresa 175
Cambodia 29, 137
Cameron, John 255, 257
Cameroon 108, 109
Canada 82
capitalism 7
  care 124, 130, 131, 137
  clothes sector 32, 44, 48, 51
  'crisis ordinary' 137
  ethical issues 84
  everyday life 11–12
  food sector 70, 76
  hegemonologue 246
  humour 243, 249, 251, 268
  I-PEEL 276
  law of value 80
  Marxist critique 11
  neoliberal 3, 45
  planetary exploitation 81
  platform 220–2, 237
  prosumer 209
  queer political economy 130
  racial 39–40, 129
  sharing economy 223, 225, 229
  social media 209
  social reproduction 13, 124
  surveillance 200–3, 206–7, 209
  urban development 168, 171, 173, 178
capitalization 221
care 21t, 120–1, 131, 147–51
  Covid-19 pandemic 7, 122, 127, 132–3, 145–6, 222
  crisis 131–4
  global economy 138–42
  harm 134–7
  hidden assumptions uncovered through social annotation 145–6
  military spouses 122–3, 129, 147, 274
  sharing economy 232
  social reproduction 123–6
  time use surveys 142–5
  valuing care work 126–8
Caribbean 166, 169, 249
Carlson, Tucker 191
carnival 249–52, 255, 258, 268
case study, urban development 176–8
cash transfers 69–70
casualization 219
Chegg 222
Chen, Katherine 202, 203
child labour
  clothes sector 41, 47
  cocoa 63–5
children
  care 122, 124, 138, 140, 142
  food consumption 60, 77
  influencers 192
  malnutrition 73
  military families 122, 124
Chile 37, 96–7, 100, 102
China
  Beijing Olympics 156–7, 158
  bike-share 228
  clothes sector 35f, 39
  food sector 59–60, 64, 85
  Healthy China 2030 strategy 61–2
  platform capitalism 220, 221
  Shanghai Expo 156
  Uighur Muslim forced labour 206
chocoholics 61, 61f, 62
chocolate 59–67, 76
Chouinard, Vera 179
Chua Beng Huat 44
Citigroup 103
city 21t, 152–3, 161, 180–4
  development *see* urban development
  global 161–9, 180
  mega-event 154–61
  privilege trail 178–80, 278t, 279
  right to the 175–6, 178–80
  sharing economy 225
civil society 20t
  humour 254–8
  sharing economy 228–32
Clandestine Insurgent Rebel Clown Army 246–7
class diets 76
class issues
  autogestion 175
  care 125, 127, 138, 142
  clothes sector 44–5
  debt 94
  food sector 70, 76, 80
  gig economy 219
  global cities 166
  humour 262
  mega-events 159
  platform capitalism 220
  sharing economy 230
  trasformismo 206
Clean Clothes Campaign 43, 47, 49
clickbait 190
Clift, Ben 273
climate change 81, 107
clothes 21t, 27–9, 37, 53–6
  construction of low-waged labour 38–40
  corporate responsibility 40–3
  desire 43–8
  developing an ethical clothing campaign 278t
  disposal 51–3, 279t
  ethical clothing campaign 48–51
  export share by country 34–5, 35f
  fast fashion 29–37
  humour 248
cocoa
  child labour 63–5
  downgrading 78

Index

market, competition and coordination in 65–7, 78
Cocoa Protocol 63, 65
codes of conduct
   clothes sector 41, 42–3, 49
   cocoa sector 65
coffee 79
Cold War 96
collateral 106
Collins, Patricia Hill 14–15
colonialism 12
   clothes sector 33, 40, 48
   global wealth chain 177
   humour 252, 258, 260–1
   state rescaling 169–70
comedy *see* humour
Comic Relief 254–8
commedification 243, 264
commodification 101
   care 127, 136
   higher education 233
   humour 243
   sharing economy 217, 222, 227–8, 232–3
   social media 198
   student debt 95–7, 100
commodity fetishism 10, 33, 47, 54
common sense 11
   social media 196–8, 206
Community Economies Collective 233
community gardens 230
community health workers 136
community mapping 234–7, 279*t*
conditions of production 80
conglomerates 226
consolidation 221
consumption
   clothes sector 43–51, 54
   food sector 78–9, 82–5, 87
   prosumers 192–204, 207, 209
   smoothing 104
   urban development 171, 172
cooperatives 80, 229, 232
corporate debt 102–3
corporate services complex 162–4
corporate social responsibility (CSR) 40–3, 47, 49, 52
corporations 20*t*
   food sector 59–61, 64–6, 76–80, 85
   global city 162–5
   humour 247, 254
   platform capitalism 221–2
   sharing economy 226
   social media 198–202, 206
   surveillance capitalism 200–1
   university education 98
Côte d'Ivoire 63, 65, 66, 67, 78
cotton 33–4
Covid-19 pandemic
   care 7, 122, 127, 132–3, 145–6, 222
   and chronic diseases 61
   clothes 29, 31, 50
   debt 103–4, 107, 111
   digital surveillance 7
   Gojek/GoTo 215
   humour 263–4, 265
   journalism 191
   key workers 6–7
   military spouses 122
   pedagogy 276
   platform capitalism 222
Cox, Robert 8, 197, 206, 272
creating activities 277, 278, 279*t*
'crisis ordinary' 137
Critchley, Simon 261–2
critical agency 190, 207–9
critical theory 8, 12
Cullen, Darren 103
cultural appropriation 48
Curtis, Richard 254

D

Daily Show, The (TV show) 243, 244, 260
Davies, Angela 127
Davies, Russell T. 130
Daviron, Benoît 79
de Goede, Marieke 249–50, 251
De Henau, Jerome 127
Dean, Jonathan 194
Death, Carl 259–61
debt 21*t*, 92–3, 101, 117–19
   cancellation vs repayment 94, 107–112, 114–17
   clothes shoppers 31, 46
   different kinds of 101–4
   humour 244–6, 251
   reasons for 104–7
   student 94–101, 105, 112, 117
   usury thought experiment 113–14
   zombie 244–5
debt relief 107
   role-play 114–17, 278*t*
debt sustainability 102, 105, 108
Decolonize the Curriculum 204
deforestation 65, 80
deliberating resistance on/to social media 206–7, 277*t*
Deliveroo 222
Deng Xiaoping 59
depletion through social reproduction (DSR) 134–7
development 20*t*, 159
   humour and foreign aid 254–8
   urban *see* urban development
dietary change and public health 60–2
dietary governance 72–7, 87
dieting 82
direct action 246

disability
  ableism 179, 181
  Paralympics 160–1
discourse 11
diverse economies 232–4, 237, 277t
documentary films 207–9, 279t
domestic violence 105, 137
Domínguez, Yolanda, 'Fashion Victims' 50–1
Dosekun, Simidele 45
Douglas, Mary 244
Dove (chocolate) 59
Dow Chemical Company 254
Dowling, Emma 133, 134
drag 251
dumping, clothes sector 36, 37
Durst, Seymour 109

E

earnings *see* wages and salaries
East Africa 52
East African Community 36
East Asia 33, 34
ecological debt 107
Economic Man 62, 224
Economic Nationalism 7, 9–10
  clothes 33
  food security 70–1
economic upgrading 78
Ecuador 175
education
  casualization 219
  inflation 96
  see also universities/higher education
Elson, Diane 133–4
embodied neoliberalism 74
emigration *see* migration
enacting activities 277, 278, 278t
English language 275
Enloe, Cynthia 6, 14, 54
entitlements 69
entrepreneurial city 168, 171, 181
environment 20t
  climate change 81, 107
  disposal of clothes waste 51–3, 54
  ecological debt 107
  food sector 80–2
  trasformismo 206
Epstein, Gerald 99
Erdoğan, Recep Tayyip 175
Escobar, Pablo 195–6
ethical issues
  capitalism 84
  care 126
  clothes sector 41, 43, 47–51
  food sector 87
  humour 249
  Islamic finance 111

podcasts 53
social media 198–9, 203
ethnicity
  clothes sector 48
  global cities 166
  humour 263
  low-waged labour 39
  'maid trade' 14
  urban development 174
  see also race
Eurocentrism 8
European Union 35f, 103–4
everyday International Political Economy *see* I-PEEL
everyday life 11–13
e-wallet 215
export-led industrialization
  agricultural sector 71
  clothes sector 34, 38

F

Facebook 192, 194, 198–9, 201, 206
  see also Meta
Fairphone 203
Fairtrade 10, 11, 65, 84–5
fake news 194
famine 68, 69
Farha, Leilani 175
Fashion Revolution 49, 51
fast fashion 29–37, 44, 50, 52
Fawcett Society 105
Federici, Silvia 13–14, 105–6, 124–5, 201
feminism 13
  care 123–4, 127, 132, 133
  clothes sector 46, 53–4
  embodied neoliberalism 74
  food sector 82
  humour 251, 266–8
  low-waged labour 38
  Marxist 124
  patriarchy 5
  'the person is political' 5
  transnational agendas 48
feminist sense 14
feminization
  assembly line production 14
  clothes sector 30–1, 38–9, 42–4
Ferguson, James 70
Ferrero 59
FIFA World Cup 156–60
finance 20t
  care 132–4
  global city 162–5
  Islamic 110–13, 117
  mobile money 280, 281
  urban development 168–9
  see also debt
financial technology (fintech) 280

financialization 101
  'crisis ordinary' 137
  food sector 66, 80
  household debt 103
  microfinance 106
  student debt 99–101
Finland 166
fiscal consolidation 109–10
fitness influencers 187–93, 274
Floyd, George 205
food 21t, 57–8, 67–8, 86–91
  autoethnography 277t
  chocolate 59–67
  consumer autoethnography 82–4
  dietary governance 72–7
  humour 248
  moral economy of a vegan foodscape 84–6
  value distribution 77–82
food banks 84, 85
food-for-work schemes 69
food riots 71, 84
food security/insecurity 68–72, 235
food sovereignty 71
foodscape 85
  University of California-Berkeley Foodscape Mapping Project 235f, 235–6
  vegan 85–6, 278t
football World Cup 156–60
forced labour 47, 206
Ford, Michele 229
fossil fuels 78
Foucault, Michel 15–16, 68, 70, 72, 82, 253
framing 146
France 33, 95, 103
Francis, Ben 187
Frankfurt School 12
free trade 33–5, 248
Freeman, Carla 45
Friedman, Harriet 76
future of work 44
Fyre: The Greatest Party That Never Happened (documentary, 2019) 195–8, 201–2, 207–9

G

G8 71, 246–7
Game of Thrones (TV series) 192
Gardezi, Saadia 258–9
Garritzmann, Julian 95, 100
GATT 34, 247–8
Geldof, Bob 256–7
gender 20t
  academic citations 18
  care 122–38, 140–7
  clothes sector 38–40, 42, 45–6, 48, 53–4
  debt 100–1, 105–6
  dietary governance 74
  everyday life 11
  feminist sense 14
  food sector 59, 74, 76, 78
  globalization 14
  heteronormativity 128–31
  humour 248, 251
  I-PEEL 4, 5–6
  low-waged labour 38–40
  markets 224
  military spouses 122–6
  mobile money 280
  sharing economy 222, 230–1
  social reproduction 13, 123–6
  see also feminization; masculinization
gendered division of labour 122–5, 127–9
General Agreement on Tariffs and Trade (GATT) 34, 247–8
General Atlantic 187
Generation Z 187
gentrification 12, 172, 174, 181, 227
Germany 64–5, 95–7, 103, 173–4
Gervais, Ricky 255–8
Ghana
  clothes sector 36
  cocoa 63, 65, 66, 78
  pineapples 78
gharar (uncertainty, Islamic finance) 112
Gibson-Graham, J. K. 230, 233
gift exchange 108, 117
gig economy 44, 217–20, 222, 229, 232, 237
Gilpin, Robert 272
global care chain 138–42, 139f
global city 161–9, 180
global financial crisis (2008–9) 104–5, 109
  care 132
  documentaries 197
  gig economy 217
  humour 243
  sharing economy 223, 226, 229, 232, 237
global governance 20t
  debt cancellation 115–17
  dietary governance 72–7
global justice 246, 254–8, 268
global value chains (GVCs) 164
  clothes sector 41
  food sector 63–4, 66, 76–80
  global city 162
  humour 248
global wealth chains 164, 177
globalization 20t
  care 138–42
  class diets 76
  clothes sector 34
  documentary films 207
  global city 162
  humour 243, 248, 251, 253, 258
  labour force feminization 14
  low-waged labour 38
  sharing economy 229

Gojek/GoTo 215, 226–7
   gig economy 217–18
   platform capitalism 221–2, 274
   resistance 229, 230
Google 193, 198–9, 220–1
   see also Alphabet
GoTo see Gojek/GoTo
gotong royong (community cooperation) 225
governmentality 72–4, 87
Grab 227
Graeber, David 107–8
Grameen Bank 106
Gramsci, Antonio 11, 196, 206
Grayson, Kyle 4
Greece 132–3
Greed (film, 2019) 47
Griffin, Lex 189
Gymshark 187–8, 189–90, 192, 193

H

H&M 44
Hadid, Bella 195
Hansen, Arve 85
Harvey, David 173, 176
Hayek, Friedrich 67
Health at Every Size movement 82
Heavily Indebted Poor Countries (HIPC) initiative 115–16
hegemonologue 246, 253
Helleiner, Eric 9
Henry, Lenny 254
Hershey 59
heteronormativity
   care 128–31
   carnival 249
   feminism 13
   mobile money 280
hidden assumptions, uncovering through social annotation 145–6, 278*t*
higher education see universities/higher education
Himmelweit, Susan 127
Hochschild, Arlie 138
HomeNet 229
homo economicus see Economic Man
homonormativity 130
Honan, Vivian 229
Hong Kong 34
hooks, bell 48
Hoskyns, Catherine 124
Hossain, Naomi 84
household debt 103, 244–6
householding 224, 237
housework 13, 124–5, 127
   time use surveys 143–5
human capital 97–8
human rights 139, 159, 232, 248
humour 21*t*, 241–3, 253–4, 268–70, 274
   carnival 249–51
   dangerous 261–4
   global justice 254–8
   meme, making your own 266–7
   parody collage 264–6
   radical comedy 243–54
   resistance 244–8
   subaltern 258–61
   subversion 251–3
hunger 68, 70, 72
Hussein, Shereen 136

I

IKEA 192
ILO 41–3, 138
IMF 102, 115
immigration see migration
Inayatullah, Naeem 82
Independent Workers' Union of Great Britain 229
India
   Bhopal disaster 254
   chocolate consumption 60
   clothes sector 35*f*, 46
   microfinance 106–7
   Mumbai's informal settlements 172–3
   New Delhi Commonwealth Games 156
   Self-Employed Women's Association 229
   student debt 98
Indonesia
   care 140, 141
   clothes sector 35*f*
   food riots 84
   Gojek/GoTo 215, 221–2, 274
   gotong royong (community cooperation) 225
   Jakarta's development 173, 174
industrial foods 76–7
industrialization 33, 101–2
influencers 195, 197, 204
   chocolate 59
   fitness 187–93, 274
informal settlements 172–5, 181
informed consent 53
Instagram 193–4, 206
interest 117
   debt relief campaign role-play 115
   Islamic finance 110, 112, 113
   sovereign debt 102
   student debt 101
   usury 113–14
internally displaced people 136–7
International Labour Organization (ILO) 41–3, 138
International Monetary Fund (IMF) 102, 115
International Olympic Committee (IOC) 154, 157
International Relations 7
International Women's Day 126

Index

intersectionality 15
   care 127
   humour 268
   low-waged labour 39
   politics 205–7
   right to the city 178–9
investment 20t
   global city 162–4
   mega-events 154, 157
   platform capitalism 221
   sharing economy 226–7
I-PEEL 2–4, 22–3, 272–3, 276, 281–2
   activating your I-PEEL mindset 276–9, 277t, 278t, 279t
   creating your I-PEEL tile 279–81
   how to study 273
   lineages 7–18
   what is studied 4, 275–6
   who is studied 5–7, 273–5
irony 243, 258, 262–4, 268
   carnival 251
   dangerous 262–4
   global justice 256
   memes 266
   resistance 245
Iskander, Harith 261
Islamic finance 110–13, 117
It's a Sin (TV series) 130

J

Ja Rule 195–6
Jakobsen, Jostein 85
Jamil, Jameela 75
Japan 96, 162
Javid, Sajid 134
Jessop, Bob 168
joint liability 107
Jourdain, Anne 216–17
journalism 191
Joyce, Simon 229
just-in-time production 31

K

Kaepernick, Colin 205, 206
Kalita, Devangana 84
Källstig, Amanda 259–61
Kardashian, Kim 188
Kenya 78, 84, 259, 280
Khamis, Susie 191
Killias, Olivia 141
KSI 188

L

Labour Behind the Label 30, 49–50
Lamm, Nickolay/Lammily dolls 202

Langley, Paul 97, 220
Lanier, Jaron 199
Last Week Tonight with John Oliver 243, 244–6
Latin America 80, 101–2, 166
law of value 80
Lebanon 140
Lefebvre, Henri 11–12, 171–2, 175, 181
leverage 104
Levi's 41
Levitz, Eric 226
Leyshon, Andrew 220
Liberalism 7–9
libertarian values 219, 223, 232
Linux 232
Lisle, Dan 159
List, Friedrich 9, 10
loan sharking 107
local exchange trading schemes (LETS) 230
Longhurst, Robyn 82
low-waged labour
   care 136
   clothes sector 30–1, 34–6, 38–40, 43, 47
   gig economy 217, 219
   urban development 174
Lula da Silva, Luiz Inácio 154, 156

M

M&M's 59, 60
'maid trade' 14
Makarim, Nadiem 215
Malaysia
   care 141
   central bank loans 105
   clothes sector 35f
   education 96
   humour 261
   resistance 229
   student debt 94
malnutrition 68, 72, 73
Marcuse, Herbert 246
market 9
   sharing economy 224–6, 237
marketing
   Black Lives Matter 206
   chocolate 59–60, 76
   clothes sector 45–8
   education 98
   humour 243, 252, 262
   place branding 155–7
   prosumers 193
   sharing economy 216, 218
   social media 188–91, 196–7, 199, 201–2, 206
marketization of everyday life 216–17, 218f, 219, 225, 237
marriage
   heteronormativity 129
   military spouses 122–3, 129, 147, 274

Mars 59–60
Marwick, Alice 188, 189
Marx, Karl 10–11
Marxism 7, 10–11
   commodity fetishism 10, 33
   dietary governance 74
   feminism 13
   food security 70
   law of value 80
   neoliberalism interpretation 67–8
   Urban Studies 178
Marxist Feminism 124
masculinization 142
MasterCard 69
MattDoesFitness 189, 190
Mauss, Marcel 108
Max Fashion 46
McCartney, Stella 48, 49
McFarland, Billy 195–7
McKenzie, Rex 164
meatification 76, 85
mega-events 154–61, 175
memes 194–5, 203, 207
   humour 243–4, 262–7
   making 266–7, 279*t*
men *see* gender
Merchant, Stephen 255–7
Meta 221, 226
   see also Facebook
methodological nationalism 161, 180
#MeToo movement 44, 204
Mexico 76–7, 95, 102
microfinance 105–7
Middle East 72, 138, 140
migration
   care 138–42, 139*f*
   clothes sector 30–1, 41
   colonialism 12
   global cities 165–7
   humour 258
   mega-events 159–60
   Paddington Bear books 4
   urban development 173–4
military spouses 122–3, 129, 147, 274
mimicry 260–1
mobile money 280, 281
mobile phones 226
Mohanty, Chandra 48
Mondelēz 59, 65–6
Mooney, Charles W. 113
Moore, Phoebe 191, 229
moral economy 65, 84–6
moral hazard 115
Morgan, Piers 191
M-Pesa 280
Multi-Fibre Arrangement (MFA) 34–5
municipal government 174
mutual aid 131

N

NAFTA 11, 76
National Debt Clock 109
nationalism, methodological 161, 180
NATO 264
negative value 81–2
neoliberal subjectivity 45
neoliberalism 3, 67–8
   debt 102, 105
   dietary governance 62, 74, 76
   embodied 74
   food sector 84
   food security 70, 71
   hegemonologue 246
   humour 253
   queer political economy 130
Nestlé 59
Netflix
   Fyre: The Greatest Party That Never Happened 195–8, 201–2, 207–9
   prosumers 192–3
   The Social Dilemma 195, 198–203, 207–9
Netherlands 95
Newswipe (TV show) 243
Nigeria 45
Nike 41, 46–7, 206
Noah, Trevor 259–61
non-binary gender identities 142
non-resident labour 165–6
North America 35, 40
North American Free Trade Agreement (NAFTA) 11, 76
North Atlantic Treaty Organization (NATO) 264
Noulin, Sidonie 216–17

O

obesity and overweight 61, 72–4, 84
Occupy Wall Street 11
Oceane, Natacha 190
oil shocks 102
Oliver, Jamie 256–7
Oliver, John 243, 244–6
Olympic and Paralympic Games 154–61, 175
Open University 98
Organization of the Petroleum Exporting Countries (OPEC) 78
originate and distribute process 104
Orwell, George 244, 247, 249
   Nineteen Eighty-Four 264
Osborne, George 110
overweight *see* obesity and overweight

P

Pacific region 138
Paddington Bear books 4
Pakistan 259

Panopticon 16
Papua New Guinea 177
Parker, Sean 199
parody 249, 257, 263
  collage 264–6, 278t
paternalism 39, 255
patriarchy 5
  dietary governance 74
  feminism 13
  labour force feminization 14
  military spouses 122
Paul, Logan 188
payday loans 103
PayPal 221
pedagogy 18–19, 23, 275–6
personal responsibility 62
Peters, Andi 257
Peterson, V. Spike 129
Pettinger, Lynne 46–7
Philippines 136–40
place branding 155–7, 166, 181
platform capitalism 220–2, 237
podcasts 53
Polanyi, Karl 223–6, 230
Policy Simulation Labs 114
Political Economy 7–8, 10
politicization 159–61
politics
  humour 243–6, 249–54, 258–9, 262–5, 268
  social media 194, 202, 204–9
Ponte, Stefano 79
Portugal 34, 227
poststructural theory 15–16
post-truth politics 263–4
potlatch feast 108, 224
poverty
  Argentinian debt crisis 110, 111
  care 135, 136, 138, 142, 143
  clothes sector 31, 33
  cocoa sector 65
  debt 94, 105, 107, 110–11, 114–17
  humour 246, 248, 255, 257, 262
  India's Self-Employed Women's Association 229
  mega-events 158–9
  mobile money 280
  right to the city 172–3
  urban development 181
pranksters 244, 246–51, 253–4, 256, 264, 268
precariat 219
prefigurative prosumers 203–4
pregnant workers 42
private governance 63, 65–6
privilege trail 178–80, 278t, 279
problem-solving theory 8
production 20t
  low-waged labour 38–40
  prosumers 192–204, 207, 209

  of state space 171–2
prosumers 192–204, 207, 209
protectionism 34
protests and activism
  austerity 132–3, 135–6
  care sector 132–3, 140
  debt cancellation 115
  food riots 71, 84
  gender issues 39, 132–3
  Greek 'rubber glove rebellion' 132–3
  humour 246–51
  mega-events 159–61
  poverty 246–7
  ride-share 229, 230
  social media 194, 204–7
  strikes 39, 126
  student debt 96–7, 100–1, 246
  tuition fees 96–7, 100
  urban development 175–6
  see also resistance
Provenance 203
Ptak, Laurel, Wages for Facebook 201
public health 60–2, 72, 77
Punch (magazine) 259
PwC 162–3, 164

Q

qard hasan (benevolent loan, Islamic finance) 110–11
Qatar 159–60
queer political economy 129–31
queer theory 251, 264

R

race
  Black Lives Matter 205–7
  care 125, 127, 141
  clothes sector 30, 48
  everyday life 12
  global cities 166–7
  humour 259, 261
  low-waged labour 39–40
  markets 224
  microaggressions 15
  obesity 72
  sharing economy 230
  social media 193
  standpoint epistemology 14–15
  student debt 94, 100–1
  urban development 174, 181
  see also ethnicity
race-making 174
'race to the bottom' 41
racial capitalism 39–40, 129
racial harassment 44
racist comedy 262

Radi-Aid 256–8
radical comedy 243–54
Raffles, Stamford 171
Raha, Nat 130–1
Rai, Shirin 124, 145
Rainforest Alliance 65
Ratajkowski, Emily 195
Realism 7–9
reciprocity 223–4, 225, 228, 237
Reclaim the Streets 258
Reddit 194
redistribution 224, 237
reflective activities 277, 277t
refugees 70
regulatory International Political Economy 3
reintermediation 220–1, 222
reputation management 191, 219
resistance
    humour 243–9, 253–4, 258, 261–2, 268
    sharing economy 229, 237
    see also protests and activism
retail sector 44
Rhodes Must Fall 204
ride-share 215–22, 227, 229, 274
right to the city 175–6, 178–80
Rivoli, Pietra 33, 35
Robinson, Cedric 39–40
Rodriguez, Robyn Magalit 139
Roitman, Janet 108
role-playing a debt relief campaign 114–17, 278t
Romania 34, 82
Roy, Ananya 172
Royal Bank of Scotland Group 103
Russia 60, 132, 164, 264
Rwanda 36, 52

S

Sajed, Alina 82
salaries *see* wages and salaries
Samaritans, The (mockumentary) 259
Samsung 221
Särmä, Saara 264–6
Sassen, Saskia 161–4, 166–8, 174, 180
satire 243–4, 254
    dangerous 263
    feminist 267, 268
    global justice 257
    memes 266–7
    resistance 244–6, 248
    subaltern 258–60
    subversion 253
Scandinavia 95, 100
Schor, Juliet B. 230
Schröder, Gerhard 96
Schwak, Juliette 207
Scott, James C. 205, 229
second-hand clothes 33, 35–7, 51–2
securitization 99, 104

self-branding 188–91, 209
Self-Employed Women's Association 229
Selwyn, Ben 80
Sen, Amartya 69, 70
sexist comedy 262
sexual harassment
    clothes sector 42, 44, 47
    #MeToo movement 44, 204
sexuality 129–31
shariah principles, Islamic finance 110–12
sharing economy 21t, 213–15, 222–3, 237–40
    alternatives 228–32
    diverse economies framework 232–4
    gig economy 217–20
    marketization of everyday life 216–17
    origins 223–6
    platform capitalism 220–2
    ride-share 215–22, 227, 229, 274
    university community mapping 234–7
    who owns what? 226–8
Sharman, Jason 177
silk 33
Simms, Andrew 107
Singapore
    care 140
    clothes sector 44, 45
    colonial district 171
    global city status 165
    Grab 215
    Marina Bay Financial Centre 165, 171
    non-resident labour 165
slavery
    biblical times 107
    carnival 249
    child 63
    clothes sector 32, 34
    humour 248
    sugar industry 169, 170
slum housing 172–5, 181
Smith, Adam 9, 10
Smith, Nicola J. 129
Smith, Robert F. 94
social annotation of policy document 145–6, 278t
Social Dilemma, The (documentary, 2020) 195, 198–203, 207–9
social media 21t, 185–6, 194–5, 209–12
    attention economy 190–2
    beauty ideals 82
    clothes sector 50
    deliberating resistance on/to 204–7
    documentary film review poster 207–9
    everyday politics 19
    food sector 59–60, 85
    humour 249, 253, 263
    'I Weigh' campaign 74, 75
    our work for 198–201
    performances of the self 17
    prosumers 192–4, 201–3

regulation 195–8
resistance deliberation 277t
self-branding 188–90
see also influencers
social reproduction 13
   care 123–6, 131–2, 134, 144–5
   depletion through 134–7
social upgrading 78
Soederberg, Susanne 173–4
Softbank 221
South Africa
   Basic Income Grant 70
   FIFA World Cup 156, 158
   fruit 78, 79
   humour 260
South Asia 72
South Korea 34, 95–6, 221
Southeast Asia 33–4, 138
sovereign debt 101–2, 108–10, 111, 113
   Covid-19 pandemic 103
   debt relief campaign role-play 114–17, 278t
   European crisis 132
space race 96
Spain 34, 157, 227
Spivak, Gayatri Chakravorty 258
Sri Lanka 43
Standard Chartered 165
Standing, Guy 38, 219
standpoint epistemology 14–15
starvation 68, 69
state 20t
   austerity and the welfare state 132–6
   autogestion 175
   care 131–6, 140, 141
   clothes sector 42–3, 52
   corporate debt 102–3
   debt see sovereign debt
   education 94, 96–7
   entrepreneurial city 181
   food sector 61–2, 70–2, 84
   heteronormativity 129
   labour standards 42–3
   mega-events 157, 159
   rescaling 168–71, 181
   urban development 168–71, 173–4
stereotypes 262, 263
Stewart, Jon 244
Strange, Susan 272
strikes 39, 126
student debt 94–101, 105, 112, 117
   four worlds of student finance 95f, 95, 100, 117
   protests 96–7, 100–1, 246
subaltern 258–61
subjectivity 16–18
   autogestion 176
   education 99
   'maid' 141
   middle class 159

   neoliberal 45
subprime mortgages 104–5
sub-Saharan Africa 72, 136
subsidies
   agricultural 76
   cooking fuel 69
   higher education 96
   military families 122
   student loans 94, 95f
subversion 251–4, 259, 261–2, 266, 268
subvertising 252
Sundararajan, Arun 217
super apps 215, 220
Superbarrio 258, 259
surplus population 174
surveillance capitalism 200–3, 206–7, 209
Sustainable Development Goals (SDGs) 42
swap shops 230
symbolic value 79
Syrian refugees 70
systemic International Political Economy 3

T

tactical frivolity 246
Taiwan 140
Tanyag, Maria 136–7
tax havens 164
taxation
   vs austerity 109
   avoidance and evasion 94
   food sector 77
   higher education 96
   redistribution 224
   sharing economy 227
   social media corporations 202
Ted Baker 44
Tencent 193, 220–1
Thailand 215
Thatcher, Margaret 168
Thompson, E. P. 84
thought experiment on usury 113–14, 277t
TikTok 193, 201
time use surveys 142–5, 144t, 277t
Ting, Chloe 190
Tokopedia 215, 221
trade 20t
   clothes 29–37
   cocoa 66
   free 33–5, 248
   global city 162
   humour 248, 268
trade unions
   clothes sector 31, 43
   food sector 63, 80
   sharing economy 229
   transformation of labour systems 43
trans identity 142
translation 275

transnationalization 138–42
Transparency International 164
trasformismo 206
Trump, Donald 191, 206, 262–3, 265
tuition fees 94–101, 95f
   see also student debt
Turkey 34, 35f, 70, 175–6
Tutu, Desmond 232
Twitter 194, 198

U

Uber 78, 191, 215, 218–20, 222, 227
ubuntu (shared humanity) 232
Ukraine 60, 164
UNICEF 72, 260
Union Carbide 254
United Arab Emirates 166–7
United Kingdom
   austerity 226
   care 132–3, 135–6
   casualization of higher education 219
   chocolate consumption 59
   clothes sector 29–34, 35f, 42, 44
   colonialism 168–71, 252
   corporate debt 103
   debt 105, 109–10
   food sector 84
   heteronormativity 129
   humour 243, 252, 262
   Independent Workers' Union of Great Britain 229
   London Olympics and Paralympics 159–61
   London's development 168–9
   London's global city status 162, 164, 166, 169
   market paradigm 224
   student debt 94, 96, 98–101, 112
   Uber 219
   urban development 168–9
   urban inequality 166
United Nations
   'Covid-19 and the Care Economy' 146
   Food and Agricultural Organization 71
   food security 68–9
   humour 248
   International Children's Emergency Fund (UNICEF) 72, 260
   right to the city 175
   simulated negotiations 114
   Universal Declaration on the Eradication of Hunger and Malnutrition 68–9
   World Food Conference 68–9
   World Food Programme 69–70
   World Summit on Food Security 71
United States
   Argentinian debt crisis 110
   austerity 226
   Black Lives Matter 205
   care 122–3, 127, 143, 147

   chocolate consumption 59
   clothes sector 30, 31, 35
   corporate accountability 206
   corporate debt 103
   food sector 63, 69, 76
   humour 243, 260, 262–3
   Los Angeles' racialized habitation 166–7
   Mexico's sovereign debt 102
   Miami's non-resident workers 166
   military spouses 122–3, 129, 147, 274
   New York's global city status 162
   obesity and overweight 72, 74
   platform capitalism 220
   potlatch feast 108
   presidential election (2020) 219
   queer people 131
   racial inequality 15
   ride-share 215, 218–20, 227
   right to the city 180
   sharing economy 227, 230, 235–6
   sovereign debt 108–9, 113
   student debt 94, 96, 100–1
   Treasury 102
   University of California-Berkeley Foodscape Mapping Project 235f, 235–6
   urban inequality 166
universities/higher education
   casualization 219
   community mapping 234–7, 235f
   diverse economies 233–4
   sharing economy 219, 233–7
   student debt 94–101, 105, 112, 117
University of California-Berkeley Foodscape Mapping Project 235f, 235–6
upgrading 78
urban development 159, 168–76, 181
   case study 176–8, 279t
   mega-events 157–9
usury thought experiment 113–14, 277t

V

value
   care work 126–8, 145
   distribution, food sector 77–82
   law of 80
   negative 81–2
Varman, Rohit 98–9
vegan foodscape 85–6, 278t
venture capital 226–7
Vietnam 35f, 85, 215
Visa 221
vulture funds 110

W

wages and salaries
   care 127, 139
   clothes sector 42, 43, 50

debt 105
food sector 65, 78
food security 69
global cities 164, 166
housework 13, 124–5, 127
social reproduction 125
university education 98
see also low-waged labour
Wall, Ilan rua 53
WALL-E (film, 2008) 171, 172
Ward, Anthony 66
Washington Consensus 102
waste, clothes 31, 37, 51–4
Watson, Matthew 9
weight discrimination 74
Weis, Tony 76
welfare state
austerity agenda 110
care 132–6
heteronormativity 129
urban development 174
West Africa
clothes sector 36, 48
cocoa 63, 66, 71
WHO 61, 72
Widodo, Joko 'Jokowi' 215
Wikipedia 231, 231*f*
women *see* gender
word clouds 273, 274*f*
working conditions
care sector 133, 136, 141
clothes sector 29–32, 38–44, 46–7, 50–1, 54
cocoa sector 65
mega-events 159–60

World Bank
debt relief campaign role-play 116
Heavily Indebted Poor Countries initiative 115
lending 104
shared prosperity 223
Washington Consensus 102
World Debt Clock 109
World Food Programme 69–70
World Health Organization (WHO) 61, 72
World Trade Organization (WTO) 34, 247–8

X

Xiaomi 221

Y

Yes Men 247–8, 254, 256
yield 101
'Your Plan, Your Planet' quiz 52
Youssef, Bassem 243
Yunus, Muhammad 106

Z

Zambia 84, 116
Zara 31, 44
zero hours contracts 44, 219
Zijderveld, Anton 253
Zizek, Slavoj 245
zombie debt 244–5
Zoolander (film, 2001) 47
Zuboff, Shoshana 200
Zwick, Detlev 192